Wall or No Wall
Barking up the Wrong Tree

Third Edition

by

John J. Bodoh

Dedicated to Jorge Antonio Paque

Table of Contents

Preface...v

Prologue 1

Chapter I, The Maya 9

Chapter II, The Origins of GSSG 20

Chapter III, Guatemala, 1524–1960.. 39

Chapter IV, The Guatemalan Spring 49

Chapter V, Civil War, 1960–1996... 57

Chapter VI, Post-War Guatemala 75

Chapter VII, GSSG 2003 88

Chapter VIII, GSSG 2004.. 98

Chapter IX, GSSG 2005 117

Chapter X, GSSG 2006.. 130

Chapter XI, GSSG 2007 165

Chapter XII, 2008 175

Chapter XIII, GSSG 2009.. 200

Chapter XIV, GSSG 2010.. 217

Chapter XV, Guatemala Today.. 220

Epilogue 226

Appendix A, The Recruiting Manual.. 235

Appendix B, Host-Family Orientation.. 246

Appendix C, Workshops... 249

Appendix D, Higher Education.. 254

Appendix E, Internships.. 256

Appendix F, Calculating the Number of Graduates................................ 257

Appendix G, An Outline of Guatemalan History.....................................259

Appendix H, Snapshots of the Students' Fortunes 261

Bibliography 266

Index 269

Acknowledgements

This book developed out of my eleven years' experience as the executive director of an organization called the 'Guatemalan Student Support Group' (GSSG). I owe a deep debt of gratitude to the many supporters of GSSG, without whose constancy and generosity of time, expertise, and financial backing GSSG would not have been possible. They fall naturally into four groups:

1) the American families that hosted GSSG's students, fed them, clothed them, helped them with their homework, wiped away their tears, got them to school on time, and dressed them up for the prom—Noreen Ordronneau, Marguerite and Francis Goyle, Joy and Dave Currens, Cathy Lambeth and Conn Herrington, Margo and Roger Peterson, Ann and Milton Machost, Michelle and Tom Bonds, Nicole and Dwayne White; Marie and Jack Lewis, Shari and Kevin Allen, Ellen Ziemer and Jerry Waddell, Kelly and Kirby Lewis, Amy and Greg Grazen, Debbie and Lee Smith, Julie and Greg Phillips, Joan and Chuck Thomas, Kelli and Rick Conlow, Mary and Scott VanderVeen, Jennifer and Justin Adair, Connie and Jim Brooks, Diane and Russell Curtis, Judy and Bill Doran, Wendy and Randy Helm, Kristin and Kent Mattson, Tracy and Steve Mulanix, Darci and Bruce Muller, Kelly and Patrick Mulry, Susan and Craig Newhof, Lori and Chris Pieri, Beth and Don Porter, Annette and Michael Yared, Martha and Rene Centeno, Lea and Paulo Chiquito, Pam and Bob Cochrane, Amy and Greg Grazen, Carolyn and Jim Heuser, Mary Jane Houlihan Smith, Donna and Robert McElcar, Tara Milenski, Ursula and Rod Ruiz, Josie and Richard Spontak, Paige and David Van Lenten, Sharon and Tim Wiwel, Michele and Brad Worthington, David and Kevin Mulhall, Lisa and Dan Efrat, Rosemary and Neil Jacob, Jack and Jane Apellido, Dori and Francis Crocco, Rosemary and Joe Czejkowski, Pilar and Steve Jennings, , Mick and David Roth, Nancy and Bill Spencer, Andrea and Tom Anderson, Carolyn and Joe Barnes, Connie and Jim Brooks, Jean and Mark Deming, Jennifer and Michael Golden, Linda and Ron Kohls, Julene and John Oxton, Evelyn Rojas and Juan Ramirez, Londa and Jeff Somers, Rosie and James Wagner, Michele and Brad Worthington, Dawn and Robert Atkinson, Kim and Luis Pop, Alma and Richard Hammer, Lynn Franz and Joe Krueger, Loree and Paul Lam, Thelma and Warren LeMarble, Debbie and Tom Lindsey, Cathy and Jim Morrissey, Amy and Brian Mulhall, Karrie and Richard Weber, Randy and Amy Poteat, Andrea and Tom Anderson, Susan DeGiralamo, Roxanne and Tracy Felder, Cathy and Rik Greenseth, Marisa and Brian Harrell, Shannon Jordan and Joe LoBuglio, Melissa and Joe Neuman, Loreen and John Postma, Dawn and Rob Atkinson, Kathy and Jim Condon, Lori and Ken Pelzel, Tim and Jill Eastman, and Marilyn and Tom Goehl;

2) sponsors who contributed $20 or more every month for a specific student, usually for years, and those who otherwise made generous financial contributions, especially Rick and Kelli Conlow, A.C. Gray, Bob and Val Reeber, Steve Gendler, Bret Gray, Matthew Siwiecki, Robert and Mary Bodoh, Dorothy Gockerman, Saeed Tavana, Francis Stankard, Russell Curtis, Bob Luddy, Jon and Linda Coleman, Steve and Denise Nordhagen, Jens and Margie Bach, Jim Stasheff, Peter Saldanha, Dave Watsabaugh, Berkeley Grimball, Brad and Michelle Worthington, Jim Wolfe, Art and Diane Belden, John Manley, Frank Takei, Ann Hamrick, Jeff and Londa Somers, Mario and Giovanni Battigelli, Joanne Van den Heuvel, Lori Schweickert, Diane Sambrick, Alvin and Brenda Bodford, Joe and Carolyn Barnes, Ann Powers, Paige Van Lenten, Steve Quint, Rev. John Wall, Rev. Douglas Reed, Julie and Bob Dermody, Dwayne and Nicole White, Anna Louise Reynolds,

David and Mick Roth, Mark Ruston, Joe McManus, Nora Howes, Ed and Patricia Cody, Jeff Taylor, Joe LoBuglio and Shannon Jordan, Yadira Rodriguez, The William Low family, Amy MacDonald, Ana Madriz, Sandra Trejos, Robert and Veronica Hadden, George Lensing, Jon and Jennifer Leonard, Bob Lind, Dick Isabel, Barbara Moran, Terri Guokas, Joannie Novak, Tracey Ocampo, Dave and Marcie Ollis, Mercedes Pannone, John and Loreen Postma, Jodi and Joe Burns, Susan Newhof, Margaret Newhouse, Carolyn and Jim Heuser, Thomas and Judy Bonds, Christine Gellings, Peter Franz, Joe Krueger, Lynn Franz, Marion Franz, Kelly Crider, Kelly Sambrick, Don Watkins, Rex Dwyer, Nancy Goodling, Donna McElcar, Richard Magnuson, Shannon Gray, Mary Kay Bondhus, Richard Tidball, Joe and Barbara Danos, Pat DeTitta, Mary Dowe, Karen Garcia, Petrus and Maria Tax, Dan and Lisa Efrat, Alejandro Francisco, Francisco Francisco, Sarah Freedman, Virginia Freedman, Kimberly Swain de Pop, James Kapuscinski, Tom and Gwen Konsler, Tish Galu, Margaret and Gene Johnson, Jo Ann Davis, Carrie Benoit Salemi, Kevin Heil, Thrivent, Mutual of America, Charles and Joan Thomas, Citibank, Wells Fargo, and the Rotary Club of North Raleigh;

3) the members of GSSG's Boards of Trustees: Pete Davis, John Yesulaitis, Pat Yesulaitis, Marguerite Coyle, Francis Coyle, John McKee, Noreen Ordronneau, Lois Macgillivray, Margaret Johnson, Sandra Trejos, Tom Bonds, Richard Conlow, Kelly Lewis, Saeed Tavana, Jens Bach, Mary VanderVeen, Jorge Paque, Bob Lind, Brent Heiser, Rosemary Czejkowski, and Joe Czejkowski, Barbara and Joe Danos;

4) gifted professionals who provided essential services: J. McLane Layton, a pro-bono lobbyist in Washington; June Kunsman, Visa Chief, U.S. Department of State (DOS); Jim Pritchett, lead attorney, Visa Office, DOS; Stanley Colvin, Director, Exchange Visitor Program, DOS; Abby Rupp, Designation Officer, F-Visa Program, DOS; Howard Betts, Visa Department Head, U.S. Consulate in Guatemala (DOS); Bob Dermody, accountant par excellence; Bill Ilgen, translator par excellence; Isabel Ferrall, M.D.; Suzanne Eismann, Melanie French, Executive Director, Academic Year in America; Rod Ruiz, Headmaster, St. Thomas More Academy, Raleigh, NC; Jim Glazier, Principal, Caledonia High School, Caledonia, MI; Bill Tschida and Wes Kapping, Principals, Holy Trinity High School, Winsted, MN; Br. Roger Betzold, Principal, McDonell Central Catholic High School, Chippewa Falls, WI; Tim Eastman, Principal, Hackett Catholic Central Prep, Kalamazoo, MI; Musicians Jeannie Rodgers and Marisa Whitesell; Optometrist Donna Hillsgrove; Richard Adelman, MD; Gabriel Rich, DDS; Optometrist Donathan Hudgins; Charles Lohr, DDS; Dempsey Smith, DMD; Uday Reebye, DMD; Margaret and Gene Johnson, for providing Internet Service; Paulo Chiquito, IT specialist, for maintaining GSSG's electronic equipment for many years; Lea Chiquito, who dealt with the quirks of a cantankerous Microsoft Word in the preparation of the manuscript for this book; Hannah Apellido, who prepared an earlier version of this book for publication as an eBook; Tom and Marilyn Goehl, who, after working with me for more than a year, agreed to take over the directorship and the bookkeeping of the organization when I retired; Klara Klein, Ph.D. M.D, for encouragement in a dark hour; and Daniel Chiquito, expert electronics technician who gave generously of his time and talent.

Everyone who has ever been involved in GSSG's program, especially the students and I, are particularly indebted to Jorge Paque, my sagacious Guatemalan Associate Director, a maven of all things Guatemalan, who selflessly contributed not only his time and talent but also his ever-cheerful disposition. Cognizant of this debt, I dedicate this book to Jorge Antonio Paque—friend, tireless worker, problem solver, and one remarkable guy.

I am also indebted to Marie Lewis, Jack Apellido, and Clark Taylor for reading portions of the manuscript in its early stages and to Dorothy Gockerman, Kelli Conlow, and Robert Bodoh for reading it in its entirety. All of them made many useful suggestions for which I am grateful.

iii

A Note on Names and the Pronunciation of Foreign Words

People everywhere are sensitive to the pronunciation of their names and Guatemalans are no different in that regard. For this reason, the pronunciation of many Spanish and Mayan names is provided, for example, Jorge Paque (HOR-hey PAH-kay), the capitalized letters representing the accented syllable. Mayan names can be particularly difficult because many phonemes in the Mayan languages have no parallel in English (and vice versa). Nearly everyone in Guatemala has four names: a first name, a middle name, and two family names,[1] the first paternal, the second maternal, without a hyphen, for example, María Ana Quej Yaxcal (ma-REE-ah AH-nah KEHH yahsh-KAHL). In this book, Guatemalans will usually be called by their first names or nicknames only, unless two have the same name, in which case the paternal family name is added; Americans generally by their last name. In the interest of privacy, some names of Americans mentioned in this book have either been changed or omitted.

As an aid to the pronunciation of foreign words, familiar English monosyllabic <u>words,</u> like *pie* and *day*, are often used to represent the pronunciation of foreign <u>syllables</u> (again, capital letters identify the accented syllable), for example, *costumbre* (kohss-TOOM-bray), *bray* representing the sound made by a donkey.

Ordinary Mayan and Spanish words are here printed in italics; the names of people, places, and languages are not. The translations of Mayan and Spanish words are enclosed in parentheses or, rarely, brackets; for example, *agua* ("water") or ["water"], depending on the context.

One final note on names. I avoid the word *Indian*. Many of the Maya regard it as a racial slur.[2]

---

[1] In parts of Guatemala, the Spanish conquerors changed some Mayan family names to Spanish family names. More recently, some Maya have done the same on their own initiative. As a result, some Mayan families have names like Vásquez, Pérez, and López, while most have family names like Quej, Tux, Co, Pop, Macz, Ich, and Cu.

[2] Diane Nelson concurs: *A Finger in the Wound: Body Politics in Quincentennial Guatemala*, 1999, p.174.

Preface

Impoverished and desperate Guatemalans, not Mexicans, constitute the largest group of illegal immigrants crossing our southern border.[3] A wall may reduce the numbers temporarily but ultimately only increase the volume of those seeking to escape intolerable conditions at home. The Maya, the desperately impoverished, terrorized, and exploited bulk of the Guatemalan population, represent a human tsunami, doubling in size with each generation, to overwhelm any physical deterrent here. A wall may be an effective expedient but it is not a solution.

The various chapters of this book examine the history, the causes and effects, the economics, the social and political issues, the geography, the religion, and, most importantly, the people of Guatemala, while the Epilogue details a plan to transform Guatemala into a country that nobody would want to leave and the deprived citizens of Honduras, El Salvador, Mexico, and elsewhere would want to call home—a solution.

Dan Saxon, concludes his preface to *To Save Her Life: Disappearance, Deliverance, and the United States in Guatemala*, with this ray of sunshine: "Perhaps in the future those who are already involved, including the United States government, may provide more effective assistance to victims of human rights violations." Such is the purpose of this book, though "compensation" may be more appropriate than "assistance," as we shall see.

---

[3] https://www.cbp.gov/newsroom/stats/usbp-sw-border-apprehensions

Prologue

Homo sapiens, having subjugated its natural predators and extended its lifespan by several decades, is unwittingly painting itself into a corner. Inevitably mankind will someday have insufficient land to feed itself.

Presidential Apology

"It is important that I state clearly that support for military forces or intelligence units which engaged in violent and widespread repression of the kind described in the report was wrong and the United States must not repeat that mistake. We must, and we will, instead continue to support the peace and reconciliation process in Guatemala."

President Bill Clinton
March 10, 1999
Guatemala City, Guatemala

The "report" to which President Clinton refers, titled *Guatemala: Memoria del Silencio*, had been published by the United Nations thirteen days earlier. It detailed the Guatemalan military establishment's strategy of terror in Guatemala's thirty-six-year Civil War. What was President Clinton apologizing for? What did the United States do that was so "wrong" as to require an official apology from the president of the United States and a promise to do better?

Background

Briefly, in 1960 the United States Central Intelligence Agency (CIA) fomented a civil war in Guatemala at the behest of the United Fruit Company, an American firm that owned forty-two percent of the land in Guatemala. The U.S. Department of State (DOS), ever attentive to the potential for communist infiltration in Latin America, provided a pretext justifying the intervention.

The war officially ended when the Guatemalan government and the opposition guerrilla forces signed the Accord for a Firm and Lasting Peace, the last of several U.N.-sponsored Peace Accords, on December 29, 1996. The process ending in that agreement had begun with an agreement by the presidents of the five Central-American governments, four of them dealing with a civil war in progress,[7] to collaborate in a search for peace. This agreement, signed in 1987, came to be called 'Esquipulas II.' Three years later, the government of Guatemala and the commanders of the various guerilla forces signed the Accord to Search for Peace by Political Means, the so-called 'Oslo Accord.' Many others followed, including, prominently: the Accord on the Identity and Rights of Indigenous Peoples, signed in 1995, the Accord on Constitutional and the Electoral Regime, signed on July 12, 1996, and the Accord on Strengthening of Civilian Power and the Role of the Army in a Democratic Society, signed on September 19, 1996. To this day, not all of the provisions of the various accords have been implemented and gangs of desperate youth, especially MS-13, terrorize the major cities.[8]

---

[7] Costa Rica, which has no army, being the exception.

[8] AppData/Local/Temp/Gang *Fact Sheet*.pdf

1

CEH

The Commission for Historical Clarification was created by the Accord on the Establishment of the Commission to Clarify Human Rights Violations, signed on June 23, 1994. The Commission's twelve-volume report, titled, as noted above, *Memoria del Silencio* ("*Memory of Silence*") was published by the United Nations on February 25, 1999. It is universally referenced not by its title, *Memoria del Silencio*, but by the initial letters of the commission's name, *Comisión para el Esclarecimiento Histórico*, CEH.[9] The report documents more than 250,000 human-rights violations intended to terrorize non-combatant Mayan villagers into submission, including particularly monstrous acts of horror, such as forcing Mayan women to watch as soldiers grabbed toddlers by their feet and smashed their heads against a rock or a tree until they split open "liked a ripe melon" (as CEH notes); burning people alive; pulling out fingernails (even small children's); keeping individuals who had been mortally tortured alive and in agony for days; slicing open the wombs of pregnant women; and similarly atrocious crimes.[10] These were not the random acts of some deranged psychopath but the result of government policy. Did the United States commit any of these surreal acts? No! The United States supplied the guns, trucks, jeeps, helicopters, planes, ammunition, and, most importantly, training (which the U.S. military had developed during the Vietnam War).[11]

The CEH concluded that, of the 250,000 individuals killed during the civil war, 93% were victims of government policy and 7% were killed by guerrilla forces. CEH also concluded that 83% of the casualties were Mayan and 17%, mixed-race Guatemalans.

The U.N. published the CEH in two formats, the full report in twelve volumes in Spanish as well as a single volume detailing only the commission's "Conclusion and Recommendations," in Spanish and in English.[12] (With regard to the twelve-volume edition, citations in this book include the notation [Spanish] or [translated]; otherwise references are to the one-volume, English edition.)

REHMI

The Guatemalan Council of Catholic Bishops created its own investigative project, called *Recuperación de la Memoria Histórica* ("*Recovery of Historical Memory*") now universally referenced as "REMHI." Bishop Juan José Gerardi Conedera, chairman of the project, had long been an activist in Mayan causes. In the spring of 1998, REMHI finished its report, *Guatemala: Nunca Más* ("*Never Again*"). The report laid the blame for 89.7 percent of the atrocities on the government (slightly lower than CEH's 93%) and 4.8% on the guerillas (slightly higher than CEH's 3%). REHMI was also published in two formats, a four-volume work in Spanish and a single volume in English. Citations here are from the latter.

Reparations

The Guatemalan National Reparations Program, created in 2005, mandated compensating victims' families the equivalent of about $3,000 per victim. Few awards have actually been made. In any

---

[9] The CEH is in the public domain. The English version uses British spelling.

[10] CEH, *Guatemala: Memory of Silence*, (1999), "Conclusions and Recommendations," #87.

[11] "[U.S.] military assistance was directed toward reinforcing the national intelligence apparatus and for training the officer corps in counterrevolutionary tactics, key factors which had significant bearing on human rights violations during the armed confrontation." Ibid., #13.

[12] Details of the process by which CEH data were analyzed are available at https://hrdag.org/guatemala

case, what monetary award can compensate a mother having to witness her child being swung by its feet against a tree until its head split open, being burned alive, or having its fingernails pulled out? Such anguish transcends calculation.

As President Clinton's apology demonstrates, the United States created its own share of blame and responsibility for compensation. What has the United States done by way of compensation? Nothing. This work will demonstrate that educational opportunity for the progeny of the victims would provide a measure of compensation appropriate to the need and commensurate with the United States' obligation, while eliminating the principal cause of illegal emigration on the United States southern border.

Map of Central America

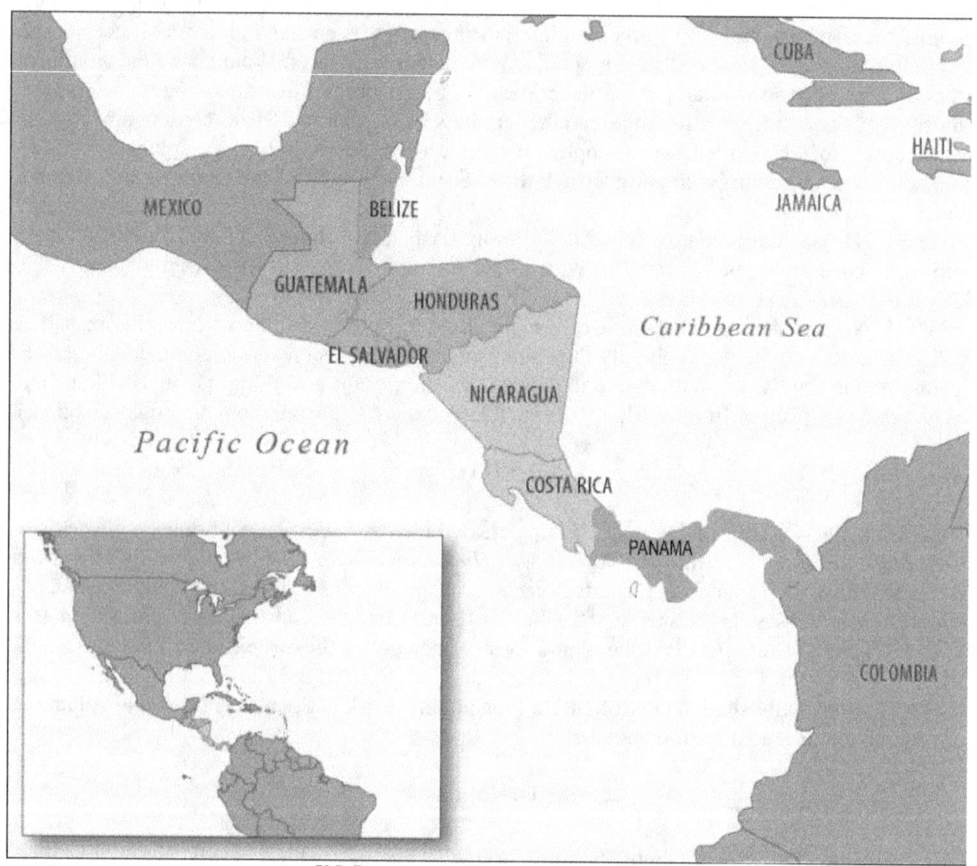

U.S. Department of State (slightly modified)

Central America, as a political term, includes neither Panama, which has been culturally and politically aligned with Colombia since the Spanish Conquest in the 1520s, nor Belize, which was once part of Guatemala but now is a member of the British Commonwealth of Nations.

With geography in hand, we may turn to recent statistics detailing the citizenship of illegal immigrants crossing our southern border.

Illegal immigrants crossing our Southern Border[13]

I) **Unaccompanied Alien Children Apprehensions by Country**
II) Numbers below reflect Fiscal Years 2013-2017, FYTD[14] 2018[15]

Unaccompanied Alien Children Apprehensions by Country						
Country	FY 2013	FY 2014	FY 2015	FY 2016	FY 2017	FYTD 2018
El Salvador	5,990	16,404	9,389	17,512	9,143	660
Guatemala	8,068	17,057	**13,589**	**18,913**	**14,827**	**3,333**
Honduras	6,747	**18,244**	5,409	10,468	7,784	1,154
Mexico	**17,240**	15,634	11,012	11,926	8,877	1,756

III) **Family Unit Apprehensions by Country**
IV) Numbers below reflect Fiscal Year 2016 and 2017, FYTD 2018

Family Units Apprehensions by Country			
Country	FY 2016	FY 2017	FYTD 2018
El Salvador	**27,114**	24,122	2,067
Guatemala	23,067	**24,657**	**5,861**
Honduras	20,226	22,366	3,497
Mexico	3,481	2,217	314

It is no accident that the largest number come from Guatemala.

Our current program, paying Mexico to intercept fugitives from El Salvador, Honduras, and Guatemala on their way north and send them back to their home counties[19] has led to disastrous consequences, as we shall soon see. First let us briefly consider conditions in El Salvador and Honduras, and then more fully in Guatemala.

El Salvador

In El Salvador the homicide rate in 2015 came to ninety per hundred thousand, making El Salvador the most world's most violent country not at war.[20]

Honduras

On July 16, 2016, the *New York Times* ran an article about Elena, a fugitive from Honduras who, at eleven, had been told by a gang member to be his girlfriend. She knew better than to say 'no,' because a friend of hers had also been told to be a gang-member's girlfriend and refused. Elena witnessed the outcome, telling the *Times* reporter, "in the blank tone of a child who has seen far

---

[13] https://www.cbp.gov/newsroom/stats/usbp-sw-border-apprehensions (highlighting added)
[14] FYTD, 'Fiscal Year To Date.' The U.S. Government operates on a fiscal year, October 1 to September 30.
[15] Bold type has been added to prominently significant statistics.
[19] https://www.nytimes.com/2016/06/26/opinion/sunday/obamas-death-sentence-for-young-refugees
[20] https://www.cfr.org/backgrounder/central-americas-violent-northern-triangle

too much," how her friend had staggered away from the resulting encounter "naked and bleeding." She had been raped and shot in the stomach. Elena did not know if the girl survived.[21]

Guatemala

In Guatemala widespread police corruption leaves the populace defenseless, while judicial immunity reigns, gang-related crime disables the major cities, violence defies calculation, and the homicide rate exceeds the highest casualty rate in any year of the civil war.[22]

In terms of land mass, Guatemala is about the same size as Honduras and Nicaragua but has by far the largest population in all of Central America, twice that of Honduras, the runner up. The citizens of El Salvador and Honduras speak mainly Spanish and, rarely, an indigenous language. Most Guatemalans, the Maya, on the other hand, speak mainly one or another Mayan language (see page 10) and, frequently now, Spanish. Political parties come and go but there is no Mayan party and no Mayan has ever been elected president; only rarely is a Mayan elected to congress.

Historically Guatemalans have been governed by dictators. In 1872 Justo Rufino Barrios, the 'Father of the Country,' seized hundreds of thousands of acres of Mayan land and sold it to foreign investors, mainly German, to start coffee plantations, obliging the previous owners, the Maya, to work the plantations at rates of pay below the poverty line.

In 1945 Juan José Arévalo, a reformer, became the first civilian president in memory (see 'Appendix G, An Outline of Guatemalan History,' page 259). He was succeeded by another reformer, an army officer, Jacobo Árbenz Guzmán. The Árbenz government purchased hundreds of thousands of uncultivated land at its accessed value, owned for the most part by the United Fruit Company, the American firm that had, over time, accumulated forty-two percent of Guatemala's land. To these purchased acres were added most of the acreage that the government itself owned together with some other privately-owned property, including land owned by President Árbenz' wife. The government then set up a system for redistributing the accumulated acreage to the poor, mostly landless Mayan farmers. As noted above (page 2), the ensuing civil war resulted in the slaughter of more than 250,000 civilians and in the restoration of all the land purchased from United Fruit and others to its previous owners.

The Mérida Initiative

The rule of law in Mexico has improved somewhat as a result of the Mérida Initiative, a bilateral partnership developed initially by the George W. Bush administration and the government of Mexican President Felipe Calderón Hinojosa (2007–2012) and enjoyed the continued support of the Obama administration and the government of Calderón's successor, Enrique Peña Nieto (2012–). Between FY2008 and FY2015, Congress appropriated almost $2.5 billion for the Mérida Initiative. In 2016 Congress added $139 million more.[24] Peña Nieto continued his predecessor's 'kingpin' strategy that resulted in the capture of "El Chapo" in February, 2014, his subsequent escape, and his recapture in January 2016. President Peña Nieto, again like his predecessor, deploys federal troops to supplement the national police. He has also reformed the judiciary. These programs have resulted in ameliorating the quality of life for many in Mexico, thus reducing the number of illegal Mexican refugees on our southern border (see the tables on the preceding page).

---

[21] Nicholas Kristof, "We're Helping Deport Kids to Die," *New York Times*, July 16, 2016.

[22] http://publications.armywarcollege.edu/pubs/2070.pdf

[24] Clare Ribando Seelke, "U.S.-Mexican Security Cooperation: The Mérida Initiative and Beyond," *Congressional Research Service*, February 22, 2016, pp.1 and 2.

U.S. Strategy for Engagement in Central America

In 2009, three months after taking office, President Obama attended the 'Summit of the Americas,' where he made it clear that he wanted to begin "a new chapter of engagement" in Latin America.[25] Not long thereafter, the White House adopted a policy initiative known as the 'U.S. Strategy for Engagement in Central America' and requested a supplemental appropriation of $3.7 billion.[26]

The Alliance for Prosperity Plan

The three presidents of the Northern Triangle played their part with a proposal called 'The Alliance for Prosperity Plan.' On July 25, 2014, President Obama met with Honduran President Hernández, El Salvador's President Sánchez Cerén, and Guatemalan President Pérez Molina to discuss implementation. In December, 2015, the Plan was launched with a $750-million appropriation for FY2016. The funds were added onto a pre-existing U.S. Government program called the 'Central American Regional Security Initiative' (CARSI) that had been initiated during the presidency of George W. Bush.

CARSI

The programs to decelerate the flow of illegal immigration, especially the programs of the U.S. Agency for International Development (USAID) and the U.S. Bureau of International Narcotics and Law Enforcement Affairs (INL), are housed under the CARSI umbrella.

In May, 2016, Vice-President Biden met with Guatemala's new President, Jimmy Morales, El Salvador's Sánchez Cerén, and Honduran President Hernández, to assess progress in implementing the specific steps of the Alliance of Prosperity Plan.

Meanwhile, CARSI had started to come under criticism in the U.S. media for supporting USAID and INL programs that were doing nothing to stem the tide of illegal immigration. A prime example is a program designed to train the national police in the target countries,[29] without demonstrable results. How does one *train* police not to use their weapon for robbery and extortion?

Root Cause

Homicide, rape, extortion, torture, robbery—none of these, singly or collectively, is the root cause of illegal immigration across our southern border; they are symptoms of a far touchier hornet's nest, insufficient land to feed Guatemala's swelling, indigenous population, doubling with each generation. The Guatemalan Military tried and failed to solve the problem through genocide. This book will propose a solution far more effective and humane than a wall and possibly more cost effective.[33] To that end, we need first to look at the geography of Guatemala.

---

[25] https://obamawhitehouse.archives.gov/sites/default/files/strategy_for_american_innovation_october_2015.pdf

[26] https://www.whitehouse.gov/the-press-office/2014/07/08/fact-sheet-emergency-supplemental-request-address-increase-child-and-adu

[29] The police forces in Central America are national, not local.

[33] The *MIT Technology Review*, in an article by Konstantin Kakaes, estimates the cost of the wall at $38 billion. https://www.technologyreview.com/s/602494/bad-math-props-up-trumps-border-wall/?utm_term=.b016f0dd7095. In a televised interview with Bret Baer (Fox News) on 1/17/2018, White House Chief of Staff John Kelly stated that the administration does not plan to build a wall across the entire border and estimates the actual cost to be about $20 billion. The next day, the President quashed Kelly's statement.

Map of Guatemala

Geography of Guatemala

The whole of Guatemala compares in size to South Carolina or Tennessee. It is divided into twenty-two *departamentos*, each larger than counties in the United States but much smaller, generally, than states.

Take note of Petén at the top, Alta Verpaz below it, and Quiché and Izabal, left and right. We will have occasion to visit these places.

Petén is both the largest *departamento* in Guatemala and the least densely populated. *Alta Verapaz* will engage much of our attention, in part because the Maya represent 93% of its population. The Maya of *Quiché*, 89% of its population and more than a million strong, are the most conservative culturally, seldom speak Spanish and otherwise preserve their ancestral heritage unflinchingly.

Izabal, to the right of Alta Verapaz, surrounds the largest lake in Guatemala and will be the setting for a fair measure of what follows. We will also have occasion to visit the *departamentos Chiquimula, El Progresso, Guatemala,*[36] and *Solola.*

Volcanoes

The isthmus of Central America was formed millennia ago when the Cocos tectonic plate forced its edge under the edge of the Caribbean plate, creating thereby the Sierra Madre mountain range and its awesome string of volcanoes in Mexico and Central America, five in a row in this illustration, in Guatemala. Many volcanoes are active and figure significantly in this narrative.

Lake Atitlán

About 84,000 years ago, continuing volcanic activity stopped up a river high in the Sierra Madres, a process that resulted in the creation of Lake Atitlán, 5,128 feet above sea level, covering an area of more than fifty square miles, and feeding two rivers that ultimately drain into the ocean.

We will spend some time in a town called *San Lucas Tolimán* on the shores of Lake Atitlán. (Photo taken from atop a two-story building in San Lucas.)

---

[36] *Guatemala* is the name of the country, the *departamento*, and the capital city.

Chapter I, The Maya

The Maya are descendants of adventurers who migrated from Siberia[37] sometime prior to 12,000 B.C., probably crossing what is today the Bering Strait but was then a land bridge connecting Siberia and Alaska during the last Ice Age when sea level was probably three to four hundred feet lower than it is today. Having worked their way south over thousands of years, some of those intrepid explorers settled in present-day southern Mexico, Guatemala, Belize, and parts of Honduras and El Salvador. We call their descendants the 'Maya,' most of whom live in Guatemala where they account for about sixty percent of the population.

Mayan Languages and Personal Identification

In the absence of roads and bridges, the mountains of Guatemala effectively isolated the primitive Mayan settlements one from another so that, over time, the parent language, Proto-Mayan (next page), developed into a number of mutually unintelligible, descendent languages (not dialects), as different from one another as, say, English and German.

If you ask indigenous Guatemalans to identify themselves, their response will not be, 'I am Guatemalan'; neither will they say, 'I am Mayan,' but rather, 'I am a Q'eqchí'-speaker,'[38] 'I am a Poqomchí'-speaker,' 'I am a Quiché-speaker,' or any other of the twenty-two Mayan language groups[39] spoken in Guatemala today.' A Mayan person's self-identification is not by country, religion, genes, or anything else but language.[40]

All languages change over time and when different groups are separated from one another, whether by water barriers, mountains, or distance, the evolution of local developments requires new modes of expression. In Guatemala, mountains serve that function (except in one case, where the island in the middle of Lake Petén developed a specific language, Itzá, that is still in use today; the island was, by the way, the last turf to be conquered, in 1697). The table on the next page represents graphically the development of Mayan languages, including those spoken in Mexico, Belize, El Salvador, and Honduras. An 'X' means extinct. The names of many of these languages are variously spelled. The seventh from the bottom, K'iche', for example, is also spelled Quiché' but is pronounced *key-CHAY* in either case and Kaqchiquel, ninth from the bottom, is also spelled Caq'chikel and is uniformly pronounced *cock-chee-kell*. More than a million people speak Quiché', the most numerous language group, and live in an area with the same name (see map above).

Most of the Maya presented in this book speak Q'eqchí' (*kek-CHEE)*, the last listed on the next page. (Two common expressions in Q'eqchí': "Chan xah QUIL," ["Hi! How are you?"] and "BantiOX," ["Thank you!"].) The first two Mayan youth we will meet, however, speak Poqomchí' (*poh-comb-CHEE*), third from the last. Many Mayan languages have dialects, that is, subsets of a single language, much as a Boston accent may differ from a Texas drawl, though both are still English.

---

[37] Charles Mann in *1491: New Revelations of the Americas Before Columbus* finds that the closest genetic relatives of the Maya are indigenous Siberians, 2005, p.116.

[38] The apostrophe after Mayan words, for example, Q'eqchí', modifies the quality of the preceding phoneme, for which English has no equivalent.

[39] Most sources list twenty-one languages but see Diane M. Nelson, *Who Counts? The Mathematics of Death and Life after Genocide*, 2015, pp. 42–43.

[40] "Mayan languages are the fundamental essences of Maya identity." Brigittine M. French, *Maya Ethnolinguistic Identity: Violence, Cultural Rights, and Modernity in Highland Guatemala*, 2010, p.30.

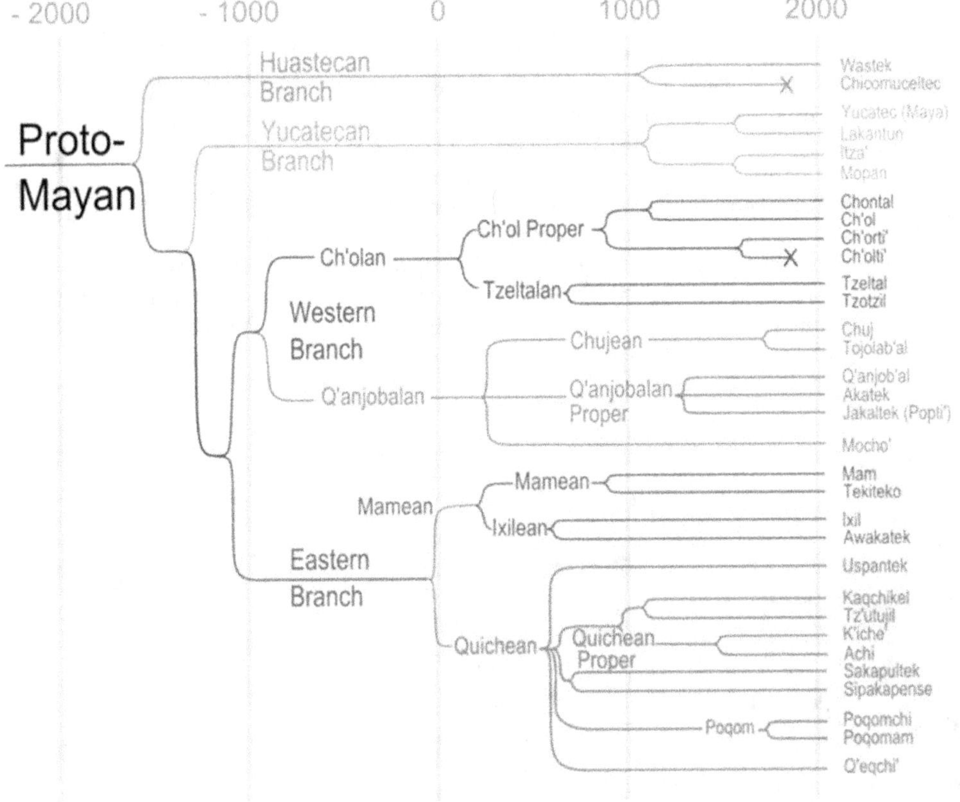

The Classic Period of Mayan History

We know very little about the Maya prior to 2000 B.C. Anthropologists divide what we do know after that until the Spanish Conquest in A.D. 1524, as follows:

1) the Pre-Classic Period, roughly from 2000 B.C. to around A.D. 250,
2) the Classic Period, from c.250 until 900 or so, and
3) the Post-Classic Period, from then until the Conquest in 1524.

The Classic Period, witnessed all the great cultural achievements of the Maya—the establishing of cities and monumental architecture, a refined system of writing, mathematical sophistication (including the concept of 'zero,' long before Europe had it), astronomy, and significant art forms. Hereditary kingships governed the different language groups. The ancient Maya conceived of the earth as flat and four-cornered, each corner a 'cardinal point': first the rising sun, then the second point in the opposite direction, and finally left and right. (When the issue first came up, I opined that the cardinal points represented east, west, north, and south. My informants vigorously denied any such attribution. In their minds, the cardinal points are not directions but sources of power, not abstract concepts but physical realities.)

The Maya of the Classic Period, unaware even of the existence of Europe, Asia, and Africa, developed a unique system of writing, using glyphs, a few of which are illustrated here. Although the various language groups thought of themselves as wholly distinct from one another, the literati all used the same system of writing because the glyphs represented, not sounds, but ideas. In the Classic Period they also attained high levels of sophistication in astronomy, using mathematical models, based on 20s rather than 10s, a system that enabled them to predict solar eclipses and provided them with a calendar having only a two-hour margin of error over its 500-year cycle. Their architecture continues to astound archaeologists, anthropologists, and historians, to say nothing of the modern tourists. During the ninth century the culture of the Classic Period collapsed, for reasons we do not know.

Museo de sitio, **Palenque, Mexico**

Temple at Tikal

The Conquest of Central America

Pedro de Alvarado, a lieutenant of Cortés, the conqueror of Mexico, established Spanish rule in the area we now call 'Central America' in 1524.[41] The Spanish named it the 'Kingdom of Guatemala' and divided it into five provinces: Guatemala, Honduras, Nicaragua, El Salvador, and Costa Rica (see also the map on page 3). As noted above, Panama was colonized from Colombia and has a history different from its neighbors to the north. 'Central America,' as a political designation, does not include either Panama or Belize.

As the capital of the Kingdom of Guatemala, the Spanish built a town in the province of Guatemala, naming it 'Guatemala' as well.

With the conquistadors came Catholic missionaries. In the resultant syncretism, many Maya came to practice both Catholicism and *costumbre* (kohss-TOOM-bray), also called the 'Old Ways.'

After independence in 1821, the Kingdom of Guatemala broke up and its constituent provinces became the independent Central American countries we know today.

Guatemala Today

Guatemala has a population of about sixteen million, far greater than any other country in Central America. The Maya constitute about 60% of the whole population and nearly all are deeply impoverished.[42] about 35% of the remainder of the population, called *ladinos*[43] (not *latinos*), are of mixed Spanish and Mayan descent and generally make up the middle class, but some are wealthy and together with Guatemalans of pure European descent comprise about 5% of the population, the upper class.[44]

Some paved roads traverse the country, notably the Pan-American Highway, but side roads often either are not paved or do not exist at all and villagers may have to walk miles to the nearest bus stop. Construction of a magnificent, multi-lane superhighway from Guatemala City to Puerto Barrios on the Caribbean coast is under construction, very likely with foreign aid. Although a couple of hundred miles of narrow-gauge rail exist, corruption, thievery, earthquakes, and hurricanes make service difficult to maintain. In any case passenger service is not available.

---

[41] We do not know if de Alvarado read to the Maya the usual notice intended to legalize the conquest, for which see Thomas Cahill, *Heretics and Heroies: How renaissance Artists and Reformation Priests Created our World*, 2013, pp.58–59.

[42] Statistics are hard to come by in Guatemala because the Guatemalan Government consistently underreports the number of Maya. See Piero Gleijeses, *Politics and Culture in Guatemala*, p.16. Sixty percent represents a familiar estimate, see: Francisco Goldman, *The Art of Political Murder: Who Killed the Bishop*, 2007, p.6; Maureen Shea, *Culture and Customs in Guatemala,* 2001," p.xiii; Victor Montejo, *Voices from Exile*, 1999, p.3; and others.

[43] *Ladinas*, if feminine.

[44] See Elizabeth Malkin, *New York Times*, "Toppling a President," September 16, 2015, citing Valerie Julliand, the representative for the U.N. Development Bank in Guatemala.

Guatemala, capital city of the old Kingdom of Guatemala, prospered. There, in the shadow of *Volcan Fuego*, the Spanish laid out streets and built large structures in Renaissance, Baroque, and Rococo styles. Between 1773 and 1776 a series of apocalyptic earthquakes wrought havoc in the city. Twenty-five or thirty miles away the Spanish created a new Guatemala (city) and the old capital, abandoned, came to be known as *Antigua Guatemala* ("Old Guatemala"). Thus *Guatemala* was the name of: a) all of Central America, b) the province of Guatemala, and c) the capital of the province and of all Central America. Today *Antigua Guatemala* is simply called 'Antigua.'

A century or two after Antigua lay prostrate, the phoenix returned to life as a tourist attraction. Some of the ruined buildings have been partially or wholly restored, even as the city has grown. Today tourism dominates Antigua. The city's ruins, its cobblestone streets, the domineering presence of the volcano, the moderate climate, the central park, and the ubiquity of Mayan handicrafts combine to make Antigua irresistible. (At right, Mayan women sell hand-made products.)

Ruined Church in Antigua

The Maya Today

Mayan culture today is as divided as it was before the Conquest. Yet some features of Mayan culture are common to all the language groups, as they were then. For example, virtually all Mayan women

wear a blouse called a *huipil* (*wee-PEEL*) but the design and the colors differ from one language group to another.

Until recently the Maya lived in squat huts with walls made of cornstalks, tree limbs, or sun-dried mud brick with a thatched roof and dirt floor. Today these huts have largely disappeared, in part because in 1976 an earthquake destroyed much of Guatemala's housing and most of the rebuilding used cement block, tin roofs replacing thatch.

Most Mayan women weave their own clothing and other textiles, the result of technical skills and artistic talent passed on from generation to generation for thousands of years. Often involving complex designs, the goods exhibit a variety of traditional motifs and colors, foremost among them the colors of the Quetzal (ket-SSAHL), that elusive bird with a red breast and green feathers, especially significant in the Mayan folklore that recounts how the Quetzal came to rest on the breast of the dying Tecún Umán, the Quiché' chief who fought the conqueror Pedro de Alvarado (page 12) in one-on-one combat in 1524, and lost; hence the bird's red breast. Quetzal is also the name of the Guatemalan currency.

Today many Mayan men wear jeans. The others wear Mayan garb that is very plain but those who have the means to do so don expensive attire (left) for special occasions. Whether simple or fancy, traditional clothing is always woven by hand.

Mayan women tote their babies on their backs in a *perraje*, even when they are working (see at right below).

Joseph C. Boone

Mayan women also carry everything (except their babies) on their heads.

Nearly all the Maya think of themselves as farmers, as they have throughout their history.

Finally, the Maya are poor, regardless of language. A U.S. State Department white paper on Guatemala attests, in part: "The wealthiest 10% of the population [of Guatemala] receives almost one-half of all income; the top 20% receives two-thirds of all income. As a result, approximately 80% of the population lives in poverty, and two-thirds of that number live in extreme poverty."[45]

Traje (TRAH-hey)

The most obvious feature of Mayan culture today is the ensemble that Mayan women wear, their *traje* (TRAH-hay)—the combination of the *huipil* mentioned above and a wrap-around skirt called a *corte*. Traditionally the colors identify a woman's language group, as numerous photos in this book will illustrate. Most of the women featured herein are Q'eqchí'-speaking and wear a white *huipil* (photo at right).

---

[45] U.S. Department of State, *Background Note: Guatemala*, May 2002, under 'Economy.'

Mayan Religion Today/Syncretism

Many beliefs and practices of the pre-Columbian Maya persist to this day, though they differ slightly from one language group to another. One important element they all have in common, even if they no longer believe it, holds that the earth is flat and four-cornered, each corner representing a cardinal point (page 10) in the creation myth whereby Xmucané' (*schmoo-kah-NAY*) and her consort, Xpiyacoc, made men out of corn. During the ceremony that precedes planting, the men gather in the field, build a fire, sprinkle incense on it, and face the four cardinal points. At the center, the planters draw energy from the four points.

Among the more conservative language groups, living in concord with nature is a religious obligation. Water is sacred, as is the earth. Their diet consists largely of corn, beans and other plants. The more conservative don't eat ham, cheese, or any processed foods. Before sowing their corn, the men ask permission of the earth. Candles represent man. They pray not *for* but *with* their ancestors reciting ancestral prayers, while evoking Mother Earth and the Sun, who is the deified heart of the sky. They believe that the Sun is a channel to the one God who wants them never to violate the rights of all of nature's products: plants, animals, and man. Rigoberta Menchú (whom we will meet later) emphasizes respect for the life, the purity and the sacredness of water, and reverence for the one God, the "heart of the Sky" (the sun). Above all, the Maya value human life.[46]

One Sunday, after Mass, I asked a young parishioner to take me to see Maximón (mah-shee-MOHN), an icon venerated in the western highlands. We entered a house and asked if we might visit him. The owner raised a ladder to the loft, brought down a wooden effigy about three feet tall, placed it on a table covered with a cloth, lit a cigar and put it in Maximón's mouth. I opined that Maximón seemed a bit short. "Yes, one year he failed to protect our crops and we cut his legs off." After a few moments, my companion knelt down to pray. Effigies of such icons are maintained by religious brotherhoods, called *cofradias* (koh-frah-DEE-ahss), and are carried in processions. Animism, a belief that ascribes conscious life to all natural objects, is particularly strong in the western highlands. Crosses, apart from Christianity, are venerated as guardian spirits, nourished by candles and incense, and function as symbols of the four cardinal points. The Mayan calendar is used in all religious ceremonies, called *costumbre* (kohss-TOOM-bray) or the 'Old Ways,' and in determining the time for planting.

The widely known author Victor Montejo, who speaks Jakaltec, remembers that, as a child, while he danced as a deer in the Xil Wej ceremony on Ash Wednesday, the local Catholic priest made the sign of the cross with ashes on his forehead[47]—syncretism.

From the Spanish Conquest in 1524 until about the middle of the twentieth century virtually the entire population of Guatemala professed to be Catholic. Today about 30% are Evangelical.[48]

On Good Friday entire towns walk the Way of the Cross. I participated in one such devotion, as did most of the town folk. For three or four hours we wove our way through the woods and through town, ending up in the church. I could not help but notice the sincerity of piety, especially among the older walkers, many of whom were barefoot. The bellowing of a trumpet with no discernable tune or rhythm appeared to annoy only me.

During Holy Week, festooned sawdust and sand paintings embellish streets and churches (see next page).

---

[46] Rigoberta Menchú, *I, Rigoberta Menchú: An Indian Woman in Guatemala*, edited by Elisabeth Burgos-Debray, translated by Ann Wright, 1984, pp.256–258.
[47] Montejo, *Voices from Exile: Violence and Survival in Modern Maya History*, 1999, p.6.
[48] Goldman, op. cit., p.151.

Catholicism

Together with the conquerors came Catholic missionaries, who "were overwhelmed by the readiness with which the Indians agreed to be baptized,"[49] in part because of attractive similarities: the cross is an important symbol in traditional Mayan rituals; Jesus' sacrifice and resurrection recall the same experience of their corn god; their 'day of the dead' corresponds to All Souls Day; religious processions are common to both religions as is the annual cycle of religious festivals. The burning of incense and the use of special garments for religious services are prominent features in both *costumbre* and Catholicism. In addition, most of the missionaries treated the Maya with respect and used their influence to protect them from the abuses of rapacious Spaniards as best they could.

The attractiveness of Catholicism continues for the Maya to this day. In accepting the Catholic religion, they believe that they have not abandoned their culture. Rather it seems to them that Catholic ritual is an alternate way of expressing themselves and confirms their belief that there is a God who is the Father of all. The New Testament relates the passion and death of Jesus Christ and the Maya draw "a parallel with our king, Tecún Umán." "Thus," says Rigoberta Menchú (the Nobel Peace Prize recipient), "we made Catholicism part of our culture."[50]

---

[49] Lynn V. Foster, *A Brief History of Central America*, 2007, p.79.
[50] Menchú, op. cit., pp.80–81.

Courtship and Marriage

Rigoberta Menchú tells of her own experience at age ten, when her parents explained to her that she was beginning her life as a woman, that she would want many things that she could not have, and that, no matter what ambitions she might dream about, she would have no way of achieving them. They gave her the freedom to do whatever she wanted as long as, first and foremost, she obeyed the laws of their ancestors. She was not to use lipstick and kiss on the street, as do the *ladinos* (mixed-race people, see page 12). If she got engaged, her suitor could visit her in her home, provided "he abides by various customs and the laws of our ancestors."

When a young man has decided he wants to marry a girl, he and his parents visit her parents, who, by custom, initially are non-committal. If their daughter is pleased, by the third visit and an exchange of gifts, they usually agree. After that, the lad may visit the girl in her home, provided at least one of her parents is present. The suitor brings a gift for her parents and is then allowed to talk with his intended directly for the first time. They may never meet on the street. If the girl does not like him, she finds things to do and doesn't talk to him. If she does like him, he may return but they are never alone. This seemingly phlegmatic ritual ensures the girl's purity, "which is something sacred, something special." The marriage ceremonies preserve four ancestral rites and adds a Catholic ritual; all of these, weeks or months apart. At the third of the ancestral rites, the couple take their vows. The fourth is called the 'farewell.' "It is a big party." If the marriage doesn't work out, the girl can go back to her parents.[51]

Cultural Vitality

The multiplicity of languages, clothing styles, modes of portage, and religious ceremonies are manifestations of Mayan culture thousands of years old. For all of that, partly in response to the recent Civil War (that will occupy much of our attention later), change has now invaded the Mayan mind-set. Many Maya today speak at least some Spanish; most Mayan men today wear jeans most of the time; nearly everyone would prefer carrying firewood, not on his or her back but in the back of a pickup; and nearly all of the Maya have adopted significant elements of Christianity. Under-lying all such developments, not only for the Maya but for everyone everywhere, is the way we human beings think about ourselves, our mind-set or mentality or, broadly speaking, our culture.

Culture determines the nature of everything we human beings do. Americans drive on the right-hand side of the road; we read from left to right and from top to bottom; we shake hands when we meet and we speak English; we eat three times a day and sit on chairs to do so; we drink coffee and eat toast or cereal for breakfast; we use a ring as a symbol of marriage and wear it on the third finger of the left hand; we stop on red and go on green, and we do all the other things that make up our particular culture simply because they are traditional, *not because they are necessary.* Else-where and in other times, other people have other customs. The Japanese sit on the floor to eat, take off their shoes at the door, speak Japanese, drink tea, use chop sticks, drive on the left, and do not use the alphabet. There is nothing in nature to validate the traditional elements of any culture. Most importantly, every culture is in a constant process of change. Consider how American culture has changed just since the advent of the computer and the Internet. A culture that is not constantly changing is, in fact, dead, like the culture of the ancient Egyptians.

Among the cultural differences which separate one people from another, the most pronounced and the most significant are found not in the realm of what we do—sit on chairs, wear rings, stop

---

[51] Ibid., pp.60–78.

on red—but in the way we think, that is, in our values and attitudes, our assumptions about life, our convictions, our principles and prejudices, our opinions, our interests, our hopes and fears, and our religious beliefs, in everything that makes us behave the way we do and do the things we do—in short our *mind-set, mind, or mentality*—the way we think.

The dominant elements in any culture, language and religion, not only *express* the way we think, they also significantly *control* the way we think. Religion rather obviously dictates certain behaviors. Christians go to church on Sundays and celebrate Christmas as a time of gift-giving. Muslims wash five times a day and pray bowing their heads to the floor. Language control is more subtle. We all prefer to speak our native language because it matches our mind-set like a glove; it is comfortable; it expresses our values and attitudes, our assumptions about life, our convictions, our principles and prejudices, our opinions, our interests, our hopes and fears, and, yes, also our religious beliefs. Every language is created by the people who speak it to express the way they think, their mind-set.

Historically, the Maya prefer to live in villages and farm rather than live in towns or cities and work at payroll jobs; sons and not daughters are expected to care for their aging parents; corn is more important to them than money[52]; women are subordinate to men; a new-born child belongs not only to the parents but to the community as well. Conservative Maya are scandalized if a woman goes to a hospital to deliver her child.[53] The Maya everywhere, liberal and conservative alike, have always preferred tortillas (made of corn) to any other food.

Because all cultures are in a continual process of change, our minds teem with innovation, ever generating new developments that alter, in one way or another, that spiderweb of values, aspirations, hopes and fears. In the United States, during the Second World War, women took over traditionally male jobs (cp. Rosie the Riveter). The traditional role of women as stay-at-home moms took a hit and, after the war, women started going to college. Today, gender equality has moved the norm far to the left in the so-called 'developed' world.

The people of any culture also borrow from other cultures. Baseball was introduced into Japan in the late nineteenth century by an American, Horace Wilson, an English professor at the Kaisei School in Tokyo. The Japanese now think of baseball as *their* national sport and are sometimes surprised to learn that we Americans also think of baseball as *our* national sport. Many Japanese brides often now wear white instead of the traditional yellow and Japanese men routinely wear business suits.

The influence of Western culture after the Conquest of Guatemala altered traditional Mayan thought in some important ways, the introduction of Christianity being only the most obvious. Today private property ownership has replaced communal land rights (but not by choice). And, in the course of the current generation, the Maya have come to value formal education. Some may regard these developments as unfortunate, as bastardizing Mayan culture. Be that as it may, change is inevitable. I make the point because the program detailed in this book will influence Mayan culture at its source, the Mayan mind-set, the way the Maya think about themselves—one of the consequences of education. Attempts to turn back the clock can only be counter-productive. "Educational reform is one of the top priorities not only of Pan-Maya discourse, but of indigenous rights discourse in general."[54]

---

[52] "Maize is the centre [*sic*] of everything for us. It is our culture." Ibid., p.54.

[53] Ibid, page 8.

[54] Michael T. Millar, *Spaces of Representation: The Struggle for Social Justice in Postwar Guatemala*, p.69.

Chapter II, The Origins of GSSG

Having retired from academe early to finish a *magnum opus* already numbering some five hundred pages, I thought to take a long-overdue vacation to some exotic place I had never visited and knew nothing about, before getting down to business. By coincidence my sister-in-law gave me a subscription to the *St. Anthony Messenger*. (She had never before given me a gift and never did so again.) The first issue I received featured an organization in Cincinnati called 'CoEd' (Cooperative for Education)[58] that distributed textbooks to schools in Guatemala because the schools there didn't have any. As a life-long teacher, I wondered about the efficacy of teaching without textbooks. The closing paragraph invited readers to join a book-distribution tour. I could not have located Guatemala on a map. I knew it was in Central America, but which was Guatemala, which Honduras, which Nicaragua, and so on, I could not say.

Having consulted a map and having paid CoEd, I boarded a plane for Guatemala City on February 8, 2002. After a few hours, the view out of my window began sporting mountains and volcanoes, thirty-three of the latter I would soon learn, the tallest an awesome 13,845 feet high.

Because of its natural beauty and its benign climate, the conquerors of Guatemala come to call it 'the Land of Eternal Spring,' a moniker undergirding Guatemala's tourist industry today. But, look at the picture—how can people farm in such a place? And the Maya are farmers! You can see why Proto-Mayan developed into many distinct languages, the different valley settlements, unable to communicate with each other easily, becoming, over time, linguistically diversified.

---

[58] CoEd is not affiliated with the Catholic Church.

As my Continental Flt. 444 began its descent into Guatemala City, *Volcan Pacaya* rose majestically into the air to dominate the view outside my window. Its awe-inspiring summit shone brightly in the morning sun, fleecy white clouds encircling its slopes in silent adoration, its base ruling the surrounding cityscape in the power and majesty of an aloof Mikado.

Approaching the runway revealed a different reality, one of Guatemala City's many slums.

CoEd

At the luggage carousel in the old La Aurora terminal, I met other Americans who were also responding to the article in the *St. Anthony Messenger*. We were soon ushered into a waiting bus and taken to the Sheraton Hotel in downtown Guatemala City, where we met the executives of CoEd, the brothers Jeff and Joe Berninger. Some years earlier Jeff had taught school in Guatemala, without textbooks, of course. At the end of that year, he and brother Joe decided to do something about the problem and created CoEd (Cooperative for Education). Jeff lives in Guatemala City now and directs operations there; Joe, the American executive, lives in Cincinnati.

The next day we toured Guatemala City, which seemed much like any other metropolis, if noisier, more congested, more polluted, and filled with children who I thought should be in school.

During the ensuing week we got into a routine. Arriving at a school, we were welcomed by the assembled students and faculty; the principal gave a speech and the students presented something they had prepared, a skit perhaps, some singing, or a dance. After these preliminaries the students lined up and we started

handing out books and school supplies. We had different books for the different grade levels and the various subjects in each grade, all published in Guatemala. Each of us had a specific task—my assignment was handing out pencils, two to each student. At the first school we visited, one of the students claimed he had not gotten any pencils. I gave him two. Then they all claimed they had not gotten any pencils.

The schools themselves, in addition to having no textbooks, also had no library, no science equipment, no typewriters, no dining facility, no musical instruments except drums, no gym, no computers, no audio-visual equipment, and no faculty offices.

As it turned out, we did not learn much about Guatemalan history at these staged events. But we spent a lot of time on the road and

Courtesy Ed Cody

our bus was equipped with a microphone. During our trips from one school to another, Joe held us captive as he unveiled the poignant details of Guatemala's history and present circumstances.

The average level of education for a Mayan woman, he told us, was one year of grade school. Teachers, even high-school teachers, only high-school graduates themselves, were poorly prepared and poorly paid, and most of them worked two jobs. Only about half of all Mayan parents sent their children to school, he said, child labor being seen as more profitable. Guatemalan law re-

quired schooling through the sixth grade but many indigenous parents did not comply because, by the time their children were old enough to go to school, they were also old enough to work. As a result, fewer than half of the children who entered first grade completed the six years required by law. Not surprisingly, illiteracy in Guatemala topped the list in Latin America, surpassed in the Western hemisphere only by Haiti.

Especially unnerving was Joe's account of the Guatemala Civil War, how the U.S. Central Intelligence Agency engineered a coup by a renegade Guatemalan officer, Castillo Armas, who in 1954 deposed a Guatemalan democratically elected president, the second such in Guatemala's history up to that point.

At the end of the week-long tour, we were back in our Sheraton Hotel, sitting down to another feast. I took a seat next to Joe. "Look!" I said, "I want to get involved here." "What can you do?" "Well, my father was a home-improvement contractor. I'm pretty good with a hammer and saw." "No good!" he replied, "All the building here now is in cement block. What else can you do?" "I taught high-school English for a couple of years. I've even taught English as second language." "Bingo!" he exclaimed. "I know just the place for you. At one of the first schools to get our books, the third-year English teacher is also the principal. You could take over his classes and not put anybody out of work. How is your Spanish?"

A refresher course in Spanish? Well, why not! The book-distribution tour took place in February, 2002. In April I returned to Guatemala and enrolled in a Spanish school in Antigua.

Tourism in Antigua

In the twentieth century, Antigua became a major tourist attraction. The cobblestone streets, unflustered by earthquakes, remained today as difficult to negotiate as they were in the seventeenth century.

The central park looks much as it did before the earthquakes of 1773–1776 (see page 13), even as some of the major colonial buildings have been either partially or wholly restored, while others—churches, monasteries, convents—tower majestically over the polyglot babble in their shadow (see next page).

Central Park, Antigua

Tecún Umán

The school I had chosen to attend, called *Tecún Umán,* after the Quiché chief who in 1524 battled Pedro de Alvarado, the Spanish conqueror of Central America, in one-on-one combat and lost (page 14). Instruction at Tecún Umán consisted largely of one-on-one conversation about the meanings of words and idioms, for a few hours every day, Monday through Friday. Many of the students at Tecún Umán would get together at a local cantina on Friday nights. Most of us were Americans but two Chinese girls and a Canadian woman who spoke only French  provided a medley of gaffes. With spirits at hand, we had an uproariously good time.

Zoila

My teacher at Tecún Umán, a young, indigenous woman, who might be called either Zoila or Josefina, was natively bilingual (Caq'chiquel and Spanish). Zoila had advanced beyond high school, taking classes at a nearby university on Saturdays.[59] Like most Mayan women, Zoila also spent a good deal of time weaving on a back-strap loom.

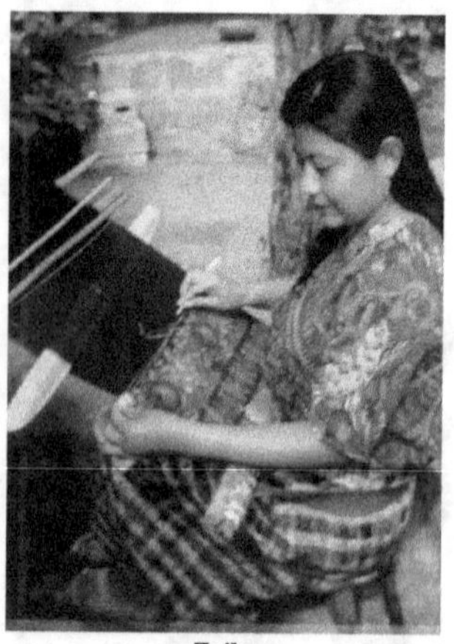

Zoila

Zoila had an older brother who, a few years earlier, while studying on the bus on his way home from school one day and greatly irritated by something in his assignment, aroused the interest of the man seated next to him, by happenstance, an American. Observing the young man's distress, the American asked what was wrong. Their ensuing conversion resulted in the American offering to put the lad through a university in El Salvador. A few years later Zoila's brother had completed his program and was looking forward to graduation two weeks hence, when he was accosted on the street and killed, apparently by thieves.

Zoila lived in a community at the foot of *Volcan Fuego* called *San Antonio Aguas Calientes* ("Hot Waters"), for good reason. In the night *Volcan Fuego* glows menacingly, belching black smoke and sometimes covering Zoila's community in a thin layer of ash. One weekend Zoila invited me to visit her family. She had told me that her father had diabetes and, lacking sufficient funds to buy insulin, the family used medicinal herbs to treat the disease. During the course of his illness he had fallen and broken a leg. Taken to a nearby medical facility, the leg was set in a cast. Gangrene set in and his leg had to be amputated. (Subsequently an American physician told me that a cast should never be used on a patient who is diabetic, for that very reason.) I met Zoila's father and his family that weekend. He struggled to conceal his pain. Most impressive was Zoila's mother, who, despite her family's circumstances, radiated a pleasant disposition, smiling, talking little but taking delight in the chatter of the progeny around her. Some months after I returned to the States, Zoila wrote me that her father had died.

First Lesson[60]

Back home and eager to learn more about this troubled land, I immersed myself in Guatemalan history and culture, starting with Lynn Foster's *A Brief History of Central America*, then Walter LaFeber's *Inevitable Revolutions*, Robert Carlsen's *The War for the Heart and Soul of a Highland Maya Town* (an anthropologist's report on the changes of character taking place in Santiago Atitlan), Sedley Mackie's *An Account of the Conquest of Guatemala in 1524 by Pedro de Alvarado* (a collection of documents from the time of the conquest), Dennis Tedlock's translation of the Mayan creation myth, the *Popul Vuh*, Victor Bulmer-Thomas' *The Political Economy of Central America since 1920* (an exhaustive account of the relation between economics and politics in the period), Lisa North and Alan Simmons' *Journeys of Fear: Refugee Return and National Transformation in Guatemala*, Gabriel Garcia Marquez, *One Hundred Years of Solitude*, Stephen Connely

---

[59] A common phenomenon in Guatemala because most of the population cannot afford taking university classes without a steady income.

[60] Parenthetical comments were made at the time and may or may not be germane today.

Benz' *Guatemalan Journey* (an enjoyable read, both interesting and informative), Jonathan Evan Maslow's *Bird of Life, Bird of Death* (the author's search for the Quetzal, the national bird of Guatemala, interspersed with some Mayan history and ornithology), Miguel Angel Asturias' *Men of Maize* (a surrealist piece involving the reader in the primitive mythology of Guatemala), Rigoberta Menchú's *I, Rigoberta Menchú*, and David Stoll's response, *Menchú and the Story of All Poor Guatemalans.*

Only one conclusion was possible, viz., that the enigmatic history of Guatemala since the Conquest is linked at the hip with exploitation. From the moment Pedro de Alvarado arrived (page 12), the Maya were reduced to serfdom if not outright slavery. Their land was seized and they were put to work producing crops for the new owners. Many were sold as slaves to be worked to death in the gold mines of Peru.

Draft animals—horses, oxen, and mules—although common in Europe and Asia, did not exist in the Americas before 1492. Wheeled vehicles and roads were equally unknown. In Guatemala goods were transported over the mountains by human porters who carried their cargo on their backs with a tumpline on their foreheads. After the conquest, these porters even carried their Spanish masters, seated in an armchair, in this fashion.[61]

Today cars, trucks, busses and paved roads have not entirely eliminated the tumpline. Because all indigenous women cook on an open fire, their sons go into the mountains every day to collect the required fuel, as seen in the photo at right. During the coffee-picking season, hundred-pound sacks of beans are carried to the nearest road in the same

way. Even women and children use the tumpline.

Sometimes the conquerors found it useful to curry favor with the royal Mayan families in the various language groups. The royals were taught Spanish and the alphabet and served as a conduit between their subjects and the Spaniards and, with their inherited authority and credibility, sometimes kept the peace and collected tribute and taxes for the state.[62]

The conquerors brought with them diseases, like smallpox and measles, against which the indigenous had no immunity, not only in Guatemala but throughout the Americas. In Guatemala alone, an estimated native population of one and a half million in 1500 had been reduced to an estimated 180,000 by 1570.[63]

---

[61] Lynn V. Foster, *A Brief History of Central America*, 2007, p .84.
[62] Ibid., p.85.
[63] Ibid., p.83.

Bartolomé de Las Casas

Bartolomé de Las Casas (1484–1566), from a well-to-do Spanish family, stands out as an early advocate of indigenous rights. Las Casas was nine when Columbus returned in 1493 from his first voyage to the New World. His father and an uncle accompanied Columbus on his second voyage. Because of his family's connections, Bartolomé, a dedicated student, received a superior education, attending first the University of Salamanca and then the University of Valladolid. He traveled back and forth between Spain and the New World several times and witnessed the treatment accorded the natives. At the age of thirty he decided that he could no longer remain an innocent bystander, became a Catholic priest, and returned to  the New World. After an abortive attempt at reform in Venezuela, Las Casas persuaded the crown, in 1537, to give him control of an area in Guatemala where the Maya had been especially violent in their resistance to 'pacification.' He and the missionaries he brought with him successfully preached Christianity and the area became known as *Verapaz* ("True Peace"); the name persists to this day (see map on page 7). Twenty-three years later, a new wave of colonists took control of Verapaz, enslaved the natives, and drove out the missionaries. Las Casas returned to Spain where he persuaded Charles V to issue new laws in 1542. Thus armed he went back again to Verapaz but, as the colonists were getting wealthier by the day, so were they also increasingly independent, and the new laws proved impossible to enforce. Las Casas returned to Spain in 1547 and spent his last years in a Franciscan monastery.

Second Lesson

The latter of the two lessons I learned from reading after returning home is simply stated but difficult to swallow, that the United States Government was deeply involved in Guatemala's civil war and morally culpable, along with Guatemala's Military Establishment, for its conduct and its consequences. My sources included: Jean-Marie Simon, *Guatemala: Eternal Spring – Eternal Tyranny*; Hector Pere-Brignoli, *A Brief History of Central America* (mostly economic history [the epilogue is excellent as is the bibliography]); Diane M. Nelson, *A Finger in the Wound*; Kay B. Warren, *Indigenous Movements and Their Critics* (largely about the Pan-Maya activist movement); Edgar Leonel Barillas Barrientos, et al., *Historia del istmo centroamericano, Tomo 1*; David Stoll, *Is Latin America Turning Protestant?*; E. F. Schumacher, *Small Is Beautiful: Economics as if People Mattered*; S. D. Houston, *Reading the Past: Maya Glyphs*; Mary Kitchel Kost, *E-Mail from Guatemala*; George E. & Gene S. Stuart, *The Mysterious Maya* (a good introduction to the classic Maya); Gaspar Pedro González, *A Mayan Life* (first novel ever written by a Mayan author, details the misery among rural indigenous, ending with self-help); Eric Holt-Giménez, *Campesino a Campesino* (on sustainable agriculture, informative but repetitive); Hugh Thomas, *Rivers of Gold* (a well-researched history from Columbus to Magellan); Stephen Schlesinger & Stephen Kinzer, *Bitter Fruit* (detailed account of the causes and events of the Guatemalan Civil War—excellent, riveting, heavily documented); Thomas R. Melville, *Through a Glass Darkly*; and Arnold Toynbee, *Civilization on Trial*.

Animated now, I looked forward to flying back to Guatemala and teaching English at the school Jeff Berninger had recommended (page 23). My *magnum opus* (page 20) would have to wait. It is still waiting.

On February 8, 2003, I flew to Guatemala for the third time. An acquaintance of mine, having heard what I was doing, wanted to donate a computer he had recently replaced with a newer model. He had bundled it up in the original packaging that, in those days, approached the size of a bathtub. At La Aurora, muscling my luggage into a cab, in the rain, I told the driver to take me to the Monja Blanca bus station,[65] where, standing in line to buy a ticket, I overheard the clerk tell the man in front of me that the bus was nearly full. The guy behind me, overhearing the same conversation, immediately jumped in front of me. As it turned out, I got the last ticket and, when I boarded the bus, the only vacant seat was next to that same guy. I had caught a cold in the rain and was not feeling well. My less than sympathetic companion, who had the window seat, and I were in the second to the last row. As soon as the bus got up to highway speed, diesel fumes began pouring in through the open window. By the time we got to Tactic, I was unquestionably sick. The driver pulled up to the curb beside the central park and set my luggage on the sidewalk, in the rain.

Cell phones were still relatively new but I had bought one in Guatemala City and now called Manuel Zamora, the principal of the school where I was going to teach. He answered and, mercifully, drove up in just a few minutes. We shook hands, etc. He explained that he had not engaged a room for me because he wanted me to approve any commitment first and suggested that I spend the night in a hotel. I readily agreed. At the hotel, I was shown a windowless room approximately eight feet square. I said it was fine. Manuel left. I took off my shoes, climbed into bed, suit, tie and all, pulled the blanket over my head, and fell asleep.

The next morning church bells woke me up; it was Sunday. The sun shone brightly. Not yet cured but certainly better, I washed and shaved, and grabbed my camera, for Sunday, I knew, is market day.

Market Street in Tactic on Sunday

---

[65] Many independent bus lines service Guatemala and each has its own terminal.

The bedlam outside reminded me of Antigua, with one critical difference—these people were not tourists. On market day, the Maya from nearby villages bring things to sell in town: weavings, for sure, but mostly vegetables of all sorts, chickens, eggs, pigs, and hand-made products, like wood bowls, both decorative and functional. Businesses, both local and those from nearby towns, also participate, hawking pots and pans, dishes, silverware, machetes, scissors, tools of all sorts, hammers, saws, planes, and pliers, hardware like nails, screws, and wire, clothing, shoes, boots, flour, sugar, salt, just about anything you can name. I marveled particularly at an impressive selection of watches spread out on a blanket, a mix of very

expensive, not so expensive, and very cheap, none of them in a box and no documentation. (Yes, your conclusion is quite right.)

The girl on the left in this photo, the seller, fled the moment she saw me taking her picture and did not return until I left. I have no idea why. Meanwhile the girl on the right completed her selection and departed.

The traditional home-made garb of Mayan women, their *traje* (page 15) has no pockets; so, as I observed, they kept their change in the only other pocket-like accommodation in their ensemble.

In the afternoon, Manuel took me to meet Miguel Ángel and Maruca (mah-ROO-cah) López—he, *ladino*

(page 12); she, Mayan and trilingual (Poqomchí', Q'eqchí', and Spanish). Miguel Ángel was the manager of a local credit union. The López home had a detached bedroom behind the house, with a bathroom but no stove or refrigerator, perfect for me. We agreed on a price for room and board.

Because Maruca was always home, ordinarily I did not need a key to the house, but on two occasions she was not home and I had to get to my room through a gate beside the house. Beyond the gate lay Bingo, chained. I get along very well with dogs, having had one almost all of my life, but Bingo would not respond to my overtures and when I got past the gate, he bit me. On the next occasion, I bought some *salchichas*, Guatemalan sausages, and gave them to him as I approached. He wolfed down the *salchichas* and then bit me.

One weekend, Maruca asked if I would like to go to a place called 'Biotopo,' a government park where the illusive Quetzal (page 14), could sometimes be seen. We went. I marveled at the beauty of the landscape and sky, but we did not see a Quetzal.

After a few days, Maruca, knowing that I was teaching English at the school, asked me if I could teach her English at home. "Do you have a blackboard," I asked. She did and we began. Maruca soon found out that my fundamental interest was in helping the poor and that teaching English simply served as a vehicle to that end. So she asked, "Would you like to meet some poor people?" "Yes! I would." Forthwith we went to visit María López (see footnote 1 on page iv) and six of her children who had survived infancy.

Unidos and *Casados*

I must interrupt this narrative to explain *unidos* ("united") and *casados* ("married"). Many Guatemalans, both Mayan and *ladino* (mixed-race) couples, never marry. Guatemalan law recognizes such informal arrangements after the first child is born. But, since a *unidos* couple were never married, no divorce is required to break their union and, in fact, many men, and some women, just walk away. En route to María's house, Maruca told me that María's husband had recently done so.

María's home (at right), a small wooden structure with no windows, was divided in two by a curtain; on the far side two mattresses on the floor identified the bedroom. For furniture, the living room had, and probably still has, a wooden bench, two plastic chairs, and a plastic table.

Below you see the bedroom, the kitchen (a lean-to in back of the house, with no appliances), and the bathroom. María's home actually belonged to her mother, who had her own house in

back. María's sister lived with their mother and when, a few years later, grandmother died, the property was divided in two. Since the property is small, María's sister has to walk through María's house to get to her own.

María provided for herself and her children by weaving small objects—shawls, napkins, baby blankets, and the like—which she sold to a middle man who in turn marketed them, probably abroad or in Antiqua. She made about two dollars a day.

A smiling María, rising from her loom, her hollow black eyes smudged with fatigue, greeted us as we approached the open door (always open in the daytime, for the house had no electricity and no windows).

Heydi (HEY-dee)

The eldest of María's children, Heydi, had attended a local Catholic grade school for four years on a church scholarship and then two more years at a public grade school that did not charge tuition. As there was no public middle school in town, sixth grade was to be Heydi's last; María could in no way afford tuition.

When we entered the home, María took the bench and invited Maruca and me to sit on the chairs. Five children stood in front of the curtain, facing us; the sixth, a boy of twelve, was working in a garage, as he had since age eight. Heydi, the cook, dishwasher, and laundress of the family, was thirteen or fourteen; the youngest child, three or four. Maruca explained who I was and why we were visiting. In the course of conversation Maruca mentioned that I was teaching English at the school and that I was also teaching her at home. Like a shot, Heydi burst in excitedly, "Can I study English with you?" I glanced at Maruca; she agreed. The next day Heydi came to Maruca's with a notebook that had a few empty pages left and the stub of a pencil. It soon became apparent that Heydi was alert and, as her quickness in asking to join us had demonstrated, eager to seize any opportunity for self-improvement.

The next day I asked Manuel, the principal, if it was too late for Heydi to register. No problem (he could use the income). So I paid her tuition for the year (ordinarily parents pay about $2.25 a month) and bought her school supplies. The next day she was back in school, seventh grade, happy as a clam.

Since María's home had no electricity, Heydi studied with the door open during the day. At night,

a single candle (unlit but visible at right) allowed her to do her homework. Outdated calendars and home-made art provided the only decoration (above left).

One day I walked into María's house and noticed that Heydi was holding her jaw with one hand while writing with the other. When I asked what was wrong, she replied that she had a toothache. "Come with me." At Maruca's house I asked if there were a dentist in town. Yes! At the dentist's, a teen-age boy answered our knock. When I told him what we wanted, he replied that his dad would only pull the tooth. "No way!" Back at Maruca's house, she replied to my question, that "Yes, there is a dentist in Cobán." (Cobán is the nearest city; see the map on page 7.) Would she take Heydi—I had to teach; I would pay the bill. "Yes." That evening I learned that the dentist in Cobán had no x-ray equipment but had determined that Heydi needed a root canal, a procedure that she (the dentist) could not perform but she knew a dentist in Guatemala City who would come to Cobán. Within a few days the dentist came. Heydi has had no further trouble with the tooth.

Meanwhile, I had started teaching at the *Instituto Mixto de Educación Básica por Cooperativa* (middle school, grades 7, 8, and 9). The building, a cement-block structure, sits on a concrete slab. Inside, a central area runs the length of the building (except for the school office at this end) and serves as auditorium and theatre (without seats), a stage at the far end. The day I arrived to begin teaching, Manuel called a general assembly. We stood on the stage while he explained that I was an American professor[66] and that I would be teaching English for a couple of months. The students applauded.

Early on, Manuel told me that he (the third-year English teacher) had learned his English twenty years earlier when he had lived for two months in New York City. He had never studied the language and could not read, write, or speak it. After I had been there a few days, the first and second-year English teacher sent two of her students to my classroom to ask what the English word *them* meant.

Over the next several weeks I learned that the other teachers, with one possible exception (a man who taught science and math), were all poorly prepared in their subjects and that all but one (a woman of some means) worked two jobs. The English textbook (yes, the one supplied by CoEd [page 22] but published in Guatemala) was so bad that after a few days I discarded it and started duplicating hand-outs of my own.

The students had little interest in studying. Indeed, they had little reason for being in school at all.

In addition to the teachers' lack of preparation, there were no substitutes and when a teacher did not show up, as frequently happened, the students, unsupervised, usually kicked a soccer ball around, sometimes outside, sometimes in the central hall. The school had no bell to signal the end of class. Manuel had a cow bell but he often forgot to ring it. My blackboard was patched with brown packaging tape. Some of the windows were broken and on one occasion a boy outside poked his head through a broken window and began chatting with one of my students inside. He was taken aback when I told him to leave. A rectangular table that served as my desk had only three legs.

Meanwhile I volunteered to teach also at Asunción, a Catholic school in the same town. The principal agreed but when I showed up for class the next day, the regular teacher did not appear. The students had no textbooks, so I asked them what they were studying. They showed me their notebooks. (The traditional mode of instruction in schools that had no textbooks involved the teacher copying from his or her textbook onto the blackboard and the students copying from the blackboard into their notebooks.) I saw that they were on verb forms, so I started in. The students were polite and eager to learn but, as the hopelessness of the situation became increasingly evident, I became disheartened and decided it would be useless to continue. After a few days, I told the principal that I would not return. In retrospect, that was a mistake I deeply regret to this day. The students were better behaved and eager to learn. Had I known what would develop in the next few weeks, I would have stayed.

---

[66] The Spanish word, *profesor*, means "high-school teacher." A university teacher is called *licenciado*.

Motivation

One day I confronted Manuel and told him I wanted him to split my class in half, that I would take the fifteen or so who appeared to have some interest in learning English (or anything else). He would have to take the rest. He agreed.

Now, how to motivate my group! Learning a foreign language can be dull stuff when you never have any chance to read anything or speak with anyone in the target language. The school had no library, much less any books in English. All of my students knew for a certainty that they would never have any need to know one single word of English. I was the only English speaker in town and I would be gone in a couple of months. So I asked my group, "How many of you would like to go to the United States?" All of the hands shot up. When I asked why, they had no idea. "All right!" I pontificated, "we are going to have a contest. Each of you will write an essay, in English, telling me why you want to go to the United States. Here are some dictionaries (they had never seen a Spanish/English dictionary but I had brought three or four with me). I will help you and I will take the winners to the United States!" Bear in mind, I was making this up on the fly. In fact, I had no idea how or if I was going to take anyone to the United States. I only knew that the prospect was motive enough.

By now the first and second-year English teacher, Tita Arrué (see below), and I had gotten acquainted. When I told her what I had done to motivate the students, she suggested that I meet Jorge Paque. "Who is Jorge Paque?" Jorge had been her teacher for her one semester of English at a nearby university (she had had no prior preparation in English) and, she told me, he had taken students to the United States. Jorge lived in Cobán, about twenty miles away (page 7). I called him; he offered to come (by minibus) to Tactic. Within half an hour or so, we met in the plaza in front of the church, found a *cantina* nearby, and ordered a couple of beers. So began a life-long friendship that would bind the two of us in a mutual enterprise, called the 'Guatemalan Student Support Group' (GSSG), for years. Tita and Jorge would have leading roles in the playbook we were about to choreograph, though we did not know it at the time.

Tita (TEE-tah) Arrué de Zamora[67]

Tita[68] Arrué, the daughter-in-law of Manuel (the principal at the *Instituto Mixto*) and the first and second-year English teacher (who had asked what the English word *them* meant), had three children, two girls and a boy, all of them teen-agers at the time. Like most teachers in Guatemala, Tita worked two jobs, one in the morning at Manuel's *Instituto*, the other in the afternoon, at another private school, in addition to being a housewife and mother of three teen-agers, with no dishwasher, washing machine and dryer, air conditioner, vacuum cleaner, or car.

Soon Tita would become an invaluable asset in getting GSSG off the ground.

Though we haven't seen each other in many years and she has no access to the Internet, we remain good friends. Once in a great while someone with a cell phone will call on Skype and surprise me by turning the device over to Tita.

Tita is *ladina*, mixed-race (page 12), middle-class.

---

[67] Married women use their father's last name followed by *de* and their husband's last name.

[68] "Tita" is the abbreviated form of *Martha* in Guatemala.

Jorge (HOHR-hey) **Antonio Paque** (PAH-kay)

Jorge Paque! Gregarious, gifted, and gallant, Jorge attracts friends like a water hole in the desert. Generous with his time and talent, always ready to pitch in, Jorge gets the job done, whatever it may be.

Like other teachers, Jorge worked two jobs, one at a public[69] middle school (grades 7, 8, and 9) and another at a private high school (grades 10, 11, and 12). Many years earlier, when he himself was in high school, he had studied to be a grade-school teacher. When he went to his first job, he was assigned to teach English in high school. He protested that he knew no English. (Since there are no colleges in Guatemala, one learns a trade in high school. Studying to be an English teacher is an option but Jorge had opted for grade-school teaching; English is not taught in grade school.) "No matter!" he was told. "Here is the textbook. Go and teach it!"

But Jorge is an enterprising guy. He organized the other English teachers in the area and persuaded them that they could teach themselves English. Somewhat later, he won a competition of some sort for an extended visit to Japan where, of course, he had no choice but to speak English. Still later, he successfully applied for a year-long job teaching Spanish in Sweden. Knowing no Swedish, he taught in English, which, like most Europeans, all educated Swedes speak as a second language. In addition, he had friends in California and visited them from time to time, and on one occasion had taken some of his students to California. Thus, he knew how to apply for visas, as I did not.

Jorge also knows the ropes in Guatemala and would subsequently be responsible for getting GSSG's candidates

their birth certificates, health records, and passports as well as seeing to money transfers, paying bills, contracting for accommodations, hiring busses and security guards, and, when necessary, sweet-talking a finicky secretary into bending the rules a bit. On one occasion, we took some students to the passport office in Guatemala City only to find a very long line ahead of us. We were told to come back another day. We could not do that. Jorge went inside and returned a few minutes later, saying simply, "Follow me!" We did so and presently found ourselves in front of an agent waiting for us.

Jorge would become highly respected and much loved by all the youngsters who would be GSSG's students. In the photo above, he is seen with Judith, the same girl in the photo on page 15); we will meet her personally shortly.

---

[69] Public schools are owned by the federal government, not the town, and, with few exceptions, only exist in major cities, like Cobán, the capital of Alta Verapaz.

Visiting the Maya in Their Homes

When the students finished their essays, I visited the winners' homes. Five lived in a village called Pasmalón, where everyone speaks Poqomchi' (poh-cohm-CHEE). Their homes, board structures with no plumbing or electricity, had an open fire for a stove, minimal furniture, a concrete sink

in back, and a bathroom in the woods. In one home, I noticed that the student's birth certificate had been altered by hand. Couldn't use that. Another family had a Jehovah's Witnesses' sign over the door. I could not risk having a student needing a prohibited blood transfusion.

Arnoldo

In the end I picked only Arnoldo, whom I would try to bring to live with me for the two and a half months of Guatemala's annual vacation, November to January (part of the coffee picking season). I decided to bring Heydi as well. She had not been in my class. Two years younger than Arnoldo, she was only in seventh grade but I took her anyway, remembering her eagerness to seize any opportunity for self-improvement in her, "Can I study English with you?" (page 32).

Arnoldo's home sat on a coffee plantation near Pasmalón and belonged to the company. His father, an overseer of some sort, made about $4 a day; his mother spoke only Poqomchi'. Arnoldo told me that one of his older brothers had committed suicide the previous year; he did not know why but life was hard, with little prospect for the better.

Years later I learned that Arnoldo was the first Mayan to attend the *Instituto Mixto* and that the other students had treated him badly, both physically and verbally. The next year other Poqomchi'-speaking youth registered and the abuse diminished. I reminded him that on my first day of class I had asked each of the students to tell me something about himself or herself, including his or her ethnicity. He remembered the event. I commented that I was surprised when one girl told me she was Spanish. That seemed unlikely and I expressed my doubt. She then acknowledged that she was indigenous. I remarked to Arnoldo that I thought some of the students were ashamed of being Mayan. He surprised me, replying, "All of them!"

The next time I saw Jorge, he floated the idea that I might take an English teacher to the United States as well as Heydi and Arnoldo, since, if the teacher learned English, his or her teaching would improve. So I asked Tita if she would like to participate. She said she would but not for three months; she had family and had to be home before Christmas.

GSSG

Back in Chapel Hill, I talked with friends and neighbors, of course, about bringing Heydi, Arnoldo, and Tita here. Some told me they wanted to get involved. So I invited them to my house to talk about what we might do. In the end we concluded that, if the way out of poverty lies through education and the Maya cannot get a decent education in Guatemala, we should create a program to get some of them here. I had already made arrangements to bring Heydi and Arnoldo for three months. Could we build on that? Jorge was on the AFS[70] Board in Guatemala. Could we bring Heydi and Arnoldo back the following year for a year of high school with AFS? Could we bring more students the next year? I wondered if we might organize under Section 501(c)(3) of the Internal Revenue Code so that those contributing money could get a tax deduction. As consensus developed, someone suggested we should call ourselves the 'Guatemalan Student Support Group.' Unanimity on these issues quickly became apparent. With that, the Guatemalan Student Support Group (GSSG) was born. The date was August 28, 2003. Attendees became the first Board of Trustees—Peter Davis, Marguerite and Francis Coyle, John and Pat Yesulaitis, my neighbor John McKee, Noreen Ordronneau, and I.

Libraries

Libraries had existed long before Johannes Gutenberg's invention of movable type but his successful production of the first printed books, about 1453, made libraries affordable. Prior to Gutenberg, copies of books had to be made by hand, a tedious and inexact method that might require years to produce a single copy, with multiple errors and at an astronomical cost. The printing press was the first major advance in the dissemination of knowledge since the creation of the literary alphabet by the ancient Greeks in the eighth century B.C.[71]

The printing press can be credited with the creation of modern libraries, institutions disseminating knowledge to substantial segments of the European population, a development largely responsible for the transformation of European culture from that of the Middle Ages to the Renaissance.

The printing press has now been succeeded by the Internet. It seems obvious that we are now on the cusp of a new era, so new, in fact, that it does not yet have a name—'The Electronic Age,' 'The Age of Invention,' 'The Information Age'? Whatever it will be called, it is already the third engine of development in the creation and dissemination of knowledge.

Can Guatemala, which has virtually no libraries, and other functionally illiterate societies skip the middle step?

---

[70] American Field Service, the student-exchange program created after the Second World War to promote international understanding and goodwill by sending American youth abroad and bringing foreign students here for year of high school.

[71] Many of the characters in the alphabet had previously been used for accounting purposes by the ancient Phoenicians, traders in the Mediterranean, but never, so far as we can tell, for literary purposes.

Libraries in Guatemala

Library collection in a town called El Estor, the focus of attention later in this book.

The big cities and some towns in Guatemala have libraries; schools do not. Town libraries serve all of the schools in town. Their collections consist almost exclusively of old textbooks. The library in El Estor (above) has, in addition, an encyclopedia and a few maps.

One study a few years ago found that the sixty public libraries in Guatemala were allocated six dollars a month for acquisitions.[72]

The libraries' holdings may not be checked out.

Library Reading Room in El Estor

---

[72] Victor Perera, *Unfinished Conquest: The Guatemalan Tragedy*, 1993, p.49.

Chapter III, Guatemala, 1524–1960

Land, Parcels, and Community

Before the Conquest in 1524, all the arable land in what is today Guatemala and Belize, as well as Mayan enclaves in Honduras, El Salvador, and southern Mexico, had been carved out of the primordial forest by the Maya who had lived there since time immemorial. The archaeological record suggests that, at some time during the Archaic Period (c.7000–1200 B.C.), the Maya began replacing the hunter-gatherer livelihood of their ancestors with agriculture, sooner in the lowlands, later in the highlands, and families began living together in villages.[73] The major innovation responsible for this development was the domestication of corn, about 3500 B.C.[74]

Living in villages fostered the development of social, economic, and political customs related to the land, its use and development, about which we can learn much not only from archaeological evidence but also from conditions in place at the time of the Conquest.

Until the Conquest, Mayan land under cultivation consisted of irregularly shaped *parcels*, owned either: a) by individual families within the community or b) by the community jointly. The parcels belonging to individual families [a)] were large enough to feed an average family, generally about twenty acres, more or less depending on the productivity of the soil, and was passed on from father to son. Titles did not then exist and boundary markers consisted of objects in nature—rocks too large to move, trees, creeks, rivers, and so on. In addition to its parcel, each family had an irregular lot in the village, large enough for a squat (so the wind wouldn't carry it away) hut with a dirt floor, walls made of cornstalks and/or sticks, and roofed by thatch or leaves. The property in the village, like the family parcel, was also passed on from father to son. The village and its surrounding farmland were governed by elders. As settlements developed into cities, governance evolved into hereditary kingships. Diego de Landa speaks of beads being used as currency in the Yucatan (in present-day Mexico) around 1550[76] but there is no evidence of any form of currency in Guatemala before the Conquest nor of domesticated animals other than dogs.[77]

The following paragraph details an issue that will be centerstage in Guatemala's political and economic drama from the nineteenth century until the present day, a foundation in sand that resulted in the mayhem of Guatemala's thirty-six year civil war and <u>illegal emigration</u> today.

The land owned by the community jointly [b)] prior to the Conquest was not worked by the men collectively. Rather it too consisted of parcels that might either be left fallow or assigned to individual families at the discretion of the community elders. Those in need (families with many under-age children, for example) would be granted usufruct of a particular community parcel but, if the elders were not satisfied with a family's care of a communal parcel or if family circumstances changed (if several children in a large family died, for example), the elders could reassign usufruct to someone else. As the number of families increased, additional land had to be created out of the surrounding forest by the community jointly and divided into parcels assigned by the elders to individual families as needed. It was the responsibility of the elders to see to it that every family

---

[73] Lynn V. Foster, *Handbook to Life in the Ancient Maya World*, 2002, p.19; Arthur Demarest, *Ancient Maya: The Rise and Fall of a Rainforest Civilization*, p. 82.

[74] Richard E. W. Adams, *Prehistoric Mesoamerica*, Third Edition, 2005, p.38.

[76] Friar Diego de Landa, *Yucatan Before and After the Conquest*, trans. William Gates, New York, 1937, p.9.

[77] Ibid., p.41.

had sufficient land to feed itself. Until the Spaniards arrived, surveying and legal evidence of ownership would have served no purpose.

The Conquest

The Conquest of Central America in 1524 had been funded by King Charles I of Spain and others. All of the land, therefore, belonged to those who funded the operation, 'by right of conquest.' The Spanish government, however, also recognized that the land belonged to the indigenous people 'by natural right.' Dealing with this obvious contradiction, government lawyers reasoned that the state had property rights only to unoccupied land, not to the lands of the indigenous who had owned it "from time immemorial."[80]

The riffraff who were released from prisons in Spain on condition they go to the New World and never come back and young peasants who fancied an opportunity to improve their fortunes also headed for the new world. Whereas the nobility who intended to stay took their wives and children along; the others simply took up with native girls. These latter sometimes improved their fortunes and sometimes did not. Their children, of course, were' mixed-race,' *ladinos* (page 12).

The upper-class created *haciendas* ("estates") and employed *ladinos* who were often bilingual as overseers to manage the Mayan labor force.

Independence (1821)

In 1821, three hundred years after the Conquest, the 'United Provinces of Guatemala,' as they now called themselves, joined Mexico in declaring independence from Spain (page 12).

The liberal policies of the Spanish nobility, now free of Spanish law respecting the 'natural right' of the indigenous to their land, came to regard that land as subject to expropriation. To stifle opposition, the liberal government expelled the clergy and seized church property.

Rafael Carrera (c.1838–1865)

In the late 1830s, Rafael Carrera, an illiterate *ladino*, led a successful uprising against the aristocracy. Though demonized by the opposition, Carrera, a devout Catholic, invited the clergy to return and restored church property. Above all he respected Mayan property rights. Under his autocratic rule, after a bumpy start, Guatemala enjoyed a long period of relative peace and stability.

In 1840 Carrera declared Guatemala independent of the United Provinces. The other provinces were similarly inclined and, after an interlude of diplomatic squabbling, the United Provinces of Guatemala evolved into the five independent countries we know today—Guatemala, Nicaragua, Honduras, El Salvador, and Costa Rica—governed by dictators.

Carrera died in 1865 and was succeeded by Vicente Cerna y Cerna, a loyal associate of Carrera, whose conservative policies he ventured to maintain.

Coffee

Coffee had been introduced into Guatemala in 1835. By mid-century, *ladino* entrepreneurs, itching for entrée into the emerging world market, were pressuring Carrera to expropriate Mayan land and sell it to them to start coffee plantations. He refused. At the time, more that *seventy percent* of the

---

[80] David McCreery, *Rural Guatemala: 1760–1940*, 1994, p.49.

arable land was still controlled by Mayan communities that had no interest in capital ventures like coffee plantations and no concept of title deeds.

By the time Cerna y Cerna's term expired at the end of 1870, the hottest political debate focused on two issues, how to dispossess the Maya of their land and how to make them work. These issues, exacerbated by the lack of a centralized title registry and a unified system of measuring land,[81] bode ill for the Maya.

Labor Relations

After 1761, when the production of indigo was king and before the introduction of coffee, the colonial government required individuals who needed labor to apply in writing to a court. Applicants had to agree to treat the laborers well, to pay them, and to pay a head tax; further, the workers had to be paid in advance, not directly to the laborers but to the village elders who were responsible for mobilizing the men and seeing to their arrival at the plantation on time. Soon the labor of certain villages came to be attached to specific plantations and passed on from owner to owner without state intervention.[82] The indigenous, of course, reluctant to abandon their own crops, resisted as best they could and frequently refused to appear at the work site. The employer, for the moment, would lose the wages he had paid in advance but the obligation to work would remain with the Maya and sometimes had to be repaid by descendants, with their own labor.

Independence in 1821 left the system unchanged. Although the conservative policies of Carrera and Cerna y Cerna favored the indigenous, some *departamento* governors unduly favored the *ladinos*, especially in *departamentos* where coffee production and profits exceeded expectations. As early as 1861 the villagers in San Felipe in the *departamento* of Retalhuleu were complaining of encroachment on their hereditary land and threatening to cut down the coffee bushes with their machetes. The government conducted a census and found that sixty-three *ladinos* had taken possession of 4,500 acres, 511 legally. Rioting ensued there and elsewhere. In 1867 the Bishop of Alta Verapaz complained to the Archbishop of Guatemala that the local governor was allowing *ladinos* to take over not only Mayan communal land but even their parcels, especially in and around the capital of the *departamento*, Cobán, as well as in Tactic (page 28) and Tucurú.[83]

Liberal Governance (1871–1920)

Miguel García Granados y Zavala, Spanish by birth to a wealthy family and well educated, succeeded Cerna y Cerna in 1871. García Granados, a historic liberal, represented the landed aristocracy that had ruled the country before Rafael Carrera's conservative revolt in 1838.

The new administration quickly made its priorities clear. In September of 1871, government representatives began expelling Catholic priests and closing convents, confiscating their property.[84] For all of that, the Liberals' primary interest lay in the development of export agriculture, especially coffee, and the integration of Guatemala's economy into world-wide capitalism as a supplier of raw materials and a buyer of manufactures. Within weeks of his election García Granados asked those aristocrats who owned plantations to express: 1) their most urgent requirements,

---

[81] Ibid., p.172.
[82] Ibid., pp.93–94.
[83] Ibid., pp.164–67.
[84] Ibid., p.182.

and 2) how they could be satisfied. Their draconian responses: 1) institutionalization of forced labor (the 'peonage' system) and 2) definitive expropriation of [Mayan] communal land.[86]

In peonage a poor person borrows money and repays the debt with his labor. In 1871, one planter expressed his frustration by saying that no matter how many workers an employer needed, he could not get them without advancing them some money, but he had to realize that the workers would never repay the loan because, as soon as they had a little, they would ask for more and, since you needed them, you couldn't refuse. For all of that, the owners wanted workers to be in debt as a means of ensuring the labor supply.[88]

[N.B. Many names and dates follow. To keep them all straight, you may want to bookmark Appendix G, An Outline of Guatemalan History, page 259.]

Justo Rufino Barrios (1872–85)[89]

The period from 1871 to 1897 is known as 'La Reforma.' Its bellwether, Justo Rufino Barrios, elected to the presidency in 1872, is celebrated today, quite rightly, as the Father of his country for he created the stage upon which Guatemalan history, both good and bad, would be played out.

In the year after his election Barrios ordered the seizure of all Church property.[90] That same year he established the *Escuela Politécnica*, a military school to create a professional class of army officers, "the breeding . . . ground for a new ruling caste."[91] He went on to recognize civil marriage and civil record keeping as exclusively valid; he built public schools,

Justo Rufino Barrios

and transformed San Carlos University from a pontifical to a secular institution. (All of these functions had previously fallen within the purview of the Catholic Church.) Barrios also introduced telegraph service and some railroad service. But land tenure kept him awake at night.

The date is January 1, 1877. The Barrios' government issues Decree 170 providing for the sale of, ultimately, all uncultivated Mayan communal land at three or four percent of its value, proceeds to be deposited with the newly created National Bank of Guatemala, that was to compensate the Mayan communities four percent of the funds received. (Since the bank soon collapsed, the indigenous probably never received anything for the seizure of their land.[92]) By the turn of the century, the depredations of *La Reforma* would amount to two-and-a-half million acres.[93] Consider for a moment the implications of "all uncultivated Mayan communal land." After Decree 170, whenever, in any given village, the existing communal parcels (page 39) had all been assigned to families in response to the growing population, any father that had more than one son would have to divide his parcel into two, three, or more sub-parcels, as would his sons and grandsons in perpetuity because, thanks to Justo Rufino Barrios, no more uncultivated communal land existed. That decree is ultimately responsible for the misery that has been Guatemala ever since.

Barrios intended to make history. To do so he needed money, a rare commodity in Guatemala. For capital he turned abroad.

---

[86] J.C. Cambranes, *Coffee and Peasants: The Origins of the Modern Plantation Economy in Guatemala, 1853-1897*, 1985, pp.120–21,

[88] McCreery, ibid., pp.186-87.

[89] The numbers following the names of Guatemala's presidents represent the duration of their terms in office.

[90] McCreery, ibid., p.182.

[91] Francisco Goldman, *The Art of Political Murder: Who Killed the Bishop?* p.141.

[92] Ibid., pp.185–86.

[93] Jean-Marie Simon, *Guatemala: Eternal Spring – Eternal Tyranny*, 1987, p. 20.

German Investors

Since the middle of the nineteenth century, the Industrial Revolution in Europe and America had been ramping up. In 1855 Henry Bessemer invented a process for making steel out of iron. In 1866 Alfred Nobel invented dynamite. Both discoveries led, in the late-nineteenth century, to Germany's dominance in the production of heavy equipment, while simultaneously acquiring much of the world's capital and looking for investment opportunities. Barrios had land for sale and Germans had money to buy it. In 1887, Germany and Guatemala conferred 'most-favored-nation' status on one another, thus removing restrictions to trade and travel between the two countries. German investors began buying expropriated Mayan land to create coffee plantations and by the end of the nineteenth century they had invested more than 200,000,000 Marks in the purchase of about 300,000 hectares (741,000 acres) suitable for the production of coffee.[96] By 1900 more than a third of Guatemalan coffee production was in German hands. Thus, German capital provided the funds for the construction of electric companies and the creation of ports and railway lines.

Today the descendants of German investors, together with the Spanish-speaking aristocracy and a few wealthy *ladinos*, constitute Guatemala's upper class, perhaps five to six percent of the population.

Cobán and Carchá[97]

By the late Nineteenth Century, German investors[98] had acquired more than 100,000 acres in Alta Verapaz, especially concentrated around Cobán, the capital, and Carchá, a Mayan *municipalidad* (a community consisting of a large number Mayan settlements). Those 100,000 acres included entire Mayan villages, whose inhabitants became *colonos* (*koh-LOH-nohss*), "resident workers," in effect the property of the new owner. Typically owners would allow each Mayan family a small patch of land that, together with its produce (corn) was and is still called a *milpa*. The Mayan cemeteries, important to the Maya for maintaining a relationship with their ancestors, were sometimes respected and sometimes not.[99]

Investment in Alta Verapaz nearly transformed Cobán into a German town, flaunting gas street lights and a movie theatre showing German films. German goods were readily available in German stores, while the German Mark served alongside the Guatemalan Quetzal as legitimate tender. After Hitler came to power in the Twentieth Century, Swastika flags flew above municipal buildings in Cobán and on German plantations.

Loss

Superficially, not much seemed to have changed. The Maya still raised their corn. The vast majority had no money but they had never had money. They still had their religion, modified by Christianity, but voluntarily so. They still spoke their native tongue, wore the same clothes, followed their ancestral customs. What had they lost? Prominently abstractions—freedom, security, ownership—the things men die for. And in time, those who still owned land would lose that too. In the late 1880s, ninety-seven Maya in Alta Verapaz still owned enough land to be considered plantations. By 1930, that number dropped to nine. In 1949, there were none.[100]

---

[96] J. C. Cambranes, op. cit., p.145.

[97] My source here is Greg Grandin's, *The Last Colonial Massacre: Latin America in the Cold War - Updated Edition*, 2011, pp. 24—25. Grandin references his primary sources.

[98] Like Erwin Paul Dieseldorff. Whenever Jorge comes to the U.S, he brings along a bag of Dieseldorff coffee.

[99] McCreery, op. cit., p.199.

[100] Greg Grandin, *The Last Colonial Massacre: Latin America in the Cold War* – Updated Edition, page 26.

Labor

After the sale of Mayan land to *ladino* and foreign investors, the government was obligated to ensure a labor force to work the plantations, especially during the harvest. The Mayan labor force, fell into three classes:

Colonos, Women at a plantation laundry

Colonos, Woman and children at home

a) *colonos* (resident workers).

b) seasonal workers who lived off the plantation but were bound to the owner in debt peonage;[102]

c) temporary workers, hired as need dictated and not in debt peonage but paid at the end of each month that they worked.

To say that *colonos* were often mistreated would be a gross understatement. In one incident, a worker testified that the brother of his employer had beat him for no reason and had beaten his wife and their baby as well and that both had died. Another protested that he had had to endure the dread experience of being hung in stocks because he had asked his employer to credit his account with the work he had done over a period of six months.[103] 'Hung in stocks' meant either having the stocks around your neck and hands as you knelt on the ground, or with the stocks around your ankles as you sat on the ground or lay flat on your back. In either case, the individual so confined, was helplessly exposed to weather, insects, hunger and thirst, verbal and physical abuse, and his own bodily discharges, sometimes for days and nights at a time.

Seasonal workers lived in their own communities. Plantation owners would hire *ladinos* as contractors to go to the villages, especially when there was a fiesta and the indigenous wanted money to buy alcohol[105] or during June and July when the supply of corn had nearly run out and prices were high.[106] The contractors would entice workers by giving them an advance on their labor

---

[102] In 'debt peonage' a person might borrow money, to be repaid by labor but seldom, if ever, liquidated his debt.

[103] McCreery, op. cit., pp.274–75.

[105] "[F]or the price of a couple of drinks, many Indians were burdened with debts they could never pay." Handy, *Revolution in the Countryside*, page 10.

[106] Ibid., p.225.

and, when the harvest was ready, round them up and deliver them to the plantation. Under the new law, local officials were authorized to jail seasonal workers who failed to show up for work.

Temporary workers had no obligation to an owner and securing their employment was a can of worms. On the one hand, at the height of the harvest, when labor was in short supply, temporary workers could demand very high wages and then sometimes disappear before satisfying their commitment. On the other hand, living in crowded conditions on a plantation, especially a plantation on the hot southern coast, temporary workers suffered from all kinds of diseases—dysentery, malaria, smallpox, cholera, and yellow fever, to say nothing of parasites—and when they returned to their villages, they carried these diseases with them.[107]

Rigoberta Menchú tells of her annual sojourn to the south as a temporary worker, travelling with about forty other people in the back of a truck, covered by a tarpaulin, for two nights and a day, together with some animals that sometimes defecated and urinated during the trip, even as some of her fellow passengers vomited and relieved themselves en route.[108]

She remembers working on a cotton plantation and waking up one night, lighting a candle and seeing the faces of her parents, her brothers, and her sisters covered with mosquitoes. Worse still, every plantation had a *cantina*. Workers could get just about anything they wanted there and charge it to their account. At the end of the month, purchases would be deducted from their pay. Rigoberta remembers her father, in despair, once drinking all night and running up a bill almost wiping out his earnings for the month.

At the end of the month, the overseer paid the workers, deducting his own pay first. No auditing, no accounting, no appeal! Before leaving, the workers were all required to make a thumbprint on a ballot, that they were unable to read, for the next election .

Because laborers acquired debt and had to make payments, they had to carry, on their person, a small account book, called a *libreta*, and because they were illiterate, they had to rely on someone else, often their *ladino* overseer, to make their entries for them. No auditing, no accounting, no appeal!

Justo Rufino Barrios was killed in battle in El Salvador on April 2, 1885, in a bootless attempt to reunite the five countries of Central America under his rule. His successor, Manuel Lisandro Barrillas (1886–1892), simply maintained existing policy.

José María Reina Barrios (1892–97)

José María Reina Barrios, a nephew of Justo Rufino Barrios, ended forced labor in March of 1894, explaining that "expansion and development" as well as "the love of work and the desire to improve oneself . . . among all social classes" had invalidated his uncle's labor laws.[109] In fact, the new law only changed the kind of work the indigenous could be forced to do, now, prominently, building roads and bridges. The law exempted: a) *colonos*, b) those otherwise essential to the plantations during the harvest season, and c) those "who knew how to read and write and were giving up their Indian costumes and customs."[110] The new law was promulgated as Decree 243.

Reina Barrios was assassinated on February 8, 1897.

---

[107] Ibid., pp.276–77.
[108] Rigoberta Menchú, *I, Rigoberta Menchú: An Indian Woman in Guatemala*, 1984, pp.21–26.
[109] McCreery, op. cit., p.190.
[110] Ibid., p.191.

Manuel Estrada Cabrera (1898–1920)

Manuel Estrada, a civilian lawyer and the vice-president, after finishing Reina Barrios' term was elected to the presidency in his own right. Early on, the quixotic Estrada initiated a kind of cult to the Roman goddess Minerva and began building public venues in imitation of Roman architecture. Pretentious to the core, he even built an opera house.

Not long after his election, Estrada Cabrera invited the United Fruit Company to purchase substantial tracts of land in Guatemala and in 1901 granted the company an exclusive contract to transport mail between Puerto Barrios and the United States. Three years later he engaged United Fruit to finish the railway line between Puerto Barrios and Guatemala City.

Estrada Cabrera proclaimed himself the first 'Education President' but when the government of Chile sent a delegation to study his reforms, they found nothing, "No teachers, no equipment, no students, not even buildings."[111]

By 1919 an opposition party had formed and in 1920 orchestrated a demonstration for March 11. On Estrada's orders, the army opened fire, a move that united all sides against him. On April 8 the National Assembly declared him insane and on April 14 he capitulated.

Bananas and Railroads

Minor Keith was born in 1848 to wealthy parents in Brooklyn, NY. When Minor came of age, his uncle, Henry Meiggs, who had built railroads in Peru, invited Minor and Minor's brother Henry to join him in constructing a railroad from the capital in San José, Costa Rica, to the port of Limon on the Caribbean coast. Henry started in San José and Minor in Port Limón. By late 1873 Henry was unable to meet the terms of his contract, which was then vacated by the Costa Rican Government. Meanwhile Minor had become a successful businessman in Port Limón. He negotiated a new contract with the Costa Rican government and construction was resumed in 1875. Meiggs, the uncle, died in 1877, leaving Minor Keith in control of the company. He completed the ninety-seven-mile rail line from San José to Port Limón in 1890.

In 1883 Keith had married the daughter of Costa Rica's president and the following year negotiated a deal with the government for 800,000 acres of land, tax exempt for twenty years, on which he planted banana trees. By 1899 he had acquired several smaller banana companies throughout Central America, creating thereby the 'Tropical Trading and Transport Company' that shipped its bananas in its own vessels to a new, thriving market in the United States.

At the turn of the century, the Keiths moved to Brooklyn. From there Minor controlled his banana empire and his railroads, including a line from Puerto Barrios to Guatemala City, completed in 1908.

---

[111] Daniel Wilkinson, *Silence on the Mountain: Stories of Terror, Betrayal, and Forgetting in Guatemala*, 2002, p.67.

United Fruit Company

By 1900 Keith had merged his Tropical Trading and Transport Company with its rival, the Boston Fruit Company, naming the new business 'The United Fruit Company,' which proceeded to buy up the competition. By 1930, United Fruit had become the largest employer in Central America.

In 1930 Sam Zemurray, "Sam the Banana Man," sold his Cuyamel Fruit Company to United Fruit for 300,000 shares of United Fruit stock, a move that made him the mammoth's largest stockholder and in 1933 he took control of the company. With Zemurray in charge, United Fruit became "the very symbol of Yankee imperialism."[112] Zemurray was at the helm of the company when, in 1952, Guatemalan President Jacobo Árbenz signed Decree 900 into law, authorizing the expropriation of more than a million acres of undeveloped plantation land (including 550,000 acres owned by United Fruit) for distribution to Guatemala's landless farmers, mostly Mayan.

To jump ahead for a moment, in 1968 Eli M. Black bought 733,000 shares of United Fruit, a purchase that gave him control of the company. We will meet him once more.

Jorge Ubico y Castañeda (1931–44)

In 1931 General Jorge Ubico y Castañeda,[113] succeeded to the presidency of Guatemala in an election in which he was the only candidate. As a child Ubico had been in an accident that left him impotent. Perhaps in compensation, he had a penchant for prodigious displays of ostentatious virility—acrobatics on his motorcycle, kicking lions in Guatemala City's zoo, and cruelty toward the Maya.

Jorge Ubico

After his election, Ubico granted United Fruit a ninety-nine-year lease on 200,000 acres of Tiquisate land on the Pacific coast and exempted it from taxation. He also curried favor with the Catholic Church by reestablishing diplomatic relations with the Vatican.

Ubico did away with debt peonage, substituting in its place a vagrancy law which required all men of working age, who did not own land, to work a minimum of a hundred to a hundred and fifty days a year on plantations or on public infrastructure, like roads and bridges. The new law applied to indigenous and *ladino* alike. Ubico also froze wages at absurdly low levels and created a law allowing landowners immunity from prosecution for anything they might do "to defend their property," that is, they might beat their workers to death with impunity.[114]

By 1944 two percent of landowners (including United Fruit) owned seventy-two percent of all of the land in Guatemala. United Fruit, the largest land owner, controlled forty-two percent.[115]

We will return to Ubico in a moment but must interrupt the narrative to focus on the National Palace and the square fronting it, the incendiary venue for anti-government demonstrations.

---

[112] Richard H. Immerman, *The CIA in Guatemala: The Foreign Policy of Intervention*, 1982, p.73.

[113] The '*y*' (meaning "and") is a sign of nobility, or at least noble ancestry. In this case it smacks of grandiloquence and borders on the absurd.

[114] Thomas R. Melville, *Through a Glass Darkly: The U.S. Holocaust in Central America*, 2005, p.95.

[115] Walter LaFeber, *Inevitable Revolutions: The United States in Central America*, 2nd edition, 1993, p.117.

The National Palace

In 1920, Acting President Carlos Herrera, with the centenary of independence (1821) closing in, ordered a national palace to be completed in three months. It was nicknamed the 'Cardboard Palace' and in 1925 burned to the ground. In 1932, Jorge Ubico ordered a new design. Construction was completed in 1943 and on November 10, Ubico's birthday, the Palace and its opulent trappings were opened for public admiration.

Courtyard in the National Palace

A Typical Room in the National Palace

Chapter IV, The Guatemalan Spring

The October Revolution

In June 1944, a series of strikes fomented by middle-class university students who perceived themselves as 'classless.' rattled the government.[118] Ubico responded by appointing his cronies to positions of authority at the university and arresting various faculty members and some students. The protests only became more strident and on June 23 the students and their supporters massed in the plaza fronting the National Palace and issued an ultimatum demanding university autonomy within twenty-four hours. Ubico ordered his security forces to fire on the demonstrators; they refused.

Ubico, who had always imagined himself to be very popular, was crushed, or so he said, and resigned (sort of), appointing a junta of three of his minions to govern until a new election could be held. The junta summoned the National Assembly to the Presidential Palace and ordered the *deputados* to elect retired General Frederico Ponce, one of Ubico's minions, to the presidency. Soon it became apparent that nothing had changed. Even the army was disillusioned and on October 20, still 1944, a group of younger officers launched a coup, led by Francisco Javier Araña and Jacobo Árbenz Guzmán.

Araña's defection won over the powerful *Guardia de Honor*. Árbenz did not actually have any troops under his command, so he armed some two thousand civilian volunteers, ardent supporters of a civilian candidate for the presidency, Juan José Arévalo. The fighting went on through the night and the following morning. Meanwhile more and more volunteers kept joining Árbenz' civilian army. At noon Ponce capitulated and by two o'clock was on his way to exile in Mexico. Árbenz and Araña asked Guillermo Toriello, a civilian businessman, to join them in forming a junta to schedule new elections to the presidency and the National Assembly. Guatemala was poised for the most revolutionary correction in its history. The elections were held in December, 1944. All adult males, including the Maya, and all literate females were allowed to vote, but few of the Maya participated. Juan José Arévalo Bermej garnered nearly universal support and became *the first popularly elected president in Guatemalan history*—a bloodless revolution. Indeed, the October Revolution initiated a decade that would become known as 'The Guatemalan Spring.'[119]

Juan José Arévalo Bermej (1945–50)

Juan José Arévalo

As a young man Arévalo had studied at San Carlos University in Guatemala and subsequently earned a Ph.D. in Philosophy in Argentina.[120] For several years thereafter he taught at various universities in several South American countries. In 1936, during the Ubico regime, he finessed an appointment to the Ministry of Education and, at the urging of other intellectuals, presented a project to the government to create a Faculty of Humanism[121] at San Carlos University. Ubico quashed the idea. Arévalo, disappointed, returned to Argentina but his popularity in Guatemala persisted, in part because he had written a variety of popular

---

[118] Susanne Jonas, The Battle for Guatemala: Rebels, Death Squads, and U.S. Power, 1991, p.23.

[119] For a full account of the October Revolution, see Richard H. Immerman, op. cit., Chapter 2, "Underdevelopment, Repression, and Revolution."

[120] San Carlos University did not then and does not now have the resources for conducting research, the object of the Ph.D.

[121] We would say a "Humanities Department."

textbooks that endeared him to teachers across the country and because colleagues of his began a campaign for the presidency on his behalf. The possibility that Guatemala's future might be in the hands of an intellectual instead of a dictator stimulated a wave of excitement never before seen in Guatemala. On September 2, 1944, Arévalo returned to Guatemala to "the most joyous, most tumultuous and most massive demonstration in the nation's history."[122]

In his inaugural address on March 15, 1945, Arévalo, a socialist, referring to Franklin D. Roosevelt, commented, "He taught us that there is no need to cancel the concept of freedom in a democratic system in order to breathe into it a socialist spirit."[123] In a subsequent speech he explained that materialism had become "a tool in the hands of totalitarian forces." Communism, Fascism and Nazism, he said, were also socialistic but "their kind of socialism gives food with one hand while with the other it mutilates man's moral and civic values."

Arévalo pledged to round up all communists but Washington was not impressed.[124]

In 1947 President Arévalo signed into law a new Labor Code that legalized labor unions and collective bargaining, including the right to strike, and eliminated the *libreta*, the little account book that indigenous workers had to carry on their person (page 45). The new law limited the workweek to forty-eight hours, six days a week, outlawed corporal punishment on the plantations, and set safety standards in the work place. It also established a minimum wage and restricted the employment of women and children.[125]

Arévalo survived numerous attempts to assassinate him. The Guatemalan constitution limited a president's term to six years. Although his popularity might have circumvented this limitation, Arévalo did not seek reelection.

Jacobo Árbenz Guzmán (1950–54)

Jacobo Árbenz Guzmán, the son of a Swiss father and a society mother, had been a brilliant student at the *Escuela Politécnica* (page 42) and, subsequently, a member of the junta that was most directly responsible for the ouster of Ubico and the election of Arévalo in the October Revolution. Árbenz had served as Arévalo's Defense Minister. In the election of 1950, with the backing of the military and the laboring class, Árbenz handily won the presidency.

Arévalo had avoided the prickly issue of land reform. In 1950 the per capita income of plantation workers was $87 a year.[126] Árbenz knew what was expected of him. In his inaugural address, he proposed converting Guatemala from a "predominantly feudal economy into a modern, capitalist state" and making the transformation "in a way that would raise the standard of living." He also admonished foreign investors that they would be obliged to abstain from intervening in Guatemala's social and political life.[127]

Jacobo Árbenz

---

[122] Stephen Schlesinger and Stephen Kinzer, *Bitter Fruit: The Story of the American Coup in Guatemala*, Expanded Edition, 1999, p.30.
[123] Ibid., p.34.
[124] LaFeber, op. cit., p.116.
[125] Melville, op. cit., p.171.
[126] Schlesinger and Kinzer, op. cit., p.50.
[127] Ibid., p.52.

Agrarian Reform

Agrarian reform drove the unflinching Árbenz' chariot. Specifically, he was determined to restore land to dispossessed Mayan farmers. To that end he introduced Decree 900, which would authorize the redistribution of all of the *uncultivated* land on estates larger than 672 acres, as well as the total redistribution of the government-owned plantations to landless peasants, who would pay for their allotment at a rate of three to five percent of production annually. The legislature passed the bill on June 17, 1952. Árbenz signed it into law the same day.

Decree 900 invited landless peasants to apply for a parcel to a 'Local Agrarian Committee' (CAL). "CALs were the thin edge of the wedge of the October Revolution's purest democratic impulse."[128] Each CAL had five members, one appointed by the governor of the *departamento*, one by the local community, and three by the peasant union. The local CAL would decide who would get what land. Landowners could appeal decisions all the way up to the President.

During the next two years, more than 2.7 million acres were distributed to about 100,000 peasants,[129] together with credit and technical assistance.[130] United Fruit, which owned some 550,000 acres, 85% of which was fallow, lost 386,901 acres.[131] In compensation, the Árbenz government offered United Fruit $627,572, the assessed value of the land. A counter offer, made not by United Fruit but by the U.S. State Department, demanded $15,854,849.[132]

Decree 900 authorized the formation of unions on the plantations. Union organizers belonging to Árbenz' Revolutionary Party held meetings on most plantations. Nearly all the workers joined the party and formed a local union on the plantations they worked, and they were free to strike.[133] Decree 900 had also established legal procedures to adjudicate rival claims.[135] The process of re-distribution did not always go smoothly. Many of the claimants—hungry, illiterate, and with little understanding of or patience for due process—sometimes took matters into their own hands before the completion of formalities and spontaneously occupied their plots. Daniel Wilkinson relates his conversation with a *ladino*, José Maldonado, who had worked for the Árbenz government to implement Decree 900. As an inspector, Maldonado visited many plantations to see to it that the law was being properly applied. In many cases it was not and the owners were not alone in attempting to circumvent the law. Some of the inspectors, for example, would tell the petitioners to take the land saying, "we'll legalize it later." [138] Another official recalled that the wheels of government could not move fast enough. The reform took too long. "Maybe if there had been fewer legal restrictions, it would have worked."[140]

Communism

After the success of the Bolshevik Revolution in 1922, Vladimir Lenin had converted Russia into a communist state. The subsequent spread of communism gave Western powers pause. In 1949 Mao Tse-tung drove Chiang Kai-chek from the mainland and China became a communist state.

---

[128] Greg Grandin, "Five Hundred Years," in Carlota McAllister and Diane M. Nelson (edd.), *War by Other Means: Aftermath in Post-Genocide Guatemala*, 2013, p.64.

[129] "The allocated plots varied in size from 8.5 to 17 acres if the land had previously been under cultivation . . . and from 26 to 33 acres if the land had been fallow." Immerman, op. cit., p.65.

[130] WRITENET, *Guatemala: Displacement, Return and the Peace Process*, 1995, 1. Introduction.

[131] Schlesinger and Kinzer, op. cit., p.76.

[132] Idem.

[133] Wilkinson, *Silence on the Mountain*, pp.149–51.

[135] Cindy Forster, *The Time of Freedom: Campesino Workers in Guatemala's October Revolution*, 2001, p.190.

[138] Ibid., pp. 164.

[140] Ibid., p. 165.

Other, lesser governments soon followed suit, including Cuba in 1959, just ninety miles off the coast of Florida. Wary Americans had good reason to be attentive.

The Guatemalan constitution that had been adopted in 1945, Arévalo's first year in office, did not disallow any political party but it did proscribe foreign political organizations and that same year Arévalo closed a school, the *Escuela Claridad*, which the Communist Party had opened. The leader of the Communist Party, José Manuel Fortuny, ran for Congress in 1952 and was soundly defeated. Arévalo and Árbenz both refrained from appointing communists to cabinet-level posts.[141]

Although card-carrying membership in the communist party, the *Partido Guatemalteco de Trabajo* (PGT), never exceeded 4000,[142] thousands of displaced farmers seeking relief climbed onto the communist bandwagon, though they knew nothing about communism, certainly had never read Karl Marx or Friedrich Engels. All they wanted was to get their land back and were ready to march for any program claiming to represent their interests. Had they known about Stalin's collectivization of peasant farms in the Soviet Union, they would have been ready to stone him. The landowners had even less interest in communism and its collective farms than did the workers and had "embraced Ubico's tyranny as the best defense against the communist and the Indian."[147] President Arévalo had espoused socialism.[148] President Árbenz followed his lead.

Since the Conquest, land had been the epicenter of Guatemalan politics. The United States, long in a position to help, had done nothing. Secretary of State John Foster Dulles, whom we will meet in a moment, knew all that. His reasons for intervening in Guatemala, as we shall see, lay elsewhere, the spread of communism providing a convenient cover.

Greg Grandin, who had worked for the CEH (p.2) confirms that, without U.S. interference, Árbenz would have remained in power. There had been far fewer attempted coups against him than against Arévalo and, in any case, as a military officer he enjoyed the loyalty of the military elite, while the landed oligarchy was too demoralized to risk the comforts they enjoyed "in a quixotic campaign against a popular and apparently secure president."[149]

United Fruit's Response

United Fruit responded to Decree 900 by hiring a clique of lobbyists and public relations firms to remove Árbenz from power. Edward Bernays, a nephew of Sigmund Freud, would lead the charge.

Bernays began by elbowing the New York *Herald Tribune* into sending a reporter, Fitzhugh Turner, to Guatemala. Turner wrote a series of articles titled "Communism in the Caribbean" after interviewing officers of United Fruit, and no one else. His articles appeared on the front page of the *Herald Tribune* for five consecutive days. The publisher of the highly influential *New York Times*, Arthur Hays Sulzberger, a friend of Bernays, sent Will Lissner, a reporter, to Guatemala. Lissner returned to New York "convinced that the Communist movement had colonized Guatemala by infiltrating cadres from Chile,"[150] a novel theory that got no traction anywhere.

Next Bernays persuaded Sulzberger to send another reporter, Crede H. Calhoun. Calhoun weighed in with a series of articles that persuaded *Time, Newsweek, U.S. News & World Report*,

---

[141] Schlesinger and Kinzer, op. cit., pp. 56–57.

[142] Ibid., p.59.

[147] Piero Gleijeses, *Politics and Culture in Guatemala*, 1988, p.6.

[148] Although both communism and socialism seek to provide for all of society's needs, communist ideology espouses state ownership of the means of production, while socialism does not.

[149] Grandin, *The Last Colonial Massacre: Latin America in the Cold War*, 2011, p.76.

[150] Schlesinger and Kinzer, op. cit., p.84.

The Atlantic Monthly and the Latin magazine *Visión* to dispatch journalists to Guatemala to document "the advance of Marxism" there.

Bernays arranged, for newsmen only, a number of 'fact-finding' junkets to Guatemala. No expense was spared to make sure that the facts they found seriously compromised objectivity.[152] In his memoirs Bernays noted that after the newsmen returned, public interest in the subject skyrocketed.

Doing its part, United Fruit commissioned John Clements to create a report on Communist infiltration into the Guatemalan government. The company paid him $35,000 for his report. Clements sent copies to members of the U.S. Congress and to some eight hundred names on a list of "decision-makers that he had assembled." Clements' 'report' eventually appeared in the State Department's 1954 White Paper on Guatemala and was quoted in various speeches at the United Nations.[153]

Operation PBSUCCESS

After President Eisenhower took office in January, 1953, the cards seemed stacked against President Árbenz. Allen Dulles, director of the U.S. Central Intelligence Agency, had been president of United Fruit in the 1930s. His brother, the indefatigable John Foster Dulles, Eisenhower's Secretary of State, also served on United Fruit's Board of Directors. Both men were major shareholders in the company. The Assistant Secretary of State for Inter-American Affairs, John Cabot, was the brother of Thomas Cabot who had also been president of United Fruit. U.N. Ambassador Henry Cabot Lodge, formerly a senator from Massachusetts, owned stock in United Fruit. Anne Whitman, the wife of Undersecretary of State Bedell Smith, was Eisenhower's personal secretary; her husband was actively seeking a position with United Fruit and later became a member of its Board. All of these people, because of their association with United Fruit, were well aware of the company's campaign to oust Árbenz and were eager to add to the calculus the overwhelming supremacy of the United States Government.

By the summer of 1953 the State Department and the CIA had developed a plan for a covert operation that the CIA would execute. In August they brought their plan to the National Security Council, which has supervision over all covert operations. The council approved. The project was code-named Operation PBSuccess, with Frank Wisner, the CIA deputy director for operations, in charge. Wisner immediately hired Colonel Albert Haney, a counterintelligence expert and a skillful liar as his field commander.

The CIA needed one more recruit, a Guatemalan military officer to lead a rag-tag 'army' in the parody of an invasion, dispatch President Árbenz, assume the presidency, persuade the country to accept him as its savior, and restore to United Fruit the land purchased by Árbenz. CIA representatives extended an offer to Colonel Carlos Castillo Armas, who had an anti-Communist reputation and had been trained at Fort Leavenworth in the United States. As an anti-Árbenz activist, he was living in Honduras, selling furniture. The CIA took Castillo Armas to Florida, where they struck a deal.

The Alfhem Affair

Árbenz, well aware of the diabolical machinations evolving in Washington, sought to strengthen his military by purchasing arms and ammunition. Knowing he would be rebuffed anywhere within the orbit of U.S. hegemony, he covertly contracted with communist Czechoslovakia for a large

---

[152] Ibid, pp.87.
[153] Ibid., p.95.

shipment of guns, ammunition, mines, and artillery. Early in the morning of May 15, 1954, the Swedish freighter Alfhem docked in Puerto Barrios. A blanket of secrecy immediately sealed off the area from the public and the press, while stevedores began transferring heavy wooden crates marked 'Optical and Laboratory Equipment' from the ship to waiting railroad cars. The arrival of the Alfhem provided Allen Dulles with just the pretext he needed to set a date for the invasion.

Invasion

On June 18, 1954, Castillo Armas led his force of about 300 mercenaries (whom the CIA had trained at its base in Honduras) across the border six miles into Guatemala as a CIA plane, piloted by an American mercenary, simultaneously dropped leaflets proclaiming liberation on the streets of Guatemala City. Operation PBSuccess was under way. The event caused no spontaneous uprising to bring down Árbenz and the CIA ordered Castillo Armas to stay put. The next day the same pilot dropped a hand grenade and a stick of dynamite from the plane's window onto Puerto Barrios. Another American mercenary strafed Cobán but ran out of gas and crash-landed just over the border in Mexico. The day after that, another mercenary pilot was assigned to knock out the Guatemalan government's radio station in Guatemala City. The pilot was advised that the transmitter of an Evangelical radio station was nearby and that two American missionary women were minding the store. "You can tell the difference," he was told, because the government station was all concrete and the Evangelical station had a red tile roof. When the pilot returned, he was asked if he was sure that he had hit the right place. "Absolutely!" he replied. "You should've seen them red tiles flying!"[156]

Field commander Haney received two new planes on June 23 to replace his losses, bringing his total fighter force to four. During the next seventy-two hours they bombed the army barracks in Zacapa and dropped incendiary bombs on nearby Chiquimula, the capital of the *departamento* with the same name (map on page 7), while Castillo Armas' rag-tag army battled government troops to occupy the town. Seventeen soldiers on each side were killed and many more wounded. On June 25, three planes strafed Zacapa, striking an ammunition dump, and in the afternoon attacked the airport in Guatemala City. During a nighttime raid, the U.S. Embassy in Guatemala City played a recording of a bombing attack over loud-speakers set up on the embassy roof. The CIA's 'Voice of Liberation' radio operators broadcast bogus news reports of large troop movements, battles, losses sustained by the Guatemalan army and growing rebel strength. At the same time, trains began delivering the soldiers wounded in Chiquimula to hospitals in Guatemala City. Pictures of the bandaged troops in Guatemalan newspapers the next day lent credence to the CIA broadcasts. Guatemala's foreign minister asked the United Nations Security Council to intervene. The Soviet Union, France, and Britain agreed but the U.S. ambassador threatened France and Britain and persuaded the Security Council to refer the issue to the Organization of American States, which the United States dominated.[158]

On Sunday evening, June 27, Army Chief of Staff, Colonel Carlos Enrique Díaz, reported to Árbenz that a group of officers were plotting a coup. Árbenz realized that without the army he could not remain in power and offered to step aside in favor of Díaz. Díaz attempted unsuccessfully to negotiate with the American ambassador, John Purifoy, who, in a gratuitous display of diplomatic legerdemain, brought Castillo Armas to Guatemala City in his own plane. The new dictator,

---

[156] Schlesinger and Kinzer, op. cit., p.176.
[158] For a fuller account, see Immerman, op. cit., pp.168–73.

on the pretext of having him searched, made Árbenz strip to his underwear on the tarmac before allowing him to fly into exile in Mexico.

On July 13 the United States officially recognized the Castillo Armas government. Secretary Dulles, went on radio lauding the "new and glorious" developments.[159] Henry Kissinger's trenchant one-liner, made in another context, suits the present as well: "The difficulty with [John Foster] Dulles' policy was not that he was wrong about communism, but that he was right about so little else." Churchill said of Dulles, "The only bull I know who carries his china shop around with him."

Carlos Castillo Armas (1954–57)

Carlos Castillo Armas

Within two months, Castillo Armas returned to United Fruit its expropriated land.[161] Even today, two percent of the population still owns more than half of Guatemala's land.[162] Castillo Armas also repealed the constitution that had been adopted during Arévalo's first year in office and appropriated to himself all legislative and executive functions.

Shortly after taking office, the dictator declared July 10 'Anticommunism Day,' alleging that communism was still a threat. The U.S. State Department sent Richard Adams, a famous anthropologist, to interview two hundred and fifty communists that the CIA had identified and Castillo Armas had jailed.[163] He found that only a handful knew anything at all about communism. What they did have in common was participation in Árbenz's agrarian reform.[164]

As many as 8,000 Maya were killed in the first two months of Castillo Armas' presidency.[165] None the less, the Eisenhower administration invited him to visit the United States in late October, where he was welcomed with a twenty-one-gun salute in Washington, a ticker-tape parade in New York, and honorary degrees from Columbia and Fordham.[166]

Soon after taking office, Castillo Armas formed a new political party, the *Moviemento de Liberación Nacional* ("National Liberation Movement"), abbreviated MLN. The party would wield considerable power even after Armas' death, as we will see.

The United States supported the tin god for the next three years. During this time his regime received some $150 million from the U.S. Treasury (while the Arévalo and Árbenz administrations, by contrast, had received a scant $600,000, total for ten years).[167] Castillo Armas' reversal of Arévalo's and Árbenz' popular initiatives sparked widespread rioting. On July 22, 1957, his former bodyguard assassinated him in the National Palace.

Miguel Ydigoras Fuentes (1958–62)

To succeed Castillo Armas, the army high command installed Miguel Ydigoras Fuentes, a move they would soon regret. In 1960, Ydigoras Fuentes granted the U.S. Government permission to

---

[159] For more detailed records of CIA involvement in fomenting the Civil War, see Nicholas Cullather, *Operation PBSUCCESS: The United States and Guatemala 1952-1954*, 1999.

[161] WRITENET, ibid

[162] Immerman, op. cit., p.198.

[163] Kirsten Weld, *Paper Cadavers: The Archives of Dictatorship in Guatemala*, 2014, p.118.

[164] Melville, *Through a Glass Darkly: The U.S. Holocaust in Central America*, 2005 p.267.

[165] Jonas, *Battle*, p.41.

[166] Immerman, op. cit., p.180.

[167] Cindy Forster, *The Time of Freedom: Campesino Workers in Guatemala's October Revolution*, 2001, p.273.

train U.S. troops for the Pay of Pigs invasion of Cuba at a location in Guatemala, outraging his senior staff. In addition, he also failed to conform to precedent in the promotion of military officers.

On November 13, 1960, a hundred and thirty army officers at the head of the troops they commanded, about a third of the entire army, rebelled, seizing the armory in Guatemala City, the port of Puerto Barrios, and the central command base in Zacapa. Ydigoras called the CIA in Washington. Within a few days the U.S. aircraft carrier *Shangri-La* and five destroyers arrived at Puerto Barrios. The rebellion collapsed.

Chapter V, Civil War, 1960–1996

Guerrillas

On November 13 of 1960, two young officers, Marco Aurelio Yon Sosa and Luis Turcios Lima, left the army and began organizing a guerrilla force called 'MR-13.'

On February 6, 1962, a large group of armed men overpowered an army post in Mariscos, took the weapons and ammunition, and withdrew. A short time later, these same men entered the military post at the branch headquarters of the United Fruit Company on the eastern coast, where the local executive was waiting for them. Having assembled his puzzled staff, the executive introduced the visitors as his friends, adding that they were going to install a government of men who were honorable and had "the balls needed to stand up for what was right and just."[168] The leader of the group was Yon Sosa.

Turcios Lima founded the EGP, the Guatemalan Army of the Poor, the most formidable of the various rebel forces that would develop during the war.[169] He was killed at age twenty-five on October 2, 1966, when his car was destroyed, apparently by a bomb planted underneath.

At about the same time, the three largest political parties—the Christian Democrats, the Revolutionary Party, and the MLN (page 55)—demanded Ydígoras resignation. Two more factions, the Guatemalan Labor party and a student organization, joined the movement and in December, 1962, these clusters merged into a coalition called the 'Rebel Armed Forces' (FAR).

Meanwhile the United States had a new president, John F. Kennedy (1961–63).

Alliance for Progress

Not surprisingly, the new American president turned U.S. foreign policy toward Latin America on its head and, scarcely three months after taking the oath of office, proposed a ten-year aid program, the Alliance for Progress, to repair U.S. relations with its Central-American neighbors. One program held out some promise for the landless Maya.

National Institute for Agrarian Transformation

The INTA, as it came to be known, would hear appeals for title to tracts of land that the Maya claimed to be theirs. Although the military-controlled bureaucracy usually denied Mayan applications, it did at least provide a mechanism for obtaining legal title and, in some cases, did grant the coveted document. Greg Grandin sites an article in *El Imparcial*, dated October 10, 1966, claiming that the INTA "in its first four years provided 150,000 peasants with land."[170] Later Grandin cites the INTA itself claiming that by 1984 it had distributed more than 650,000 acres to 18,535 beneficiaries in Alta Verapaz.[171]

---

[168] Thomas R. Melville, *Through a Glass Darkly: The U.S. Holocaust in Central America*, 2005, pp.303–4.

[169] Greg Grandin, *The Last Colonial Massacre: Latin America in the Cold War* – Updated Edition, 2011, p.204.

[170] Ibid., p.251.

[171] Ibid., pp. 256—7, note 76.

Enrique Peralta Azurdia (1963–65)

To succeed Ydigoras the military now installed Peralta Azurdia as president. Soon the Guatemalan press began reporting the discovery of unidentified bodies with signs of torture. The U.S. State Department put pressure on Peralta Azurdia to hold elections; he scheduled the voting for March 6, 1966.

Julio Cesar Méndez Montenegro (1966–70)

Julio Cesar Méndez Montenegro, dean of San Carlos University's law school, won the election as a stand-in for his brother Mario, who had been murdered. The army compelled Méndez Montenegro to sign a written guarantee that the armed forces—not he—would rule the country.[174]

Death Squads

Unlike the army, death squads carried out the torture and execution of specific individuals. To do so they needed intelligence—names and addresses. In 1966, the Guatemalan government created a special office in an annex of the National Palace to coordinate intelligence gathering, using "tactics developed by the U.S. military in Vietnam."[175] The Orwellian task of this special office was to prepare lists of persons to be "disappeared," supply the coordinates, and, adding a macabre touch, publicize the lists.

An example of their work in San Antonio Aguas Calientes particularly caught my attention because Zoila, my Spanish teacher (page 25), lived there. One day in December, 1982, the mayor was returning home from Guatemala City. He noticed a pickup that seemed to be shadowing the bus. To lose it he got off in Antigua (page 13) and mingled with the jostling crowd in the market. After half an hour or more he boarded another bus for San Antonio. The pickup reappeared and, a couple of miles out of town, forced the bus to pull over. Some men in civilian clothes got on and walked down the aisle demanding to see the papers of every passenger. When they got to the mayor, they took his papers and told him to get off the bus. At the door, he yelled, "Tell my wife they've got me!" The bus driver, ordered to move on, pulled away. Three days later, the mayor's mutilated body was found in some bushes outside of town.[176]

Carlos Arana Osorio (1970–74)

In 1972, Guatemala purchased $6.5 million worth of military supplies from the United States, much of it on credit.[177] President Nixon (1969–74), in a truculent speech the year he took office, declared that the United States would "deal realistically with governments in the Inter-American system as they are," death squads be damned.

[To keep the names and dates in order, turn to Appendix G, An Outline of Guatemalan History, page 259.]

---

[174] REHMI, p.197.
[175] Daniel Rothenberg, *Memory of Silence: The Guatemalan Truth Commission Report*, 2012, p.xxviii.
[176] Sheldon Annis, "Story from a Peaceful Town: San Antonio Aguas Calientes," in Robert W. Carmack, *Harvest of Violence: The Maya Indians and the Guatemalan Crisis*, 1988, p.167.
[177] Walter LaFeber, *Inevitable Revolutions: The United States in Central America*, 2nd edition, 1993, p.203.

<h1 style="text-align:center">Kjell Eugenio Laugerud García (1974–78)</h1>

In 1974 the military chose Kjell Eugenio Laugerud García to succeed Arana. The Laugerud government allowed the INTA to issue titles to a number of Mayan petitioners.[178]

In February, 1976, Guatemala was shaken by an earthquake measuring 7.5 on the Richter scale. The quake left 22,000 to 25,000 dead and another million, almost a fifth of the population, homeless, all in about 40 seconds. Laugerud García's failure to provide assistance to those left homeless would have profound consequences in the Mayan mind-set.

<h2 style="text-align:center">Liberation Theology</h2>

In 1891, Pope Leo XIII had published *Rerum Novarum,* an encyclical letter defining the moral rights and mutual responsibilities of the rich and the poor, of capital and of labor, insisting that some remedy be found "for the misery and wretchedness pressing so unjustly on the majority of the working class." The Second Vatican Council (1962–1965) loosened the constrictions on innovation in the application of Catholic doctrine, a development which lead to a theological congress at Cartigny, Switzerland, titled "Toward a Theology of Liberation." After the second general conference of the Catholic Bishops of Latin America, held in Medellin, Colombia, in 1968, the phrase, 'Preferential Option for the Poor,' became the central axis of Liberation Theology in Latin America.[179]

Concomitant with these developments, a world-wide program called 'Catholic Action' promoted the training of laymen as catechists to teach Catholic doctrine and practice to others who were nominally Catholic but knew little about the faith, as well as those seeking to become Catholic. In remote parts of Guatemala, where individual priests served vast stretches of difficult terrain, these catechists proved to be essential to the Church's implementation of its 'Preferential Option for the Poor.'

The earthquake in 1976 (above) marked a turning point in Guatemala's history. What the Laugerud García government failed to do, international relief agencies did do. They also brought with them ideas foreign until then to Mayan culture, prominently Liberation Theology. This concept, warmly endorsed, practiced, and preached by Catholic priests, both Guatemalan and foreign, introduced the concept of legal title to indigenous parcels, a development fiercely resisted by major landowners. In 1978 the matter came to a head in a place called *Panzós*, not far from Cobán (see map on page 84).

<h2 style="text-align:center">Panzós</h2>

Q'eqchí'-speaking families had populated the valley around Panzós, probably for millennia. Much of the land in the area had been expropriated by Justo Rufino Barrios and sold to German investors in the early 1880s to create coffee plantations (page 42). In the 1960s, beef had also become a highly profitable export commodity and, in the absence of legal titles, what land the Maya had left was vulnerable.

Panzós itself, a river town and the head of a rail line to Puerto Barrios, had become the transit point for coffee and cattle shipments from the valley to the coast. Maya in the area had for several months been soliciting the INTA (page 57) for titles to their land because, they alleged, some powerful landowners, backed by the military, had forced them off much of their ancestral inheritance.

---

[178] Grandin, op. cit., p.125 and 144.

[179] The guerrilla movement saw in Liberation Theology an opportunity to extend its base for many catechists and priests were victims of the violence. (CEH, "Conclusions and Recommendations," #16.)

May 28, 1978, dawned brilliantly clear over the valley. Several hundred Q'eqchí' were assembling in the plaza as part of their protest or, possibly, at the invitation of the mayor. A local army unit was standing by. A capacious ditch had been dug a few days earlier on the outskirts of town; no one knew why. Some pushing and shoving served as a pretext for opening fire. More than a hundred indigenous were killed.[181] Walter LaFeber calls the massacre the "triggering event" which moved the indigenous to organize.[182] Greg Grandin calls it a "prelude to genocide"[183] and a "watershed" with "far-reaching consequences . . . that rang through all levels of society."[184]

Liberation Theology had instructed the indigenous in property rights and galvanized the movement to pursue title to their land assiduously through legal channels rather than violence which, in any case, ran counter to Mayan cultural norms. When the news of the massacre reached Guatemala City, tens of thousands marched in protest against the state.[185]

That same year (1978), the Guerrilla Army of the Poor, the EGP (page 57) coalesced into a formidable force, attracting large numbers of Mayan foot soldiers.

Fernando Romeo Lucas García (1978–82)

In 1978 General Romeo Lucas García became the president of Guatemala after a fraudulent election. The new president had grown up in Alta Verapaz and spoke not only Spanish but Q'eqchi' as well, a circumstance that suggests growing up with neighborhood kids who spoke Q'eqchi'. Yet, when the Carter Administration sent General Vernon Walters to meet with him, the Machiavellian Lucas García advised him that "he had no intention of respecting human rights."[186] During his time in office, two events further galvanized public opposition.

Bus-Fare Protest

In October of 1978, an increase in bus fares united the general public and university students in a massive protest. The bus-drivers struck in support of the protest, crippling the capital. During the first twelve days, at least thirty people were shot and killed, three-hundred and fifty survived gunshot wounds, and six hundred were arrested. On October 20, the anniversary of the October Revolution (page 48), at a raucous rally in the square in front of the National Palace, one of the speakers, the president of the Association of University Students, was machine-gunned to death as police looked on.[187]

Burning of the Spanish Embassy[188]

On January 31, 1980, a delegation of about four hundred Quiché-speaking *campesinos* (farmers), after having been denied a hearing in the legislature to protest a slaughter in the *departamento* of Quiché, assembled at the Spanish embassy, which was known to be sympathetic to indigenous

---

[181] Shelton H. Davis, "Introduction: Sowing the Seeds of Violence," in Robert M. Carmack (ed.), *Harvest of Violence: The Maya Indians and the Guatemalan Crisis*, 1988, pp.19–20.

[182] LaFeber, *Inevitable Revolutions: The United States in Central America*, 2nd edition, 1993, p.258.

[183] Grandin, op cit., p.132.

[184] Ibid., pp.155—6.

[185] Deborah T. Levenson, *Adiós Niño: The Gangs of Guatemala City and the Politics of Death*, 2013, p.3.

[186] Beatriz Manz, *Paradise in Ashes: A Guatemalan Journey of Courage, Terror, and Hope*, 2004, p.23.

[187] Stephen Schlesinger and Stephen Kinzer, *Bitter Fruit: The Story of the American Coup in Guatemala*, 1999, pp.249–50.

[188] For an exhaustive treatment of the subject, see Myrna Ivonne Wallace Fuentes, "The Spanish Embassy Occupation and Assault: History and the Partisan Politics of Memory Since 1980 in Guatemala," in *A Contra Corriente: A Journal of Social History and Literature in Latin America*, Fall 2012, pp.265–412.

causes after the murder of several Spanish priests by the Guatemalan army. The protestors entered the embassy and asked Spanish Ambassador Máximo Cajal y López to mediate their demands, making it clear they had no intention of harming anyone. Over the ambassador's objections, President Lucas García decided to evict the protestors. Shortly before noon, a SWAT team entered the embassy and cleared the first and third floors, while thirty or so of the protestors barricaded themselves on the second floor with the ambassador, some of his staff, and some Guatemalan officials with whom the ambassador had been conferring about another matter. The SWAT team breached the defenses on the second floor. No one knows how the fire started but only Ambassador Cajal y López and one of the demonstrators, a *campesino*, Gregorio Yujá Xoná, escaped through a window, both badly burned. The fire department arrived and extinguished the blaze. Thirty-seven people had been burned alive, including Rigoberta Menchú's father.

Ambassador Cajal y López and Gregorio Yujá Xoná were taken to a hospital. The next morning a band of masked men entered the hospital and kidnapped Yujá Xoná. His mutilated body was found on the campus of San Carlos University with a note that read, "Brought to Justice for Being a Terrorist." Spain severed diplomatic relations with Guatemala, restoring them four years later.

Terror as a Strategy[189]

In 1981–82, a group of younger officers, 'Gramajo's boys' as they were called, adopted a plan to terrorize the indigenous into submission. The plan, known as the 'Project,' was the brainchild of General Héctor Gramajo, Vice Chief of Staff and a graduate of the School of the Americas in Fort Benning, GA. The heart of the Project called for massacring 30% of the Mayan populaton in order to terrorize the remaining 70% into submission. Gramajo later quipped that the Project was humanitarian, because "Earlier the strategy was to kill 100%."[190] To implement the Project, Gramajo's boys created an army unit, the 'G-2,' and provided it with sophisticated methods of intelligence and psychological, rather than physical, warfare.

The Project called for a civilian president, a lapdog to project a façade of legitimacy onto a de facto military dictatorship.

(After the war, Gramajo went to Harvard, where he submitted his 'Project' as a Master's thesis in Public Administration. Gramajo and his son died in March, 2004, having been attacked by a swarm of African bees that, incidentally, killed a number of people as far north as Texas.)

Torture

Torture became the method of choice in the implementation Gramajo's Project, carrying out its mandate both through acts of physical violence, like hacking people with machetes or burning them alive, and through acts of psychological violence—raping women, forcing them to watch as their children's fingernails were being pulled out, smashing toddlers' heads against a tree (leaving their mothers catatonic), forbidding burial of murdered relatives (a particularly traumatic outcome in light of the Mayan deep believe in death as a continuation of life and in the bond between them

---

[189] "Human rights violations have been used as a strategy of social control in Guatemala. . . . More than simply a byproduct of armed confrontation, terror has been the goal of a counterinsurgency policy that used different means at different times." REHMI, p.4, under "A Strategy of Terror."

"What we have seen has been terrible: burned corpses, women impaled and buried as if they were animals ready for the spit, all doubled up." Ibid., p.9, under "Climate of Terror."

[190] Jennifer Schirmer, "The Guatemalan military project: an interview with Gen. Hector Gramajo," *Harvard International Review*, Vol. 13, Issue 3 (Spring 1991).

and their ancestors that depended on proper burial [page 73]), forbidding the Maya to speak their language or practice their religion, cutting down their corn crops, and forcing men in the PACs (see below) to torture and kill, sometimes their own relatives and neighbors.[193] Psychological warfare!

PACs

One of the adjuncts to the Project was a program designed to break the connection between guerrillas and the indigenous villages that supported them by placing on the villagers themselves the burden of keeping the area free of guerrilla influence. Basically, this program required every male between the ages of sixteen and sixty to participate for at least twenty-four hours every week in the *Patrullas de Autodefensa Civil* ("Self-defense Civil Patrols"), PACs for short. (Priests and Evangelical ministers were exempt.) The PACs are said to have included one million peasants, "one-fourth of the adult population."[194] They became an essential component to the success of Gramajo's Project.

Massacres

The CEH provides a haunting introduction to massacre (italics in the original [British] English).

> The Army's perception of Mayan communities as natural allies of the guerrillas contributed to increasing and aggravating the human rights violations perpetrated against them, demonstrating an *aggressive racist component of extreme cruelty that led to the extermination en masse, of defenceless Mayan communities purportedly linked to the guerrillas - including children, women and the elderly - through methods whose cruelty has outraged the moral conscience of the civilised world.*
>
> These massacres and the so-called scorched earth operations, as planned by the State, resulted in the complete extermination of many Mayan communities, along with their homes, cattle, crops and other elements essential to survival. *The CEH registered 626 massacres attributable to these forces.*
>
> *The CEH has noted particularly serious cruelty in many acts committed by agents of the State, especially members of the Army, in their operations against Mayan communities. The counterinsurgency strategy not only led to violations of basic human rights, but also to the fact that these crimes were committed with particular cruelty, with massacres representing their archetypal form. In the majority of massacres there is evidence of multiple acts of savagery, which preceded, accompanied or occurred after the deaths of the victims. Acts such as the killing of defenceless children, often by beating them against walls or throwing them alive into pits where the corpses of adults were later thrown; the amputation of limbs; the impaling of victims; the killing of persons by covering them in petrol and burning them alive; the extraction, in the presence of others, of the viscera of victims who were still alive; the confinement of people who had been mortally tortured, in agony for days; the opening of the wombs of pregnant women, and other similarly atrocious acts,*

---

[193] "And that officer told us that if we didn't kill them, they were going to kill of us. And that's how it came about that we had to do it. I don't deny that, yes, we had to do it, because they threatened us." REHMI, Case 2267, page 8.

[194] Jonas, *The Battle for Guatemala: Rebels, Death Squads, and U.S. Power*, 1991, p.150 (emphasis in the original). See also Rothenberg, op. cit., p.xxxi.

were not only actions of extreme cruelty against the victims, but also morally degraded the perpetrators and those who inspired, ordered or tolerated these actions.[195]

Many of the massacres have been the subject of anthropological research and book-length publications. A few may be summarized here.

Santa María Tzejá[196]

In northern Quiché, a serpentine, muddy path wends its way through a mountainous rain forest toward the Mexican border. In 1970 a hundred, landless, Quiché-speaking families slogged their way along this 150-mile trail to take advantage of a land grant from the Guatemalan government intent on colonizing this remote area, known as the Ixcán (eesh-KAHN). The immediate objective was the creation of a new village, Santa María Tzejá (see map on page 84).

Twelve years later (1982) a column of government troops worked its way along that same path, weighed down with cumbersome combat gear. The villagers in Santa María Tzejá had heard that the army had slaughtered the inhabitants of a nearby village two days earlier and had, therefore, set up sentries along the path, who, at first sight of the military column, ran to the village. The inhabitants scooped up their children and fled into the forest.

When the column reached its destination, the soldiers found tortillas cooking on open fires. During the next few days, they put everything of value in their knapsacks, killed the domesticated animals, and set fire to all of the homes, the church, and the school and then, shouldering their gear, headed toward the next village. On the way they heard a dog bark. Investigating, they found a pregnant woman cradling an infant and two boys, all of whom they shot. Soon they found a second group, a pregnant woman, her eight children, and their grandmother, all of whom they sprayed with gunfire. The villagers were now running deeper into the jungle, pursued by the soldiers. A six-year-old boy remembered, years later, that he had hidden behind a fallen tree. When the soldiers left, he found his little sister, her stomach slit open, and his older sister, decapitated.

The villagers who escaped the slaughter had no idea what to do. They could not return to the village and in the forest they were reduced to eating whatever they could find and sleeping on the ground. As the months went by about half of them made the forty-mile trek to Mexico, where they would remain for more than ten years. A few returned to the village, now under tight military control. Soon the government brought in a new group of landless families from Alta Verapaz, who spoke Q'eqchí; the original inhabitants spoke Quiché.

The village would survive but those who had fled to Mexico, like many others, had no home to which they might return after the war (see 'Refugees,' page 71).

Cuarto Pueblo[197]

On March 7, 1982, a government helicopter flew over the community of Cuarto Pueblo, in the *departamento* of Huehuetanango (see map on page 84), just a few miles south of the Mexican border. A week later, a Sunday, market day was in full swing (like a market day in Tactic, page

---

[195] CEH, #s 86 and 87.

[196] For the full and gripping account, read Beatriz Manz', *Paradise in Ashes: A Guatemalan Journey of Courage, Terror, and Hope,* 2004, from which this abbreviated account has been taken.

[197] These few paragraphs are an abbreviated rendering of a full account by the Rev. Ricardo Falla, *Massacres in the Jungle: Ixcán, Guatemala,* 1944.

28). The community was crowded with farmers from outlying settlements displaying their chickens, eggs, tamales, vegetables, pigs, hand-made clothing, and house-hold products, while merchants from nearby towns hawked watches, kitchen utensils, hand-driven mills for grinding corn, tools, dishes, Pepsi, clothing, sugar, salt, and more. The men jawed over coffee with brothers and friends, while the women gabbed about their children, clothes, and up-coming weddings as their young frolicked about their skirts. Many of the crowd were attending religious services, both Evangelical and Catholic.

The market of Cuarto Pueblo was situated in a hollow surrounded on its north, west, and south sides by a crescent-shaped hill and on its east side by a river. Seven paths converged on the market. Unannounced, an army unit entered from the northeast and spread out in a pincer movement, a shorter arm curving to the east and south and a much larger arm curving to the west and south. As they converged toward the southeast to close the escape routes there, the soldiers opened fire on the villagers fleeing in that direction.[198] In the mayhem, two witnesses found places to hide, one in the northern part of the market, near the Evangelical chapel, the other a little further off. Neither knew of the other's presence.

After the escape routes had been sealed, the army separated the men from the women and the terrified children hiding behind their mothers' skirts. One soldier, seeing a small child crying next to its dead mother, grabbed it by one leg and smashed its head against the ground. That same day, both of the hidden witnesses overheard soldiers rounding up groups of people and subsequently several volleys of gunfire. Not long afterwards, they caught the acrid smell of burning flesh. In the evening some buildings were set afire. During the night both witnesses heard women screaming as the soldiers raped them. One of them later heard two of the soldiers flaunting their exploits.

On Monday morning, the commanding officer gave a pep talk to his men, ranting that they had to obliterate this entire village, while he unfurled a list of other villages to be destroyed as well. He admonished his men to have no fear of the guerrillas because, "we're going to win." He raved that, thanks to the United States, a helicopter would join them.

That same day, the children were taken from their mothers and locked in a building that was then set on fire. On Tuesday, the witness who was close to the Evangelical chapel could tell that the soldiers burned a structure with the bodies of a lot of the women inside. The few women who were not murdered served as cooks and sex slaves. Many of the men had been killed on Sunday. Later that day, the witnesses could hear the sounds of the rest of the men being killed singly, perhaps after questioning.

Early Wednesday morning, the surveillance somewhat relaxed, the two witnesses escaped. Of the inhabitants, only the cooks and the two witnesses survived. Three hundred and twenty-four people had perished in the massacre.

Efraín Ríos Montt (1982–83)

José Efraín Ríos Montt, the avatar of Gramajo's Project (page 61), was born June 16, 1926, to an aristocratic Catholic family in Huehuetenango. Another son, Mario, became a priest and, later, a bishop. Efraín's military career began in 1946 when he enrolled in Guatemala's *Escuela Politécnica* (page 42) and in 1951 he attended the School of the Americas in Fort Benning, GA. In 1978

---

[198] As Fr. Falla notes, the tactics used at Cuarto Pueblo parallel those used by the United States military as described by Jonathon Schell in *Village of Ben Suc* (1967). See also page 38 above, under 'Death Squads.'

he joined the Church of 'The Word' ("*El Verbo*").[199] On his assumption of power, the stentorian Ríos Montt trumpeted, "I am trusting God, my Lord and King, to enlighten me. For He is the only one who gives or takes away this authority."

President Reagan (1981–1989) met with Ríos Montt on December 4, 1982, and later dismissed reports of human rights abuses published by Americas Watch, Amnesty International, and others as a "bum rap." Reagan, despite his disclaimer, surely knew that in declaring, "President Ríos Montt is a man of great personal integrity and commitment," he was dancing with the devil.

Ríos Montt was overthrown in another coup on August 8, 1983. The military's unremitting grip on power, is nowhere more evident than in the fact that, almost twenty-five years later, in 2007, Ríos Montt was elected a member of the Guatemalan Congress, thereby gaining prosecutorial immunity from a pair of long-running lawsuits alleging war crimes during his time as president. His immunity ended on January 14, 2012, when his term in Congress ran out. On January 26, he was formally indicted for genocide and crimes against humanity and on May 10, 2013, was convicted of genocide against the Ixil and crimes against humanity and sentenced to 80 years in prison. Ten days later, his conviction was overturned. Retrial began in January, 2015. The addled dictator died on April 1, 2018.

On the day after his meeting with President Reagan, Ríos Montt took to the airwaves, assuring the nation that he would rule "in peace, with the help of God Our Lord and with your consideration. . . . No longer will corpses be thrown on the roadside." Anyone who violated the law would be executed. "Let's have no more murders. We want to respect human rights and defend them." The massacres continued without interruption.

In May Ríos Montt issued a decree making June a month of amnesty for all who would lay down their arms and report to the army. "An estimated 20,000 former guerillas and sympathizers enrolled . . . in the first year."[202]

In June the dictator announced that a 'state of siege' would begin in July and last for six months. The state of siege would give him the power to suspend habeas corpus, ban all political activity, empower the army to enter homes and offices without a search warrant, to arrest and to try civilians in military courts and impose the death penalty. Ríos Montt justified his suspension of civil rights declaring that in the past ten years, without a state of siege, 150,000 people had been killed. "With the state of siege, all executions will be legal."

[199] *El Verbo* is the Guatemalan branch of the Gospel Outreach Church in Eureka, California, a magnet for pot-smoking hippies in the Sixties, by this time converted to evangelizing by the Assemblies of God lay preacher, Jim Durkin.

[202] Jennifer Schirmer, *The Guatemalan Military Project: A Violence Called Democracy*, 1998, p.52 (quoting Roberto E. Letona, "Guatemalan Counterinsurgency Strategy," U.S. Army War College Study Project, 1989).

<h1 align="center">Sebep[204]</h1>

On Tuesday, July 13, 1982, a hundred and fifty soldiers in camouflage uniforms surrounded the village of Sebep. Of the village's one hundred families, some were Evangelical, some practiced the traditional Mayan religion, and some were Catholic but there were no resident clergy. The advancing soldiers were Mayan but not from the area; the officers, as usual, *ladino*. By noon, all of the men and boys had been corralled in the village center. One of the officers, despite a ski mask over his face, was soon recognized as a defector from the EGP (page 57).

The soldiers had the men and boys walk single-file past the masked commander. Whenever he signaled with his right hand, several soldiers would grab the individual so indicated and tie him up. Twenty-seven individuals, including four boys, the youngest only ten, were thus bound.

Finally, the masked officer told his men to untie five of his prisoners. Next each was given a club. Then another five were singled out and placed in front of the five with clubs. The officer ordered those with clubs to pulverize the skulls of the men in front of them. "If you hesitate," he admonished them, "your wives and children will be next." The five men with clubs stood paralyzed. The officer screamed, "NOW!" Approaching their five relatives and neighbors, one struck a glancing blow. The others, trembling, did the same. The officer bellowed, "I want to see their fucking brains on the ground. HARDER!"

When the five heads had been battered beyond recognition, the barbarian ordered his men to tie up the five who had just done his bidding. "Congratulations!" he smirked. "You've saved your wives and children! But now you must pay the penalty."

At his command, the soldiers untied five other prisoners and handed them the clubs; the macabre procedure proceeded as before, several times. When only seven prisoners remained, including the four boys, the officer ordered, not his soldiers but the local PAC (page 62), men from the same village, into action. They performed as required to save their own lives.

The next day, half the soldiers, led by that same officer, set out for Yolcultac, a village an hour away. The other half set out for Petenac, also an hour away. Before leaving, the officer told his terrified prisoners that they were not to bury their dead until he returned, something he never intended to do.

San Francisco

San Francisco was built on land owned by a certain Colonel Bolaños. The sixty families who lived in the village were sharecroppers and took care of the colonel's cattle in return for being allowed to farm. Francisco Paiz García, one of the villagers, supervised the tending of the herd. San Francisco had a grade school but few children advanced beyond the second grade. The Catholic church was not large enough to accommodate all of the faithful. San Francisco, like Sebeb, had no resident clergy.

On July 17, 1982, a large troop of soldiers dressed in camouflage uniforms were approaching San Francisco from several directions, requiring everyone they encountered to move ahead of them, ultimately to the soccer field.

Soon a helicopter circled the village and landed. Five soldiers piled out. The commander immediately ordered his men to gather up the women and children and lock them in the church. Next he obliged a man who had caught his eye to approach. "With only a curse at the man's ancestry by way of explanation," the officer whipped out his machete and sliced it across the man's face.

---

[204] For the full and riveting accounts of this and the episode that follows, read Thomas R. Melville's *Through a Glass Darkly: The U.S. Holocaust in Central America*, 2005, from which these summaries are taken.

He then turned his attention to a group of five men standing behind a desk and asked who they were. When one of them answered, he shot him in the face. He queried another and when he answered, he shot all of them in the face. At the same time, the cries of terrified children indicated that the church had been set on fire.

Late that day, the commandant departed San Francisco in his helicopter, leaving behind the remains of more than 350 San Francisco's residents scattered about the village center and in the ashes of the church. Outside the church were the bodies of two infants; one had been shot and the other, "a mash of flesh where its head had been," had been swung by its feet against a tree, its head shattered "like a ripe melon." Fifteen men remained penned up in the office; three would survive. Francisco Paiz García (see above), a stake driven into his rectum as he was being driven along a path toward another village, also survived!

The Family of Vicente Menchú[206]

In her autobiography, Rigoberta Menchú relates how her father struggled for twenty-two years to preserve their village's land rights. It all started one day when representatives of the Garcia family came and began measuring the land. "They brought inspectors, engineers and Heaven knows who else," who claimed to represent the government. Rigoberta's father, a village elder, called a meeting and collected the signatures (thumb prints) of the men. Thus armed, he went to the appropriate government office in Guatemala City where he was asked to sign a paper that purported to guarantee the villagers' rights. He could not read it and innocently affixed his thumb print. When the truth turned out to be just the opposite of what he had been led to believe, Vicente engaged a lawyer to represent the village. He was now told, "You must get engineers to measure the land and then you'll be the owners." The villagers were ecstatic but soon the Garcias arrived again with their engineers, who said they had come to help them measure the land but would depend on the residents to feed them while they were there. The villagers knew their unwelcomed guests would not be satisfied with tortillas, so they killed chickens, collected money from each household and went to town to buy rice, oil, eggs, meat, coffee, and sugar. The engineers stayed a week. In the end the government said that the land belonged to the nation; the villagers could stay and work for the Garcias or they could leave. When it became apparent that the villagers were not going to leave, the Garcias' men arrived, ransacked the homes, took what they wanted, and smashed the earthenware pots, plates, and cups. Then they killed the animals, even the dogs. Still the people would not leave. A month or two later, the process was repeated. Eventually, representatives of the government arrived saying that they were going to give the villagers titles to their land and provided papers for them to sign. The year was 1967. Two and a half years later the engineers showed up again, bringing with them the 'titles' the villagers had signed. In reality the 'titles' said that they had agreed to stay for only two years.

Mr. Menchú refused to give up and spent the rest of his life gleaning support from various sources and staging protests. He was arrested, tortured, and imprisoned more than once, and died in the 'Burning of the Spanish Embassy' (page 60).

Rigoberta relates that her mother also became an activist, was arrested and raped. In the end, her tormentors cut off her ears, then sliced her body all over with machetes. Worms set in. She was left in the open for four days, without food, water, medication, or company. As she lay dying, the soldiers urinated in her mouth. Her body was left to be eaten by wild animals.

---

[206] After Rigoberta Menchú's account in *I, Rigoberta, Menchú: An Indian Woman in Guatemala*, 1984, pp.102–116, 122–30, 172–87, and 195–200.

Excerpts from CEH and RHEMI

The CEH (page 2) took the testimonies of more than eleven thousand individuals to create its database. (Many of the witnesses struggle to express themselves in Spanish; bracketed additions are my own.)

While one guy had intercourse with her, some masturbated, others were feeling her. Some put their hands on her breasts, slapped her on the face; others extinguished their cigarettes on her chest. She lost consciousness several times and each time she was able to recover her senses. [Then] another man came to have intercourse [with her]; at least about 20 men raped her. She was [lying] in a puddle of urine, semen, [and] blood.[207]

Both the bodies [both men] burst into flames. They were able to run around for a few meters in the courtyard but fell down, rolling on the ground for about ten minutes, and finally they did not move; they remained [they were] dead, and for fifteen minutes more bodies [more men] continued to [be] burn[ed]. When the fire was out the bodies shrugged [continued to twitch] and the commissioners ordered some patrol soldiers [PACs] to carry the fully burnt bodies, taking them to a ravine that was in the community, which was used by the patrol [PAC] as a body dump.[208]

Two soldiers arrived at the girl's little lemonade stand[209] and asked her to go with them; she was taken to the house she was living at. They locked her parents up in one of the rooms and took the nine-year-old girl to the next room where she was raped there. . . . She remained on the floor almost dead with a heavy bleeding.[210]

I remember. . . we went to the kitchen and there was the whole family, my aunt, my daughter-in-law, her sons and daughters; there were two little children hacked to pieces with machetes. They were still alive. The boy, Romualdo, lived for a few more days. The one who couldn't last any longer was Santa, the one with her guts hanging out. She only lasted half a day.[211]

There are women hanging. Well, the stick goes into her private parts and then the stick comes out of her mouth.[212]

And when I got there they only had one of the boys left, and they were cutting off his head.[213]

---

[207] CEH, 1999, Tomo III, p.27, #2399 [translated].

[208] CEH, op. cit., p.69, #2512 [translated]. The witness, surely Mayan, struggles to express himself in Spanish.

[209] The Spanish just says that the soldiers came to the girl's *venta* (stand) but, for American readers, the nuances are better conveyed as translated here.

[210] CEH, op. cit., p.45, #2453 [translated].

[211] REMHI, *Guatemala: Never Again!* (one-volume summary in English), Case #9014, p.17.

[212] Ibid., p.79.

[213] Ibid., p.131.

68

<h1 style="text-align:center">Recollections</h1>

The war was still fresh in people's minds when I first went to San Lucas Tolimán in 2003 (page 91), where I heard a number of stories about the war.

In one heinous incident, an army unit approached a village and assembled the inhabitants. The commander advised them that he knew there were four guerillas in the village and that he and his men would return the next day and, if he did not find the bodies of the four guerillas laid out on the grass, he would kill everyone in the village. The next day, the army unit returned and found the bodies of the four men who had volunteered to kill themselves. There had been no guerrillas; the officer knew that.

On another occasion, while an army unit was rounding up the inhabitants of a village, one little girl, separated from her mother in the mayhem, was kneeling on the ground, sobbing. An officer approached and told one of his men to shoot her. The soldier hesitated. The officer grabbed his gun and shot her in the head.

Fr. Greg Schaffer (page 91), living in San Lucas Tolimán on the shores of Lake Atitlán (page 8), learned that his name was on a Death-Squad list (page 58) and had had to leave the country. The husband of the cook at the parish had 'disappeared' about that same time.

The story of another priest, Fr. Stanley Rother, living on the other side of Lake Atitlán, was widely talked about in San Lucas.

<h2 style="text-align:center">The Assassination of Fr. Stan Rother[214]</h2>

Thirteen Catholic Priests were killed by the military during the war. One of them, Fr. Stanley Rother, a priest from Oklahoma and the pastor of the only church in a town called Santiago Atitlán, on Lake Atitlán in the *departamento* of Sololá (see map on page 84), was killed in his residence by a Death Squad (page 58) during the night of July 28/29, 1981.

More than a century earlier, the government of Justo Rufino Barrios (page 42) had expelled all foreign priests. In the early 1960s, Pope John XXIII asked the North American Bishops to respond to the shortage of priests in Guatemala and elsewhere in Central and South America. The American Bishops established communication with their counterparts in Latin America to assess specific needs. Upon receipt of responses, they canvassed their clergy for volunteers, offering them the opportunity to serve in specific parishes for a specific length of time. Many priests responded, including Fr. Greg Schaffer (page 91), a priest of the New Ulm Diocese in Minnesota, who was offered an opportunity to serve in San Lucas Tolimán in the Diocese of Sololá for three years. At the end of the three years, he did not want to leave and remained until his death nearly fifty years later. Many other priests responded in the same way.

The Bishop of the Oklahoma Diocese arranged with the Bishop of Sololá to send clergy to a parish across Lake Atitlán from Fr. Greg, in a town called Santiago Atitlán, a parish that had had no priest since Justo Rufino Barrios' expulsion of all foreign priests more than 100 years earlier (page 42). When the new clergy arrived in Santiago Atitlán, they set about, with the aid of several nuns and lay personnel, establishing a hospital and a radio station as well as a project to translate

---

[214] Details are, for the most part, provided by María Ruiz Scaperlanda, *The Shepherd Who Didn't Run*, 2015.

69

the New Testament into Tz'utujil (*tzoo-too-HEEL*), even as they themselves struggled to learn this difficult language. (The indigenous, here as elsewhere, did not speak Spanish.)

Stan Rother had been ordained a priest in 1963 and served in the Oklahoma diocese until 1968. In the fall of that year, he volunteered to minister in Guatemala and, together with a friend, drove his Ford Bronco, with a trailer in tow, to Santiago Atitlán, coming to a stop in the town square, facing the stately colonial church of Santiago Apóstal, that had been built by Franciscan Friars between 1541 and 1547, the oldest church in the Diocese. Fr. Stan, now thirty-three, initially resided with an indigenous family to learn Tzutuhil, while simultaneously providing new leadership for the hospital, the radio station, and the translation projects.

Santiago Atitlán and its neighboring villages were among the poorest in all of Central America. Men earned 25 to 70 cents a day as hired farm hands, and more than half of all the children died before the age of six. The most common causes of death were malnutrition, diarrhea, flu, and measles. Most adults had intestinal worms from drinking lake water.[215] Writing home, Fr. Stan described the squat huts in which his parishioners lived. He could not help but notice the contrast between the beauty of the area (see page 8) and the misery of the people.

One of Fr. Stan's predecessors had sent two Tz'utujil young men to the Francisco Marroquín Language Institute in Antiqua (page 13) to learn how to modify the alphabet to accommodate the sounds of Tz'utujil, subsequently creating a dictionary and a grammar.

In addition to his religious and educational activities, Fr. Stan worked with the men, planting and harvesting, his childhood experience as a farmer's son enabling him to introduce innovation. Like other priests, Fr. Stan benignly tolerated *costumbre*, even Maximon (page 16).

On October 21, 1980, the army arrived in Santiago Atitlán. Two days later, during the night, five soldiers entered the hut of a young community leader and the director of the radio station. A soldier smashed his face with the butt of his gun; the young man fell to the floor. The soldiers began stamping on him and then dragged him outside. His body was never found. Over the next few days, the Danteque scene was repeated several times, leaving the entire population traumatized. Then the radio station was destroyed.

In December, 1980, Fr. Stan finished a letter about conditions in Santiago Atitlán, saying, "The shepherd cannot run at the first sign of danger."[216] One Saturday evening, the parish's lead catechist, Diego Quic, a young man whom Fr. Stan had educated, was abducted. The priest later wrote, "that makes 11 members that have been kidnaped and all are presumed dead."[217] Later another seven bodies, badly brutalized, were found on the shore of the lake.

On Monday, July 27, 1981, Fr. Stan made plans to donate blood the next day for one of his parishioners who would have surgery to remove two bullets from his hip and he planned to take two parishioners with him in the expectation that at least one of the three of them would have the right blood type. At 5:00 o'clock that afternoon he celebrated Mass as usual and then spent the evening with two friends on his staff, retiring about 10:30. Around one o'clock in the morning, some men broke into the rectory. Fr. Stan fought fiercely, as the abrasions on his knuckles would demonstrate. He suffered multiple blows to his abdomen. His head hit the wall hard enough to leave bloody marks and his body had multiple knife wounds. Ever the shepherd, he never screamed or called for help, no doubt to make sure that the nuns did not try to come to his assistance and be killed as well.

In 2016 the Vatican declared Fr. Rother a martyr.

---

[215] Ibid., pp.91–92.
[216] Ibid., p.186.
[217] Ibid., p.189.

Refugees

The first large-scale arrival of Guatemalan refugees seeking a safe haven in Chiapas, Mexico, took place in May and June 1981.[220] As the volume of refugees surged, the Mexican Government found itself unprepared and disagreement about how to deal with the influx resulted in problems both for Mexican officials and for the refugees. The United Nations High Commissioner for Refugees intervened in March of 1982 when an estimated 36,000 Guatemalans had crossed into Mexico. In 1983 the number rose to 46,000, eventually peaking at about 200,000, living in camps along the border and supervised by Mexican officials. Soon the camps developed a political and social structure of their own, electing individuals to oversee community projects such as cutting down the forest, building roads, housing, community centers, clinics, churches and schools, even roads and airstrips.[221]

The lives of the refugees, however, were far from idyllic, not least of all because Guatemalan army units sometimes crossed the border and worked havoc in the camps. For this and other reasons, the Mexican Government eventually decided to move the camps away from the border but met with resistance from the refugees themselves, who wanted desperately to return home and balked at moving further away. In addition, Chiapas had once been part of Guatemala and many refugees had relatives living there. Moreover, the refugees had made improvements to their temporary homes and the area (see above), in one case planting 3,000 mango and citrus trees.[222]

In the end, however, the refugees had no way of resisting. The Mexican Government loaded them into buses and transported them to the Yucatán.

The new camps were laid out in a grid with a central square, where houses, a school, church, clinic, market, and community center had already been built. The houses were all the same size but had differing floor plans. No Guatemalan army units would suddenly appear to terrorize the inhabitants. No matter; nearly all of the residents affirmed that they would have preferred staying in Chiapas, not least of all because in the Yucatán they were completely cut off from knowing what was happening back home and were now simply dependents of the Mexican state.

During the Cerezo Government (page 75), those who had fled to Mexico began to return but found that their homes and land had been sold by the government to new tenants. Jorge (page 35) and I visited one of the communities that had been created to accommodate some of those thus dispossessed. The aid worker in charge told us that, for the most part, the families could not communicate with one another because they had no language in common. In addition, they had cultural differences which created discord.[223]

Genocide

The legal framework adopted by the CEH to analyze the possibility that acts of genocide were committed in Guatemala during the civil war was the Convention on the Prevention and Punishment of the Crime of Genocide, adopted by the United Nations General Assembly on December 9, 1948.[224] The convention had been ratified by the Guatemalan Government in 1949, eleven years before the beginning of the civil war. "Considering the series of criminal acts and human rights

---

[220] Beatriz Manz, *Refugees of a Hidden War: The Aftermath of Counterinsurgency in Guatemala,* 1988, p.146.

[221] Ibid., p.147.

[222] Ibid., p.152.

[223] For a fuller account of the trials associated with repatriation, see Beatriz Manz, *Repatriation and Reintegration: An Arduous Process in Guatemala*, 1988, Chapter II: "The Process of Repatriation."

[224] CEH, "Conclusions and Recommendations," #108.

violations which . . . were analysed for the purpose of determining whether they constituted the crime of genocide, the CEH concludes that . . . agents of the State of Guatemala . . . committed acts of genocide against groups of Mayan people."[226] Rios Montt (page 64) would subsequently be specifically convicted of the crime.

Óscar Humberto Mejía Victores (1983–85)

In August 1983 General Mejía Victores, Ríos Montt's Defense Minister, engineered a coup, justifying his act by saying that "religious fanatics" were abusing their positions in government because of "official corruption." By that time the counterinsurgency under Lucas Garcia and Ríos Montt had largely succeeded in implementing Gramajo's Project (page 61), thus depriving the guerrillas of civilian support. That same year Rigoberta Menchú's autobiography, for which she won the Nobel Peace Prize, ineluctably shaped public opinion around the world. Under international pressure, in 1984 Mejía Victores allowed an election for a Constituent Assembly to draft a democratic constitution. On May 30, 1985, after nine months of debate, the Assembly presented its document, which by agreement took effect immediately. The G-2 (page 61) made its displeasure known. In April that same year, the mutilated corpses of Rosaria Godoy, a leader in Guatemala's human rights movement, [228] her younger brother and her two-year-old son, were found in a ravine on the outskirts of Guatemala City. Mrs. Godoy's breasts had been bitten and her underwear was stained with blood.[229] The two-year-old's finger nails had been pulled out.[230] A police report claimed they died in a traffic accident.[231] No one was ever charged.

To digress for a moment, imagine the scene, the terror in the two-year-old's screams as the officer took out his nail puller, ordered one of his men to lock on to the child's arm, and yanked out the first nail. As the paroxysm shot through his tiny body, the child must have shrieked in terror, "Mommy! Mommy!" The officer, clamping onto the second nail, yanked it out. "Mommy! Mommy! Mommy!" Just six feet away, his mother, struggling to free herself from the iron grip around her, could only sob, "Mommy's here. Mommy's here, my baby. Mommy loves you. It will be over soon. It will be over soon, my baby." Her tormenter might well have stopped, cast a sadistic smile her way, lit a cigarette, and after puffing leisurely for a while, jammed his nail puller onto another finger. "Mommy! Mommy! Mommy!" Imagine her pain, as the officer, enjoying her helplessness, tore out the nail, then another, and another. She had to keep looking straight at her terrified child, hoping against hope that he would see the pain in her weeping eyes and somehow understand, but she knew he could not understand.

When only ten bleeding stumps remained and the child had lost consciousness, the officer no doubt splattered its brains on the ground and, turning on the Mrs. Godoy, pistol-whipped her, ripped off her underwear, and raped her. Finally, when his men had had their way with her, he probably jammed his revolver into her mouth also and pulled the trigger.

---

[226] Ibid., #111 and #122.

[228] Mrs. Godoy, like most of the leadership in the rebellion, was not Mayan. Few of the Maya had any experience or skill in political leadership.

[229] Francisco Goldman, *The Art of Political Murder: Who Killed the Bishop?*, p.148.

[230] Piero Gleijeses, *Politics and Culture in Guatemala*, 1988, p.10, citing a CIA document. See also CEH, Vol. 1, Annex 1, #35 [Spanish].

[231] Kirsten Weld, *Paper Cadavers: The Archives of Dictatorship in Guatemala*, 2014, p.139.

Cultural Genocide

Arjuno3

Years later, we can look back on the Guatemalan Civil War and wonder, what was the object of all that carnage? It had little to do with the guerrillas, who never constituted a significant threat to the government.[232] Still less was the war about rooting out communism, a simple red herring. Rather the military government had a more existential objective.

Language and religion dominate every culture, especially in Guatemala where language is front and center. During the war, speaking a Mayan language could result in being shot. Religion is more subtle. Among the Maya, a proper burial has deep religious overtones because of their respect for ancestors. They do not just remember their ancestors; they believe that a sacred bond exists between the living and the dead and they renew that bond in religious ceremonies that go back, probably, millennia. That bond, however, depends upon a proper religious burial. For this reason, after a massacre, the army forbade villagers to bury their dead. Those who had been forced to flee into the jungle and returned several days later would encounter the miasma of their loved ones' rotting bodies being eaten by wild animals. The destruction of more than six hundred villages and, often, forced resettlement elsewhere after the war, eviscerated a core element in Mayan cultural heritage. REHMI (page 2), as an instrument of the Catholic Church, naturally had a penchant to deplore the Guatemalan army's Machiavellian dismemberment of Mayan beliefs and practices. "In Mayan culture, death is not understood as the absence of life, and relationships with the ancestors are part of daily life."[233] The position of the body at the moment of death and the preparation of the corpse as well as the objects to be buried with the deceased are especially important to the Maya.[234]

Other elements of Mayan culture also presented opportunities for genocide. "The rape of women, during torture or before being murdered, was a common practice aimed at destroying one of the most intimate and vulnerable aspects of the individual's dignity."[235] The bellies of pregnant women were sliced open. Men and boys were forced into PACs and sometimes obliged to kill people in their own villages. "The use of their own norms and procedures to regulate social life and resolve conflicts was prevented; the exercise of Mayan spirituality and the Catholic religion was obstructed, prevented or repressed."[236]

"The massacres, scorched earth operations, forced disappearances and executions of Mayan authorities, leaders and spiritual guides, were not only an attempt to destroy the social base of the guerrillas, but above all, to destroy the cultural values that ensured cohesion and collective action in Mayan communities."[237] That was the object of all that carnage. But why?

---

[232] CEH, #24, p.22.

[233] REMHI, p.14.

[234] Ibid., p.15.

[235] CEH, #91, p.95.

[236] CEH, #88, p.35.

[237] CEH, #32, p.23.

The civil war had begun over the issue of land. If the Maya could be made to abandon their cultural values, their languages, their dogged adherence to ancestral values, their belief in the sacredness of the earth and the obligation of fathers to pass on their parcels to their sons, if they could just be normal people, give up their precious land, find employment as factory workers and shop keepers, if they could just be normal people, get married, have three or four kids, spend their working lives paying off a mortgage and helping their children get a start at repeating the cycle, if they could just be like us—that's what all that carnage was about. It didn't happen. The issue remains unresolved.

Sequel

In 1958 the United Fruit Company lost an anti-trust suit in U.S. Courts, a judgment eviscerating its assets. In 1972, United Fruit sold its remaining assets in Guatemala to Del Monte. On February 3, 1975, the president of United Fruit, Eli M. Black (page 47) went to his office on the forty-fourth floor of the Pan Am Building in Manhattan, smashed the window with his briefcase, and jumped out.

Jacobo Árbenz Guzmán left Mexico and went first to Switzerland. his father's homeland, then France, Czechoslovakia, Russia, Uruguay, Cuba, and Mexico again, where he died on January 27, 1971, at the age of fifty-eight.

Juan José Arévalo served as Guatemala's ambassador to Chile and France. He died at age 86 on October 6, 1990, in Guatemala City. Arévalo's most famous book, *The Shark and the Sardines*, a bitter diatribe directed at U.S. foreign policy in Latin America, was published in an English translation in 1961.

Chapter VI, Post-War Guatemala

1985

1985 marks a turning point in the war. The guerillas realized that they could not defeat the opposition juggernaut supported by the United States and, though not disbanding, were content to stay out of sight. The army knew it had won and tempered its ferocity. Harrowing violence still occurred, like the massacre at the village of San Andrés Ixtapa in 1988 and that at Xamán in October 1995 but 1985 saw the election of a civilian president, albeit with limited power, and in 1986 the State of Emergency was lifted. Nevertheless, before leaving office outgoing president Mejía Victores (page 72) signed "a general amnesty for military officers" in his final days in office.[240] More importantly, 1985 saw the drafting of a new constitution.

Unfortunately, the civilian governments that followed governed poorly. Diane Nelson quotes one official, saying, "The government has no plan, no money, and no clue."[241] More importantly, the psyche of individuals who had survived the conflict left people in doubt about themselves. "In other words," Nelson avers, "if people make war, war also makes people."[242]

Vinicio Cerezo Arévalo (1986–90)

Victor Cerezo Arévalo, the winner of the 1985 election, a civilian and the son of a supreme court judge, had participated in the student protests at San Carlos University against the Ydigoras government (page 55) and in 1968 had graduated with a degree in law. At his inauguration in January, 1986, President Cerezo announced that his top priorities would be ending the violence and establishing the rule of law. His government would respect habeas corpus and court-ordered protection. In addition, his government would create the Office of a Human Rights Ombudsman.

A test of his authority soon presented itself when he attempted to appoint a retired general who no longer had ties with the military as director of the National Police, because the constitution mandated police independence from the military. But Cerezo's Defense Minister, General Héctor Gramajo (page 61), negotiated the appointment of General Caballeros Seigné, a career intelligence officer close to Gramajo. Thus, the military would continue to control the National Police. A detective confided to Jennifer Schirmer that, although publicly the army and the police operate independently of each other, in fact there are always two investigations operating in tandem, "that of the police and that of the G-2 [page 61] watching the police."[245]

Cerezo did have some successes early on, prominently the creation of the Office of a Human Rights Ombudsman, but the final two years of his presidency were marked by a failing economy, strikes, protest marches, and allegations of widespread corruption.

The constitution of 1985 provided that presidential and congressional terms be limited to four years. Cerezo survived coup attempts in 1988 and 1989, and in 1990 handed the government over to his successor, Jorge Serrano, another civilian.

---

[240] Kirsten Weld, *Paper Cadavers: The Archives of Dictatorship in Guatemala*, 2014, p.143.

[241] Diane M. Nelson, *A Finger in the Wound: Body Politics in Quincentennial Guatemala*, 1999, p.83.

[242] Diane M. Nelson, *Reckoning: The Ends of War*, 2009, p.xiii.

[245] Jennifer Schirmer, *The Guatemalan Military Project: A Violence Called Democracy*, 1998, p.180.

Esquipulas II

In August 1987, the five Central American presidents, at the instigation of Oscar Arias of Costa Rica, met in Esquipulas [ess-key-POO-lahss] in the *departamento* of Chiquimula (see map on page 84) to work out a plan for parallel peace negotiations in Guatemala, El Salvador, Honduras, and Nicaragua, a plan known as 'Esquipulas II'; civil war had been raging in all four countries for years. (Costa Rica has not had an army since 1948; not surprisingly, it has also not had a civil war.)

Anticipating the possibility of a negotiated settlement, the four largest guerrilla groups in Guatemala—ORPA, EGP (page 57), FAR (page 57), and PGT (page 52)—joined together to form a new organization, the URNG (*Unidad Revolucionaria Nacional Guatemalteca*).

An initial meeting between military representatives of the Cerezo government and the URNG took place in October, 1987, in Madrid, but the army had recently launched a new offensive, resulting in the massacre at the village of San Andrés Ixtapa in 1988 (preceding page). Cerezo subsequently set up a government agency, the National Commission for Reconciliation, in accordance with Esquipulas II. In March of 1990, the Commission met with the URNG to prepare the groundwork for direct meetings among the government, the URNG, and the army, which now realized that its recently launched offensive, resulting in the massacre at the village of San Andrés Ixtapa, had failed to achieve its objective.

Jorge Serrano Elias (1991–93)

As a youth, Serrano had studied in Switzerland. Returning to Guatemala, he graduated from San Carlos University with a degree in engineering and subsequently earned a doctorate at Stanford in California. Returning to Guatemala again, he worked for the government and got involved in politics, publishing a document describing the miserable conditions in which the Maya lived, a move that resulted in death threats. Serrano found it prudent to return to the United States but soon went back to Guatemala to work for fellow Evangelical, Ríos Montt (page 64), only to become disaffected. He ran for the presidency in 1985 and lost.

The collapse of the Soviet Union in 1991 brought an end to the Cold War and the threat of communism. That same year Serrano became the first civilian president in Guatemala's history to succeed another civilian president. (See Appendix G on page 259.)

In April, 1991, in Mexico City, the army signed an accord establishing an agenda that became the basis for the Peace Accords (see page 1). Negotiations continued on the specifics but were deadlocked on the accord to create a truth commission (CEH [page 2]) and an Accord on Human Rights. In May of 1993 the government/army broke off further dialog, threatening a renewal of hostilities.

On May 25, 1993, Serrano, irritated by the lack of progress, suspending the constitution, dissolved Congress and the Supreme Court, intending to solve the problem himself. President Clinton threatened to withhold all financial support. With that the entire country turned against Serrano and he had to flee for his life. The Guatemalan Congress appointed the country's human rights ombudsman (see preceding page), Ramiro de León Carpio, to finish Serrano's term as president.

Ramiro de León Carpio (1993–95)

After obtaining his law degree, Ramiro de León served in various government departments and corporate businesses. He was elected to Congress in 1984 and the following year participated in the drafting of the constitution of 1985. Pursuant to that constitution, Cerezo had appointed de Leon to fill the Office of Human Rights Ombudsman (see above) and when Serrano fled, the National Congress elected the congenial de León to finish out Serrano's unexpired term.

De Leon enjoyed immense popular support. With the wind at his back, de Leon, in an attempt to rid the government of corruption, demanded the resignation of all the members of Congress and the Supreme Court. Taken aback they refused. In the end, the matter was resolved by a popular referendum in January, 1994. New elections followed, a new congress was seated, and de Leon was elected president in his own right.

Now, with support from the U.N. and the Organization of American States, De León immediately opened negotiations with the URNG and on March 29 he and the commanders in the URNG signed the "Accord on Human Rights."[246] In June, the "Accord on Resettlement of Displaced Persons" and the "Accord on the Establishment of the Commission to Clarify Human Rights Violations" were both signed. But signing documents is not peace itself. The violence continued and on April 1, 1994, the chief justice of the Supreme Court was murdered. The talks continued nevertheless and on June 23 the accord establishing the "Commission for the Historical Clarification of human rights violations and acts of violence which have caused suffering to the Guatemalan people" (CEH [page 2]) was finally signed, but the army had agreed only on the condition that individuals responsible for the violence not be named. On March 31, 1995, the Accord on Indigenous Rights was also signed.

Much remained to be done—four accords had failed to be signed and more had not yet even been discussed, but the 1985 constitution limited the president's term of office to four years and de Leon's term had run out.

Alvaro Arzú Irigoyen (1996–99)

In 1996 Alvaro Arzú Irigoyen, a successful businessman and a member of Guatemala's European elite, ran for the presidency. He had been mayor of Guatemala City and was well liked there. Arzú succeeded de Leon in office, but hardly in spirit.[247] The civil war was effectively over but Arzú had no program to address the cause of the war, insufficient land to feed the population. As a result, the level of crime during his term in office rose sharply.

Peace

On December 29, 1996, in Guatemala City, President Arzú (fulfilling a promise he had made during his campaign) and the representatives of the UNRG put their signatures to the "Accord for a Firm and Lasting Peace," the last of the Peace Accords. Yet, in spite of the significant number of Mayan guerrillas who had served during the war, no indigenous commanders representing the guerillas had been invited to participate in the talks.[248] At the official presentation of the CEH (February 25, 1999), President Alvaro Arzu publicly rejected the report.[249] He also refused to implement most of the CEH's recommendations.[250]

---

[246] Which, among other things, specified the disbandment of the PACs (page 59).

[247] See James Black's, "Scorched Earth in a Time of Peace," 2015, https://nacla.org/article/scorched-earth-time-peace

[248] Nelson, *Finger in the Wound*, p.59. Rigoberta Menchú made the same complaint (cf. Nelson, ibid., p.86, n.12).

[249] Susan Fitzpatrick-Behrens, "Angels in Guatemala: Confronting a Legacy of Official Terror," in *NACLA* (2014), https://nacla.org/news/angels-guatemala-confronting-legacy-official-terror

[250] Rachel Sieder, "War, Peace, and Memory Politics," in Alexandra Barahonda de Brito, Carmen Gonzáles-Enríquea, and Paloma Aguilar (edd.), *The Politics of Memory: Transitional Justice in Democratizing Societies*, 2001, p.178.

MINUGUA

To oversee implementation of the Peace Accords, the U.N. created MINUGUA, the "United Nations Verification Mission in Guatemala."

Signing documents is one thing; carrying out the details, another. To take but one example, the leadership of the URNG (the guerilla forces) had agreed to demobilize. What then? Are their men simply to turn in their guns and go home? All of these men had been killers. How would they be received back home, if home still existed? In many cases, their villages had been destroyed and their families massacred. They had no skills beyond farming and fighting and now they had no land and nobody to fight. Where were they to go and how were they to support themselves? How could they be protected from vengeance by the army, which did not disband?

MINUGUA was created by an act of the United Nations General Assembly on September 19, 1994; its mandate, overseeing the implementation of the Peace Accords, would run for ten years. The URNG, with MINUGUA oversight, created eight 'Assembly Points' for decommissioning their forces; the army was kept at a distance and guerrillas, virtually all Mayan, turned in their arms and were turned out onto the streets, many of them, perhaps most of them, destitute and homeless.

In its final report, MINUGUA noted that resolution of problems regarding Mayan rights "has been more formal than substantive" and "many key *land-related* legal reforms have not been carried out" [emphasis added].[251]

Land

In traditional Mayan religion, the Corn god created men out of corn, the staple of the Mayan diet, and when Mayan men perform their planting ritual (page 10), the crop they are about to plant is corn, and the calendar they use to tell them when to plant is the ancient Mayan calendar (page 11).

Traditionally a Mayan father passes his farmland onto his son. If he has more than one son, he must divide it or acquire an additional parcel or parcels (page 39). The problem now is that since January 1, 1877 (see page 42), no more land has been available, even as the Mayan population has continued to double with each generation. Between 1950 and 1970 alone, the number of families living on parcels too small to provide enough food for a family rose from 308,070 to 421,000 and the average size of farms decreased from 20 acres to 14 acres.[252] In the highlands, where most of the Maya live, the shortage of land is particularly acute. "The average size of farm units in this area . . . decreased from 1.3 hectares (3.2 acres) per person in 1950 to less than 0.84 hectare (2 acres) per person in 1975."[253] Between 1950 and 1979, the category of 'peasant not self-sufficient' increased from 47 to 60 percent.[254] A report issued by USAID in 1979, demonstrated that 89.8 percent of family farms in Guatemala did not meet the minimum required to support an average family.[255] Think about it for a moment—most of the Maya did not have enough to eat in 1979. The population of Guatemala in 1979 was 6,843,875; today it is 16,856,938.[256] In desperation, young Mayan men and women in search of work flood into the major cities, where the unemployment and underemployment rate is around 50% [my estimate]. And what do they find in

---

[251] Nelson, *Reckoning*, 2009, pp.297–98.

[252] Shelton H. Davis, "Introduction: Sowing the Seeds of Violence," in Robert M. Carmack (ed.), *Harvest of Violence: The Maya Indians and the Guatemalan Crisis*, 1988, pp.14–15.

[253] Ibid.

[254] See Beatriz Manz, *Repatriation and Reintegration: An Arduous Process in Guatemala*, 1988, p.14.

[255] WRITENET, *Guatemala: Displacement, Return and the Peace Process*, 1995, 1. Introduction.

[256] Source, http://www.countrymeters.info/en/Guatemala

their new environment? *Violent crime! Gangs! Drugs! Starvation! Homelessness! Rape! Racism! Torture! Police Corruption! Criminal Immunity! Death!*

The Guatemalan Government Response

Today the government of Guatemalan is installing a national land registry, using the various municipalities' records as a basis for issuing nationally valid deeds.[257] The result places the traditional system at odds with the system replacing it. We saw the traditional system earlier:

> "The cultivated portion consisted of irregularly shaped parcels, owned either by the community jointly or by individual families within the community. The parcels belonging to individual families were large enough to feed an average family, probably about twenty acres, more or less depending on the productivity of the soil, and was passed on from father to son. . . .
>
> "The land owned by the community jointly . . . consisted of parcels that might either be left fallow or assigned to individual families. . . . As the number of families increased, additional land had to be carved out of the surrounding forest by the community jointly. It was the responsibility of the elders to see to it that every family had sufficient land to feed itself. Until the Spaniards arrived, surveying and legal evidence of ownership would have served no purpose" (page 39).

It's not that the Maya are unwilling to adopt the use of title deeds. Read again Rigoberta Menchú's account of her father's and neighbors' heroic and ultimately unsuccessful efforts to acquire deeds to what property they still had left (page 67).

Under the new law, land can be mortgaged to fund some project or other and, if the owner cannot pay off the mortgage, the bank may seize the land and sell it to a complete stranger, a total violation of Mayan tradition. In a recent case which I know personally, the father of a large family, living in a village that had schooling only through sixth grade, wanted his children to get a better education. His tiny parcel could not produce enough corn to feed his family. He had steady work on a plantation but did not make enough to pay all of their bills if they went to school in town, where instruction goes through twelve grades. (Nearly all schools in towns are private and charge tuition; books and school supplies, including uniforms, must be purchased.) To finance the education of two of his children, he mortgaged his parcel intending that, when the children finished school and got jobs, they could help him pay off the loan; meanwhile he would make minimal payments himself. Initially all went well but one day, without warning and for reasons unknown, the plantation on which he worked fired all of the men from this man's village. Since he could no longer make payments, the bank notified him that it intended to seize his parcel. Fortunately, an American learned of this development and intervened to save the parcel—a temporary expedient but no solution.

---

[257] Curtis W. Dabb, James H. McDonald, and Walter Randolph Adams, "A Land Divided without Clear Titles: The Clash of Communal and Individual Land Claims in Nahualá and Santa Catarina Ixtahuacá" in John P. Hawkins, James H. McDonald, and Walter Randolph Adams (edd.), *Crisis of Governance in Maya Guatemala: Indigenous Responses to a Failing State*, 2013, p.121.

If land is center stage in Guatemala, what does land in Guatemala look like?

This photo illustrates in the foreground an area of good farmland. Not all the parcels are of uniform size, all of them having been divided, some several times. Almost no buildings and absolutely no roads take up valuable space. Crops, therefore, must be carried on one's back to the nearest road. The dark foliage sprinkled here and there are coffee bushes, planted to provide a small cash income.

The mountain in the background presents a stark contrast, most of it impossible to access, much less to cultivate. Imagine a group of families setting out to create a settlement in such a place. There are no roads, of course; just getting there would take weeks of slashing undergrowth steeply up the mountainside with no trail. Then imagine felling trees and building houses, a school, and a church with only hand tools. Finally, imagine the isolation, getting sick in such a place, breaking your leg or an arm, planting crops, putting out a fire, surviving a storm, replacing a pair of boots, dealing with ants and other vermin. Although this mountain is in Alta Verapaz, it is not unlike the land the government ceded to families to create Santa María Tzejá in Quiché (page 63), a project that took twelve years.

The cleared area on the left in the photo on the next page gives you an idea of what a resultant parcel might look like in such a place.

Farmland is surely the most burning issue for the Maya in Guatemala. Piero Gleijeses concludes *Shattered Hope*, quoting the 1988 Pastoral Letter of the Guatemalan Bishops: "The cry for land is, without any doubt, the loudest, the most dramatic and the most desperate sound in Guatemala."[258]

Mining

Between 1957 and 1960 the Hanna Mining Co., a subsidiary of the Canadian-based International Nickel Company (INCO), discovered sizable nickel deposits near El Estor (see map on page 84). During the dictatorship of Peralto Azurdia (1963–66), INCO obtained from the Guatemalan Government a lease to export 30 thousand tons of nickel annually for forty years. "The project promised a major shift in Guatemala's economy."[259] Because of fluctuating prices on the nickel market, operations did not begin until 1977. The first stage of the process, called 'strip mining,' removes the top soil, thus destroying the farmland.

Sixteen Q'eqchí'-speaking farming communities lived there. Violence erupted as soon as the strip mining began. Guerrilla forces moved in to protect the villages. In reply the government of Laugerud García (page 59) sent in the army. The company ceased operations in 1981. In 2004, INCO sold its mining rights to Skye Resources. Operations resumed in 2005. HudBay Minerals bought Skye Resources in 2008.

Guatemala's bloody civil war had ended in 1996. The Peace Accords provided for the return of Mayan lands to their rightful owners and restricted the employment of both military and private

---

[258] Piero Gleijeses, *Shattered Hope: The Guatemalan Revolution and the United States, 1944–1954*, 1991, p.387.

[259] Susanne Jonas, *The Battle for Guatemala: Rebels, Death Squads, and U.S. Power*, 1991, p.52.

security forces throughout the country, on paper. In 2010, HudBay security forces, in response to a demonstration demanding that the land be returned to its rightful owners, killed Adolfo Ich, a community leader, and drove the demonstrators off. Mr. Ich's widow, with international legal assistance, filed suit against the company in Canadian court. In June, 2013, the court found her case admissible. As of this writing, it is still pending.

Diane Nelson[260] provides abundant detail of a mining operations on the other side of the country, in San Marcos and Quiché' (see map on page 84). I can only summarize her findings here.

After the civil war, Goldcorp, also a Canadian company, secured a license from the Guatemalan government to open a gold mine in San Marcos and began operations in 2005. Four years later, the company applied for a license to open another gold mine further north. In response, the Catholic Church's Peace and Ecology Commission organized a meeting to show to the residents living in the area around the site of the proposed second mine, what had resulted from opening the first mine. The lead speaker, a man named Vinicio, had brought with him a PowerPoint presentation and began to show pictures. The first image illustrated the massive destruction that had replaced a mountain top with a lagoon, green with cyanide, the result of a process that treats the oar with a cyanide-and-alkali solution to extract the gold.

When the vertiginous shock of his hitherto languid audience subsided, Vinicio related the history of the 2005 mine. In 1996 the company had sent representatives to the mayor of the community in that area offering 'development,' and saying that the company would pay the residents handsomely for permission to mine there and would employ local men to work at the mine, paying high wages. (The 1985 constitution required mining companies to secure the approval of local residents before beginning operations.) The residents readily agreed. Now, ten years later, the cyanide lagoon was poisoning the air and the water. Many people, especially children, were sick, nothing grew, and the promised financial enticements had not materialized. Vinicio's audience, aghast, soon organized to prevent a similar outcome in their backyard.

Already in 1975, the army had begun operations against the Maya in an area known as the Northern Transversal, where oil had been discovered and high-ranking military officers were buying up the land.[262] Today more than a third of Guatemala has been licensed for exploration.[263]

Alfonso Portillo Cabrera (2000–2003)

Alfonso Portillo first gained a measure of prominence when he ran for the presidency against Alvaro Arzú in the election of 1995 (page 77) and lost. In 1999 he took advantage of the swelling crime rate that had developed during Arzú's term in office and campaigned on a tough-on-crime slogan called *mano duro* ("iron fist"). He won on the first round. In fact, for all its pretense, Portillo's government was awash with scandals involving drugs and corruption. On leaving office he fled to Mexico. When he returned, he was tried but the court ruled that insufficient evidence had been presented and the case was dropped. Subsequently, he was extradited to the United States, tried, and found guilty of money laundering.

Óscar Berger Cabrera (2004–2007)

Óscar Berger, like Arzú, came from a wealthy business family and had, again like Arzú, been mayor of Guatemala City, but his performance as president could hardly have been more different.

---

[260] Nelson, *Reckoning*, Chapter 6.

[262] Schirmer, op. cit., p.41.

[263] Ibid., p.216.

As one of his first acts, President Berger cut the size of the army by more than forty percent, as required by the Peace Accords. Not long thereafter, he acknowledged the government's complicity in the 1990 murder of human rights activist Myrna Mack, a Guatemalan anthropologist who had documented many of the army's massacres in the highlands.

CICIG

The International Commission against Impunity in Guatemala, created by the U.N. and President Berger in 2006, CICIG (its Spanish acronym) is charged to investigate cases in which criminals are thought to have infiltrated government institutions since the end of the civil war. CICIG has some notable achievements, prominently in the arrests and convictions of President Pérez Molina (see below) and his Vice-President, Roxana Baldetti.

Alvaro Colom (2008–2017)

A well-to-do business man, Alvaro Colom ran successfully on a platform of reducing the crime rate by reducing poverty. On February 25, 2009, at a rally of some 18,000 survivors of the war and relatives of the victims, in the plaza fronting the National Palace (page 48), Colom publicly accepted the CEH, as Arzú had refused to do (page 77), and apologized. In 2010, he appointed Helen Mack, Myrna's sister (see above), to head investigations into police corruption, with no observable results.

Otto Pérez Molina (2012–2015)

During the 1990s, before entering politics, Pérez Molina served as Director of Military Intelligence, as Presidential Chief of Staff under President de León Carpio (page 76), and as the representative of the military in negotiating the Peace Accords. Campaigning with Portillo's slogan 'mano dura' ("iron fist"), he won the election of 2011, the first military officer (though retired) to be elected to the presidency since Mejia Victores in 1983 (page 72), even though he was accused by Ixil-speaking indigenous of massacres in 1982.

In April, 2015, U.N. investigators uncovered evidence of a corruption ring (discounting tariffs in exchange for bribes from importers) and, in August, prosecutors presented the evidence to Guatemala's Supreme Court. A month later, the Guatemalan Congress stripped Pérez Molina of his immunity as president after weeks of relentless protests in the square fronting the National Palace (page 48). He resigned the next day and the day after that was arrested and sent to prison. The Vice President was appointed to serve the remainder of his term.

Pérez Molina's criminal activity continues from behind bars.[264]

Jimmy Morales (2016–)

Jimmy Morales, a professional entertainer and the candidate of the *Frente de Convergencia Nacional*, the political party of retired army officers, is the first Guatemalan president to come from a lower-class background. President Morales is in trouble for ordering the expulsion of the UN's anti-corruption chief in Guatemala[265]; see CICIG above. *Prensa Libre* (a leading Guatemalan newspaper) reports that there are not enough votes in the Guatemalan Congress to strip him of his immunity.[266]

---

[264] http://www.insightcrime.org/news-briefs/guatemala-ex-president-and-vp-still-wield-power-from-jail-report
[265] Elisabeth Malkin, *New York Times*, Aug. 29, 2017.
[266] http://www.prensalibre.com/Tag/Jimmy-Morales/48823

Guatemala's System of Education

Guatemalan law requires parents to enroll their children in *primaria* (grades 1 through 6), a step in the right direction but education, broadly defined, does not begin with first grade; it begins in the home. I digress, again, for a moment.

Chapel Hill, NC, where I lived for many years, has a fine public library, as do nearly all cities in the United States. I sometimes visited a room in which one of the librarians reads to pre-school children, generally fifteen to twenty kids at any given session. As the librarian reads, the children's eyes sparkle with wonder, so focused on the story that they can hardly contain themselves, their little imaginations creating worlds that exist nowhere else. Periodically the reader asks a question.

All the hands shoot up; many of the children cannot sit still and jump up waving their hands excitedly. Inevitably, when I went to check out my books, any number of moms and their preschoolers were standing in line ahead of me, with an armload of children's books to take home.

In Guatemala, there are no public lending libraries. Let me repeat that. In Guatemala, there are no public lending libraries; zero! Libraries, yes, a few. but you cannot check any books out!

The first level of formal education in Guatemala is called *primaria* (*pree-MAH-ree-ah*), grades 1 through 6.

The next higher level, corresponding to our middle school, is *basico* (*BAH-see-koh*), grades 7, 8, and 9. The standard curriculum in *basico* includes: Spanish, math, social studies, natural sciences, English, industrial arts for boys and home economics for girls, physical education, music,[268] art, and, typing. (At the *Instituto Mixto* [page 33] I was teaching English in *tercero basico*, "third basic," i.e., ninth grade.)

Diversificado (*dee-ver-see-fee-KAH-doh*) corresponds, more or less, to our high school, that is grades 10, 11, and 12. The curriculum includes many of the same subjects as ninth grade together with a variety job-related skills, like accounting, computer science, electrical, plumbing, and others. The object of *diversificado* is a *carrera*, a "job"). Nine to eleven subjects are the norm. Neither Spanish nor English includes any literature, only grammar (which the teachers do not know) and vocabulary (which they do not have).[269] Social Studies includes history but none of the students I knew could answer even the simplest questions about the history of Guatemala. And, for the vast majority of students who want to get a job, *diversificado* is the only preparation they will have.

Those studying to become teachers had, until recently, a curriculum called *magisterio* which involved four years of study replacing the three years of *diversificado*. In 2013 the government replaced *magisterio* with a program called *bachillerato*, which adds another year. (When I told Niceh [page 211] of this development, she laughed, "Adding another year isn't going to make any difference.") Most recently the government made another bootless attempt at resolving the education problem by requiring teachers to study for three years at the university level. When this requirement was passed into law, the teachers marched in rebellion, closing major highways. In any case, it is difficult to see how the requirement can be enforced, since the vast majority of teachers have only been through *magisterio*, high school, and the vast majority of Guatemalans have neither the preparation nor the means to undertake university studies.

Traditionally, in the absence of textbooks, teachers copied from their textbooks onto the blackboard and the students copied from the board into their notebooks. Today most schools have textbooks, but their quality is questionable. It took only a week or two before I discarded the one I had been given, back in 2003, and started mimeographing my own lessons for the next day (page 33).

There are no colleges in Guatemala, as we understand the term—four years of study between high school and graduate or professional school. Someone wanting to become a physician, a lawyer, or an engineer in Guatemala enters medical school, law school, or engineering school directly after *diversificado*, high school. Medical schools grant the M.D. In all other fields the *licenciatura* (*lee-sen-see-ah-TOO-rah*), 'licentiate' in English, adds five to eight more years of job training. In other words, the entire curriculum, from start to finish, is devoted entirely and exclusively to job training. There is no shortage of trained workers. The quality of job training, i.e., absent research, appears at this level to be comparable to that in the United States: bridges do their job and last at

---

[268] I have never met a Guatemalan who knows how to read music. The only school bands I ever saw consisted entirely of drums, though I saw pictures of bands that had other instruments as well, but even they play by ear.

[269] A Guatemalan administrator advises me that the national curriculum includes the reading of some specific books other than textbooks but that the teachers are not qualified to teach them "and limit their teaching to what is easy for them."

least as long as bridges in the U.S.; medical care includes open-heart surgery, lawyers successfully prosecute high-ranking public officials, etc. Job training works very well in Guatemala. But life is more than a job. What Guatemala needs is new leadership, people with an active imagination to get Guatemalan patent production off the floor (page 228), to develop new industries, to promote capital ventures, and to give meaning and excitement to human life. In short, what Guatemalan needs most, right now, is a generation of readers and thinkers. And for that Guatemala needs a generation of college graduates whose training includes coursework in the humanities, as in the United States.

Humanities

W.E.B. DuBois, a free black man born in 1868, studied philosophy, history, economics, and sociology at Harvard University, graduating with a B.A. in 1890. After two years of study in Berlin (Germany), DuBois returned to Harvard for his Ph.D. and joined other educated blacks in founding the NAACP. He died in 1963. In *Darkwater: Voices from Within the Veil*, DuBois writes about education, "We must not seek to make men carpenters but to make carpenters men."[271] He is talking about the role of the humanities. To understand the nature of the humanities, we must ask, 'what does it mean to be human?'

One can easily identify some characteristics that human beings share with the higher species of animals. Like them we are, physically, vertebrates and like them we eat, sleep, reproduce, experience anger, fear, and companionship. But some characteristics are not shared. The most obvious is our ability to reason—to figure out the complicated solution to some knotty problem, a problem in algebra, perhaps, or in engineering. We also have the ability to laugh at a sitcom on TV or to cry when we read a particularly sad book, to enjoy music and art, to organize a charity drive for a child that needs an expensive operation. Since these things are so, we may conclude that human beings are by nature partly animal and partly something else, something superior to animals.

The ability to perform some activity, whether physical (like shoveling snow, playing basketball, or eating pizza) or non-physical (like remembering someone's telephone number, solving a quadratic equation, or figuring out *whodunit* in a murder mystery) is often referred to as a 'faculty.' The specifically human faculties have names: 1) intellect, 2) will, 3) speech, 4) imagination, 5) aesthetic sense, and 6) some specifically human emotions, like passion and empathy.[272]

The faculties by themselves are just abilities; they do not do anything unless something stimulates them. Everyone has the ability to enjoy music but, unless one is actually listening to music (or humming it to oneself) that ability just sits at the ready, dormant. The faculties are stimulated by 'fields.' A field is simply a body of related material that has the potential to activate one or more of our faculties: mathematics, physics, art, music, literature, medicine, law, anthropology, biology, chemistry, accounting, management, and a host of others. It is obvious that many fields correspond more or less closely to contemporary academic disciplines (for obviously good reasons) but some—art, music, literature, religion, commerce, sports, and others—existed long before colleges and universities arrived on the scene. There is no one-to-one correspondence between the faculties and the fields that stimulate them. The number of our faculties is fixed but the number of fields is limitless and they sometimes come newly on the scene (computer science, for example) and sometimes go into oblivion (long dead languages of which no record survives, for example).

---

[271] AMS Press, 1969 (originally published, 1920), page 210.

[272] The source of this list and the detail that follows is *Experiencing the Humanities*, an unfinished textbook I prepared over the course of the eight years during which I taught a two-semester course in the humanities.

Some fields deal with things physical—physics itself, of course, but also chemistry, biology, geography, computer science, and many more. Other fields deal with things non-physical (some of which correspond to academic subjects and some do not): philosophy, literature, music, art, religion, language, history, jurisprudence, love, marriage, and others, all of the fields that make human life worth living. These are the humanities and, as W.E.B. DuBois suggests, these should be the primary focus of education. These are what Guatemala is, tragically, missing.

The upper class in Guatemala has its own schools. I visited one: the language of instruction was English; the school year began in September; the textbooks were American; the language of instruction was English (from first grade on), and most of the teachers were Americans. For college, upper-class families often send their sons and daughters to the United States or Europe. I got to know one of them, who was, at the time, a senior at the University of North Carolina in Chapel Hill.

Foreign Students in the U.S.

The fact that foreign students flock to American colleges and universities needs no documentation. Graduate students, of course, seek to take advantage of the superior resources for research available here, but what about undergraduates? Why do they come here? The lead article of the April 21, 2017, issue of UNC's *The Daily Tar Heel*, reported that incoming freshmen from China give two reasons: one, they can explore a variety of subjects and change majors easily, while at home they would have to stick with their initial choice even if they subsequently prefer something else, and, second, they are attracted by the "liberal arts curriculum." A senior assistant director in the Admissions Office concurred, saying, "a number of international students are attracted to the freedom and flexibility of a liberal arts education," that is, prominently, the humanities.

Chapter VII, GSSG 2003

On September 7, 2003, I flew back to Guatemala. Heydi (page 32) and her parents, Arnoldo (page 36) and his parents, Tita (page 34), and Jorge (page 35) were waiting for me at the airport. We put up at Hotel Ajau (*ah-HAH-oo*), cheap but serviceable accommodations in down-town Guatemala City. The next day we took taxis to the U.S. Embassy to apply for visas. (Jorge had previously gotten Tita, Heydi, and Arnoldo their passports.)

We need to pause for a moment to say something about passports and visas because without them, no Guatemalan is going anywhere.

Passports and Visas

(This is really boring; you may want to skip it, but if you don't know the difference between a passport and a visa, maybe you should read on.)

A *passport* is a document issued by your home country as proof of your citizenship. If you are returning from abroad, you need your passport to get back in. A *visa* is a document issued by the country you intend to visit. Since you need a visa to enter that country, you have to get it at that country's Consulate in your home country before leaving. Normally you cannot successfully apply for a visa to visit another country if you don't have a passport from your own country. Jorge had helped Tita, Heydi, and Arnoldo with their passports; they now needed visas, issued by the U.S. Consulate in Guatemala (which is physically located in the U.S. Embassy there).

The United States Government issues many different kinds of visas—the "A" visa, for example, is issued to foreign diplomats—ambassadors, their families, and their staff; the "B" visa is for visitors and business people; the "F" visa, for foreign students (mostly college students); the "H" visa, for temporary workers; the "J" visa, for exchange students; etc.

Only three visas concern us here: 1) the B Visa, that is, the *visitor's visa*, 2) the F Visa, that is the *student visa*, valid as long as the student is in school, and, 3) the J Visa, that is, the *exchange visa*, which is issued to exchange students but is only valid for one year. In order to get any of these, the petitioner had to present several paper documents (much of the process has since been digitized):

For the **B Visitor's Visa** the applicant had to present:
    a passport issued by his or her home country,
    a completed application form for a visa (Form DS-156),
    a 2"x2" full-face, recent, color photograph with a white background,
    a receipt for the SEVIS fee (see below),
    Form I-134, an Affidavit of Support.

For the **F Student Visa** the applicant had to present:
    a passport issued by his or her home country,
    a completed application form for a visa (Form DS-156),
    a completed Form I-20, issued by the school the applicant wished to attend,
    a 2"x2" full-face, recent, color photograph with a white background,
    a receipt for the SEVIS fee (see below), and
    Form I-134, an Affidavit of Support.

For the **J Exchange Visa** the applicant had to present:
    a passport issued by his or her home country,
    a completed application form for a visa (Form DS-156),

a 2"x2" full-face, recent, color photograph with a white background,

a receipt for the SEVIS fee (see below), and

Form DS 2019, issued by an exchange program in the U.S.

SEVIS stands for **S**tudent and **E**xchange **V**isitor[276] **I**nformation **S**ystem. The Department of Homeland Security (DHS) created SEVIS to keep tabs on all foreign students in the United States. Each student is assigned a SEVIS ID, which is printed on his or her I-20 (see under **F Student Visa** above) or DS-2019 (see under **J Exchange Visa** above). In the early years, we had to pay the SEVIS fee in cash at any branch of Banco Industrial in Guatemala. Today the money can be transferred electronically.

Form DS-160, an application for a visa interview, had to be submitted online well before the desired interview date. Jorge assumed responsibility for filing this complicated form, each application taking him an hour.

After depositing the application fee (about $100) in the embassy's bank account, we had to buy a visa-application telephone card. With the number on the card we could call the embassy call center (which is actually located in Mexico) to arrange a suitable date for the interview. The telephone card allowed only five minutes. If we were lucky we could make appointments for two students on a single card.

The Secretary of State, who is ultimately responsible for the issuing of visas, carries out his or her responsibilities in accordance with the Immigration and Nationality Act of 1961, often amended and usually referred to as the 'INA.' For us, the relevant portion of the INA was Section 214(b) that read: "Every alien . . . shall be *presumed to be an immigrant* until he establishes to the satisfaction of the consular officer, at the time of application for a visa, . . . that he is entitled to nonimmigrant status under section 101(a)(15)" [emphasis added], which means that the U.S. Government assumes that everyone applying for a visa really intends to stay in the United States illegally and the burden of proving otherwise in on the applicant, not on the United States Government. In other words, the various U.S. embassies abroad are charged to issue visas only to people who can prove they are not going to stay, not just who *say* they are not going to stay.

With respect to the **Visitor's Visa**, still another book, the Federal Affairs Manual (FAM), came into play. The relevant section for us was 9FAM41.31, which said: "In determining whether visa applicants are entitled to temporary visitor classification, you [the consular officer] must assess whether the applicants: (1) have a residence in a foreign country, which they do not intend to abandon; (2) intend to enter the United States for a period of specifically limited duration; and (3) seek admission for the sole purpose of engaging in legitimate activities relating to business or pleasure." FAM summarizes these requirements into one, that is, that the applicant has to have "binding ties" which ensure his/her return home. "Binding ties" include title to a property, a bank account, a family, and a job.

The INA also stipulates that to get a **Student Visa** or an **Exchange Visa** to attend a public school (but not a private school), the applicant must be in at least ninth grade.

The interviewing officer has final authority in granting or denying visas and there is no appeal; one cannot even take the matter to court. The impression created by the number of people leaving the Embassy in tears is that the vast majority of applications fail.

As our own fortunes will demonstrate, some applicants may be granted visas, while others, in identical circumstances, are denied. Even some highly-regarded organizations, like the National Academy of Sciences and the Quakers are known to have experienced significant difficulties in bringing foreigners here for meetings or conferences. Two or three years after we brought Tita,

---

[276] The inclusion of the word *visitor* here is unfortunate, since the system does not include visitors.

Heydi, and Arnoldo here, a local physician in Chapel Hill, who had been interested in GSSG from the beginning, was convinced that bringing Guatemalan teachers here would be more effective than bringing students and offered to provide whatever was needed to test the hypothesis. Accordingly, Jorge identified a mature English teacher who readily agreed to participate. She, Jorge, and the American physician supplied the necessary paperwork, demonstrating: (1) that she owned her own home in Guatemala, had investments in Guatemala, and had a six year-old son who was wholly dependent on her and whom she would leave behind if she came to the United States; (2) that she had a job in Guatemala; 3) that she would be in the United States for five months only and that she would leave on a specific date; (4) that she would devote herself entirely to improving her English skills while she was here and not work illegally; and (5) that ample funds were available for the project. She was denied a visa.

Visas for Tita, Heydi, and Arnoldo

Jorge had prepared the necessary forms; I had secured the necessary financial documents; and we had called the appointment center (which is actually in Mexico) to schedule the interviews. On September 8 (still 2003), Tita (page 34), Heydi (page 32), her mother (her father had meanwhile died), Arnoldo (page 36), his father and mother, Jorge (page 35), and I presented ourselves at the U.S. Embassy before an officer and handed him the required paperwork. The officer was sympathetic but told us that we were submitting applications for the wrong visa. We had prepared applications for B Visitor's Visa (page 88). He advised us to return the next day with applications for Student Visas, adding that there were people across the street who had typewriters and all the forms and could fill out the F (Student) Visa quickly. Crossing the street, we found a man with a typewriter and the forms, had him fill them out, and paid him. We stayed overnight at Ajau and got in line at the embassy again the next day. This time we had a different officer, who told us that we had had the correct forms the day before. Fortunately, we had them with us. He told us that we could pick up the visas the next day (September 10, 2003). We stayed at Ajau again, picked up the visas as scheduled, and went our separate ways. Tita, Heydi, and Arnoldo would come to the United States in October, as we shall see.

In the interval between my second trip to Guatemala, to take a refresher course in Spanish in Antigua (page 25) and my third trip, to teach in Tactic (page 33), a high-school friend of mine, now a priest, had come to visit me at home in Chapel Hill. In the course of our conversation I mentioned my interest in Guatemala. He replied that I should visit Fr. Greg Schaffer, a priest from Minnesota who had been pastor in a Guatemalan town called *San Lucas Tolimán* for a long time. I took my friend's advice and contacted Fr. Greg, making arrangements to visit him on my next trip to Guatemala.

Since it was now (after getting visas for Tita, Heydi, and Arnoldo) early September and I would not be bringing Tita, Heydi, and Arnoldo to the United States until October, the opportunity to visit Fr. Greg was at hand.

San Lucas Tolimán

Back in the hotel, I called Fr. Greg. He told me that the parish had many visitors who come and go and that the parish sends a car or a minivan to the airport in Guatemala City almost every day. He told me where I could find it. Four or five hours later I arrived in San Lucas Tolimán.

During the next few days I learned that Fr. Greg had been pastor there for forty years. He had come initially on a three-year hitch but when the three years were up, he did not want to leave. He also told me that in those forty years he had raised fourteen million dollars, mostly in Minnesota, and had built a hospital (below) and put an indige-

nous young man through medical school in Guatemala City, adding that the young man, having just completed his M.D., was killed when the pick-up in which he was riding crashed. Still needing a physician, Fr. Greg offered the same opportunity to one of the doctor's younger brothers, who also completed the program and is now Dr. Tun (*TOON*), the only resident physician in the area.

Fr. Greg had also built a grade school. Well-lighted and attractively furnished with books, maps, a globe, and other essentials, the school compared favorably with schools in the United States. Sr. June, the American sister he had engaged as principal, showed me around. I could not judge the quality of instruction, which still had to conform to Guatemalan law.

Some years earlier, Fr. Greg had purchased a coffee plantation and divided it into plots and given them (or perhaps sold them at affordable rates) to various families in the area. He had then helped the owners organize, build their own processing facility, and develop a marketing plan. (I have purchased their coffee in the United States on more than one occasion.)

The parish had many other projects ongoing. One planted 50,000 trees a year. Since nearly all Guatemalan women cook on a wood fire, erosion plagues the countryside. Another project took a gang off the street and put the boys to work building houses. At another, a farm, the seedlings for those 50,000 trees were raised and many other agricultural initiatives were under way.[278] Still another project provided medical care in remote villages. Regardless of the nature of the project, nothing got to the drawing board without the approval of Marcos Tun, the town's leading elder.

Dinner in the Biblioteca

At any given time, there would be from 20 to 200 volunteers at the parish: doctors, dentists, nurses, teachers, scientists, priests, students taking a gap year, and a variety of other people like myself, mostly Americans. The volunteers all ate in a large room at the parish, called the *Biblioteca* ("library"), that had a modest collection of books. All the volunteers had jobs. I asked Fr. Greg what I could do. He saw my camcorder and suggested I make a video of all of the projects.

One day I accompanied a retired American physician, Cliff Starr, and his wife Nancy, a nurse, on a trip to a remote village. For transportation, the parish had a four-wheel drive pickup seating six with a cargo bed in the back for supplies. Our excursion started at the hospital, where we loaded two large plastic containers full of medicines and other supplies into the bed of the pickup. An employee of the hospital, Jesus (*hey-SSOOSS*), had two long boxes which contained all of the records of all of the patients in that village who had ever been seen by any physician from the

---

[278] I visited the farm several times and on one occasion noticed that the right foot of one of the workmen was backwards. I would encounter many correctable but uncorrected birth defects during the ensuing years.

parish. We also had a driver and a translator who spoke four Mayan languages and Spanish. Cliff spoke Spanish but the villagers did not.

We arrived at the site and entered a large, cement-block structure with windows, a few wooden benches, and three or four tables but no lights. Jesus set his boxes of records on one of the tables near the entrance. Nancy dragged another table to one side and set up her pharmacy. Cliff pulled a bench over to a window and sat at one end. The villagers had known that Cliff was coming and the women and children had lined up quickly in front of Jesus, as soon as we arrived. Only one man was there, at the head of the line. Cliff motioned to him and asked him to sit down. The man had a problem with one of his eyes. Cliff examined him and told him that he did not have the means to treat him but would refer him to a facility in Guatemala City. The man, of course, would

have no way of getting to Guatemala City on his own. Cliff would make arrangements for him to travel in the parish minivan to the capital.

Next in line, a woman with three children approached. Greg motioned for the patient, a girl, to sit down. Through the translator (extreme right), he learned that she had a problem with one of her feet. Cliff examined the foot and wrote out a prescription. The translator told the woman to take the prescription to Nancy who read it, put the appropriate medication in a plas-

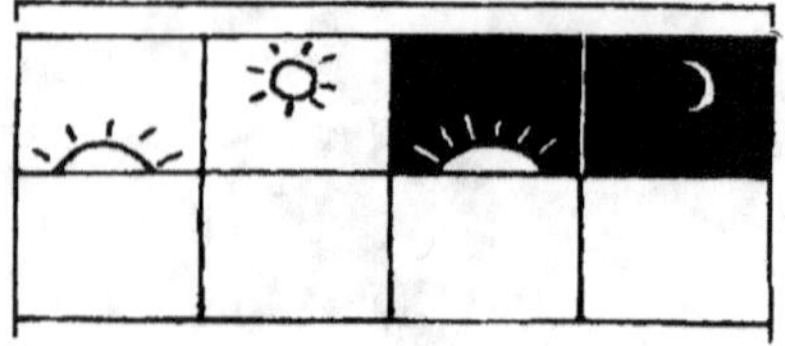

tic sandwich bag, attached the label you see at left, acted out applying the medication to the foot, put a mark under the appropriate icons, not with numbers but with vertical lines, pointed to the sunrise and sunset icons, held up held up two fingers, and gave the bag to the woman, who nodded that she understood and with a smile left with her children. Cliff saw twenty-five or thirty people that day.

Eunice An

Eunice An, a Korean American from California who majored in Spanish, had been at the parish a couple of months before I arrived. She had two jobs there. One took her to a village a few miles away to teach I am not sure what, for the children were of different ages from, perhaps, six to twelve, and their activities seemed to focus on making things appropriate to their age. Anyway, one day I went with Eunice and an indigenous young woman, perhaps a teacher, to the school where the children were assembled. I started filming. At one point, a girl of eleven or so approached me and asked for something, using a word I did not understand. We went to see Eunice. She did not know the word either. So the three of us went to see the indigenous young woman, perhaps a teacher. She laughed and told us it was the Caq'chikel word for 'coin'; the girl wanted to draw a circle.

Eunice's other job was teaching youngsters of school age, but not in school, how to read.

Blanca

One evening at dinner, I told Eunice that I wanted to videotape her reading project. So the next morning we walked over to a house owned by an American woman who was not a volunteer at the parish but, for reasons unknown to me, lived in San Lucas doing good deeds on her own. We set up a table and some chairs outside and soon seven or eight children arrived. The lesson began and I began taping. Peering through my view finder I was particularly impressed by the intense concentration of a girl of about seven or eight with whom Eunice was working. That evening at dinner I asked Eunice about the child. She told me her name was Blanca and that she was an orphan.

Subsequently I learned that Blanca's mother had died very early in Blanca's life and that her father refused to acknowledge paternity. Blanca was taken in by her maternal grandmother, who died four years later. She was then taken in by an uncle, Moisés (*moh-ee-SSESS*), and his common-law wife (see *unidos*, page 31). A day or two later, the American at whose house I had videotaped the reading lesson told me that Moisés and his wife had two or three children and that the wife's sister, who also had a couple of children by different men, lived with them. Illiteracy reigned.

Later I would visit Blanca's home. It had two bedrooms, one for Moisés and his family, the other for the other woman, her children, and Blanca. Blanca kept her few clothes in a cardboard box on the floor.

Eunice was particularly fond of Blanca and would sometimes invite her to come for dinner in the *biblioteca* (page 92).

When I first met Blanca, she did not know her age. No birth certificate was known to exist. Moisés, her uncle, remembered that she was born on May 28 but could not remember the year. The child had never had a birthday party. I always brought with me a few gifts, mostly small toys for children. So, when Eunice, Blanca, and I were eating dinner the day before I left, I said, "Blanca, you have never had a birthday party, have you?" She acknowledged she had not. I continued, "I propose that today is your birthday and that we celebrate," and I gave her the one gift I had left, a men's wrist watch from Walmart, cheap but wrapped. Blanca opened it, screeched, and jumped into my arms. The child's unaffected joy would have melted a stone.

Eunice and I decided to see if we could get Blanca adopted in the United States. Eunice herself would be off to graduate school in a couple of months and could not adopt her. Over the next several years, I would work on that project and ultimately fail (not for lack of families wanting to adopt her; four readily came forward) and not for lack of funds (raising money for her was easy) but because no legal documents existed to prove that she or her mother ever existed.

Despite all odds, Blanca would one day come to the United States and graduate from high school but getting her here would unroll in a maddening sequence of events to be detailed as this narrative unfolds.

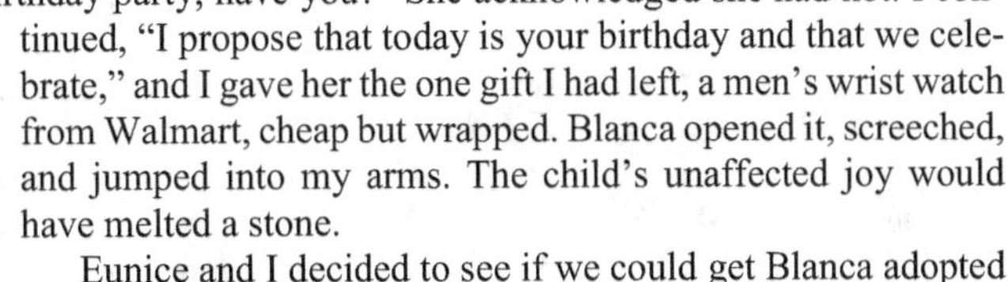

Path to Blanca's home

Heydi and Arnoldo in Phase 1

I stayed in San Lucas for two months and then returned to Guatemala City, bought tickets for Tita, Heydi, and Arnoldo and the next day, November 1, 2003, we boarded a plane for North Carolina. Heydi and Arnoldo could hardly contain their exhilaration. We were seated toward the rear of the plane and many of the seats were empty. As the thrust threw us back in our seats, the kids excitedly asked if they could move to window seats. We were still climbing and the seat belt sign was on, but I nodded "O.k." They catapulted to the nearest windows. On landing at RDU we found the GSSG board members waiting for us. Many questions kept me busy translating while we waited for my luggage. (The kids had their few possessions in paper bags.) Noreen took Heydi home, the Coyles took Tita, and Arnoldo went home with me. The next day everyone came to my house for lunch. GSSG (page 37) had gotten off the ground.

For the remainder of 2003 Noreen delivered Heydi to my house every morning before going to work and picked her up on her way home in the late afternoon, while the Coyles ferried Tita to and from my house as well. Heydi, Arnoldo, Tita, and I studied English at my kitchen table every morning but in the afternoons we went everywhere together, to the grocery store, the post office, the bank, the library, church—everywhere.

Church was interesting. Arnoldo is not Catholic. I asked him what church he wanted to go to. He said, "Any church that has *Apostolic* in its name." We consulted the phone directory and found one. On the first Sunday after arrival he and I drove to that church and went inside. The service was just beginning. We were the only two white faces there. Everyone smiled pleasantly and someone offered us hymnals. We sang lustily along with everyone else, who looked our way periodically to check on our level of our spiritual edification.

On the way home, Arnoldo asked if he could play guitar at my church. I checked with the choir director. From then on, he did, every Sunday.

Many other people provided a wealth of other experiences. John McKee, my neighbor and a board member of GSSG, took us for a tour along the Blue Ridge Mountain Drive, much like Guatemala.

On the Blue Ridge

The Coyles took us to a performance of the *Ballet Gran Folclórico de Mexico* at the Carolina Theater. (Heydi and Arnoldo had never seen the inside of a theater.) One day I took the three of them on a tour of the UNC campus, the oldest State University in the United States, with its two quads and their hundred+-year-old trees, the Wilson Library proudly displaying its stately neo-classical architecture and its collection of rare books, some first-editions. We also visited Davis Library, with its eight stories housing some eight million volumes. Other days I took them to a show in the Planetarium and to the North Carolina Museum of Art. Several people invited us into their homes, taught Heydi and Arnoldo to play chess, and otherwise opened windows that these impoverished youngsters had never even dreamed of.

Tita returned to Guatemala on December 17 to be with her family for Christmas.

On January 12 we had a snowstorm. Heydi and Arnoldo, who had never seen snow, had their first snowball fight and made their first snowman.

A young Korean couple, Danny and Soonae Kim, friends of mine, had us over for dinner (below). The Coyles took Arnoldo to a protest at the infamous School of the Americas in Fort Benning, GA, where Ríos Montt (page 64), Laugerud García (59), Turcios

Lima (page 57), Perez Molina (page 83), and many others had been trained.[279] John Yesulaitis took Arnoldo to a UNC football game in November. Donna Hillsgrove, an optometrist, gave them eye exams. (Heydi needed glasses.) Noreen took Heydi to a performance of the *Nutcracker*, hired a personal trainer to work with her at the gym, and taught her yoga. In early December Heydi and Arnoldo spent a day attending classes at East Chapel Hill High School with a friend's son and an exchange student from Chile. I took Heydi and Arnoldo to get their booster shots.[280] We went to a parade. A friend

took Arnoldo to a UNC basketball game in December.

---

[279] http://www.soaw.org/about-the-soawhinsec/soawhinsec-grads/notorious-grads/239-notorious-graduates-from-guatemala
[280] Most Guatemalan children, although born at home, receive shots sometime after birth, but never any boosters.

I had given Heydi and Arnoldo some money to buy Christmas gifts. Heydi, frugal from birth, used the money to make her gifts. A day or two before Christmas, my son Miguel (far left) drove down from Pennsylvania.

In January I took Heydi and Arnoldo to a dentist. Heydi had four cavities and needed an extraction as well as a second root canal (for the first, see page 32). Over a period of several days Arnoldo had seventeen cavities filled, two extractions, and a root canal.[282]

Several people invited us for lunch or dinner, often having Heydi, and sometimes Arnoldo, try on various articles of clothing and accessories.

One day on our way to the post office, when I stopped at a red light, a police car pulled up beside us. Arnoldo looked at me and asked, "Aren't you afraid?" I understood his concern. When I left San Lucas earlier that year, my driver and I passed an overlook, high in the mountains, with a view of Lake Atitlán (page 8). A police car was parked there. I asked the driver to stop. He replied, "Not with the police there!"

On January 31, Heydi and Arnoldo returned to Guatemala, in time to get back into school. They were speaking tolerable, if limited, English. Jorge met them at the airport and took them home.

GSSG had put its toe in the water.

---

[282] Some years later I asked one of our girls, "What do you do if you have a toothache?" She replied, "You live with it." I asked, "Can't you take an aspirin?" Her response: "If you have enough money to buy one." One aspirin!

Chapter VIII, GSSG 2004

Those who had met informally at my home on August 28, 2003, for the organizational meeting of GSSG (page 37), met again on February 4, 2004. The first item of business—the election of officers, whose names I would need in order to apply for tax-exempt status. That done, we moved on to nail down some particulars of our new program. Phase 1, we decided, would last for the three months of Guatemala's annual vacation, mid-October to mid-January, during which our clients would learn English by immersion while living with American host families. Heydi and Arnoldo had just done that. Phase 2 would be four years of high school in the United States and Phase 3, four years of college in the United States. Since we had no experience bringing high-school students here, we decided to pay the $6000 fee to bring Heydi and Arnoldo back with AFS as Exchange students (see the footnote on page 37).

A month earlier I had applied online for an EIN. EIN stands for "Employer Identification Number" and is required of any organization having any kind business with the federal government, whether it has employees or not (we did not). An electronic reply was generated the same day. Armed with an EIN, we could now apply for corporate status in the State of North Carolina. Our application was approved. With both an EIN and corporate status in hand, we could apply for tax-exempt status under Section 501(c)(3) of the Internal Revenue Code.

Mission

Applying for tax-exempt status involves filling out a lengthy form and supplying detailed information and data on a variety of topics, crucially a mission statement. With the approval of the Board, I provided the following (as slightly updated later):

> The mission of the organization is to support poor Guatemalan youth, that is, for the most part, descendants of the ancient Maya, in the pursuit of an education to First World standards in the United States. Job training is not the object. Neither is the immediate relief of poverty. Rather, the organization seeks to give its direct beneficiaries an opportunity to acquire a knowledge of history and world affairs, of politics and jurisprudence, of philosophy and economics, and of science, literature, and the arts sufficient to enable them to transform the conditions in which their forebears have historically lived. In short, the organization's objective is the creation of a network of knowledgeable leaders, of thinkers and writers, of professionals and entrepreneurs, in sufficient numbers to effect significant socioeconomic development in Guatemala.

Our petition was granted in early March. Anticipating approval, in February I had published the first issue of *GSSG news*. The text began: "Welcome to the first issue of *GSSG news*, an occasional publication of the *Guatemalan Student Support Group* (*GSSG*), a new non-denominational, tax-exempt charity incorporated in the State of North Carolina. Enjoy!" The text went on to illustrate conditions in Guatemala and featured articles on Heydi, Arnoldo, and Tita.

In April the Board met for the third time, welcoming two new members, Sr. Lois Macgillivray, who had been the president of a college in California, and Margaret Johnson, a physician and the local representative of AFS (page 37).

I proposed we recruit four new students for 2004. The Board agreed.

Seven Criteria

The first step in recruiting students would be to establish criteria by which we might determine who among the applicants were likely to possess the attributes requisite to fulfilling GSSG's mission. To that end, all agreed that the first requirement would be *poverty*, because GSSG's mission statement (see above) so determined. Next, *honesty* came easily to mind; liars accomplish nothing. And if honesty, why not *integrity*, consistency in a superior set of moral values? Yes, of course! *Personality*, a shoo-in. *Character*, how you behave whether someone else is looking or not. Yes! *Intelligence*, of course. And, finally, *Leadership Potential*, a prerequisite to fulfilling GSSG's mission. From now on our selections would be based on these seven criteria and, as we shall see, we would soon develop instruments to measure applicants against them. Years later we would add two more: *Imagination*, the ability to think outside the box, and *Will*, the ability to make decisions.

The second step would be to make sure that the youngsters we selected understood these criteria, for they would determine not only whom we selected but also who would advance through the three phases (see the first paragraph in this chapter). Thus armed, we could proceed to recruiting candidates for 2004. But first we needed host families to receive them.

A Pool Party

In May I got a call from Joy Currens in Cary, NC, telling me that she had heard about GSSG and would like to host one of our students. I visited the Currens a few days later, we chatted, I took some pictures, and they filled out the 'Host Family Information Form' that I had prepared. A few days after that, Joy fell in conversation with Cathy Lambeth (they both had children at the same pre-school). Cathy said she wanted to host as well. I visited Cathy and her husband. They filled out a 'Host Family Information Form.' A little later, John and Linda Coleman, who had a Guatemalan daughter, invited me to a pool party for families with adopted Guatemalan children. After an hour or so of friendly jabber and an array of pot-luck, John asked me to tell the group about GSSG. I'd brought along an arsenal of print and photos. When I finished, Margo Peterson told me that she and her husband would like to host. I visited their home and we had our third host family. A few days later Cathy Lambeth called to say that she had a friend with an adopted Guatemalan child and would like to host; so I visited the Machosts. We had our four host families.

In 2003 Heydi, Arnoldo, and I had sat around my kitchen table drilling English verbs, diagramming, and engaged in vocabulary-building conversation and reading. The four new kids in 2004 would all live in Cary and Apex (adjacent communities not far from Chapel Hill); my kitchen table wouldn't do. One day Joy called: "I've talked with people in the office at St. Francis Methodist Church in Cary and they have a classroom you could use. Would you like to see it?"

About the same time, I had a message from Shannon Hathaway, saying she was a friend of Margo Peterson, who had told her about GSSG. She and her husband would like to host. "All four of our Phase 1 youngsters have been placed," I replied. "How would you like to have Arnoldo? He's in Phase 2." Soon Elizabeth Wilson called to say that she had heard about GSSG and that she and her husband would like to host. "How would you like to have Heydi?"

We now had six new host families. I asked them to meet with me as a group to share with them GSSG's procedures, provisions, and caveats—health insurance, clothing allowances, legal limitations, time-table of coming events, booster shots, house rules, homesickness, GSSG rules (no physical punishment, no proselytizing, no TV in the student's bedroom), dating, limitations on phone calls (especially to Guatemala), avoiding the word *Indian*, etc. Henceforth the Host Family Orientation would be part of our annual routine. For more detail, see Appendix B, page 246.

Heydi and Arnoldo in Phase 2 (for Phase 1, see page 95)

In August, still 2004, Jorge (page 35) called to say that Arnoldo's brother had committed suicide. Stunned, I had no idea what to do. Arnoldo and Heydi had plane tickets for the next day. School would start two days later. Arnoldo had no phone. With only bad options, I had no choice but to let events play out as they would.

Heydi would live with Elizabeth Wilson and Ross Jackson and their two children. Well-traveled, polyglot, and comfortable in a lifestyle energized by a world of ideas, replete with books, art, and children's toys, the Wilson-Jackson home offered a rich environment for an eager young woman from Guatemala.

Heydi would attend Chapel Hill High. She was two years younger than Arnoldo, two years behind him in school, and her English was less fluent than his. English became an issue when school started. To help her, Heydi's advisor at Chapel Hill High put her in some classes that did not involve much reading. She did well until, several months into the school year, the superintendent of the district found out that Heydi was not enrolled in the standard freshman classes and immediately ordered her to be taken out of the classes she was in and put into the regular program. Of course she failed. Back home in June she returned to school at the *Instituto Mixto* (page 33), graduated, and got a job. A few years later, still working, she started taking classes at the Cobán branch-campus of San Carlos University and is now well on her way to graduating with a degree in Social Work. Tuition is free but she has other, school-related expenses and receives support from GSSG.

On his return, Arnoldo lived with Shannon and Gary Hathaway and their two teen-age boys, off and on, over a period of three years. He started out attending Green Hope High School in Cary, NC. After a year at Green Hope, he finished high school in Guatemala but came back to attend Wake Tech Community College in Raleigh. Meanwhile, he had fallen in love and returned to Guatemala before graduating. He got a job at a call center in Guatemala City and married. He has since found a better job but hates living in the metropolis.

In the fall I wrote to Eunice (page 93), asking if she would join me in recruiting the four new students the Board had authorized for 2004. She readily agreed. Jorge met us at the airport. Tita had arranged suitable accommodations in the home of a Guatemalan man who lives most of the year in Canada. The next day we started visiting the applicants whom Jorge and Tita had identified.

Giovanni

We first visited one of Jorge's students, Giovanni, a lad of sixteen, the eldest of seven children, in Carchá, not far from Cobán where Jorge lives. Giovanni's father collected scrap metal, which he periodically took to Guatemala City to sell at a recycling facility. Unfortunately, he drank and frequently abused his wife and children. Giovanni told us that one rainy night his father had kicked him out of the house and he had no choice but to spend the night outside in the rain.

The family home is a board structure, with electricity but no appliances other than a radio and TV, which did not work. The family shared an outhouse with several other fami-lies. Four of the seven children shared a bedroom with their parents, three girls sleeping in one bed and the youngest child with his parents. Two younger boys shared a room and Giovanni had a cubbyhole.

Giovanni's father had no fixed income and the family often did not have enough to eat. Giovanni was in the eleventh grade, ranked third in a class of thirty-four, yet he could not multiply 10 times 12, did not know whether the United States is north, south, east, or west of Guatemala, and had no idea why Guatemala is a poor country.

For all of that, he remained unflustered by his obvious ignorance of common knowledge and presented a persona mature beyond his years. He had no desk, chair, or lighting by which to study and had to work when he was not in school. His aspirations appeared to be limited to finding a job and disengagement from his father. He said he did not want to marry, because children cost too much.

Giovanni's parents had a sixth-grade education; the older children speak Q'eq-chí' (*kek-CHEE*) but Spanish is the family's language of choice now.

Giovanni told us that his mother did not want to marry his father. She was only thirteen but his father's parents, eager to curb their son's behavior, persuaded her parents to agree. I asked, "Why didn't she simply refuse?" He replied, "You don't understand the Maya."

María Candelaria

The next day, Tita, Eunice, and I visited the home of María Candelaria, one of Tita's students. María, 15, the second eldest of nine children, was in the eighth grade. Her father, a janitor at the school where I had taught the previous year, was paid less than $100 a month. He had a fourth-grade education. Her mother had no schooling and the family spoke only Poqomchí' at home, which had four beds, all without mattresses, just blankets on top of boards. There were no appliances. The kitchen had a table, an open fire, and a bench (at left).

The home was innocent of any sign of electricity.

María Candelaria, pleasant, a bit shy, and hardworking, got got grades, but appeared to be without aspirations and could not comprehend the objectives of GSSG.

Unlike most of the Maya, María Candelaria did not live in a village. Her home, in fact, lay just a short walk outside of Tactic on the main road. Its wattle and daub construction (to be illustrated more fully later) allows for holes in the walls to admit light and fresh air. The corrugated tin roof makes conversation impossible

during Guatemala's torrential rainstorms.

In the foreground (above right) you see the family *pila*, the concrete sink that serves as dishwasher, washing machine, and shower for all poor and most middle-class homes in Guatemala. Homes in or near towns generally have running water, as was the case here.

Inside, beds without mattresses competed for room with the kitchen (see above).

The bathroom (right) provided its services a short distance into the woods behind the house.

Edgar

That same day we visited Edgar, fifteen, his mother, a widow, and his younger brother, Wilson. The boys' father, a baker, had been murdered when Edgar was four or five but the family lacked sufficient resources to prosecute a suspected relative. Edgar's mother has no home and lives rent-free in a concrete structure (right) which has electricity but no appliances. Water is brought in through a long hose attached to a neighbor's house. There are openings in the rear of the house but no windows. The home has no furnishings beyond beds, a couple of chairs, a bench, and a gas hot plate.

Edgar's Home

After her husband's death, Edgar's mother began making candles for a living. Now Edgar's life consists of going to school and making candles, earning about twelve dollars a week.

Both Edgar and Wilson appear to be unusually bright and math questions posed no problem for either of them. Edgar,

another of Jorge's students in Carchá, readily attributed the country's poverty to corruption and injustice. Bravo!

Karina

On Saturday we interviewed Karina in Carchá. Though poor enough not to have even a gas hot plate, the family runs a little store and has enough to eat. Karina, sixteen (she would be seventeen in September), was the eldest of four children. She spoke reasonably well and seemed to have a plan for her life. Eunice opined that Karina may end up a feminist ac-

tivist. She impressed us by saying that she would someday like to build an institution to take homeless kids off the street and educate them. She would also like to provide care for the elderly. She responded to questions about her future by saying that she anticipated delaying marriage and children until such were feasible and that she would continue working outside the home after having children. She also correctly answered all of the usual questions about matters of common knowledge.

Elio

Elio's Family

That same day we visited Elio and his family, also in Carchá. The family home was a board structure with a dirt floor. Elio's father drank and beat his wife. His mother tried to raise money by selling food on the street. Elio had an older sister and two younger brothers. Of these, the youngest broke his right arm when he was six. Repeated attempts by a series of doctors to set the arm properly all resulted in failure and the boy lives in constant pain, especially intense at night.

This is the sort of encounter that makes working in Guatemala so difficult. Often one has no choice but to walk away and live with what one cannot change.

Elio himself was inordinately shy. He had no questions and his diffident responses to our questions persuaded us that a Personal Interview would be fruitless.

Edy, Edy, and Sergio (*SAYR-hee-oh*)

The next day, Sunday, Tita, Eunice, and I visited the homes of three applicants identified by Tita, two brothers, Edy, seventeen, and Sergio, fourteen, and another Edy in another family, also fourteen. They live in a village called *Chijulhá* (*chee-hool-HAH*) a few miles from Tactic, high in the mountains. By coincidence Noreen Ordronneau (page 37), Heydi's host mom the year before and a GSSG Board member, was in Guatemala for a nursing conference and I asked her to join us. Walking along the mountain paths for a couple of hours proved exhilarating—where does one find such scenery as this, mountain tops modestly hiding their beauty in downy-soft clouds, while their slopes yield a bountiful fare to Mother Nature's providence!

The village had gotten electricity five years earlier but few of the fifteen to twenty homes had any appliances. Edy's and Sergio's home (at left) was a *bajareque* structure with a dirt floor and a tin roof. An open fire dominated this home and probably all of the others. The parents could not read or write and spoke only Poqomchí', the boys translating for us. A variety of domestic fowl wandered in and out of the home.

At Tita's request, we did not talk about GSSG on this trip. Rather we would come back on Tuesday. I believe there existed some social issue that required Tita to be circumspect. On this occasion, our object was simply to get acquainted, take pictures, and set people at ease, as in fact did happen.

Bernardina

In the photo above you see a girl seated on a stool and holding a child (not her own). Her name is Bernardina. She has two knees on each leg. I asked her if I might speak with her about her disability and she demurely agreed. She showed me her legs and let me photograph them. She has a long scar on one leg, the result of an operation which had produced no results. I asked Noreen, who is a nurse, to examine Bernardina's legs. She found that the upper knees are functional. (I have video showing Bernardina flexing the upper knees.) Noreen opined that the lower knees might be fused so that Bernardina could walk.

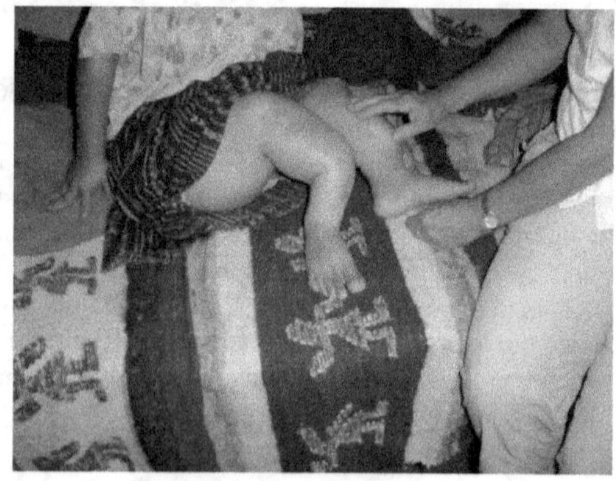

While we talked, Bernardina never uttered a word of complaint nor displayed any self-pity. She spoke softly and agreeably but did not initiate conversation, ask any questions, or in any way seek to draw attention to herself. I asked if she had any pain. She replied that her pain was constant but not intense. I gave her a small bottle of aspirin that I often had along and asked her to take no more than one a day. For two or three years thereafter, I tried to find funds to bring Bernardina to the United States, at least for an examination, without success.

Edy's and Sergio's mother (seen at left) had borne thirteen children. All of them, remarkably, survived. Some older children were married but nine still remained at home and slept in three beds.

Because the family owns a parcel and the land, although mountainous, is remarkably fertile, malnutrition is not an issue. Indeed, the mother, jabbering away happily in Poqomchí', which none of us understood, offered up a fair wealth of victuals—soup, chicken, tamales—of which Eunice and I partook only to the extent of not seeming rude. (Despite having eating almost nothing, I found it prudent to remain indoors the next day.)

We learned that the boys earn some money on weekends and holidays by cutting firewood, hauling it on their backs to Tactic, and selling it for about $1.75 per load. The younger children frolicked delightedly with the balloons we gave them. The youngest child had, apparently, never seen a camera and was terrified when we started taking pictures.

We returned on Tuesday, as planned. Unfortunately, the boys could not respond well to our questions and apparently could not comprehend what GSSG was trying to do in Guatemala, remaining, despite our overt prompting, narrowly focused on their own family income. When Eunice pressed the seventeen-year-old Edy, the most likely candidate of the three, for a better response, the only way he could think of helping other indigenous people was to give them food. When Eunice asked one of the boys if there are any indigenous leaders, he was unresponsive. She prompted him by mentioning Rigoberta Menchú, the Nobel Peace Prize recipient. He affirmed that he had heard of her but in response to my questioning, it was clear he did not know that she had authored a book and had no idea how a book could change anything. Eunice explained to him the expression, "The pen is mightier than the sword," but he could not comprehend it.

I asked Bernardina if the aspirin had relieved her pain. She replied gently, "A little." This time I had brought along a bigger bottle to give her.

The family of the other Edy, fourteen, also lives in a board structure, with his parents and three other children; the youngest, a girl of three or four, was also terrified by my camera. Edy's mother had asthma and had been largely confined to her bed for the previous six years. The father speaks very little Spanish and everyone else in the family, except Edy, speaks only Poqomchí'. Edy, though quite personable and with a sense of humor, could not respond meaningfully to our questions. During our treks up and down the mountain sides, I had a chance to talk with him alone at some length. When I asked him how conditions might be changed in Guatemala, he guessed that outsiders would have to come in and help. When I asked if the indigenous could help themselves, he simply replied "No!" He readily acknowledged that the political situation in Guatemala does little for the indigenous. I explained the basics of the political process to him and pointed out that there is no indigenous political party. He seemed not to comprehend that with some leadership the indigenous might organize and become a factor in Guatemalan politics.

To our great disappointment, we left Chijulhá empty-handed. The boys cheerfully accompanied us back to town.

Bajareque (bah-hah-REK-[k]ay)

Since I have good photos of Edy and Sergio's home, its wattle and daub construction may conveniently be illustrated here.

Construction is straight forward. After leveling an area the size of the projected structure, the builder first sinks a series of posts into the ground about four to six feet apart; you can see one on either side of the boys' dad in the photo above. Next a series of horizontal poles or reeds are attached both to the outside of the posts, as seen above, and to the inside, as seen below. (Because the posts are sunk directly into the earth and thus rot, all of these houses eventually collapse.)

107

Any strong filament may be used to bind the poles to the posts. The space in between is then filled with a combination of mud and pine needles.

Once the walls are stabilized, the roof rafters can be structured. The roof itself may be either thatch or what we call 'tin,' *lamina* in Spanish. The noise on a tin roof in a rain storm surpasses thunder. A thatch roof is quiet and cooler but harder to construct and maintain.

Two of our students' *bajareque* homes fell down, one in 2008 and the other in 2009.

Rigoberta Menchú records that the house she lived in as a child had walls made of cane stuck in the ground and tied together with *agave* fibers. Most of the homes in her village, however, had walls make of cornstalks. The roofs, made of leaves, lasted two years. "The houses are not very high because, if there's a lot of wind, it can lift the house and carry it all away." With no partitions to provide privacy, everyone slept in the same space.[283]

Nataly

On Monday, August 30, still 2004, Eunice, Jorge, and I visited Nataly, and met her parents, her older brother and adopted sister. Nataly was fourteen.

The family's home, in Carchá, is made of concrete and has a concrete floor, but a large kitchen made of boards attached in the back and an unfinished room across the front completed the building. On the inside were three bedrooms and a dining room. The house had electricity but Nataly's mother cooked on an open fire.

Like most Mayan women, Nataly's mother married young and had two children, before her husband died. Out of necessity she remarried. Nataly was born of this second union. Her father has a job but spends all of his income in a bar. (Indig-

enous widows have few options in Guatemala.) Nataly's sister is married, lives nearby, and helps her mother some, when she can, as does her son, but Nataly and her mother were living in deep poverty.

Though obviously nervous, Nataly impressed us with her self-control, readily answered all of our questions, and manifested a surprising facility in thinking outside the box. Left alone while Jorge and I took pictures, Nataly responded when Eunice asked her why she wanted to participate in the program by saying that she wanted to become "someone" and, without participating in the program, she simply could not continue her education. "We are too poor," she added. Pressed for specifics, Nataly replied that she wanted to become a doctor so that she could treat people who are too poor to be able to pay for medical services. Asked about marriage, she said that she wanted to marry after she completed her education and was financially able to do so but that she intended to continue working after marriage.

---

[283] Rigoberta Menchú, *I, Rigoberta Menchú: An Indian Woman in Guatemala*, 1984, pp.46–47.

Vivacious, talkative, happy, and excited, Nataly makes great company. Jorge, who was her teacher, added that she was the top student in her class. In a largely illiterate society, Nataly is a voracious reader. Although there are no public lending libraries in Guatemala, a monastery in her town had a private library and the monks were happy to let Nataly use it.

Claudia (*CLOW-dee-uh*)

Eunice conducting the Family Interview with Claudia and her parents

Although our recruiting for the year was technically complete (we had our four candidates), on October 4, Eunice, Tita, and I visited a girl in the village of Chiallí (*chee-ah-YEE*), a two-hour walk from Tactic. Claudia seemed like an ideal candidate. I considered taking her in place of Karina, whose constant eating in the bus on the way to Guatemala City to get passports had suggested a want of self-control, something Eunice also noticed. My failure to act here has troubled me deeply ever since. By dint of hard work and grit Claudia would go on to higher education in Guatemala.

Passports for Giovanni, Nataly, Edgar, and Karina

On a day selected by Jorge, we shepherded our four candidates and their parents onto a bus (at 4:00 A.M.) for the trip to get passports in Guatemala City. Karina's and Giovanni's applications were nearly turned down because only one parent accompanied each of them and Guatemalan law requires that both parents be in attendance. Karina's step-father did not come because he had to work and Giovanni's mother could not come because there was no one to care for the younger children. Jorge had foreseen this development and had obtained documents from a lawyer certifying these circumstances. But the passport agent was not satisfied and it took two hours of telephone calls to persuade him that the documents were genuine. Finally, we trudged over to the national TB center and had the youngsters' chests x-rayed for TB and then headed home.

Visas for Giovanni, Nataly, Edgar, and Karina

On a given Sunday we again shepherded our candidates and their parents onto an afternoon bus and arrived at Hotel Ajau in time to practice for the visa interviews the next morning. At 7:30 the next morning, the four applicants, their parents, and I stood in line, while Jorge and Eunice paced outside. Eventually we were motioned to approach one of the interviewers' windows, where a young woman was waiting for us.

I explained what GSSG was and who these youngsters were and I showed her a letter I had written months earlier to the U.S. Consul General in Guatemala. She asked me a few questions and then said she would talk to the first candidate, who happened to be Nataly. After speaking with her briefly, in Spanish, she turned to me and said, in English, "I think she is lying. I have never known a Guatemalan who does not have relatives in the United States and she tells me she does not." I pointed out that we had gone to considerable trouble to identify these youngsters, that among the documents Nataly had presented were: a) a sworn statement from the Currens, her potential host family, that they intended to see to it that she returned to Guatemala in three months, on January 25; b) an affidavit of support, and c) a statement from GSSG's bank affirming that the organization had sufficient funds to fulfill its financial obligations. I also repeated that Heydi and Arnoldo had returned to Guatemala as scheduled the previous year. She asked some questions about Heydi and Arnoldo, then asked me to explain the program again, then questioned Nataly again, and finally sighed, "All right." The others' interviews went smoothly. We bought plane tickets for October 15.

A Birth Certificate for Blanca

Since Eunice, Jorge, and I had time on our hands until October 15, we went to San Lucas to visit Blanca (page 94). Her magnetic joy at seeing us again moved all of us. Blanca eagerly took out one of the books we had given her the year before, *Pinocho* (spelled thus in Spanish), and with much seriousness showed us how she could read, pointing to each word in turn and pronouncing it very deliberately.

I had not forgotten my quest to get her adopted and four families had come forward. The next step would be getting her a birth certificate, without which we could not apply for legal guardianship for her uncle, without which she could not be adopted. Accordingly, Jorge and I went to El Jabalí, on the Pacific coast, where she had been born and where an aunt of hers lives. We found the aunt's family. Her husband, rather obviously illiterate, carried a an enormous Bible with him everywhere. Blanca's cousin, a teen-age girl, had a tattoo. Two smaller children played in the yard, one of them, a boy, nearly naked. The aunt did not know when Blanca was born. Jorge found the mayor of El Jabalí who told us that the area records office was in a nearby town called *Santa Lucía Cotzumalguapa*. We went there and were helped by a very obliging clerk, who looked through all of the birth records for a five-year interval on either side of what we guessed might be the year of Blanca's birth, twice, without success. We visited the local church to see if there might be a baptismal certificate, with the same outcome. Disappointed we returned to San Lucas and I hired a lawyer to get Blanca a birth certificate. He said he would send her to Dr. Tun (page 91) but first asked me how old I thought she was. I guessed eleven. Jorge, conscious that she was already overage in school, said ten. Blanca immediately retorted "Twelve!" Dr. Tun subsequently judged that she was eleven.

Arrival 2004

Giovanni in Phase 1

Giovanni had manifested considerable unhappiness when we first interviewed him at home. Given the circumstances, we assumed that his father was the cause (page 101) and that living with Margo and Roger Peterson and their children, the very antithesis of that environment, would make him glad to be alive

Margo and Roger cheerfully endured his dour behavior for the three months of Phase 1.

Edgar in Phase 1

Edgar's affable personality (see page 103) endeared him to Cathy Lambeth, her husband Conn Herrington, and their two kids.

Edgar would get sick during Phase 1 and, much to our dismay, would not return for Phase 2, but Cathy still communicates with him, now more than a decade later.

I would see Edgar in Guatemala from time to time, happy as ever.

Nataly in Phase 1

Joy Currens has a special place in GSSG's history; she was the first to contact me about hosting (page 99). Husband Dave initially made learning English easy for Nataly, by pausing between words, as I had suggested. She caught on quickly. The children made it fun.

Karina in Phase 1

Ann and Milton Machost and their daughter shared their home with Karina and tried every which way to help her succeed. But Karina spend most of her time watching Spanish TV and, though I reduced her to tears over the issue, she never did learn any significant English and would not return.

Every weekday morning, the moms brought Giovanni, Edgar, Nataly, and Karina to the classroom that Joy had found for us (page 99). I taught them English all day and returned them to their hosts on my way home.

Support

Two members of the North Raleigh Rotary Club, Jeff Taylor and Ed Cody, both of whom had been to Guatemala, invited us to one of the club's regular lunches. I was given a few minutes to talk about GSSG and introduce the students. North Raleigh Rotary would make significant contributions, both monetary (annually) and professional. Drs. Adelman, a physician, Rich, a dentist, and Hudgins, an optometrist, all members of North Raleigh Rotary, provided their services pro bono.

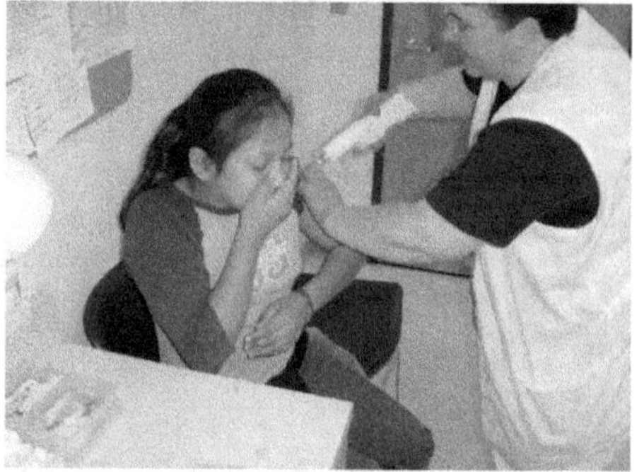

Nataly getting her shots

After a few weeks, Edgar complained one day of chest pains. Cathy rushed him to Urgent Care but the doctor could find no cause. Over the next several weeks the pain recurred twice, with the same outcome. I tried to tell him what psychosomatic illnesses are but he could only reply, "No, it is real. I'm not imaging it." "Yes, Edgar. It's real but the cause is psychological, not organic." He couldn't understand. We could not bring him back the next year. A few years late, I met him in Guatemala and asked him if he still had that pain from to time. He said he did not.

Giovanni, Edgar, Nataly, and Karina returned to Guatemala on January 25, 2005.

Learning by Doing

During the course of 2004 it had become clear that we had to do a better job of recruiting. Responding to this observation we made a list of baseline requirements to give to the principals who now began calling Jorge, asking that we recruit in their schools. Our list stipulated that the applicants had to meet nine baseline requirements; the applicants:

1) could be no older than 15 as of September 1;
2) had no reputation for lying, cheating, stealing, or mischief;
3) appeared to have an aptitude for academic achievement;
4) had no impairments which would prevent full participation in the program;
5) would have completed at least two years of English in Guatemala by September 1;
6) had a pleasant personality;
7) must agree never to seek to live permanently in the United States, legally or illegally;
8) could communicate reasonably well in Spanish; and
9) would agree to obey GSSG and host-family rules.

More importantly, we prepared a "Recruiting Manual" that established specific procedures for assessing applicants' merits vis-à-vis our criteria (see Appendix A, page 235).

With the manual as our guide, we soon got into a routine. Briefly, on a mutually suitable date, Jorge, I, and usually Tita (page 34), Stella (page 134), or Eunice (page 93) would travel to a school from which Jorge had received an invitation. After introductions, we would join the assembled

applicants and conduct what we now called our 'Group Interview.' With the applicants seated in a semi-circle and ourselves at the open end, we had them write in large letters their name, birth date, and grade level on a sheet of paper and pin it to their shirts. If the data on any applicant's sheet were not in accord with the list above, he or she was asked to leave. The team members then helped the applicants to fill out our *Forma de datos familiares* ("Family Information Form"). When these had been collected, the team leader (usually Jorge) asked each applicant to rise and tell us about himself or herself, while each of us took notes on the pages provided in the Recruiting Manual, notes not only about the applicant who was speaking but also about the response of the other students—did what the speaker was saying hold their attention, were any of them trying to embarrass the speaker (if so, a note on that student's record as well as the speaker's), and so on.

Next we gave them three tests: an aptitude test which we had composed, a commercially produced IQ test, and a seventh-grade American math test translated into Spanish (the applicants were in ninth grade). Having dismissed the applicants, we graded their tests and shared our individual notes. The results usually reduced the number of applicants by half or more. Jorge would then make arrangements for us to visit the homes of those selected.

In the homes we conducted a Family Interview, first explaining who we were and why we had asked to visit. Inevitably the father and sometimes the older sons, had questions: "How long will my child be gone?" "Will he or she be able to work?" "Will you send my child home if he/she gets sick?" and so on. We too had questions, of course, some of which were intended to tell us indirectly something about the parents as well as the child: "Does he/she ever lie?" "How does he/she get along with your other children?" "Have you ever had to beat your child," etc. I also asked about the Civil War but got few responses.

The Family Interview over, one of us would take the applicant aside for the Personal Interview (Eunice, Tita, or Stella, if a girl), while another of us engaged the parents in conversation and the third blew up some balloons or otherwise played Pied Piper to keep the other children, often including neighborhood children, occupied and out of ear-shot. Meanwhile, we all took pictures.

After repeating this process x-number of times, we would meet, usually on a Sunday afternoon, evaluate the results of the three tests and our own notes, while reviewing our pictures to make sure that, at any given time, we were all talking about the same individual. We then separately rank ordered the candidates in light of our criteria (page 99). If we all agreed on a number equal to that authorized by the Board of Trustees, regardless of their order, we were finished. If not, we would then share our reasons for our rankings, each of us offering detail that the others may not have noticed. We then voted again. If we agreed, we were done. If not, we would accept as many as we did agree on and then proceed to another school and repeat the entire process, doing so as often as necessary to reach the number of candidates authorized by the Board. (For greater detail see, Appendix A, the "Recruiting Manual," page 235.)

The "Recruiting Manual" responded to our need to tighten and regularize our recruiting process. Two years' experience had also taught us that three months of immersion were insufficient to give our students enough English to start school in the United States. Accordingly, Jorge and I decided to extend Phase I to six months. I ran the change by the Board. They approved.

Workshops

A day or two before Nataly, Giovanni, Edgar, and Karina flew to the United States, I had conducted an orientation explaining what we expected of them during their time in Phase 1. The following year I enlarged the orientation to teach all of the students (both seasoned veterans and raw recruits) some American history, how to pronounce various English words like *through* and *cough*, the meaning of idioms like "just in case" and "the coast is clear," and other essentials to fluency. By 2008 these orientations would morph into workshops lasting several days, which not only provided the students with an opportunity to get to know one other and to practice giving speeches to their peers but also a venue for me to teach them subjects not usually included in a school curriculum, like the history of Islam and 9/11, how the stock market works, the different kinds of insurance, taxation, and much more. In addition, never having read a book while growing up, the students did not know how to see unexpressed relationships in what they read, how to 'connect the dots,' or 'think outside the box.'

The most important of these workshops, in 2008 and 2009, took place between Christmas and New Year's Day; attendance was mandatory, regardless of where the students were living or what phase they were in. These winter workshop became an essential part of the program (see Appendix C, Workshops, pages 249ff). That in the winter of 2009 was the most successful of all, thanks in part to the generosity of Jo Ann Davis, who generously offered, as our venue, her large and beautiful home on the North Carolina coast. Jo Ann told me that we might use the facility at any time.

The Wall Street crash in 2008 made it impossible for GSSG to continue bringing Guatemalan students to the U.S. for high school and college.

We also conducted a shorter, 3-day workshop in Guatemala before our aspiring scholars left for the United States in the fall and again when they returned home in June. Attendance, again, was mandatory.

Chapter IX, GSSG 2005

Recruiting our 2005 cohort had actually begun in 2004, even though we did not know it at the time. When Eunice and I were living in Tactic selecting the applicants for 2004, from time to time I engaged a man, whom I knew only as Juan Pablo, to take us here and there. I had heard of a hydroelectric dam on the Chixoy River and wanted to see it. So one day I hired him to take us there.

Raquel

When Juan Pablo arrived to pick us up, his daughter Raquel was in the front seat beside him. Eunice got in back with someone to be dropped off en route to Chixoy and I got in front beside Raquel, who moved over to a non-existent seat between her father and me.

On the way I got out to take some pictures of the mountains and left my hat on the seat. Raquel stayed in the car and when I returned picked up my hat so that I would not sit on it. "My goodness," I thought, "what a considerate ten-year-old," and we fell in conversation. I had for some time wanted to experiment with bringing a younger child to see how much difference age would make in learning English by immersion, and retaining it. Talking with Raquel, I had, quite accidentally, conducted a Personal Interview. A few days later we visited Raquel's home and did the Family Interview.

The Dam at Chixoy

Luis Fernández (*lwEESS*)

Tita knew that Raquel's brother, Luis, had a reputation for high academic achievement. He was also reputed to be a weapon on the soccer field. Luis had not gone with us to Chixoy but I took the opportunity to talk with him while Jorge was doing the Family Interview.

Raquel's and Luis' family is *ladino* (page 12). They lived in a rented, cement-block home in Tactic. Juan Pablo is usually unemployed. Their mother, of course, sells food on the street.

Pablo

Pablo's parents and their six children live in the house you see at right that has, as I recall, only two windows and two bedrooms.

Pablo's home is in 'San Pedro Carchá,' often abbreviated 'Carchá,' just a twenty-minute drive from Cobán, Jorge's home town.[284] Jorge taught school in Carchá and Pablo was one of his students. Pablo's father had a regular job driving a delivery truck for a wholesale food distributor. Pablo's mother had a refrigerator and made frozen treats, always in

demand in a Mayan community where few homes have a refrigerator.

Virtually all the population of Carchá speaks Q'eqchi' natively, an important point because Carchá is a *municipalidad*, that is, a community consisting of a large number Mayan settlements, in this case forty-eight villages and two-hundred and nineteen *caserios* (unincorporated hamlets), altogether about 245,000 people.

The residents of the villages and *caserios* generally do not speak Spanish. Carchá provides the opportunity for

those thousands of Q'eqchí'-speakers to conduct business and find goods and services in their own language.

Carchá is the third largest *municipalidad* in the country. Only Guatemala (which is the name not only of the country and the capital city but also of a *municipalidad*) and Mixco are larger.

The *Popul Vuh*, the atavistic Mayan folklore composed initially well before the conquest, speaks of Carchá as the site of a lionized contest at the famous ball court there.[285]

Central Park and Church in Carchá

---

[284] Giovanni, Nataly, Edgar, and Karina (see previous chapter) also lived there.

[285] See the second note to page 94 in Dennis Tedlock's monumental translation to the *Popul Vuh*, 1996, p.255.

Ana Pop (*AH-nuh POHP*)

Ana, also a Q'eqchí'-speaker, is the sixth of eight children, all still at home. Ana's family lives in the house you see at right, a board structure with a dirt floor and no appliances, on a street subject to flooding, with effects inside (see arrow below). Not long after we vis-

ited Ana's home, her family had to move in, temporarily, with relatives because of flooding.

Ana did not get good grades in *basico*, though the cause probably had more to do with the quality of in-struction than Ana's proficiency. Her English teacher, who does not speak English, gave her a failing grade.

Ana, always cheerful, industrious, and helpful, radiates respect both for others and herself. I would one day, a year later, attend her fifteenth birthday party, a coming-of-age celebration for Mayan girls.

Rubén (*roo-BAYN*)

Rubén, also a Q'eqchí'-speaker, is the second eldest of nine children, one of whom had died. Rubén's family lives in a town and is, therefore, bilingual. The structure at right is the family bedroom.

Rubén's father tried to earn a living by making jewelry; his equipment is seen below at right. At left below you see the kitchen.

The simple joys of a kid's life. The same everywhere.

Rubéns's little sister, who stole my heart.

Jairo lived in this house, together with his mother, father, and two sisters, whom the father is reputed to rape. Jairo's home is in a village outside Carchá accessible only by a rough, unpaved road. The house itself can be reached only by a long, steep set of steps carved into the mountainside (see below).

Inside, the house is divided in three by card-

board partitions. In one part Jairo sleeps with his brother and their parents; in another, the two girls. The third is the kitchen, living room, and dining room. Furnishings consist of a gas hot plate, a table, and three or four chairs. There are no windows. The home has electricity. A plastic curtain provides privacy for the shower outside.

At the time of our visit, Jairo's pride and joy was a television set that he won when Jorge bought raffle tickets for his students. Jairo cheerfully turned on his set for us. The resultant image mimicked a December snow storm in Buffalo.

Werner

Werner, though this photo hardly does him justice, was the most promising student we met that year (with the possible exception of Nataly). Werner's is the only lower-class home in which I have ever seen books. His family's apartment, one of several units strung together in a row, provided the basest of necessities; both the kitchen and the bathroom facilities were shared by the residents in all the units.

Werner, a *ladino*, had an intoxicating sense of humor. Bright and adult beyond his years, he could see the funny side of something that left others wondering what he was laughing about, a

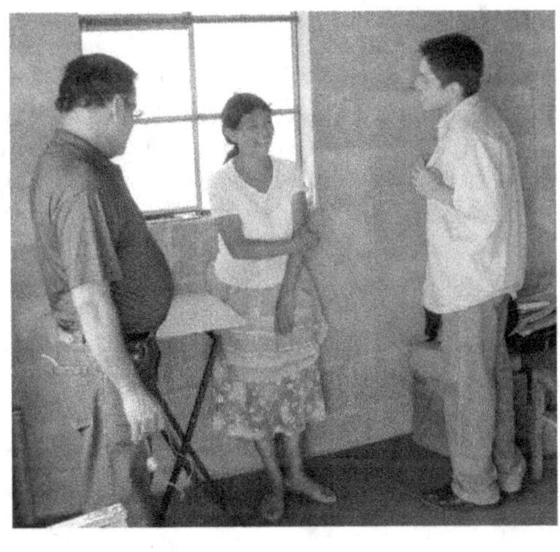

trait apparently inherited from his mother. As it turned out, we could not take him because many schools will not admit students who will turn twenty-one in their senior year. Werner was seventeen.

Werner's father had established a business, buying soap from a wholesaler and marketing it on the street.

Two years later Jorge told me that Werner had developed his own soap business on his father's model and had married. Not long after that Jorge wrote again, saying that Werner had been murdered on his way to purchase soap from a wholesaler, for he had money in his pocket.

Lidia

Tita had recommended a girl named Lidia whose home (at left) sits recessed from Market Street in Tactic (page 28). The house is subject to flooding and various pieces of concrete serve as stepping stones throughout the house. We were satisfied with Lidia but

her mother would not let her go, perhaps, like others, believing that *gringos* take Guatemalan youth to the U.S to harvest their organs.

2005 Selection, Passports, and Visas

In April Jorge, Tita, and I made our final selection and settled on Raquel, Luis, Pablo, Ana, Rubén, and Jairo, whom we took to Guatemala City to get their passports and chest x-rays. That same day we made visa appointments for April 25. The candidates would be applying for B (Visitors) Visas. I had brought with me the necessary financial documents and Jorge had prepared the legal documents. I had also paid the candidates' SEVIS fee (page 89). Jorge had rented a 12-passengeer van and made hotel reservations in Guatemala City for April 24th.

On April 15th Rubén's father, who had only recently found a job, was killed when a trench he was working in collapsed and buried him. The funeral took place the next day (the poor cannot afford embalming). Rubén's family was now reduced to desperation, supported only by Rubén's older brother, who worked at pumping gas at a filling station. Jorge and I attended the funeral.

The students got their visas. I bought plane tickets with a departure date set for May 25 and then notified the host families that the visa applications were successful, and I gave them our ETA. However, just getting a visa does not necessarily mean that you have hit a home run—you still have to satisfy ICE (Immigration and Customs Enforcement) when you land in the United States. To get the students through ICE, I always supplied a letter addressed to any Immigration Officer at the Port of Entry, whether in Houston or Miami, and we never had a student turned away.

The day before departure we bunked at Ajau, our favorite, cheap hotel, and the next day flew to RDU, where the host families were waiting for us.

Ana Pop in Phase 1 (see page 119 for Ana at home)

Ana would live with the Petersons (left), who had hosted Giovanni the year before. The Petersons' large, boisterous family suited Ana very well indeed, like being at home.

Luis Fernández in Phase 1 (see page 117 for Luis at home)

Luis lived with me, my son Pete, our Golden Retriever, and, for a month or so, Jorge as well.

In June, the four of us published Volume III, Number 2 of *GSSS news* (page 98). As we were affixing the stamps to the envelopes Luis asked, "What are these for?"

No one in the families of any of our students had ever sent or received a letter or anything else by post. During our Group Interviews we distributed forms on which the applicants supplied family information, including their home addresses, some of them noteworthy, "Across the street from the gas station," "Last house before the cemetery," and the like.

Pablo in Phase 1 (see page 118 for Pablo at home)

Well before Pablo arrived, Tom and Michelle Bonds had contacted me about hosting. The Bonds had two children, the older, a boy, two years younger than Pablo.

Pablo's birthday occurred shortly after his arrival. Michelle invited neighbor kids to celebrate. Pablo, overcome by it all, could hardly hold back his tears.

By this time our sponsorship program was in high gear and soon after Pablo's arrival, I wrote to Bishop Gossman about our program and asked if I could bring Pablo to meet him. He invited us

to the Chancery and gave us a tour. Bp. Gossman, until his death, sponsored Pablo.

At a fund-raising party, I asked each of our youngsters to give a little speech. They did. Pablo concluded his by saying that he wanted to become the president of Guatemala. He would change his mind but in years to come would twice be elected president of GSSG's student organization.

The day after we arrived in North Carolina, I took Raquel, Rubén, and Jairo to PA.

Jairo in Phase 1 (see page 121 for Jairo at home)

Dwayne and Nicole White, having three Guatemalan children of their own, had contacted me several months earlier to ask about hosting and when I offered Jairo, they happily agreed. At first all went well but when I visited later, Dwayne related to me that Jairo claimed he had lost the new pair of shoes they had just bought for him, in an attempt to get another pair. Dwayne found the shoes on the roof outside Jairo's window. Nevertheless, Dwayne and Nicole would be particularly active in promoting GSSG, hosting the entire group in their home whenever possible, organizing activities, recruiting host families, finding schools, and raising funds. They continued to treat Jairo as one of their own.

The next day Raquel, Rubén, and I continued north to New Bethlehem, PA, where the Lewises and the Dietzes were waiting for us.

My daughter, Marie, her husband Jack, and their daughters, Sarah and Rachel, welcomed Raquel to their country home.

The abundance of wild life, especially deer, added a novel element to Raquel's life. When winter arrived, the novelty took a quantum leap.

The Lewises' Home

Raquel in Phase 1 (see page 117 for Raquel at home)

Rubén in Phase 1 (see page 120 for Rubén at home)

Michelle and Jeff Dietz and their two boys happily took in Rubén. The Deitzes are farmers and Rubén enjoyed working alongside Jeff all day doing farming.

The Dietz Farm

I had taught Michelle to say a few words of welcome in Spanish. When Rubén and I entered the house, she performed beautifully. Rubén, assuming he would not understand anything said to him, did not understand. The resultant laugh broke the ice. Over the summer, the boy at left in the photo was seriously injured in an automobile accident.

We had all arrived in North Carolina on May 25. After a month Jorge and I thought we should visit Jairo, Raquel, and Rubén. So on June 24 Jorge, Ana, Pablo, Luis and I all piled into my car and headed for Pennsylvania. Ana, Pablo, and Luis played Monopoly in the back; Jorge and I switched off driving.

Dwayne and Nicole White (page 165) had arranged for all of us to spend the next afternoon at the Pittsburgh Zoo, a first for our students. To say they had a good time would be nihilistic.

The next day the Lewises invited everyone to their home for a picnic and, for sure, soccer.

Jorge and I switched off driving back to North Carolina and the next day he returned to Guatemala.

In July, I took Ana, Luis, and Pablo for eye exams. Dr. Hudgins discovered that Ana had neuralgia. She was not in any pain and did not even know that she had it until he held a mirror for her. She could see that the right side of her mouth was askew. Fortunately, the problem went away in a day or two. Nobody needed glasses.

In August my daughter, Marie, called to say that Raquel was suffering a good deal of homesickness; she was, after all, only eleven. Could Luis, her brother, come to live nearby; a friend, Shari, had said she would take him in. We executed the plan.

The local schools would start soon. Marie called again to suggest that the kids might sit in on some classes to see what going to school in the United States was like. It seemed like a capital idea to me. Marie took Raquel and Luis to talk with the principal, who also readily agreed. The next day they started sitting in on classes. They did not have to take any tests but did so anyway and got all A's. The teachers fell in love with little Raquel, as did her classmates. Soon Rubén was doing the same in another school not far away. The kids never got any grades; we never paid any fees. The experiment's only result was a quantum leap forward in their English and their happiness at studying in a school with resources they had previously never seen. But a dark cloud hung over the experiment, as we shall soon see.

Rick and Kelli Conlow

On September 10 (still 2005) I flew to the Twin Cities to speak at pool party hosted by Rick and Kelli Conlow. No volunteers came forward other than the

Rick and Kelli with Dania and Brian

Conlows themselves, who had two adopted Guatemalan children and would soon become very active in GSSG.

The Many and the Few

Before taking Raquel, Luis, Pablo, Ana, Rubén, and Jairo back to Guatemala, I administered the SLEP (Secondary Language English Proficiency) test. Little Raquel walked away with the prize.

The next day, November 22, 2005, the youngsters' parents met us at the airport in Guatemala City and took them home, where, among their poverty-stricken neighbors, they soon became objects of wonder—"Your child has been to the United States!" "How much did you pay the *cayote*?"[286] "Why did he come back?" "Does she have all her organs?"[287]

Jorge then went to the records office looking for the death certificate of Blanca's mother (for Blanca, see page 94), but came away empty handed. That evening I gave a presentation to a group of upper-class Guatemalans at the invitation of an acquaintance I had met earlier in Chapel Hill, where he has a second home. His only proviso was that I could not ask for money. I reasoned that I could still suggest changes in the socioeconomic structure of the state which, if implemented, would work to the advantage of everyone. I chose to use the seventeenth-century Netherlands as a model of a small country with limited resources that rose, through innovation, to economic and trade eminence by importing raw materials such as cotton and uncut diamonds, processing them into finished products, transporting them around the world in its own vessels and selling them at a profit, and by creating industries that required no raw materials, such as map making, banking, and the stock market, to say nothing of Rembrandt, Vermeer, and company.

My presentation sparked some discussion but, alas! resulted in neither social nor economic stirrings.

---

[286] Many, perhaps most, illegal aliens pay someone familiar with the process to help them to and across the border.
[287] Most impoverished Guatemalans believe that Americans who offer to take their children to the United States do so in order to harvest their organs for the black market in organ transplants.

The next day Jorge and I left early for Santa Lucia on the Pacific coast and spent the afternoon looking for a death certificate for Blanca's mother, possession of which would move legal guardianship for her uncle off dead center. Foiled again, we moved on to El Jabalí!

El Jabalí

We had previously scouted El Jabalí (page 111), where Blanca

was born, looking for her birth certificate. Now we were hunting her mother's death certificate. This time we met the sister of Blanca's father. This pleasant woman lived in a house made of bamboo (above). In the course of conversation, she mentioned that Blanca's mother had not died in Guatemala City, as we had previously been told, but in San Miguel Petapa. Jorge, eternally optimistic, seized on this new bit of information, but in the end it came to naught.

When I next went to Guatemala, I took the first volume of *Harry Potter*, in Spanish, along with me and give it to Blanca. She replied that she didn't like to read, but I left the book anyway. Sometime later I heard from her that she had finished the book in record time and asked if I could get her the next volume? Thereafter she devoured several more books. Blanca and Nataly (page 109) are, I believe, the only GSSG students who had ever read a book other than school textbooks before coming to the United States.

Giovanni in Phase 2

Of the four students who had come for Phase 1 in 2004, Karina (page 104) could not return because she had learned nothing; Edgar (page 103) could not return because of his psychosomatic illness; and Nataly did not return because she had a scholarship in Guatemala. That left Giovanni (page 101).

Giovanni had not conducted himself well in Phase 1 (see page 112). We would give him a second chance.

Heydi and Arnoldo had returned for Phase 2 with AFS in Guatemala (page 98) and found the arrangement satisfactory. So we now engaged AFS to do the same for Giovanni. He would live with Ellen Smith and attend the same public high school as Ellen's son.

Giovanni struggled for a few months in the fall but did much better, especially in math, in the spring. He did not, however, comport himself well with his host family. For Christmas Ellen gave him a new Sony CyberShot, 5-Megapixel camera. He also received some money and after Christmas bought a Sony CyberShot 7.5-Megapixel camera. Ellen, of course, was dismayed, as was I. When I took the matter up with him, he only replied, "It's my money. I can do with it what I want." He would not return to the United States again.

Chapter X, GSSG 2006

Chamíl

Jorge had arranged for us to recruit in a large village called *Chamíl* (*chah-MEEL*). We parked in Chamelco and took a minibus, equipped to hazard the impossible road to Chamil. Imagine my astonishment when I stepped off the bus and a young man approached me saying, "My name is Maynor. I speak English."

Seven to eight hundred people live in Chamíl, all Q'eqchí'-speaking. The village did have electricity but few homes had any appliances, though most had a light bulb. One would hunt in vain for a post office, though Maynor had a cell phone; satellite overhead. Maynor had learned English because Jorge had recommended him for a scholarship known as *Becas Cass*, a USAID-funded program which brings Central American youth who appear to have leadership potential to a college campus in the United States for two years of study, in this case, Georgetown.

Chamíl occupies a valley as well as the surrounding mountain sides. Our first trek took us up a series of dirt stairs carved out of earth to the local school high up on one side of the valley, with a spectacular view of seemingly endless ranges of peaks and valleys (see above). Five boys whom Maynor had selected were waiting for us to conduct the Group Interview, outside

the school, for it was locked. We had them prepare the usual information sheet telling us their names, birth dates, and year in school. Then we proceeded with our routine, first asking each boy to tell us something about himself, his home, and his family, while we made notes in our copies of the Recruiting Manual (page 114). Because the school house was locked, we could not administer our three written tests—aptitude, math, and IQ. Improvising, we asked a number of questions and recorded the answers. We dismissed the boys saying that we would visit some of them later. After they had left we selected three of the five for the Family Interview: Willy (second from the right in the photo above), Bayron (extreme right), and Alfonso (second from the left).

With Maynor as our guide, we picked our slippery way down and then up the opposite mountainside to his home, a board structure with a dirt floor and no appliances. His mother had prepared

"Mayan sandwiches" (pink or purple beans between two tortillas) and coffee for our lunch.

In addition to Willy (the youngest), Maynor's family included their mother, who cannot read or write, another brother, two sisters, and a grandmother. Maynor's father had died some years earlier.

Willy

After lunch we conducted the Family Interview, in which all of the family members eagerly participated, Maynor providing a running translation in Q'eqchí' for his family and in English for Jorge and me. Jorge briefly explained the purpose of GSSG and I explained its three phases. Jorge then went into greater detail with Willy's mother and asked her a good many questions about the family. Finally, while Maynor showed me around the house so that I could take pictures, Jorge conducted the Personal Interview.

Bayron

Another hike up and down the mountain sides brought us to Bayron's home (just visible in the photo at right). The house resembled Willy's except for the presence of a television set, a stereo, an electric typewriter, and other commercially made products. The interview process proceeded as before but in the end we decided that Bayron's family did not satisfy our first requirement, poverty (page 99).

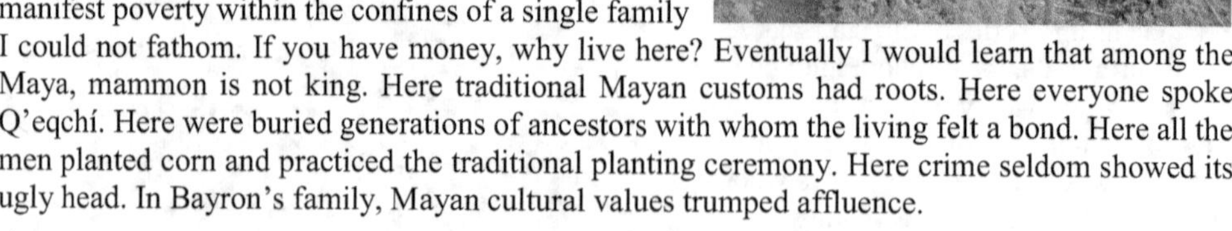

The incongruity of manifest wealth allied with manifest poverty within the confines of a single family I could not fathom. If you have money, why live here? Eventually I would learn that among the Maya, mammon is not king. Here traditional Mayan customs had roots. Here everyone spoke Q'eqchí. Here were buried generations of ancestors with whom the living felt a bond. Here all the men planted corn and practiced the traditional planting ceremony. Here crime seldom showed its ugly head. In Bayron's family, Mayan cultural values trumped affluence.

Alfonso

About 4:30 in the afternoon, once more we climbed up the mountainside, to Alfonso's house. This time Maynor took pity on my sagging sinews and offered to carry the case containing my shoulder-mount camcorder and related paraphernalia.

Alfonso's family circumstances paralleled those of Bayron.

Since we had not administered our aptitude, math, and IQ tests, we left them with Maynor and asked him to do so and get them to Jorge sometime before my return to the United States. He agreed but, as it turned out, never did.

At dusk we made our way back to the village center to catch the last minibus to Chamelco. We stood around for an hour waiting, eventually bidding good-bye, bone weary, to Maynor and Chamíl.

Cobán

Because Phase 1 would now last for six months (see page 115), participants would come in May instead of October. Accordingly, I flew down to Guatemalan in April. Jorge had made arrangements for us to do a Group Interview at a school in Cobán, the *Instituto Emilio Rosales Ponce*. After the Group Interview we selected two students for the Family Interview, Yohan, *ladino*, and Leonardo, Mayan.

Yohan

Yohan, 14, and his parents lived in a one-room home, with a single bulb.

When we began our Family Interview, the chicken who also resided there got into an altercation with a mouse that emerged under the wall from the outside (see below).

Yohan's parents impressed us greatly. Though obviously desti-

tute, they talked candidly about their poverty, making no excuses and seeking no assistance. Literate and socially conscious, they understood that the haunting conditions in which they lived were beyond their control and they accepted their lot, casting aspersions on no one. Their chief concern centered on Yohan who seemed to have health problems and they worried that he might not be able to continue in school. (Their fears would be realized, as we will see.)

Leonardo

The other applicant, Leonardo, lived in a village so remote that, to go to school, he had to stay with relatives in town during the week. Jorge made arrangements for us to take him home one Friday after school so that we could conduct the Family Interview. At two o'clock we picked up Leonardo and set out. Within half an hour we had left the highway and found ourselves bouncing along, slowly, over a remarkably rough road, for two and a half hours, until at last Jorge's little car could take no more, steam erupting ominously from under the hood. We were miles, hours actually, deep into desolation. It was obvious from such few homes as we had seen that they had neither electricity nor running water. We were, however, within striking distance of the path that would take us to Leonardo's house, a forty-five-minute hike from the road. Leonardo told us that there was but one bus, that it traveled in only one direction, making a circuit once a day, and that it had already passed us en route. Leonardo could walk the rest of the way home but Jorge was still teaching one class, on Saturday mornings, and we wanted to attend the wake for Rubén's father that night (see page 120). In addition, we had Family Interviews scheduled for the next day.

In the midst of dealing with this quandary, we found a stream, filled the radiator, and drove a mile or so before seeing a house on one side. A friendly farmer emerged from the house and fell in conversation with Jorge. The man sent his son to fetch a bucket of water. Then, as his understanding of our circumstances increased, so did his interest. He and Jorge first tried to get the fan to move, turning it this way and that by hand, and otherwise poked around under the hood. Meanwhile I saw a big beer truck, like the Coke and Pepsi trucks you see everywhere in the States, approaching, empty after the day's run. I hailed it down. Three burley *hombres* emerged from this cavernous machine and joined the resident and Jorge already under the hood. Faced with the prospect of watching five well-developed behinds presumably attached somewhere to hands and heads, I turned my attention to the farmer's three or four children who had probably never seen a *gringo* before. I took out my stash of balloons, blew some of them up, and gave them to the kids. Inevitably one of the balloons exploded loudly close behind the five derrières, thus startling the five attached torsos, which caused the five attached heads to bang up smartly against the underside of the hood, which set the five attached heads cursing loud expletives, which set the farmer's dogs barking, to whom the farmer bellowed, "Shut up," all of which sent the children, feeling guilty, scattering in all directions. The men gave up their task and parted into the darkening shadows of late afternoon. The driver offered us a ride, in the back of his steel monster.

The empty cargo space, into which Jorge and I now clambered, had no sides and no deck (floor) either, just an ample supply of polls, struts, and chains by which, presumably, the ambrosial gift of the gods is normally conveyed to mortals. Clinging to these iron sinews for dear life, we tore along at high speed for nearly two hours, the driver apparently intent on reaching home in advance of the devil, while the noise of the diesel engine soon made both Jorge and me deaf and the diesel fumes sent our eyeballs spinning and our stomachs churning as we struggled to maintain our stance on the struts, clinging for dear life to random sets of chains.

We had asked the driver to let us out at the first gas station. When at last he pulled over, we tumbled out of the ogre. The last time I was so glad to touch Mother Earth had been years earlier when, after a nine-day voyage aboard the U.S.S. Everglades in a storm, the ship docked in Naples.

Chamelco

The principal at the *Instituto por Cooperativo Basico* in a town called *Chamelco* had contacted Jorge about recruiting in his school. Jorge asked Stella to join us.

After the group interview, we did not select any students but let me introduce Stella.

Stella María Valverdi

Stella and her husband, a physician, had four children, two older boys and two girls, one four or five and the other nine or ten at the time. When I visited, only the youngest and Stella were at home. Shortly the child disappeared while Stella and I talked but soon reappeared with a gift that she had just made for me. The other daughter came home a little later, apparently after school, and greeted me politely. After a brief conversation the girls excused themselves but re-emerged, when I was leaving, to say good-bye.

Stella's parents had been very involved in civil rights and humanitarian causes, noblesse oblige. Her father was mayor of Coatepeque, in Quetzaltenango. The likeness of her great uncle, Mariano Valverde, a famous composer, appears with two other musicians on the Q.200.00 bill.[288]

The Group Interview at the *Instituto* in Chamelco. Stella is seated at left.

---

[288] 'Q.' stands for 'Quetzal,' the name of the Guatemalan currency, as does '$' for our currency.

Byron

We have already met Byron's family for he is the younger brother of Claudia (page 110) and the second youngest of their parents' ten children, all born at home.

Byron's extended family lived in a Poqomchí'-speaking village called Chiallí (*chee-ah-YEE*), a couple of miles up the mountain from Tactic. Byron walked to school in Tactic every day, leaving his house at 6:00 AM and returning at 3:00. Back home, he would go into the forest every day to collect firewood so that his mother could make dinner.

Byron's board house had a dirt floor, no appliances, and two light bulbs. Byron's mother, like all indigenous women, cooked over an open fire but in this case on a concrete stove which his father, a mason, had made. Byron's older siblings live in the same village and their children often spend time at grandma's house. Byron's mother and the little ones spoke only Poqomchí'. His father had two years of schooling; his mother, none, but she had learned to print her name and happily affixed her signature to our documents.

Byron's father also made the family *pila* (at left).

As mayor, he had got the men together, located a spring in the mountain, diverted it into a tank, and run a line down to the village.

Byron, a quiet lad, earned good grades and set high standards of comportment for himself. Unobtrusively ambitious, he probably had the talent to succeed in any profession, if he had the means to prepare for it.

Byron attended a private school on a scholarship to pay his tuition but he had to pay for his books, uniform, and supplies, and he had a job that provided sufficient income.

Ericka

Ericka, Byron's cousin and also sixteen, lived with her mother and younger sister in the same Poqomchí' village.

Ericka's tiny house with a dirt floor had room only for two beds, a small table, and one chair. There were no mattresses on the beds; the kitchen was a lean-to outside (below); there were no appliances, no *pila*, and no bathroom.

Like Byron, Ericka walked to school every day, because riding in the back of a pickup cost about twelve cents. Ericka is also quiet, unpretentious, and industrious.

When we first met Ericka's mother, a pleasant woman with three years of schooling, she was working as a maid and only earned enough money to provide the barest of necessities. Subsequently she got a job in a drug store in Tactic, which paid a little better.

Ericka had no father in her life.

San Cristóbal

Students on their way to school. Fare = 1 Quetzal (12.5 cents)

Stella (page 134) was with us when we conducted a Group Interview in a town called 'San Cristóbal Verapaz,' at the invitation of Señorita Lucero, an English teacher and a friend of Jorge's. It seemed that we had arrived during recess, for the children were all playing outside. Ms. Lucero received us cordially and took us to a large room with a goodly supply of plastic chairs. Twenty-four youngsters followed us in. Jorge briefly explained why we were there and we began our Group Interview, but throughout the next couple of hours the noise of children playing outside continued.

The initial part of the Group Interview required the applicants to rise and tell us about themselves, their families, and anything else they wanted to say. Of the twenty-four applicants, seven had been abandoned by their fathers; the mother of another one of those seven was dead and the father had abandoned his children after her demise. In four cases, the parents were separated. Two had alcoholic fathers living at home. One was an orphan, taken in by some nuns and living in a convent. One said she had no father and one other opined that her father might be dead. When the last student, a girl named Silvia, got up to tell her story, the teacher, who was seated next to me, whispered, "This is a special case." I thought to myself, "Good grief! How much more special can a case be?" The girl dropped to her knees as she slid to the floor in front of us and, sobbing and shaking, told us her story. Briefly, her father had committed suicide a year or two before. Last year, when she was thirteen, she had been raped by her brother, who threatened her with her life if she ever told their mother. In addition, her mother lavished such affection as she possessed on another daughter, ignoring Silvia.

When we finally left the building, we noticed that the students were still playing outside. Jorge asked about this anomaly and was told that the other teachers were all drinking.

Knowing the last girl to be a special case, we called Kelli Conlow (page 128), who wanted very much to host any one of our youngsters. I told her about Silvia and asked if she was interested. She was, all the more so because of Silvia's special circumstances.

Subsequently we went to Silvia's home to conduct a Family Interview but were rebuffed. The mother intoned that her father, Silvia's grandfather, would not allow the girl to go. Jorge knew the grandfather and doubted he would be involved at all. The brother who had raped the girl threatened us. We had no choice but to leave. Disappointed, Kelli sent me a letter, which Jorge translated, to give to Silvia. In her letter, Kelli expressed her sorrow and told the girl to contact her if she ever needed anything. She never heard from her.

After the Group Interview, we selected six whose homes we wished to visit: Alba, Hamilton, Lily, Nancy, Pedro, and Tita. Silvia would not have been our first choice but we would probably have selected her as well. Were her theatrics genuine distress or a well-crafted ploy?

<h1 style="text-align:center">Alba</h1>

A few days after the Group Interview, we conducted the Family Interview and the Personal Interview in Alba's home.

Alba, 15, was the youngest of seven children, the eldest of whom, a boy, died in infancy. Her mother died three months after giving birth to Alba. Her father, Israel, took his other five daughters and disappeared into the bowels of Guatemala City's slums, leaving Alba with his sister-in-law, who happened to be nursing a child of her own at the time.

Alba's *bajareque* house, out in the woods along with those of several other squatters, in an area with no streets, no electricity, indeed no services of any kind, would collapse a few years after this picture was taken.

To take a shower, outside, in a plastic enclosure, the bather dips water out of the yellow bucket and pours it over his or her head while standing on a rock. On one occasion, as we approached the house, we heard a female voice call out from the shower, "Don't look in here."

Hamilton

Seven months after his birth, Hamilton's mother died. His father subsequently re-married (*unidos*, page 31). The couple had three other children.

Hamilton's step mother treated him as her own son.

Like most homes in Guatemala, Hamilton's is sparsely furnished and Hamilton shared a bedroom with his siblings.

Lily

Lily, 14 when we first met her, is the third eldest of eight children. Her family lives, in the photo at right, in the fourth house on the left in a complex built by Habitat for Humanity. Lily's mother is obligated to make monthly payments, which she cannot do, her only income deriving from the food she makes to sell on the street. Lily's father works in a town twelve hours distant by bus, where he has another family. On those few occasions when he visits, Lily rejoices to see him.

Lily's family has to buy water from barrels at the end of the street in the dry season; in the rainy season they collect rain water. The family diet consists entirely of beans and tortillas; usually only tortillas and salt. The first time we met Lily, she and her younger brother had seasonal work helping their mother prepare calendars (by candlelight) for shipment (right).

Rossy

Rossy, fourteen when we recruited her, is the second eldest of seven children. Her father had died some years earlier and her mother subsequently remarried. Rossy's step-father, a teacher, worked two jobs, as do nearly all teachers in Guatemala, but he was barely able to support his family.

Rossy's house sits behind the houses on the street or, if you will, in somebody else's back yard. To reach it you have walk through a long, narrow, passage (left) between the houses in front. The home, made of block, has only bedrooms. The kitchen, a lean-to, has no appliances. Such furniture as they do have is badly worn (right).

Rossy, the best student in her class, long expressed her desire to become a physician.

Nancy

Nancy had an older sister and a younger brother but no parents. Her mother had died in 2000. Though she knows who her father is and on rare occasions sees him on the street, they have

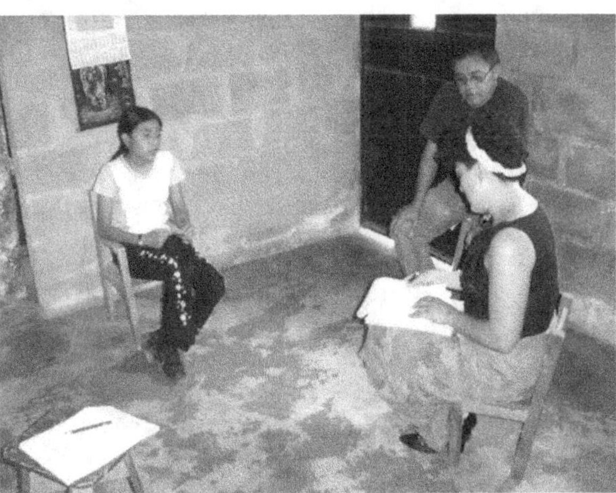

never spoken. Nancy and her siblings live on the same street as Lily (see photo on the preceding page). In the photo above, Stella (page 134) and Jorge are seated to the right.

Nancy's mother was in the process of buying the house, built by Habitat, before she died. Nancy's older sister worked as a teacher in a village out of town in the mornings and as a soccer referee in the afternoons. Between the two jobs she was able to make the Habitat payments.

The nuns at a local Catholic school provided tuition and school supplies for Nancy and her brother.

Nancy's family, like Lily's, had to buy water from barrels at the end of the street in the dry season and collected rain water in the rainy season.

Pedro

Pedro, 13 when we met him, is a *ladino* (page 12). Ordinarily *ladinos* belong to the middle-class; many, however, are as poor as the Maya.

Pedro's mother attended school through six grades. Abandoned by their Nicaraguan father, Pedro, his younger brother, and their mother had no house but occupied one small room in the home of Pedro's grandmother. Determined that her sons will get an education, Pedro's mother, a cheerful and energetic woman, ekes out a living cleaning houses, taking in laundry, collecting bottles and cans, running errands on her bicycle, making tortillas to sell on the street, and the like.

Pedro's situation was complicated by the fact that Guatemalan law requires both parents to be

present when a minor is applying for a passport. Hearing this, his mother replied, "I'll find him," knowing only that he was in Petén (page 84). Subsequently she not only found him but got him to agree to come to Guatemala City and go with his son to the passport office. Unfortunately, the thought of going to the U.S. Embassy eventually scared him off. The poor woman had sold what little jewelry she had to make the trip to Petén—all in vain. Her husband disappeared again. Jorge went to court and, with financial support from GSSG, secured sole guardianship for Pedro's mother.

Heidi

Heidi (*HEY-dee* not *HIGH-dee*), is the last of the seven recruited in San Cristóbal. Her family's home, inherited from her grandfather, has a dirt floor, two bedrooms, a kitchen without appliances, and a living room, whose furniture consists of a bench, a table, and two car seats (see below, at right). Heidi had a scholarship which paid half her tuition and excelled academically.

Heidi's father collects junk to sell to

dealers in Guatemala City. To supplement his meager income, the family owned a small mill for grinding corn, charging 17¢ per use.

In the picture to the left you can see that Heidi's house is precariously situated and in danger of falling, as it might.

In the photo at right, Jorge is explaining GSSG's requirements that Heidi's little sister apparently found more inspiring than the applicant.

Heidi is proud to be indigenous, a counterweight to Arnoldo's "All of them" (page 36).

Chitomáx

A few days after conducting the Home and Personal Interviews for the seven students in San Cristóbal, a friend of Jorge's, Moisés Ramos de la Cruz, a retired teacher, called and asked if we might recruit in a very remote place called Chitomáx (chee-toh-MAHSH)[289].

Accordingly, Jorge picked me up at 5:00 A.M. one day, with Giovanni in tow. Why Giovanni? Ramos had advised Jorge that people Chitomáx believed that Americans come to Guatemala to recruit youngsters and take them to the United States to harvest their organs for the black market. Giovanni would function as our credibility factor. He had been in Phase 1 of GSSG's program the year before and still had all of his organs.

Giovanni had ridden his bicycle from Carchá to Cobán in a drizzling rain. He arrived early, soaked and cold. As soon as possible (about an hour later), we found a restaurant just opening.

At 9:00 we arrived in Cubulco, where Moisés lived, and were greeted cordially. We all piled into his Susuki Sidekick and headed out of town. For the next two hours we bounced along a mostly one-lane, dirt road carved out of the mountain sides, nearly straight up on one side and straight down on the other, dirt serving as guard rails. An occasional house perched precariously on the side of a mountain left us wondering who could live here and why anyone would choose to do so. The only traffic we encountered, a guy on a bicycle, only doubled our wonderment— where could he be going?

The road ended abruptly at the school. We tumbled out of the Sidekick. On the other side of a deep valley, far below our perch, we could see the answer to our "who would live here and why," a stretch of greenery made productive by a broad river meandering leisurely through the heavily

cultivated bottom land, now green with ripening corn but no trees because, we would learn, in winter the water level rises about thirty feet, inundating the valley floor.

All of the housing lay on the opposite side of the river because the fertile bottomland is there and, in the absence of a bridge, that is where the farmers had to live, largely isolated from the rest of the world. The anthropological implications boggle the mind. Among other things, the way in which they build their houses is likely much the same as the way their ancestors built theirs, thousands of years ago. Only a tin roof adds a modicum of modernity.

The structure on the left is a home (see the baby pen). That on the right appears to be a community oven.

A Canadian religious organization had, in relatively recent times, built a foot bridge about ninety feet above the water. Unfortunately, the cables holding up this aerial trapeze are not quite the same length so that the platform upon which we were supposed to cross leans menacingly to one side. Worse still, many of the slats in the walkway are missing (or have rotted away?) and here and there one has to jump and pray simultaneously. No proper handrails existed but some fencing had been stretched along the sides and fastened to the cables with barbed wire. O.K., so I cut my hand. To complicate my passage, my shoes did not have rubber soles. Worst of all, the students, boys and girls alike, fairly danced across, laughing and jabbering, as if immortal.

The school, a permanent structure, had to be built on the near side of the river because the road ends there and no roads exist on the other side. So the students have to cross the bridge twice a day.

All the children who attend this school live on the far side, in hamlets accessible only by mountain paths, wherever water can be found.

Once on the other side we were met by a small group of men and the area teacher, Francisco Rosales. We had brought along some copies of *GSSG news* (page 98). The men could not read but the pictures showed that self-same Giovanni with his host family in North Carolina. He talked with us in English and he still had all his organs.

The teacher, Rosales, was born and raised in a hamlet called Pichal. When he was a boy, before the school was built, Francisco would walk to a grade school in a neighboring place, Chivaquito, and his father would beat him for thus wasting his time. But the young man persisted through six grades, doing his homework at night (after his father had gone to bed) by the light of a fire he would kindle with *ocote*. This phase of his life evolved during the *violencia*, that is, during the early 1980s, when the horrors of the civil war reached their apogee. At age twelve he was obliged to become a *patrullero* (see PACs, page 62) in Chivaquito.

After grade school and with help from his teachers and in defiance of his father's orders, Rosales, now fifteen, attended a middle school in Cubulco, where a resident gave him shelter while he himself earned money for food by teaching reading and writing in a literacy project there.

Having graduated from middle school, Rosales, passionate to learn, attended *magisterio* (page 85) in Salamá, the capital of the *departamento*. Successful there, he entered the local branch of the public university, San Carlos, subsequently earning the *licenciatura* (page 85) in education.

After meeting the village elders and having heard Francisco's story, we re-crossed the bridge, at one point suffering the indignity of being passed by a man carrying a load of wood on his back and a boy, apparently his son, similarly encumbered. The school is used in the morning as a primary school; the afternoon, *basico*. Schooling ends at ninth grade. With Francisco's concurrence, we assembled the ninth graders, both boys and girls, and started our Group Interview. The local language here is Achí but middle school instruction by law must be in Spanish. Jorge spoke for us in Spanish, Francisco helping out now and again with a word or two in Achí.

Soon, however, it was time for school to begin. This afternoon's first lesson offered instruction in native dance. We interrupted our recruiting to watch. A marimba band (three musicians performing on a single instrument) had been procured to provide music and the students, all boys, proceeded to do their best with the footwork, trying in vain to emulate the movements of the instructor, the man in the hat.

The initial dance having been concluded, we applauded heartily and then withdrew in order to proceed with the Personal Interviews of the five boys selected a half-hour earlier. We had no choice but to skip the Family Interview because of the great distances involved—two of the five boys we selected had to walk for three hours, each way, to go to school.

These five boys were uniformly polite, straight-forward, innocent, and a bit shy. Our principal task was not to find out about their honesty or their character, for all of the children are raised on the same standard, but to find out which among them were the brightest and the most likely to become leaders in their society. Jorge interviewed three of the boys; I interviewed two. A couple of the questions I asked both boys were, "What would you do if you had a 1000 Quetzales" (about $130) and "What would you do with a million Quetzals (about $130,000)?" To the first they both spoke of things they would buy for people in their hamlets, shoes being first on their list. Beyond that they seemed to be lost. The second boy, Chico, in response to my second question, replied: "I cannot imagine such a sum and cannot give you an answer." I asked if he himself could ever become a leader in the communities. He replied, "No." Taken back a bit, I pressed him. He said that a leader has to have ideas and that it is impossible in their communities to think of anything new. Everybody thinks the same things in the same way. Nobody knows how to do anything different. Novelties like television, which they have never seen and can barely comprehend, and telephone, which they do not have, were invented by other people, not their kind of people. If my task was to find someone bright enough to become a leader, then Chico had my vote.

Unable to conduct the Family Interview but reluctant to leave empty-handed, we selected two boys, Chico and a lad named Balbino. A few weeks later Jorge would get a message that Chico had died of brain cancer. Impossible! More likely, his parents believed that we would harvest his organs. We would have other instances of parents turning us down and for the same reason.

Chisec

Not long after our visit to Chitomax Jorge received a request from the principal in a town called 'Chisec.' We conducted the Group Interview at the school and selected two students for the Family Interview.

Flor

Flor's family lives in a house built by Habitat for Humanity. Her grandmother worked for thirty-seven years as a teacher and her accumulated savings accrued to Flor's father, who used the money to buy furniture for their house.

Flor's father is the principal at the local school. They have no car. Both parents and all three daughters make food to sell on the street in the evening. Flor is unusually bright and easily passed all of our tests.

The other girl, Ana Cecilia, could have won a Miss Congeniality contest hands down but her family could in no way be considered poor.

Marvin

Marvin, 14, and his siblings are the offspring of Francisco Rosales, the teacher at Chitomax (see above).

Marvin's mother, a lovely young woman, has three years of schooling and speaks mainly Achí, a language group severely victimized during the Guatemalan civil war.

Marvin, an agreeable boy, quick, sharp-witted, very sociable and eager to talk, had a sense of humor. His father, as mentioned above, had been beaten for going to school but had persisted and, against all odds, worked his way through Guatemala's teacher training program and returned to the same area to teach in Chitomax. Marvin showed much promise and, we hoped, might well join his father in attempting to lift the area out of extreme poverty, but his family was not particularly poor. We considered him anyway in hopes that he would take inspiration from his father's example.

We now had thirteen candidates who would need visas for 2006: Willy (page 131), Alfonso (132), Yohan (132), Byron (135), Ericka (135), Alba (138), Hamilton (139), Lily (139), Nancy (140), Pedro (141), Balbino (149), Flor (149), and Marvin (149). Our next step would be to assemble the documents required to get them visas (page 88).

A Passport for Alba

Guatemalan law requires that both parents be present when a minor applies for a passport; if one parent is deceased, a death certificate must be provided. The first challenge presented itself when we asked Alba's surrogate mom (page 138) for the death certificate of Alba's biological mother. Hah! Jorge would try to get one.

It had been raining all day when we arrived in the metropolis and checked into Hotel Ajau on December 11, 2005. Alba and her mom had preceded us and soon came to the lobby, accompanied by a slender man, whom I guessed was too young to be Alba's father. He grinned and shook my hand. *Me llamo Juan* ("My name is John"). I took his hand, no wiser for the introduction but soon learned that he was Alba's uncle, her (deceased) mother's brother, and that he had the phone numbers of Alba's five sisters, whom her father had taken with him thirteen years earlier when he had deserted Alba and moved into the slums of Guatemala City.

Soon Juan was on the phone, first calling Sandra, who lived in Zone 1.[290] No answer. Next he tried Olivia. No answer there either. Then Suzana. María answered, saying brusquely that Suzana lived far away and she didn't know when she would see her. Next Veronica, Alba's cousin. No answer. Juan then called Luis in Mixco, a suburb of Guatemala City. Luis was a brother-in-law of Alba's mom. He told Juan to call back in five minutes. He did and Luis gave him the number of Chuz, the ex-husband of one of Alba's five sisters. Juan immediately called him; he replied, "I know where he is. Don't go anywhere. I'm coming." Alba had never met any of these people except Juan.

Moments later Chuz arrived. Jorge, Hector (our driver), Juan, and Chuz emptied their pockets and put their watches and phones on my bed and departed, leaving me alone with Alba and her mom. Shortly thereafter came a knock on the door. It was Zoila and her sister Olga. Zoila had been my Spanish teacher in Antigua (page 25). I had told her I would be in town and they had come to visit, adding that they had run from the bus station to the hotel, for they were afraid.

Hours passed without a word from the men. We ordered pizza and drank coffee. Finally the phone rang. I answered it—wrong number. We waited. It rang again. It was Jorge: "We've got him!"

A bit later the men reappeared and told us their story. They had located Israel in Zone 18, a slum. He was drunk and would let no one in except Juan, who was, of course, his brother-in-law. Jorge, Hector, and Chuz stood outside. A woman soon emerged from an adjacent door and clucked, "It's not safe for you fellows to be standing out there. You'd better get in here."

Meanwhile Israel and Juan were arguing. "What do you want? Have you got a gun? Are you from the police?"

---

[290] Guatemala City is divided into "zones," which have come to represent different segments of the socioeconomic fabric of the metropolis. The foreign embassies, the big hotels, and the upscale stores and restaurants fill Zone 10. Until 2001 one could walk around Zone 10, alone and at night. Not anymore.

"No, I'm not from the police and, no, I don't have a gun. Alba, the daughter you haven't seen since she was an infant, has an opportunity to go to school in the United States. She's a minor and needs you to go with her to get a passport and a visa."

"I won't go anywhere. They'll find out who I am. They'll arrest me and put me in jail. Get out!"

"No, I won't get out. You have nothing to fear. No one is going to arrest you. It has nothing to do with the police. Since her mother is dead, you have to go with her to get a passport and a visa. She's a minor. That's all."

"They'll know my name. They'll take my picture. They'll arrest me."

Juan imposed discipline. "You, son of a bitch, listen to me! You're a bloody nobody and nobody's interested in your whereabouts. Your name isn't on any list. No one's going to take your picture. Nobody's going to arrest you. You've been a bum all of your life. You've never done anything for Alba before; now she needs you. She's a sweet girl and she's your daughter. You owe her this much. For her, it's the opportunity of a lifetime. You'll meet her and see for yourself what a pleasant young woman your daughter turned out to be, no thanks to you. You have my word; nobody's going to arrest you. We'll pick you up tomorrow."

"No, not tomorrow! I can't do it tomorrow. I'll go with you a week from tomorrow."

"O.k. We'll be back in a week."

Zoila and Olga listened to all of this in amazement. They knew none of these people and had only come to the hotel to meet me again after a hiatus of three years.

Every one departed. Jorge and I were left alone to ponder the road ahead for Alba. Would she eventually get her visa and come to the United States?

Israel had been living on the wrong side of the law for many years and feared that, if he showed his face in any government office, he would be arrested. The question now was, would he show up in a week?

The hunt for Alba's father was over but turned out to be only the beginning of a tense journey. For starters, Alba's application for a passport was rejected because her mother's name appeared as "Elena" on Alba's birth certificate but as "María Elena" on her mother's death certificate.

Jorge engaged a lawyer to prepare the required documents, make the correction, and file the papers with the *procuraduría*, the quasi-court that deals with such matters in Guatemala. A day or two later we went to the *procuraduría* to pick up Alba's amended birth certificate, only to be told that other inconsistencies had turned up and that the application had been sent back to the lawyer. The lawyer fixed the problem, or so he thought, but when he sent the papers back to the *procuraduría*, they were rejected again, this time because the mother's age was given as 30 on her death certificate but 38 on Alba's birth certificate. The lawyer now filed the paperwork for the third time. By this time, two months had elapsed and I had had to reschedule my return home for Christmas, twice.

I did go home for Christmas and returned to Guatemala on February 26. Rick Conlow (128), Alba's potential host dad, who travels a lot, had already used some of his miles to purchase tickets for Alba and me to fly on March 10 from Guatemala to the Twin Cities, where the Conlows live.

Jorge and I took a hard look at the calendar. First of all, we had to take into account that you cannot get a passport, which is issued by the Guatemalan government, and a visa, which is issued by the U.S. government, on the same day, because the procedures for getting a visa require the applicant to call the U.S. Embassy, give the number of his/her passport to the agent who answers the phone, and then hope that the agent, who is actually in Mexico, schedules an appointment for a relatively early date. The embassy website says that one can get a visa appointment in one day but I had grave doubts since in the past it had usually taken two weeks. In addition, we had to take into account that you do not actually get your visa on the day that it is approved. Rather the embassy sends it by *Cargo Expreso* to your home. Finally we had to take into account that, while the *procuraduría* is in Cobán, the passport office and the embassy are in Guatemala City, a four or five hour drive away.

Back to the calendar. Alba and I had plane tickets for 6:30 A.M. on March 10. So, the following time-line appeared to be our best shot at success. On March 7 we would pick up Alba and her uncle, Juan, drive to Guatemala City and meet her father, Israel, at the passport office that afternoon. If she got her passport, we would call the embassy right away, give the agent her passport number, and plead for an emergency appointment the next day, a scenario based entirely on wishful thinking. If we should happen to be blest with success, we would stay in the city overnight and meet Alba's father at the U.S. Embassy the next morning. If Alba's application for a visa turned out to be successful, we would then make the trip back to Alba's home and wait for her visa to be delivered by *Cargo Expreso* the next day, then make the trip back to Guatemala City again that afternoon or evening, stay overnight, and catch our plane early the next morning, March 10. Odds are better in Vegas. Here is what actually happened.

Alba still did not have a passport because her mother's corrected death certificate had not yet been issued. On March 2, the lawyer, Jorge, and I went to the *procuraduría* and asked for approval. We were told that, although the death certificate was now in order, it and the supporting documentation could not be sent to the Registrar (all court documents have to be recorded in the office of the Registrar, in Cobán, the capital of the *departamento*) until Monday (the 6th). On Monday, Jorge, Luis (a friend of Jorge's), and I went to the registrar's office. The corrected death certificate and supporting documentation were there but would have to be copied by hand into the official record and would not be available until Wednesday, the 8th—too late. Alba still had to get a passport and a visa and you can't do both on the same day and we had plane tickets for the 10th. So Jorge offered to copy the documents into the registry himself. Contrary to regulations, the registrar, a woman whom Jorge knew and with whom I had been exchanging furtive glances, accepted the offer. Meanwhile, Luis had been reading the documents and noticed a slight error, which he surreptitiously corrected (a big no-no but the documents were all in long hand; so he just did it). Jorge finished copying what he needed to do just at 5:00, when the office closes, and was told he could pick up the corrected death certificate the next day, Tuesday, the 7th, at 10:30.

Jorge and I agreed that, after picking up the newly minted death certificate, we would go to the capital with Alba and Juan, pick up Israel, who had agreed to cooperate, and get her passport. At 10:00 the next morning Jorge was in the registrar's office. At 11:00 he was handed Elena's (Alba's biological mother) corrected death certificate. At 11:30 he picked me up. We loaded my suitcase into his miniature car and headed for San Cristóbal, where Alba lived, a 40-minute drive away. He had called Juan and told him that, to save time, they should meet us at the intersection where our road and the road to San Cristóbal converge. Agreed, but when we arrived, they were nowhere to be seen. We careened into town and found them. Alba had all of her possessions in a half-empty backpack. Jorge peeled rubber. Juan had contacted Israel and instructed him to meet us at the passport office at 4:30; it closes at 5:00. We arrived just at 4:30. Israel was not there.

Back to the calendar. If we could persuade the embassy not to ship Alba's visa by Cargo Expreso to her home in San Cristóbal but rather give it to us the same day it was issued, Thursday, the 9th, we could gain a day—our only chance of catching our plane early on Friday, the 10th. Plan B!

We decided we could not stay at Hotel Ajau, as we usually did, because Jorge had seen on television the day before that thieves were openly victimizing people on the street two blocks away, with no response from the police. So we decided to stay in Zone 10, where most of the foreign embassies, including the U.S. Embassy, are located and the only zone in Guatemala City where you could walk the streets at night without looking over your shoulder. We checked into a Best Western (at seven times the cost of Ajau) and had dinner. Jorge and Juan then left me in charge of their watches, cell phones, and money and set out for the slum to get Israel. They returned a couple of hours later; they had found him and persuaded him to be at the passport office the next morning (Wednesday, the eighth), at 8:30.

The next morning, Alba, Jorge, Juan, and I piled once again into Jorge's car and descended upon the *oficina de pasaportes*. Israel soon appeared. Plan B was working. Alba looked at this strange man, the father she had never met, but did not speak, nor did he. They entered the building and twenty minutes later emerged victorious.

Visas for Alba & Hamilton

Hamilton (page 139) had gotten his passport without difficulty weeks earlier. So, after Alba got hers and Israel had left, the rest of us returned to our hotel and asked if we could call the U.S. Embassy from our room. "No!" To call the embassy you have to have a phone card issued by one certain company and the hotel phones used a different company. So, leaving Juan and Alba to watch the ever-depressing local news on TV, Jorge and I went in search of the right kind of phone. We found a phone booth for the right company on a busy street not far away and, amidst the din of passing diesels, horns, and motorcycles, I called, hoping to make appointments for Alba and Hamilton the next day. It was now Wednesday afternoon. I explained to the agent that we needed an emergency appointment the next day, Thursday, because we had plane tickets for early Friday morning. The agent asked a few questions about GSSG and a few more about Alba and Hamilton and then made the appointment—7:30 AM, Thursday, March 9. Hurrah! The agent then told me that I would have to call back to make Hamilton's appointment because each appointment has to be made on a separate call. He added that I could ask for him and, as he already had most of the required information, the second call would be a snap; he gave me his name. So I hung up and called again. I asked for so-and-so and, after a fairly long delay, he came on the line. He started to take Hamilton's information when, suddenly, the phone went dead—my special phone card had run out.

This development presented a problem. The card one has to buy to call the embassy costs $25 and neither Jorge nor I had that much cash on hand. (You never want to walk around Guatemala City with much cash in your pocket.) So we headed for an ATM; it wasn't working. Plan B was starting to unravel. We saw a bank nearby and entered. The line was long and it took nearly an hour before I was able to get a traveler's check cashed. We hurried back to the phone. I called again. I asked for the same agent. He had gone to lunch. Another agent cheerfully told me that she would be glad to help me. I gave her the information; she found that Alba had already been approved for 7:30. She took stock of Hamilton's application and approved his appointment for the same time, 7:30 A.M. the next morning. I hung up. Jorge and I dropped to our knees. Plan B was back on track.

Jorge now called Hamilton and told him that he and his father should be at our hotel by 7:00 the next morning, Thursday, the ninth. His father would have to take off work. Juan had previously told Israel that he and Jorge would pick him up the next morning at 5:30.

Back in our hotel, Jorge logged on to the U.S. State Department website and downloaded and completed the forms needed for Alba's and Hamilton's visa appointments. I had the GSSG documents. By now it was evening and we (Alba, Juan, Jorge, and I) went out for dinner, relieved, if somewhat wobbly, with the unfolding of the day's events.

Early Thursday morning (the 9th), Jorge and Juan once again deposited anything of value on my bed and left to get Israel. Meanwhile Hamilton and his father arrived by bus, having left home at 2:00 A.M. Shortly, Jorge and Juan reappeared with Israel. After a complimentary breakfast we called a taxi and set out in fear and trembling to face our last high hurdle.

While Jorge hunted for a parking space, Alba and Hamilton, their two fathers (we now had death certificates for both their mothers), and I divested ourselves of all metal objects into Juan's hands and got in line. An embassy official checked the kids' names on a list, looked at their documents, discovered that Alba had not signed one of hers, and told us to step out of line. Alba signed, the official let us back at the head of the line and we entered the labyrinthine bowels of the embassy's lower floor. We passed security, then the computer checks of the kids' papers, and emerged into the courtyard of the embassy compound.

Entering the upper floor, we joined several dozen others waiting apprehensively for their interviews. Eventually Alba's and Hamilton's names were called and we got into a line facing the bank of windows, behind which sit the consular agents who decide the fate of the nervous petitioners before them.

The U.S. State Department is concerned not only that visa applicants may be in actuality clandestine terrorists but also that foreigners may enter the United States legally but remain and work illegally upon the expiration of their visas or have insufficient funds to support themselves and thus become a burden on the public purse. U.S. Law unequivocally affirms the assumption that all applicants really wish to remain illegally in the United States and that it is the responsibility of the petitioner to disprove that assumption.

Like our applicants in previous years, Alba and Hamilton each had a sheaf of papers to support their applications:

1) a copy of a notarized letter which I had written a few weeks earlier to the U.S. Consul General in Guatemala, explaining the mission of GSSG, naming all of the youngsters who had previously participated in Phase 1, supplying their names and passport numbers and affirming that all had returned to Guatemala as scheduled (facts which any officer could easily check), that GSSG would ensure that the petitioner never became dependent upon the state, and that I would personally accompany the petitioner on his/her return to Guatemala, on schedule, as I had done in the past;

2) a notarized affidavit from GSSG's bank affirming that the organization has a history of unimpeachable fiscal responsibility and sufficient funds to carry out its responsibilities in the present case;

3) a sworn statement from the applicant's prospective host family that they would provide for their guest and treat him or her as one of their own children and that they would see to it that he or she would leave the country on schedule;

4) a notarized affidavit from a financial institution affirming that the host families had the means to do what they said they were going to do;

5) a page of photos of the host families and their homes, something I always included gratuitously and caused considerable excitement with the kids;

6) the student's sworn statement that he or she would never seek to live in the United States permanently but fully intended to return to Guatemala to live and work for socio-economic development there;

7) a lengthy statement, signed by the applicant's parents and witnessed, that they understood GSSG's program and that they would hold harmless in the event of accident, injury, or any other untoward event, including death, a) GSSG, b) the host family, and c) any school, church, or other organization or individual supplying support or services for their child in the United States;

8) documentary evidence that GSSG arranges for health insurance for its youngsters; and

9) a document signed by the applicant's parents granting temporary guardianship of their child to GSSG, with the right to re-assign guardianship to the host family. (This document had no legal standing in the United States but we used it nevertheless, without pretending that it was enforceable; it proved to be useful.)

Despite these assurances, approval is by no means certain and I, at least, faced the consular agent each time I took students to the embassy with more hope than confidence.

In this case, as in previous cases, the agent took the greatest interest in my letter to the Consul General, asked me more about the program, asked the youngsters a few questions, asked their fathers if they were really their fathers, consulted someone else about something, and finally said, *Su solicitud está aprobada.* ("Your application is approved.")

With a sigh of relief, I asked if we could get the visas the same day because there was no time now to drive back to the kids' home town and pick them up the next day; our plane would leave at 6:30 the next morning (Friday). The agent replied that we could pick them up at the Cargo Express office in Guatemala City *after* 9:00 that evening. I made sure, "*After* nine?" "Yes. After nine." "This evening?" "Yes, this evening."

We thanked the agent, went to the Cargo Expreso desk, paid the freight, and left the embassy. Once outside, we—Alba, Hamilton, their fathers, and I—huddled with our arms around one another and gave thanks to God. Breaking up our huddle, I gave a thumbs up to the expectant Jorge and Juan, who had seen us emerge, and we rejoiced with them outside the fence which encircles the compound. Alba hugged her father and thanked him for helping her. I couldn't be sure, but I think I saw a tear in his eye. Israel left to go to work. I do not know if Alba ever saw him again.

The rest of us now returned to the hotel. Ever-on-top-of-it Jorge called Cargo Expreso and asked what time they closed. "7:00 P.M." "Can we pick up our visas at 9:00?" "Yes." Next we had to buy plane tickets for Hamilton and Jorge. Alba and I were going to Minnesota the next day (because her host dad had used his miles to buy us tickets a couple of months earlier) but Hamilton and Jorge would go to North Carolina on Monday. We went online looking for the cheapest fares, had some trouble, but eventually found what we wanted. The hotel printer, however, was not working, so we found an Internet café to complete the transaction.

After lunch Jorge took Hamilton and his father to the bus station about 3:00. Alba, Juan, Jorge, and I spent a couple of hours unwinding in a mall, where Alba rode an escalator for the first time. We had dinner and then went to Cargo Expreso and got the visas.

Alba in Phase 1

The next morning, March 10, 2006, Jorge took Alba and me to the airport at 4:30. The line at check-in seemed unusually long, an oddity I attributed to the large group of Canadian teen-agers ahead of us, some of whom were sleeping on the floor. Nothing seemed to be moving and after an hour or so we heard that we were being delayed because of a storm in Houston, our transfer point. Finally, an airline agent approached me and asked if we were with the Canadian group. When I said no, he asked us to follow him and took us to the head of the line, checked our luggage, and found a new flight for us from Houston to Minneapolis/St. Paul, for we had already missed our connection.

Finally our plane was cleared for take-off, five hours late. I tried to call the Conlows, Alba's prospective host family, on the plane's built-in phone system but could not get through. In Houston we were told that we were on stand-by, first in line, and that there was only one seat left. I said, "No thanks! We have to fly together." The agent observed that they were already boarding but advised me to wait. I dashed to the nearest phone and left a message on Kelli Conlow's cell phone, returning to the gate just as the last passengers were boarding. The agent said we were in luck; he had one empty seat and one no-show—there were now two seats for us, not together, but what would it matter?

After the captain turned off the seatbelt sign, I went to check on Alba. The lady seated next to her recognized us and we fell in conversation. She was the grandmother of a family that we had seen at the gate in Guatemala with a newly adopted infant. She offered to change seats with me.

During the flight to MSP I asked the stewardess if she had a cell phone (no built-in phones on the smaller planes). It turned out that she was Guatemalan. She said that cell phones do not work during the flight but that I could use her phone when we landed. After all of the other passengers had disembarked, I called Rick, who said they would meet us at luggage. Within minutes Alba and her new mom were embracing.

As we got out of the car at the Conlows' home, Alba, pointing to the ground, asked,

¿Es nieve esto? ("Is that snow?") When I responded that it was, she delightedly picked some up, played with it, and quickly dropped it.

I could not remember the last time we had eaten. Kelli solved the problem in a jiffy (see photo above). The Conlows had been expecting Alba for Christmas; so Alba woke up the next morning to Christmas in March.

Rick became one of GSSG's strongest supporters and twice served as Chairman of its Board of Trustees.

Hamilton in Phase 1

Two days after I took Alba to Minnesota, Jorge took Hamilton to North Carolina. When they got to Immigration in Houston, the ICE officer (page 123) before whom they presented themselves and who did not speak Spanish gave Jorge a hard time: "Why is he coming to the United States?" "Why North Carolina?" "Why is the program there?" Jorge replied, "Well, that's where it was started." "Why was it started there?"

Hamilton and Jorge were met at RDU by Hamilton's temporary host family, Tom and Michelle Bonds and their children. They had hosted Pablo the preceding year (page 124) and were looking forward to Pablo's return in the fall, but they would host Hamilton for the summer.

Form I-539

In the days that followed I found out that it is possible for someone, who is in the United States with a B Visitor's Visa, to apply for a "change of status" and get an F (Student) Visa without having to go home. The process involved submitting a form called the I-539. Right away I asked Kelli to help Alba fill out the form and send it to me. Success could make a difference in our program—our students could transition from Phase 1 to Phase 2 without having to go home to get a new visa. The only hitch was that, whenever the students did go home, they would have to go to the embassy and get new Visas. O.k. we can deal with that.

Over the next several weeks I was busy with what was by now a daily routine, keeping the bookwork up-to-date, preparing and sending out Receipt/Reminder Forms, processing receipts, responding to inquiries, visiting potential host families, raising funds, composing various documents, copying and filing, even taking Giovanni to the dentist. Fortunately Jorge stayed with me for a month after delivering Hamilton to the Bonds. He was by now skilled in all aspects of the office routine.

In May (still 2006) I flew to MSP. Kelli and Alba picked me up. We visited Hill-Murray and Concordia high schools and were given tours of both facilities. Back at the Conlows' house, I had a chance to find out how Alba was progressing. She had nearly finished the seventh-grade math book that we gave all our students but her English obviously needed a lot of work. She did appear to be socializing well. In light of this assessment I concluded that she should certainly not go home for the summer and approval of the I-539 now became imperative.

On May 28 I returned to Guatemala.

Outlook for 2006

In 2006 we received our first five-figure contribution from a single donor. Our fund-raising banquets and other sources were yielding significant returns. We had nine candidates and host families eager to receive them. GSSG was on a roll.

Visas appointments for Byron (page 135), **Ericka** (135), **Lily** (139), **Rossy** (140), **Balbino** (149), **Flor** (149), **Pedro** (141), **Marvin** (149), **and Yohan** (132)

Maynor had not returned any tests for Willy and Alfonso (page 131); Alba and Hamilton were now in the States; Nancy would come later. Of the initial fourteen candidates, nine remained. Jorge made visa appointments for 7:30 A.M. on Tuesday, May 30, 2006. He had also engaged a twenty-six-passenger bus for the nine students, their parents, and us, for the four to five-hour trip to Guatemala City where we put up at Hotel Ajau, as usual, and prepped the candidates for their visa interviews.

The next morning, we waited in line outside the embassy for the usual hour and then another hour in the Consular Section. Finally our group was at the head of the line. I approached the waiting officer with the first student, Flor, as I recall, and her parents. Each student had a packet of nine documents. The documents were intended to overcome "the presumption in law that every visitor's visa applicant is an intending immigrant" (page 89), that is, that he or she intends to remain in the States illegally. The officer began to read the cover letter which I always provided and which explained the nature of GSSG's program and its history of ensuring that its clients returned to Guatemala. Before long the other officers also were interviewing one or another of our students. Soon the other officers left their stations and began conferring with Flor's officer, who occasionally asked me a question. After one such question, she forgot to turn off her microphone. I could not help but hear her say, "Of course, they will stay." She glanced at me, saw that the mic was on and turned it off. After more conferring, she motioned to me and said that the students would have to come back six days later, together with the six students who had been in the United States the year before—Raquel, Luis, Ana, Pablo, Rubén, and Jairo. I asked if the parents had to return as well. "No."

We left the embassy and reported our tale of woe to a worried Jorge. After breakfast at a McDonalds nearby, we returned to our hotel. The students and their parents gathered up their belongings, piled into the bus and left for home.

A Birthday Party for Blanca

Jorge and I set out for San Lucas, where we had intended to go after the visa interviews, to celebrate Blanca's birthday. On the way Jorge suggested that we buy some party things and a cake. Arriving at Blanca's house we greeted her family but Blanca was not yet home from school. So we blew up some balloons, got out some funny hats, and set out the gifts which her prospective adoptive families had sent along.

Blanca was not expecting us. When she opened the door, she jumped for joy and ran to embrace us. I gave her the gifts while Jorge distributed candy to the little kids. It was, I believe, Blanca's first, real birthday party.

The next day we returned to Jorge's modest home in Cobán. I kept track of the time, nine hours to travel two hundred and thirty-three miles.

Catastrophe

Six days later, on June 5, 2006, we returned to the embassy with our nine candidates and the six students from the year before, as directed. As soon as the first candidate and I approached the first available officer, the same woman who had caused us trouble the week before, she asked me if we had brought the six. I replied that we had. She told me that we should all sit down and that we would be called later. After another hour Luis was called. An officer, a man I had never seen before, asked him his name, etc., and then some questions about his experience attending classes in the United States (page 127), which he answered. Then Raquel, Pablo, and Jairo were called in succession; Ana and Rubén were not called. A short time later the same woman who had caused the problem six days earlier summoned me to the window and told me that not only would our current applicants not get visas but that the six could not return either and that our organization would never get any visas again because some of the six had taken classes and that was illegal. I explained that they were only visitors, had only sat in on some classes for a few weeks to see what school is like in the United States, had not registered, had received no grades and that we had we paid no tuition or fees. The officer was adamant and there was nothing to do but leave. It appeared that GSSG was dead, the only hope that any of our young clients had for a better life, dashed. Many were in tears.

We took the group to a nearby restaurant. While Jorge and the students ate their breakfast, I paced outside, trying to get my mind around what had just happened. When I thought it time to leave, I went inside. At the same time, we got a call from someone at the embassy who wanted to talk with Pedro's mother. The caller told her that Pedro had to return to the embassy to be fingerprinted. We returned to the embassy and I took Pedro inside. That same woman again now fingerprinted Pedro. I took the occasion to ask again about the denial, adding that I had written to the Consul General before taking the six the year before, that the officers then had read my letter and granted the visas. The woman replied that she had not been an officer the previous year and that last year's officers had made a mistake in granting the visas. I responded that the kids were being punished for someone else's mistake. She remained adamant, repeating acerbically that not only had the six broken the law and would not be permitted to return but also that the current candidates would not get their visas and that future applications would also be denied because trust had been broken. I asked how trust could be restored. She suggested that GSSG build a school in Guatemala and staff it with American teachers and then use AFS (page 37) for a year of high school. I observed that such was not the mission of our organization. Further discussion being obviously futile, Pedro and I left.

We all got back in the bus and set out. En route I asked Luis what questions the man interviewing him had asked. He replied, "'What was your favorite subject at that school in Wisconsin?' I told him, 'Math'." The next day I sent an email to the host families telling them the bad news. I also started a letter to Senator Elizabeth Dole, finished it the next day and emailed it to her. The day after that, I went home to North Carolina.

Nataly's Interview

In late July, 2006, I sent the required paperwork to get an F (Student) Visa for Nataly so that she could return for Phase 2, high school. We had not brought her back for Phase 2 in 2005 because she had been offered a scholarship to finish *diversificado* (grades 10, 11, and 12) in Guatemala. Given her family's circumstances, the possibility of employment in three more years beckoned. The scholarship was offered only once, on a now-or-never basis, so the family decided to take it. A year later, however, they had changed their mind. So we moved forward with the application for an F (Student) Visa, in spite of the catastrophe a month earlier, about which Nataly's family was fully aware. Jorge made the appointment for July 31, 2006. After the interview, I asked Nataly to write down what had happened.

Nataly: "Good morning." [in Spanish]

Officer: "Good morning. Let me have your documents." He looked the documents. He was silent; there was a pause of about 2 minutes. Then he asked me, "What kind of visa are you applying for?

Nataly: "Student visa."

Officer: "Did you bring some other documents?"

Nataly: "Yes, I did." I passed the letters to him. He read them and asked me,

Officer: "Do you speak English?"

Nataly: "Yes, I do."

Officer: "How did you meet your host family?"

Nataly: "At a pool party for adopted Guatemalan children."

Officer: [switching to English] "How long were you in the United States?"

Nataly: [in English] "One hundred days."

Officer: "Did you have exams?"

Nataly: "No I didn't." The officer gave the documents back to me and started to talk to a woman at another window. She was blond and thin. The officer said to me:

Officer: [switching back to Spanish] "Give me your papers again." He talked to the blond woman for about 2 minutes. She looked at the papers and snickered when she saw my passport. She told him not to give me the visa. They continued chatting and turned the microphone off twice. The male officer said to me,

Officer: "I'd believe that you were there two or three weeks but not three months. I don't trust you. I'm sorry I can't give you a visa now. I don't trust you." And the officer was constantly looking at his watch.

Nataly: I asked him why he could not give me a visa. He answered,

Officer: "I don't trust you. The visa is denied." My mother talked to him begging for another kind of reason for the visa denial. She emphasized our economic condition and the opportunity that they were giving me in offering me to study in a Catholic school. He said he was sorry and left.

In August Nataly's parents transferred title to their property to Nataly (see "binding ties," page 89); so I made an appointment for her to go back to the Embassy again on August 23. After lunch Jorge called to say that she was denied again.

After this second rejection, I emailed the other people involved. Kirby Lewis, Nataly's prospective host dad, called to suggest that I call Senator Burr (NC). Greg Phillips, Byron's host dad in WV called about contacting Senator Byrd. Jim White, a physician in Louisiana whom I had met in Guatemala, called to say that he had contacted Senator Vitter, who had been in touch with Senator Elizabeth Dole and that he, Senator Vitter, would call President Berger of Guatemala and ask him to contact the embassy. Soon I got a call from Tom Bonds, GSSG's president, asking me to approve a long email he was sending to Senator Dole's office. A few weeks later I received a reply, by email, from Senator Burr's office, saying only that there was nothing he could do.

I had written to Congressman David Price, from my district. In the next couple of years, I would meet him three times, the first with one of his financial supporters and a strong contributor to GSSG. On this and a subsequent meeting, I would have two of our girls with me, *in traje*, that is, wearing their native garb. Some months later I happened to run into Representative Price in the Harris Teeter (food market) parking lot. On all three occasions, he expressed much interest in GSSG and promised to provide assistance. That was the last I heard from him.

Later I found on the Internet a paper by the National Academy of Sciences lamenting the fact that even foreign scientists, responding to invitations from the NAS to participate in scientific conferences, are subject to the same capricious treatment as everyone else, and frequently denied visas.

In the fall I wrote to Condoleezza Rice, then Secretary of State, the President, members of Congress, and anyone else who I thought might have some influence. All of these initiatives, not only mine but those of others as well, proved in the end to avail nothing.

Alba in Phase 2, part 1 (for Alba in Phase 1, see page 156)

That fall, Kelli enrolled Alba in Hill-Murray High School in suburban Saint Paul. At the end of the year Alba went home to Guatemala for the summer. In accordance with the provisions of the I-539 (page 157), Jorge took her to the embassy for a new F Visa, only to be rebuffed.

Hamilton in Phase 2 (for Hamilton in Phase 1, see page 157)

At the end of the summer I took Hamilton to Zanesville where he would attend Bishop Rosecrans High while living with Chuck and Joan. He was quickly on the Honor Roll but in the spring got into trouble with his host family. At the end of the school year, I picked him up and took him back to Chapel Hill, because his return ticket specified RDU to GUA (see page 157). He would return.

Finding Host Families for 2007

In mid-October 2006, Jorge and I set out on a marathon automobile trip to visit all of the potential host families that we would need if we got visas in 2007 for the kids who had been denied visas in the catastrophe of 2006 (page 159). I had prepared a Power Point presentation and had GSSG's digital projector and screen with us. The first day we put on 566 miles and got a hotel room in Greensburg, IN. The next day we passed through Chicago and the Twin Cities on our way to St. Cloud, MN, where we spent the night. In the morning, we set out for Thief River Falls, ND, eighty miles from the Canadian border, where Denise and Beaver Nordhagen and their two delightful little girls greeted us warmly. The Nordhagens would have made a great host family but I had to tell them we could not place one child alone, so remote from others in the program. Denise would try to find another host family in the area. The following day we drove to Stillwater, near St. Paul, to visit Alba and the Conlows. We gave Alba her SLEP test (page 128). After visiting Hill-Murray High School, we left for central Wisconsin where my sister and brother, both GSSG supporters, lived. My sister and her husband had moved, after his retirement, to his parents' farm and built a new house. Jorge particularly enjoyed sleeping in the old farm house, eating pears picked from the tree, examining all the old farm equipment, and poking around in the woods. The next day we hopped over to Appleton and spent the day with my brother and his wife, who had given me the gift that took me to Guatemala in the first place (page 22).

Mary VanderVeen

A month or so earlier I had received a call from a woman who identified herself as Mary VanderVeen. She explained that she had an adopted Guatemalan child, as well as two biological teen-age boys. She had heard about GSSG online and wanted to host. I asked where she lived. "Alto, MI." "Could you find any other families in the area because having one student alone would be good neither for the student nor for us?" She thought she could.

We left my brother's home and headed for Alto. With the vastness of Lake Michigan standing between us and our destination we either had to take a ferry across the lake or drive through Chicago. Arriving in Milwaukee we found it was too late in the season for the ferry, so we took the Dan Ryan through Chicago to Gary and thence to Alto, arriving about 5:00. Getting to the VanderVeens' home, out of town and out in the woods, presented a challenge. But, as we got

Mary & her daughter, Maria

near, Jorge called Mary on his cell phone. She guided us from one turn to another until we finally heard her voice on the phone, "Oh, I see you! I see you!" The next morning sixteen families assembled in Mary's parents' large home next door, many of them with children, about forty people in all! Mary introduced us. We showed our PowerPoint presentation. A lot of people had questions, some for me, some for Jorge. For the most part, we had answers. Jorge and I passed out copies of our 'Host Family Application Form.' After the families left, we counted—thirteen had signed on!

Our procedures required us to visit the home of every potential host family; so between 11:00 A.M. and 11:00 P.M. the next day, Mary drove us around to visit all thirteen, to get acquainted, see the house, take pictures, and answer questions. Visas being so iffy, we put off our host-family orientation (page 100).

The next day we parted company with the VanderVeens and drove on to Fowlerville, about two hours distant. There, thanks to Beth, we gave a presentation at the United Brethren Church. We had lunch with Beth's family and then visited Justin and Jennifer who had asked us to stop. They also signed on. Thence, two days to get home.

Matt

In late November, still 2006, Matt Bernhard, a German physician whom I knew from his student days at UNC, flew in to celebrate Thanksgiving with my family, as he had in his student days, and to go with me to San Lucas (page 91) in December.

On Saturday, December 2, my son Pete took Matt and me to RDU at 4:00 A.M. We landed in Guatemala City about noon and found Jorge, who would join us. Arriving in San Lucas, we met Fr. Greg and, subsequently, Blanca and her uncle, Moisés. An employee of the parish told us that the parish would take us on an excursion across the

lake the next day. We put up at Hotel Iquitiú, as usual, which had a balcony with a view of the lake from the second floor. In the course of conversation with some Canadians who had rooms on the second floor, I mentioned that Moisés had to walk for two hours to get to work and two hours back every day and could use a bicycle. The Canadians chipped in. During the day I bought a bicycle. That evening we asked Moisés to come to the dining hall and gave him the bike. Illiterate and self-conscious, Moisés gave a little speech, to the plaudits of his benefactors.

Matt wanted to see how medical care is provided out in the villages. We visited Dr. Tun (page 91) at the hospital. With Jorge translating, Dr. Tun and Matt talked medicine for a while. Dr. Tun made arrangements for Jesus (page 92) and a driver to load the hospital's pickup with medical supplies and take us to a village called *San José*. With Jesus' help, we set up shop outside someone's home near the road and got into a routine. The women and children lined up in front of Jesus, who checked them in and sent them to Matt, Jorge standing to one side to translate. The same disease had, apparently, affected the entire village, for each woman repeated the same symptoms

to Jorge, who translated them into English for Matt, who then prescribed such-and-such a medication which Jorge dispensed. After a while, Jorge tired of the routine and, once the women had told him the symptoms, simply gave them the medication with the same instructions. Soon the women started calling him, "Doctor," which tickled him to no end. Matt and 'Dr. Jorge' saw about twenty-five patients in the morning and several more after lunch.

Back in Cobán we visited a friend of Jorge's whose son Hans, about six or seven, had been ill for a long time. Matt examined the boy and determined that he had trichinosis, a parasitic roundworm disease often affecting the brain. Unsure whether medication was available in Guatemala, Matt said he would send it from Germany. He continued to do for years. Hans in now a healthy young man. Trichinosis is fairly common in Guatemala[291] but, I am told, many victims go through life untreated.

On the twelfth we dropped Matt off in El Rancho, where he caught a bus for Puerto Barrios on his way to visit other friends in Latin America. The next day I flew home.

Visa Appointments for Arnoldo, Nataly, Byron, Ericka, and Flor

On my next trip to Guatemala, in December, 2006, we took Arnoldo, Nataly, Byron, Ericka, and Flor to the embassy for visa appointments. Arnoldo had graduated from *diversificado* in Guatemala and needed an F Visa to attend Wake Tech in Raleigh, NC. Nataly was applying for an F Visa for the third time. Byron, Ericka, and Flor were applying for a B Visa (their first). Arnoldo got his visa, the others did not because, the officer intoned, "They are students. Even though they do not register for classes, they are going to the United States to learn English and that is the same as going to school." He suggested that GSSG apply for recognition as a Sponsoring Organization, perhaps as an organization which brings Au Pairs to the U.S.; then they could even go to school. Back home I checked out the officer's suggestion and found several reasons why such a move could not serve our needs: a) Au Pairs have to be fluent in English before they come here, b) they have to be at least 18, c) they have to complete at least six credits of college courses while here, and d) they cannot return to the United States until at least two years have elapsed after their departure.

Before the New Year I received a message from Robin Freeman in the Virgin Islands saying she wanted to host. I told her we had to have more than one family. We kept in touch for a couple of years but nothing ever came to fruition.

---

[291] http://www.rightdiagnosis.com/t/trichinosis/stats-country.htm

Chapter XI, GSSG 2007

On the first of January, I received an email from Jean in Ohio. She had very much wanted to host but her husband had reservations. None the less, Jean's name was among those I had previously interviewed and to whom I had written about the catastrophe (page 159). In her email, Jean gave me a link to a U.S. State Department address which she had found on the Internet and which lead me to a series of other links ending in a page explaining how to obtain "Designation," together with an email address, which I pursued straightaway. The resultant page listed various categories of Designation without elaboration. I left a message.

   The next day I got a reply telling me that I had to apply for a login name and gave me a number to call. I called. A woman answered the phone and gave me a login name. I asked her if "Trainee" was the right Designation for a foreign student. She said she didn't know but gave me a number to call. I called, got a voice mail, and left a message. The next day a woman identifying herself as Sally Lawrence called me back. She said she did not think the Exchange Visa Designation was appropriate and speculated that the Visitor's Visa Designation might be right but, as she only dealt with questions about the Exchange Visa Designation, she would refer my inquiry to Abby Rupp, who was in charge of Visitor's Visa Designations and she called Abby right then and there, while I was still on the phone. Abby was not in but Sally left a message asking her to call me. The next day Abby called. I told her briefly about GSSG and that our students had been denied visas because the previous year some of them had sat in on some classes. She commented warmly on GSSG's program and asked me to send her the names of those students who had been denied visas. I did so.

Abby

On the twelfth Abby sent me an email saying that she had not forgotten about our issue. She had four questions, which I answered. On February 23 she replied:

Hi John,

Thank you for your patience. I verified with our legal folks that yes, the students in Phase 1 are permitted to do what you describe on B visas. The post[292] is aware of that as well. The difficulty, I think, will be in establishing that these children plan to return to Guatemala after their time in the U.S. Being able to show the officers a track record that the students who went in previous years have returned to Guatemala would be useful.

Best regards,

Abby

This positive development picked my psyche up off the floor. I called to make visa appointments for Byron, Ericka, Lily, Rossy, Flor, Pedro, and Marvin on March 7. (Meanwhile Yohan in ill health (page 132), had failed his grade, becoming thus ineligible GSSG's program.) I succeeded in making appointments for Byron and Ericka March 7 but, when I tried to make appointments for the others, I was told that the next available date would be March 15; I took it. On March 6, I flew

---

[292] By "post" she means the consular staff at the U.S. Embassy in Guatemala City.

back to Guatemala; Jorge met me at the airport. At Hotel Ajau, Byron and Ericka and their parents joined us. We prepped for their interviews the next day.

B Visitor's Visas for Byron and Ericka

Jorge had prepared the necessary papers and the next day we took Byron and Ericka and their parents back to the embassy for another try. We waited for three hours because most of the staff were on duty elsewhere, preparing for President Bush's arrival on the eleventh. Only one officer, whom I had never seen before, manned the windows. We presented our papers. After questioning me and the parents briefly, the officer granted Byron and Ericka their visas.

Catastrophe 2

On March 15, just a week later and buoyed by Byron's and Erick's success, we returned to the embassy with Lily, Rossy, Pedro, Flor, Marvin, and their parents. Abby Rupp had warned me, "The difficulty, I think, will be in establishing that these children plan to return to Guatemala after their time in the U.S. Being able to show the officers a track record that the students who went in previous years have returned to Guatemala would be useful." Accordingly, I had prepared and now presented a table with all of the data required to overcome that hurdle.

After what seemed an interminable wait, first Rossy and then Flor were called to the windows. The same woman who had rejected the applications in June recognized me and asked for all of the papers, disappeared with them, returned, and told me that we should all sit down and wait. In the end, each candidate was rejected on the grounds of Section 214(b) (page 89). We left the embassy about noon and checked out of our hotel. The students and their parents took busses home. Jorge and I drove. Back in my room, I drafted messages to the potential hosts, most of whom lived in Michigan.

Back home in Chapel Hill a few days later I wrote to Abby:

March 22, 2007

Dear Abby,

Thank you for talking with me today; a friendly voice from the State Department goes a long way to assuage frustration and restore confidence in our government's commitment to fairness. Here are the details of our recent experience in the embassy as you requested.

On March 7, I took Ericka and Byron to the embassy. The consulate was short-handed that day because much of the staff was engaged in preparing for President Bush's visit to Guatemala and only one officer was at the windows. The youngsters provided him with a sheaf of documents and, this time, a copy of your email to me about the ruling you obtained [sitting in on classes does not constitute a breach of Visitor's Visa restrictions]. The officer did not know about the ruling but, upon reading your final email to me, seemed satisfied. He also saw the table that, following your suggestion, I had prepared. He then granted the visas, adding that he did so specifically because we were sponsoring the children and that without our involvement they would not qualify.

On the 15th I took the remaining five candidates to the embassy. This time there were officers at all of the windows. The first student was called to the window of the same young woman who had denied our clients their visas in June. She recognized me, took the documents to the back of the room. Somewhat later, all were rejected and on grounds of Section 214(b).

As I mentioned to you on the phone, it seems significant that one officer is responsible for all the disruption resulting from these rejections. On all previous occasions [except 2006], the officers have granted the visas and, when I pointed out this fact to her, she only replied that they were all wrong. It seems that the officer is determined to shut us down. One has to wonder why. Could it be that, since the organization she had founded apparently failed, all others have to fail as well?

Sincerely,

Byron in Phase 1

Four days after this second catastrophe Jorge and I flew with Byron and Ericka to RDU. The next day we drove to West Virginia and delivered them to their host families, in Byron's case, Greg and Julie Phillips. After a couple of months, the Philips moved (new job, I believe). I picked Byron up and brought him home with me.

I knew that the public high schools in Chapel Hill and Raleigh would not take any of our students and our experience with Giovanni in Durham had not ended well. Our best hope would be a private high school and that meant Raleigh. So I asked Kelly and Kirby Lewis, who lived in Raleigh, if they would host Byron.

The next day Byron, Kelly, her teen-age daughter, and I visited St. Thomas More Academy. We met the Headmaster, Rod Ruiz. I explained GSSG's program. Rod gave us a tour. Kelly and her daughter were so taken with the school that not long after this visit, Kelly enrolled not only Byron but both her son and daughter as well. I asked Rod if he would admit Byron without tuition. He said he would take the matter to the Board. He did and the Board approved.

Ericka in Phase 1

On the same trip that Jorge and I delivered Byron to the Phillips, we also delivered Ericka to Lee and Debbie, also in West Virginia. We arrived late and hungry. Debbie soon wrestled up some victuals. As we sat around chatting, Lee asked Jorge to translate for him. He wanted to tell Ericka that this was her home now and they wanted her to feel at home. He continued, "If you get hungry in the middle of the night, you just get up and help yourself to anything you want. You don't need anyone's permission. This is your home." The next day Ericka had a dental appointment—thirteen cavities.

Learning How to Study

In May (still 2007), when Byron was living with the Phillips (see above), I made a trip to West Virginia to attend the annual picnic of a group of adoptive parents (not just those with Guatemalan children), at the invitation of the group's founder. Later, in the evening, Ericka, Byron, and I were together. In the course of conversation, I asked them why they knew so little math. They replied that in Guatemala the teachers all teach to the slowest students and everybody else has to wait until they get caught up; there are no tutors. I quickly saw that they had never been required to memorize the multiplication tables and could not easily do long division. So I wrote out the multiplication tables up to 12 and had them memorize them. They caught on easily. Then we took up long division. No problem; it was easy. Next I asked Ericka to show me what she had done in her copy of the math book we gave all of our students when they first came to the United States. I saw at once that she had not done any of the word problems and Byron acknowledged that he had not done them either. The cause turned out to be partly their insufficient English but mainly fear of 'word problems.' So we worked our way through the first set; they saw that the problems were in fact not all that difficult. Then they themselves solved several problems in the second set; they agreed they understood and did not need to do them all. The third set, the fourth set, and so on followed suit. In the end I asked them to go back to the beginning and finish all the problems, because they needed the exercise; they affirmed that they would, feeling confident now that they could. It was obvious that they had never before studied in the expectation that they would actually learn the material. They were visibly happy now at having learned how to study.

After the Phillips moved (see above) I brought Byron home to live with me. I wanted to teach him English grammar and he was eager to learn. He is still the only student in the program with an active knowledge of grammar, a skill that proved useful all through high school. We also spent a good deal of time sitting on my patio, just talking and enjoying life. His English improved dramatically.

Update on Blanca

Meanwhile, Jorge had kept working on Blanca's adoption. She could not be adopted without a legal guardian, for she was underage. Her father's name would not appear on a birth certificate, even if we could find one, because he never acknowledged paternity. To have her uncle, Moisés, made her legal guardian, we first needed evidence that her mother was dead. Jorge had tried to get a death certificate first at the records office in Guatemala City without success, then in Santa Lucia, where the birth certificates of children born in El Jabalí are kept, again without success.

The law provides that, in such a contingency, a social worker would visit the siblings of the deceased to verify his or her demise. Accordingly, in June of 2007, Jorge investigated, found that the nearest social worker lived across Lake Atitlán in Panajachel. But when he called her, she replied that she would not cross the lake; Blanca's aunt and uncle would have to come to her. Blanca's aunt in Jabalí (page 111) said she would come to San Lucas, if we paid her expenses, but would not cross the lake. Deftly plying a few subtle blandishments, Jorge cajoled the social worker into crossing the lake after all, on the condition that both Moisés and his sister would be there. On the appointed day the social worker appeared and shortly Moisés' sister arrived by bus, with one of her children. She got off the bus, announced that her child was sick, got back on the bus, and disappeared. The social worker left in a huff.

Back to the drawing board.

AYA

Not long after the first catastrophe (page 159), I visited the home of Jack and Jane, one of the families interested in adopting Blanca. At the time, Jack and Jane had nine children; they now have fourteen, twelve of them adopted and eight of those from Guatemala. Most of the adopted children had special needs. Jane told me that three of their Guatemalan children had tested HIV positive in Guatemala. U.S. Law stipulates that persons who are HIV positive cannot enter the United States but Jane had contacted J. McLane Layton, a pro-bono lobbyist in Washington, who secured a waiver for these three children. After bringing the kids home, Jane had them tested again. In all three cases the Guatemalan test results proved to be false. Jane suggested I contact McLane about our visa problem. I did so. She agreed to help us, pro bono.

After a good deal of investigating different options, McLane got an appointment for September 5, 2007, for Rick Conlow (page 156), chairman of GSSG's Board of Trustees and Alba's host dad, myself, and herself with June Kunsman, Visa Chief at the State Department, Jim Pritchett, the lead attorney in her office, and Stanley Colvin, Director of the Exchange Visitors Program. On the appointed day, McLane, Rick, and I walked from McLane's office to the State Department, successfully negotiated our way through layers of security, and were shown our way to the Visa office. June, Jim, and Stanley greeted us pleasantly. After chatting a bit, I explained that GSSG brings its impecunious young scholars to the United States for schooling because the abysmal state of education in Guatemala does not result in socioeconomic mobility and that we had been stymied by a single officer at the consulate in Guatemala (pages 159 and 166). June commented that the officers at the consulate do not have the authority to determine the outcome of future visa applications and asked me for the name of the officer in question. I replied that I did not know. I had not thought it my place to ask for names. I did tell her that the officer volunteered that she herself had started a charitable organization in Guatemala and advised me that, if I wanted to do some good, I should start a school. I wondered aloud why, if she had started a charitable organization in Guatemala, was she working in the consulate? I figured that June would connect the dots.

In the end, June told us that we could bring our students initially as Exchange Students for their first year with a J Visa and, after that, they would be eligible to return as Foreign Students with an F Visa. The J Visa is valid for twelve months and not one day longer. Usually Exchange Students come in the fall for nine months of schooling and then take a vacation for three months after school is over, often traveling around the country to see the sights until their visas expire. The law requires that all students, no matter what kind of visa they have, know English before coming here. Our students all had two years of English in *basico* (though in fact they had learned virtually nothing). Technically that would satisfy the law. June suggested that, if we reversed the order and brought our youngsters in June for three months of immersion first, then enrolled them in school for the fall, and sent them home when school ended in the spring, the State Department would be satisfied that the law had been met. Once back in Guatemala, they could then apply for an F Visa and return to finish high school and go on college. (The F Visa expires when a student has completed his or her program and is no longer in school.) June advised us that, although we were unlikely to encounter any problems getting J Visas for our young clients, we still had to satisfy the interviewing officers in Guatemala to get their F Visas. She mentioned no one in particular but I understood that the woman who had given us so much trouble might continue to do so. The officers have, by law, the final word. If denied a visa, you can't even go to court.

One problem remained, a requirement that a J-Visa holder cannot return to the United States as a student for two years. June told us that that requirement would be waived for our students.

When we had finished, we chatted for a few more minutes and I mentioned the ruling that Abby Rupp had obtained (page 165), namely, that sitting in on classes did not constitute a violation of the B Visitor's Visa limitations. With a smile, Jim, the attorney, commented, "I wonder who made that ruling?" They all chuckled.

In the afternoon, we met with Stanley to work out details of our new program. Since GSSG is not an exchange organization (we don't send any American students abroad), Stanley told us that he would arrange for us to partner with one. During our discussion, I commented that three months of immersion, June through August, would not result in sufficient fluency in English to start school in the fall. Stanley retorted, "It-will-be-enough."

Not long after we returned home I heard from Melanie French, Executive Director at Academic Year in America (AYA). She explained that Stanley had called her and that she had agreed with his suggestion that AYA and GSSG might work together to our mutual benefit. She told me that AYA has representatives, called 'Local Coordinators' (LCs) in most areas of the country, who supervise the placement, well-being, and progress of the Exchange Students locally, visit them monthly, and submit monthly reports on each student separately. I asked if I could become an AYA Local Coordinator in the Triangle of North Carolina. She replied that I would have to take a training course and pass a test. In due course, I did and became the AYA Local Coordinator in the Triangle (Raleigh, Durham, Chapel Hill). Melanie advised me that if we wanted to place a student in an area in which AYA had no Local Coordinator, it would be my responsibility to find someone who would be willing to go through the training, pass the test, visit the students monthly, and submit the monthly reports. We would also have to find the host families, who would have to fill out an AYA application, and that it would be our responsibility to make arrangements with the schools. (Schools, in turn, have to be approved by the State Department, that is, by Stanley's unit. Part of the approval process, in addition to filing the requisite forms and paying a fee of several thousand dollars, involves an on-site inspection.) Finally we would have to pay AYA's standard fee for each student. The amount of the fee differs from country to country, because it includes air fare. In the case of Guatemala, it would be $6000. The fee would cover air fare, health insurance, and the visa fee. We would still have to get the schools to apply for approval to receive foreign students, if they were not already approved. (Over the years, those that were not already approved successfully applied.)

The J (Exchange) Visa is good for only one year but many of our students, after their freshman year, would get an F (Student) Visa and return to the same school for their sophomore, junior, and senior years as well. We maintained three folders for each student (Phase 1, Phase 2, and Phase 3). The first included biological-family documents: the *Forma de datos familiars* ("Family Information Form"), birth certificate, parent's death certificate, if any, etc.), grade reports, Guatemalan health records, if any, etc. Phase 2 folders included documents related to their sophomore, junior, and senior years in high school. Phase 3 folders would contain documents related to the students' admission to and progress through college. We also maintained a folder for each host family, for each school, and for each financial supporter. Finally, we had multiple folders for GSSG itself— forms, records, plans, etc. In many cases, these folders were both paper and electronic. After several years I would end up with eight large file drawers full of paper, a hard drive, and an accounting program.

Guatemalans are short and my filing cabinets were five-drawers high. I bought a stool for Jorge, who also worked in my office when he was here.

Alba in Phase 2 (continued from page 161)

Alba worked hard, stayed far away from trouble, and graduated from Hill-Murray High School in 2010. It appears that *Alba is the first impoverished Guatemalan youth ever to graduate from an American high school after four years of study, while maintaining continuous residency in Guatemala.* (There have been thousands of Guatemalan youth graduating from high schools in the United States but, unlike Alba, they make their home here.)

Alba in Phase 3

Alba went on to get an AA degree at Century Community College in MN and is now a graduate student in Computer Engineering at Maríano Gálvez University in Guatemala.

Through it all, Alba inconspicuously served as a model of honesty, integrity, personality, character, intelligence, imagination, will, and leadership (page 99). She was the first president of the student organization, elected to the post by her peers.

Much of the credit for Alba's success in raising herself from extreme poverty to potential status in Guatemala's middle class goes to Rick and Kelli Conlow (page 128), without whose dedication and financial support Alba might never have left Guatemala.

Byron in Phases 2 and 3 (for Byron in Phase 1, see page 167)

Byron had come in March (2007) with a B Visitor's Visa. To matriculate in a school, he would need and F (Student) Visa. It was now June. So the Lewises (page 167) filed Form I-539 (see page 157) to get his status changed. July went by and no word from the State Department arrived. Shortly before school was to start, Kelly, Kirby, Byron, and I called the State Department. After working our way through a series of menus, a live voice greeted us. We explained our situation. The friendly voice said, "If you haven't received word that your application is rejected, wait!" We did and approval eventually came through.

St. Thomas More Academy is a private high school founded by Bob Luddy in 2002. In his freshman year Byron would read a number of the Greek and Roman classics: the *Iliad*, the *Odyssey*, three Greek plays (*Agamemnon, Oedipus Rex,* and *Antigone*), and selections from Ovid's *Metamorphoses*, all in English. He would also take four years of Latin and other subjects typical of private high schools in the U.S.

Byron graduated in 2011 (see below). Bill and Nancy Spencer had hosted Byron during his first three years and Paul and Loree Lam during his senior year.

GSSG did not have sufficient funds to enroll Byron in a senior college. Arnoldo had gone to Wake Tech and thrived. Byron studied there for a year and a half but then went home to take care of his mother, who was terminally ill. (In the Mayan culture, sons, not daughters, are obligated to care for their aging parents.)

Never idle, Byron took this opportunity to start a pet project, an English Academy for the poor in his area. Laying the groundwork for his academy, he enlisted Ericka (below), Tita Arrué (page 34), and Heydi (page 100) to read children's books in English to the pre-school children. The little ones, who had never seen a book before, were excited and easily understood because the words and the pictures tell the same story.

At the same time, Byron started a business. Historically, an enterprising *ladino* goes around to the villages, buying coffee beans from indigenous families who have just a few bushes (page 80) and, when he has enough, sells what he has collected to a coffee company. Byron, having raised sufficient start-up funds on the Internet, recently bought some storage equipment and organized the families in and around Chiallí to pool their production and sell it directly to a coffee company, thereby cutting out the middle man. The profits accrue to the growers.

Byron graduated at Wake Tech in the spring of 2017 with a major in business administration, supported by GSSG, and returned to Guatemala to manage his coffee business and his English Academy.

Ericka in Phases 2 and 3

As Byron needed to submit an I-539 (page 157), so did Ericka. Debbie filed the form and waited. The application was denied. So Debbie filed an appeal. Wheeling Central allowed Ericka to register, pending the outcome.

The appeal was denied in the fall. The denial allowed three options: 1) file a new application, 2) file a motion to reopen, and 3) go to the embassy in Guatemala and apply for an F Visa. We chose the third option and in December Ericka went home. Jorge took her to the embassy and she got her F visa.

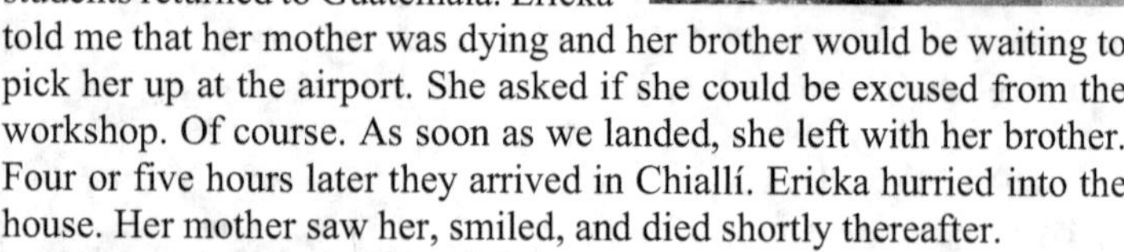

I had made plans for a three-day workshop in June of 2009 when all the students returned to Guatemala. Ericka told me that her mother was dying and her brother would be waiting to pick her up at the airport. She asked if she could be excused from the workshop. Of course. As soon as we landed, she left with her brother. Four or five hours later they arrived in Chiallí. Ericka hurried into the house. Her mother saw her, smiled, and died shortly thereafter.

After graduation in 2011, Ericka returned to Guatemala and worked as an English teacher for three years, not earning enough to support herself and her sister. In 2014 she rejoined GSSG and, still working, studied law at Rafael Landívar University, with support from GSSG, but has since had a child and left the program.

Nataly in Phase 2

We sent Nataly back to the embassy in November of 2007, her fourth try. Howard Betts (page 219) granted her the F (Student) Visa she had so long sought (pages 161 & 164). We bought her a ticket for December 5. Nataly started at Cardinal Gibbons High School in Raleigh as a second-semester freshman, Phase 2.

Nataly with Jessica

Initially Nataly lived with Greg and Amy Grazen and their daughter, Jessica, also a student at Cardinal Gibbons. When she returned as a sophomore she lived with Tara Mylenski, seen below with Nataly, for two years and then with Jim and Cathy Morrissey and their daughter, Abby, also a student at Cardinal Gibbons, during her senior year.

Nataly graduated in the spring of 2011. GSSG's program included support only through college at the undergraduate level. But in Guatemala there are no colleges. Those who can afford to do so go directly from high school to graduate or professional school (page 84). In light of her mother's desperate need, Nataly told me that she intended to withdraw from

Nataly with Abby and Cathy

from GSSG and attend medical school in Guatemala.

Nataly knew at the outset how difficult would be the path she had chosen. She would work to support herself and her mother and go to medical school full-time, and she knew that GSSG did not provide support for graduate studies.

Nataly was surely one of our most promising students. Her engaging personality, her dedication to learning, her fluency in three languages, the poverty of her youth, and her first-hand knowledge of suffering will endow her ministrations with compassion.

Chapter XII, 2008

We had not recruited any new students since the catastrophe in June of 2006 (page 141). Byron and Ericka had gotten visas in March of 2007. That left five still hanging—Lily, Rossy, Flor, Pedro, and Marvin. Marvin had not shown up for the visa appointments in 2007 but had not been disqualified thereby. Yohan (132) had failed his grade and was disqualified. Thanks to Mary Vanderveen (page 162), we had an abundance of potential host families.

I flew to Michigan in January, taking with me multiple copies of the AYA (page 149) brochure and its application form as well as our own. Mary had arranged that the next day I would conduct a combined AYA/GSSG Orientation at Caledonia High School. Most of the families that Jorge and I had interviewed in 2006 came, together with two couples who were new. I explained the new policies and procedures. The families filled out the required forms. Mary and I subsequently visited the homes of the new families. We were satisfied that we had enough hosts to accommodate our needs even if we recruited more students.

El Estor

In February I flew back to Guatemala. Jorge and I drove directly to a town called *El Estor* where Paco, a friend of Jorge's and a grade-school teacher, had made arrangements for us to recruit

El Estor lies comfortably on the shore of Lake Izabal (see map on page 84), the largest lake in Guatemala, enchanting in its vast serenity of it turquoise waters. Some years ago, the lake had been stocked with tilapia, which flourished, and more than once we enjoyed the fare and the view at a lakeside restaurant just off to the left in the photo above, the waves whispering to our wonder.

In the morning Paco, Jorge, and I visited the first middle school on Paco's list, one that impressed neither Jorge nor me. At the next interview we met Br. Francisco Perez,[293] principal at *de La Salle*. He had done graduate work in Spain, understood GSSG's program and its implications immediately, and spoke enthusiastically about the possibilities it presented for his students. In the afternoon, we visited *Aj Awinel Central* and later that same day *Liceo Vocacional Coactemalan*, both principals expressing considerable interest in our program. In the evening we met Cesar Marroquin, principal at the *Insituto por Cooperativa*. An evening class was in session. In a lengthy speech Mr. Marroquin explained that the Guatemalan Constitution requires that education be free, a puzzling gesture since the schools in El Estor, including his, are private.

We had given each of the five principals our base-line requirements (page 114). The principals collectively recommended some thirty to forty applicants. Br. Francisco offered us the use of a large, open-air room furnished with tables and chairs (see below). At a designated time the following day, all of the applicants began assembling for our Group Interview. Jorge made the introductory remarks but we did not have the students rise, tell us their names, etc. and speak one by one but rather got right to the Aptitude, Intelligence, and Math tests. In consequence of scoring these tests, we had a list of fourteen applicants whose homes we wished to visit. Of these, ten would remain after the Family and Personal Interviews.

---

[293] Br. Francisco is a member of an order of celibate Catholic laymen dedicated to teaching, called the 'Christian Brothers.'

Mario

Mario was raised by his great grandmother. His mother had left to find work in a larger town, three months after giving birth to Mario.

Great grandmother's house (at right) is made of *tabiche*, the product that results from cutting the trunk of a *tabiche* tree in half lengthwise. The house has a dirt floor and a tin roof. The beds, of course, have no mattresses. The kitchen (below) has no appliances.

Mario's mother had not seen her son in years. When Jorge located her, she told him that she

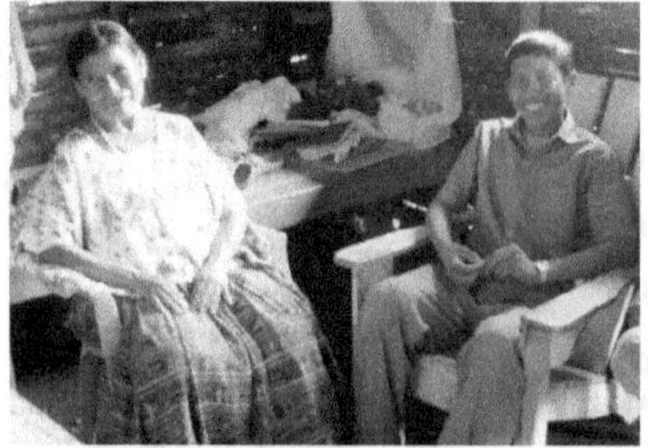

had recently married and that her husband had legally adopted Mario, all of which was news to Mario.

José

José Manuel Ich Choc lived with his parents and siblings in this *tañil* (a plant similar to sugarcane) house with a dirt floor and a tin roof. The entire structure consists of two bedrooms, one for the parents and one for Jose and his siblings. Inside, newspapers cover the walls to provide privacy and keep the sun out.

Jose's father, Adolfo, a teacher in *primaría*, had graduated from *magisterio* (page 85). His mother attended school through fifth grade. One day a fellow teacher asked Adolfo if he would co-sign a loan. He agreed and shortly thereafter the woman disappeared with the money. The bank garnisheed 100% of his wages and took his home, so that the family had to move into the grandparent's home (above).

José would be among those who came to the United States in 2008 but, through no fault of his own, would have to sit out 2009 and return in 2010.

On September 27, 2009, his father, Adolfo Ich Chamán, a community leader well known for his outspoken defense of indigenous rights, arrived unarmed at the scene of a large demonstration in response to the latest eviction of indigenous families from their land by a mining company (page 82). As he was helping some children who had taken refuge in a ditch, Adolfo was recognized by the company's security force, who surrounded him, beat him, and attacked him with machetes, nearly cutting off one arm. The head of the security force then shot him in the head. José witnessed the killing of his father and ran to try to pick him up. As he did so, his father's severed arm dangled by its skin.

At each of our workshops, the students practiced giving speeches. At a workshop in 2010, José told his story. Never was a speech more effective (see Appendix D, Workshops; 2012 December Workshop; Saturday 12/29 [page 252], 04:45–05.45).

José's mother, with international legal assistance, filed suit in Canadian court (see page 82).

Luis Coc (*lwEESS COHK*[294])

Luis is the fifth eldest of eight children, all born at home. His father died in 2001. Because the family does not own a parcel (page 39) Luis' mother tried to provide for her family by selling tortillas on the street, as do so many Mayan women. As a result, Luis' family often went hungry.

The family home (right), like many homes in El Estor, is constructed of *tañil*. It consists of one large, sparsely furnished, room. The beds have no mattresses, there is no electricity, and an open fire serves as a stove.

Luis, a pleasant, but quiet, lad, like virtually all of the indigenous in the El Estor, speaks Q'eqchí' and Spanish natively. At a workshop in 2012, during a meeting of the student organization, the president resigned in frustration that he could not get his fellow students to act on a motion to give their organization a name. The room fell into a stubborn silence, no one knowing what to do. Without a president, no one was in charge. Luis finally spoke up, saying that the group had to elect a new president. He called for nominations and a new president was elected. To my surprise, no one nominated Luis.

Abner

Abner, a *ladino*, lived with his father and a younger brother and sister. Two older brothers were in school elsewhere. The house, like José's and Luis', is made of *tañil*. There are three bedrooms and no other rooms. The three residents participate in cooking in grandmother's kitchen nearby.

Abner's father works as a high-school teacher of math, physics, and accounting (subjects he himself learned in high school), earning Q1,500 ($187) a month, enough for food but little else. Abner's mother lives in Guatemala City but comes to El Estor about twice a year.

---

[294] Like *Coke*, short for *Coca Cola*.

Ana Macz (*AH-nah MAHX*)

Ana's parents have nine children, the first six born at home. The family speaks Q'eqchí' in the house because Ana's mother knows very little Spanish. Her father works for the town of El Estor as a garbage collector.

Ana's house actually consists of three small, one-room structures. One, the dormitory, has a concrete floor. The family eats beans and tortillas three times a day. They seldom have chicken, meat, fish, or even fruit but they also seldom go hungry because Ana's father owns a parcel (page 39). Ana was student-body president in her small school at the time of our meeting. She says she likes dancing and that she dances well. She lists punctuality as one of her good qualities and she did very well on our tests.

Fritman

Fritman's parents had, in addition to Fritman, a younger son and a thirteen-year-old daughter. Though Fritman's parents are both indigenous, they speak different Mayan languages, his father, Caq'chiquel and his mother, Q'eqchí'. The ordinary language of the household, therefore, is Spanish. None the less, Fritman is natively trilingual. His father has never been to school and does not own a parcel; his mother had one year of schooling.

The family's one-room, rented home, measuring about 12' by 15', is part of a row of several homes (see above), each separated from its neighbors by a *tañil* wall. Fritman's home has one light bulb. Only the parents' bed has a mattress. There is no dresser, closet, or cabinet of any kind. One bathroom serves nine families as does the community stove (left).

Fritman's father earns between $1.33 and $5 as a day laborer; sometimes he has no work. The rent is $26.66 a month. Despite grinding poverty, Fritman excelled in school.

Sandra Coc (*SAHN-druh COHK*)

Always happy, energetic, and active, Sandra simply radiates life. She was born in 1992, the fourth eldest of eight children, all born at home.

Sandra's father never attended school and works as a guard keeping people from disposing of their garbage on public property. Her mother had minimal schooling. Q'eqchí' is Sandra's mother tongue but, like the others who live in town, she also speaks Spanish.

A day or two after the selection process was complete, Jorge went back to Sandra's house for some reason and discovered that the family did not have enough money for the *boleto de ornato*, something like a town beautification tax, amounting to a couple of dollars. Jorge paid the tax. As it would turn out, most of the families had not paid the tax and Jorge ended up paying for all of them.

Sandra's father does not have a parcel. No doubt, somewhere along the line, his family did but after Justo Rufino Barrios seized Mayan communal land (page 42), many had to do without.

Griselda

Griselda's parents separated years ago but live in the same town and, I was told, hate each other. Griselda's stepmother treated her and her sister so badly that they ran away to find their birth mother, but their stepfather, who is not Mayan, began abusing them.

Stepfather's home is also made of *tabiche*, has a concrete floor, one window and two doors, and is partially divided into two rooms by a plastic curtain. The smaller of the two rooms, entered through the front door, contains a wooden table, a home-made bench, and two plastic chairs.

The other room, the bedroom, has a triple bunk bed, without mattresses, for the children, and the parents' bed.

Griselda's stepfather makes a living buying their night's catch from fishermen on the lake and selling it in villages up in the mountains.

Remarkably, Griselda seems to be perennially happy, if a bit coquettish.

Griselda told me that her stepfather had been shot in the head by thieves and that the bullet is still there. I expressed my doubt; she insisted.

Villages

From the outset, I had one objective, the poorest of the poor. Joe Berninger (page 22) had said that, in simplest terms, three socioeconomic classes comprised Guatemalan society—the Maya, the *ladinos*, and the aristocracy and that they lived in villages, towns, and cities respectively. I had been to some villages—Pasmalón (page 36), Chiallí (page 110), and others. Although these villages are poor, they are within walking distance of a town and profit economically from that proximity. They are still poor but not the poorest of the poor.

During the Group Interview, the students always had to fill out our *Forma de Datos Familiares* ("Family Information Form"), including their home address. When we set about reading these documents after the Group Interview in El Estor we noticed that three of the girls had given as

their addresses the names of three remote villages. We asked them about this exhilarating anomaly. They confirmed that their homes were indeed in those villages but that their fathers had sent them to town for middle school because schooling in the villages only went as far as sixth grade, adding that their fathers worked on a plantation and that the expenses of going to school in El Estor (tuition, room, board, books, school supplies, uniforms) consumed their *entire* annual income, but each owned a parcel and their families did not starve.

I could hardly believe this serendipitous revelation. Here were three girls in grade nine, as required by U.S. Law for Exchange Visas, whose homes were in villages so far from town that they could not commute and their families survived because they owned parcels—the poorest of the poor. We had never been able to recruit in villages because schooling there went only as far as sixth grade and we were seeking ninth graders. Suddenly we had a game changer.

A day or two later, the mayor of El Estor sent the town's four-wheel drive pickup and a driver to take us to these three villages. Jorge jumped in front. The girls jumped in back and I jumped in with them. After an hour or two, we arrived at Nueva Esperanza, Judith's village. (See the map on page 84.)

Judith

Nueva Ezperanza has no streets. The thirty or forty board homes are arranged in no obvious order, each apparently situated in such a way as to avoid the dirt floor turning to mud in a rain storm. Chickens wander in and out. A pig roots in the yard. Various species of vegetation, including coconut palm, adorn the hill sides. The arrival of a pick-up this day brought dozens of children, none of whom had ever been out of the village, scampering to see what was going on. That an American, six-feet tall and very white, got out of the pickup left them wide-eyed with wonder and expectation.

The two buildings pictured below are Judith's home: the farther structure, the bedroom; the nearer, the kitchen/dining room/living room combination. Two home-made lanterns provided such

light as illuminated Judith's windowless home. In the bedroom, boards and ham-mocks served as beds.

Judith's parents had nine children at the time (2008); they now (2016) have twelve. Her father had three years of schooling, her mother none.

Judith's family greeted our party with a friendly "*chan-xa-quil*."

The language of instruction in the village primary school is, of course, Q'eqchí'. For this reason, Judith did

not learn Spanish, indeed had not even heard it spoken, until she started seventh grade in El Estor.

Judith's grandfather had had to buy a parcel for Judith's father because her uncle had inherited the family parcel.

The women in Judith's family get up at four in the morning to make enough tortillas for the day and in time for the men to take lunch along when they leave at 6:00 for the two-hour trek to the ba-nana plantation.

Judith talked non-stop as she gave us a tour so we could take pictures, which is also my preferred method of conducting the personal interview, because the students do not know they are being interviewed. A gaggle of children gamboled behind us, understanding not a word of our conversation in Spanish.

Judith's radiant personality would make her our poster child for years to come.

Marley

Marley lives in Socelá, about an hour's walk from Judith's village. Their mothers are sisters.

Marley's home also consists of two buildings, both made of boards. The larger (at right) includes the kitchen, dining room, and living room. In the bedroom, a smaller building, bare boards served as beds. Nary so much as a light bulb anywhere.

Both villages are set well back from the

main road; the side roads leading to them, undeveloped and, without a four-wheel drive, impassable. Even at that, our four-wheel drive met its match in the turn below.

Marley is the eldest of seven children, all born at home. Her

beautiful smile, the manifestation of her guileless character and gentle disposition, never disappears.

Marley's father has two years of schooling; her mother, three.

Years later our group (seven other Americans had joined me) would walk from Socelá to Nueva Esperanza, the girls having arranged for their brothers to carry our bags. A river, only calf-deep but concealing a bed of slippery stones, dared us venture across. We rolled up our pant legs and emerged on the far bank, I last of all, to loud applause. Clambering up the steep embankment carved out by the river on the far side, we vaulted over the edge into a grazing herd of cattle.

The candidates got their passports and their AYA (page 169) Exchange Visas without a hitch. On the fourth of June, we all assembled at a retreat house near San Cristóbal that Jorge had engaged for a three-day orientation/workshop. Before we left, we took a picture.

Left to right, standing: (child), **Heidi**, **Jorge**, **Lily**, **Marley**, **Rossy**, **Judith** (hidden behind Rossy and Flor), **Ana** (behind Flor)**, Flor**, **Mario**, **Griselda**, me, **Sandra**, **José**, **Pedro**, **Marvin**, **Fritman**, **Abner**, **Nancy** and, kneeling: **Arnoldo** (who was no longer in GSSG but had joined us at my request to share with the students his experience at Wake Tech; at this point he was the only GSSG student who had any college experience), **Luis Coc, Luis Fernández, and Pablo**.

We were all on the same plane as far as Houston. From there Jorge took the Michigan group to Grand Rapids. I took the rest to North Carolina.

Reception in Michigan (Mary VanderVeen, page 162, in front facing the camera)

Reception in North Carolina

Marley in Phases 1, 2, and 3 (for Marley at Home, see page 184)

Mary, Scott, their children, and Mary's parents fell in love with Marley right off and she quickly became part of the family. Initially knowing no English, she spoke little, quietly observing details of her new environment, smiling always. Over the summer she became sufficiently fluent in English to attend Caledonia High School in the fall, where most of our Michigan students studied during their first year.

As the years went by, Marley became one of GSSG's most reliable young adults. I was particularly impressed by the leadership role she played two or three

years later, when I asked the Q'eqchí' speakers to translate our parental orientation into Q'eqchí'. She took charge, tactfully managing those avoiding the job.

Marley graduated from Caledonia High in 2012 (see the photo on the next page) and enrolled at Grand Rapids Community College, while holding two jobs and driving herself back and forth to school. In the summer she works full time and goes home during the Christmas break.

Marley works hard at her studies, enjoys her classes, and is doing well. The VanderVeens, with whom she has lived since she first arrived, love her sense of humor, her bright and positive outlook.

When she finished her program at Grand Rapids Community College, Marley enrolled at Davenport University, majoring in international business.

On arrival in 2008 Lily lived with Bill and Judy Doran and their daughter while attending Caledonia High.

In 2010 Lily transferred to Grand Rapids Christian

and was invited to live with John and Loreen Postma and family (left).

In 2012 Lily graduated from Grand Rapids Christian (see below) and is now in pre-med at Cornerstone U, while living with Jim and Connie Brooks and their two sons.

Lily also has two jobs and drives herself back and forth to school. She is on track to graduate in 2017 but will have to return to Guatemala for medical school, where costs are significantly lower than here.

Abner Lily Rossy Marley

Rossy in Phases 1, 2, and 3 (for Rossy at home, see page 140)

Don and Beth Porter, their daughter, and their two dogs, warmly welcomed Rossy into their home. During her four years of high school Rossy attended Byron Center High, Caledonia High, and Grand Rapids Christian, where she graduated in 2012 (see above).

Rossy now lives with the VanderVeens and studied at Cornerstone University, where she held many positions of leadership, had four different jobs on campus, and still managed to get all A's. She graduated in Social Work in 2016.

Abner in Phases 1 and 2
(for Abner at Home, see page 179)

Abner lived for two years with Russ and Diane Curtis and their son and daughter (right), subsequently moving in with the Postmas (above), all the while attending Grand Rapids Christian High School.

After graduation in 2012, Abner did not return for college but found a job in El Estor. Abner and Tita Caal (page 204) are now married and have a child.

Mario in Phase 1 (for Mario at Home, see page 177)

Mario, generally one of the most affable teen I ever met, lived with Chris and Lori Pieri and their children, while attending Caledonia High but had trouble getting home on time and sometimes locked himself in his room, refusing to talk with anyone. Twice I had to reduce him to tears but the results were short lived. After two years in the States Mario returned to El Estor. For all the trouble he caused, Mario and the Pieris still correspond amicably. He is now married, has a child and has become a responsible adult. Affable as ever, he sometimes writes me.

Mario speaks English well and got a job as translator for the mining company (page 81). Once the company sent him to the Ukraine on business.

José in Phase 1 (for José at Home, see page 178)

In 2008 Steve and Tracey Mulanix and their children hosted José while he attended Caledonia High along with the others (see above and below). He got on well with the family and did well in school but Steve and Tracey could not host again in 2009 and, as I had no other home for him, he sat out a year. During that year, his father was murdered (see page 178).

Luis Coc in Phase 1 (for Luis at Home, see page 178)

In his freshman year, Luis lived with Kent and Kristin Mattson and their three young boys, while attending Caledonia High.

Some health issues intervened, requiring Luis to return to Guatemala after the spring semester. Like José, he sat out the next year.

Ana Macz in Phases 1 and 2
(for Ana at Home, see page 180)

Brad and Michele Worthington and their children happily welcomed Ana to live with them on their cattle farm in Iowa. Ana attended Pella Christian High School and shared a bedroom with one of the Worthington girls but, unfortunately, did not get along well with anyone.

When Ana was a junior, Michelle contacted me and offered to host all of the students in the Twin Cities and in Michigan for a get-together between Christmas and New Year's Day. The families arranged transportation and on Sunday, December 27, drove their guests to the Worthingtons' farm. All of the boys, including Brad and Michele's boys, bunked at Brad's parents' home next door; the girls all slept at the Worthington's.

Michele wrote: "That night the students had pizza for supper and caught up with each other. Monday morning we loaded up a large van and headed to Des Moines for shopping and a movie. We returned home where the girls prepared a spaghetti supper for 22 people. It was a huge pan of noodles! That night we played card games, video games, and watched a movie.

"Tuesday we had an early lunch and then went to the pond for an ambitious game of ice hockey and ice soccer. Don't underestimate the ability of Guatemalan students on the ice. . . .

"Tuesday night we went to the school gym for a dodge ball tournament. We were amazed at the students' indoor soccer skills. To even the playing field we then played scooter soccer.

"Wednesday we had pancakes all together and then loaded everyone up for the long trip back to Minnesota and Michigan. We had a wonderful time hosting the students. They are truly an amazing group of kids."

Ana, however, had been a poor hostess, often going off by herself to sulk. Much as she regretted having been unable to bring Ana around, Michelle could not keep her for her senior year. A new GSSG board member, Louise LeGrand, offered to take Ana but by mid-year, she too had had enough and I had no choice but to send Ana home, just a few months short of graduation, the only GSSG student to complete three years of high school and then not graduate.

Back in Guatemala Ana completed *diversificado* (grades 10, 11, and 12) and is now studying law at the Cobán campus of San Carlos University, with GSSG support.

Fritman in Phase 1 (for Fritman at Home, see page 180)

Randy and Wendy and their two teenagers were happy to welcome Fritman into their home for the 2008–2009 school year, while he attended Caledonia High. Like most of the others, he came back for his sophomore year but accessed objectionable Internet sites and had to be sent home.

Flor in Phase 1 (for Flor at Home, see page 149)

Like the others, Flor lived with a loving family that bent over backwards to make her feel welcome while she, like most of the others in Michigan, attended Caledonia High. Flor began the year as a freshman but school officials soon advanced her to sophomore status. None the less, Flor got into trouble. She acknowledged the problem and returned to Guatemala.

Somewhat later Flor wrote to me saying that she was married and expecting a child.

Marvin in Phase 1 (for Marvin at Home, see page 149)

Bruce and Darci Muller rejoiced at the prospect of sharing their family life with a youngster in need but, from the start, Marvin was morose and uncooperative. Bruce and Darci tried everything to raise his spirits, including hosting a pool party for all the GSSG kids in Michigan, all to no avail.

Marvin alone in the group spoke Achí. He had not known any of the other students until we gathered for the orientation in San Cristóbal (page 137). His parents had just broken up and his father had taken a new woman.

Feeling very much alone, all Marvin ever said was, "I want to go home." The day after the pool party I bought him a ticket. The Mullers took him to the airport. Jorge made sure he got home.

Luis Fernández in Phase 2 (for Luis at Home, see page 117; for Phase 1, see page 123)

Luis attended a variety of schools while living with different families. In his junior year, Joe and Carolyn Barnes and their three boys, provided a perfect environment for him.

In the spring Luis developed a relationship that led him to staying out late. One rainy night, getting home past his deadline and probably driving too fast, he crashed the Barnes' car. Carolyn and Joe, ever understanding, were willing to absorb the cost and give him another chance. Meanwhile some compromising photos surfaced on the Internet. Soon thereafter the school year ended. We had a workshop in Guatemala City that gave me an opportunity to talk with Luis face-to-face. Unsatisfied, I removed his name from the roster. My successor would reverse that decision.

Luis is now studying medicine at Rafael Landívar University with GSSG support.

Griselda in Phases 1 and 2 (for Griselda at Home, see page 181)

Jim and Carolyn Heuser happily took Griselda in and registered her at the Emerson Waldorf School, a private institution not far from their home. The non-traditional curriculum at Emerson Waldorf fit Griselda's personality to a T. The next year Jim and Carolyn would also take in Sandra (page 181).

Griselda's and Sandra's birthdays are two weeks

apart and every year Jim and Carolyn put on a birthday party. Griselda loved parties.

Griselda graduated from Emerson Waldorf in 2012 and returned to El Estor. She is now married and has a child. She is not in school.

Issues

From the beginning, it had been my custom to visit all of the students in the United States at least twice a year. The large group in Michigan had arrived in June, 2008. In August I flew to Grand Rapids and rented a car. In the course of conversation with Mary (page 162), I learned that Sandra (see next page) and Judith (page 183) were spending the week at a lake-front cottage with Patrick and Kelli Mulry, a family I did not know but Mary knew well. She gave me directions.

Sandra's host parents had attended the second host-family orientation (at Caledonia High School, page 175). Mary and I had visited their mobile home the next day. Sandra would share a bedroom with the couple's teen-age daughter.

After I arrived at the lake-front cottage and some pleasant chit-chat, I took Sandra aside to talk with her privately, as I did with all of the students whenever I visited. I asked her how things were going. She replied that everything was fine. Then I asked her how things were really going. She burst into tears. "Nobody talks to me, not even the girl." "What else?" Ordinarily about the first thing that host moms did, especially for the girls, was buy them some clothes. (GSSG provided a clothing allowance.) Sandra replied to my "What else" by saying that the only clothes she had were what she had arrived with and that her only bra had a broken strap.

Next I took Judith aside and asked the same questions. In response to my "What else," it turned out that she was deathly afraid of her host mom. One day, she told me, when Sandra was visiting, the woman had overheard them talking Q'eqchí'. She laced them out, yelling that they were here to learn English and that if she ever heard them talking Q'eqchí' again. . . .

Returning to the group around the picnic table, I asked the owners of the cottage if I could speak with them privately. We left the table. I explained that Sandra needed a new home and asked if they would take her in. As it turned out, they had, since meeting Sandra, been eager to host her. We went back to the picnic table and told the girls. Sandra jumped for joy and the whole troop went dancing around the premises, laughing and singing.

The next day Sandra would go home with her new family.

Next I visited Judith's host parents. After some difficult conversation, they agreed that Judith should move. I bought her a ticket to RDU on the same flight as my own. We flew to North Carolina the next day. School was just getting underway.

Sandra Coc in Phases 1, 2, and 3 (for Sandra at Home, see page 181)

Patrick and Kelli Mulry hosted Sandra while she attended Caledonia High. Late in the year Kelli developed back trouble and asked me to find another home for Sandra. Griselda (see above) had pleaded with me to find another girl to live with her, so I asked Jim and Carolyn (see above) if they would take in Sandra as well.

When Sandra returned in the fall, she joined Griselda at Emerson Waldorf. Sandra has an artistic bent and would sometimes dance just for her own enjoyment, oblivious of the world around her, but her absorption in the mystical quality of her moves attracted attention.

Sandra's artistry extended to painting as well, as you can see in this original at left.

The girls had never owned a robe, so one day I took them shopping. Excitedly they tried on all the different

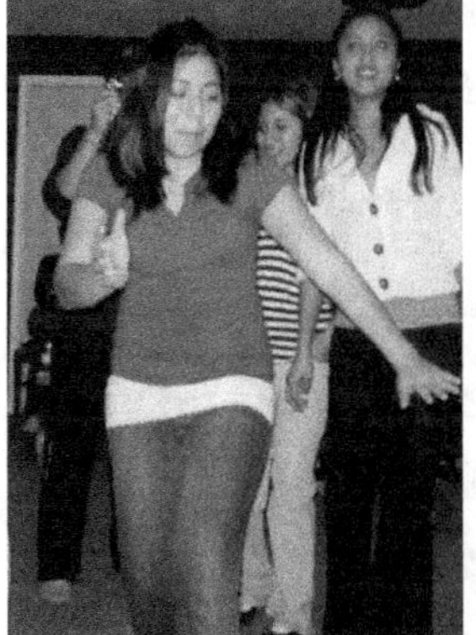

styles, eventually made their selections, and wore them virtually night and day for a week.

Sandra also graduated from Emerson Waldorf in the spring of 2012 and is now, with GSSG's support, studying Social and Legal Sciences at Mariano Galvez University in El Estor. Career choices are limited in Guatemala and Sandra's manifest talents may not be fully appreciated there.

Judith in Phases 1, 2, and 3 (for Judith at Home, see page 183)

When Judith and I arrived on our flight from Michigan, I had no host family for her and she was not registered at any school. The next day, we went to St. Thomas More Academy, where five of our students were already enrolled (Byron, Pablo, Nancy, Tita, and Pedro). I explained Judith's situation to the new headmaster. He replied that school had already started. I appealed to the Gospel. He said he would have to take the matter up with Mr. Luddy (page 172). While Judith and I waited in my car, I told her that she might have to return to Guatemala. She burst out sobbing, "I don't want to go back to Guatemala." Her family's ticket out of pov-

erty was slipping through her fingers. I made no reply, an eloquence in our mutual silence. In the end, she was admitted. Dave and Paige Van Lenten provided a loving and caring environment perfectly suited to Judith's personality.

Earlier I mentioned a pool party I had attended at the home of Jon and Linda Coleman (page 99). The Colemans had an adopted Guatemalan daughter, Chloe, then in her early teens. The child died a year or two later. In early December, 2008, Linda contacted me, saying that she and Jon wanted to do something in memory of their daughter and would I come to visit them. When I arrived, they told me more of the tragic circumstances related to their daughter's death and asked if I might suggest an appropriate memorial. In reply, I proposed that they sponsor Judith and offered to bring her to meet them. A few days later, I returned with Judith. The Colemans, with remarkable generosity, became her sole financial sponsors and paid all of her bills until she graduated from high school four years later (see below).

Early in June, 2009, I fell in conversation with Joe and Rosemary Czejkowski about hosting Judith. Moving in with the Czejkowskis meant changing schools; their children attended Cardinal Gibbons (page 173). In 2007 we had gotten Nataly (page 173) into Gibbons but when I tried again, none of my arguments availed for aught. I men-

tioned this to Rosemary and Joe. They made no comment but later informed me that Judith had been admitted. She graduated in 2012 and now has a job in Guatemala. She takes one

The Czejkowski

Judith with the Colemans

class on Saturdays with some GSSG support.

A few years ago, the management at the banana plantation, where the men in Judith's and Marley's villages worked, fired all the men from the girls' villages and hired replacements from elsewhere. I do not know why. Some of the men were subsequently rehired. Others found employment in other places, but Judith's father remained unemployed for several years and now has a menial job in El Estor, returning home on the weekends.

At the invitation of the Czejkowskis, Judith returned for a visit over the Christmas holidays in 2016 and I had an opportunity to take her out to lunch. She is working to help support her large family and pursuing a licentiate in social work part-time.

Heidi in Phases 1 and 2 (for Heidi at Home, see page 142)

Sharon

When Heidi arrived in the United States in June of 2008, she was taken in first by Donna and Robert McElcar but, through no one's fault, we had to find another home for her. Sharon and Tim Wiwel and their children filled the bill and enrolled her in St. Thomas More Academy.

During the ensuing four years, every Christmas Heidi made tamales as she had made them in Guatemala, on an open fire, for a well-attended holiday bash hosted by Sharon and Tim. The McElcars were delighted to come every year.

Heidi graduated at St. Thomas More Academy in 2012 and returned to Guatemala. With GSSG support, she is now in her final year of nurses' training. Heidi recently married and has a child. Sharon and her family, who went to her wedding, remain close.

Nancy   Pablo   Heidi

Nancy in Phase 1, 2, and 3 (for Nancy at Home, see page 140)

Nancy also graduated at St. Thomas More Academy in 2012 (see above).

When she first arrived here, Nancy lived with Paulo and Lea Chiquito, their two sons, and a daughter.

Within a few days of her arrival, the ever thoughtful Chiquitos celebrated Nancy's birthday. Pedro, Jorge, Heidi, Griselda, and I joined in the fun.

Paulo has a Masters Degree in Computer Science and serviced GSSG's electronic equipment, replacing elements as needed, all gratis, making life easier for everyone.

In her junior and senior years, Nancy lived with Dawn and Rob Atkinson and their children (see below), happy as ever.

After graduating from St. Thomas More Academy, Nancy matriculated at Durham Tech Community College, living once again with the Chiquitos. She studied for two years at Durham Tech and expected to complete her AA degree in another semester but, because of a serious shortfall in GSSG's resources, returned to Guatemala and is now a student at Rafael Landívar University pursuing a licentiate (page 85) in forensic criminology, with some GSSG support.

Nancy will always be remembered for her gentle manner, respect for others, and quiet friendliness. GSSG's mission was to create a leadership corps in Guatemala. Nancy leads by example.

Pablo in Phases 2 & 3 (for Pablo at Home, see page 118; in Phase 1, page 124)

Pablo had been living with the Tom and Michelle Bonds since he first came to the United States in 2004, attending St. Thomas More Academy (page 172). He, like the others, could not return in 2006 and 2007 because we could not get visas (see page 159). He did return in 2008 and graduated in 2012 (page 196).

Tom's parents live in New York State and know Pablo well. They also know the past president of Sienna College in Loudonville and arranged for Pablo to meet him. He encouraged Pablo to apply for admission and for financial aid. He did, was accepted, and received aid in the form of a job on campus. Though a diligent student, Pablo found the combination of work and study too much. GSSG did not have the funds to pay his tuition and Pablo had little choice but to continue his studies at San Carlos University in Guatemala, where he is pursuing a licentiate in engineering, with support from GSSG.

Pedro in Phases 1, 2, and 3 (for Pedro at Home, see page 141)

Pedro also attended St. Thomas More Academy for four years. During the first two, he lived with Bob and Pam Cochrane and their children. During his junior and senior years, he lived with Dick and Alma Hammer.

Following what I judged to be a display of arrogant racism at a workshop in 2012, I removed Pedro's name from GSSG's roster. My successor reinstated him. Pedro graduated from St. Thomas More Academy in 2012 and matriculated at Waynesburg University in PA, graduating there in 2016 with a major in business administration, his tuition and other expenses covered by generous supporters. He

now has a one-year internship at the University of Pittsburgh. Whether he will return to Guatemala is unknown.

If you have trouble keeping all of the students straight, turn to Appendix H, Snapshots of the Students' Fortunes, page 261.

Fund-Raising

Several times a year we had fund-raisers in communities where our students were living. The attraction at our most successful event took place in Chapel Hill in the winter of 2011–12. The students and I had agreed that they would put on a Mayan skit. Griselda (page 193) took over as director. The girls dressed up in *traje* (page 15); the boys put on shorts and war paint. Together they performed a folk dance in which a wounded warrior is cured by *Xmucané* (page 16). The audience gave them a standing ovation, clapping and cheering.

Most of these events were held at either St. Thomas More Church or the Newman Catholic Student Center Parish in Chapel Hill, without charge, thanks to the support of Fr. Scott McCue at the former and Msgr. John Wall at the latter. Much of the planning, preparation, and implementation was performed by Carolyn Heuser, Nora Howes, and Priscilla Otto.

Chapter XIII, GSSG 2009

The New Year began with seventeen Guatemalan youth already in various U.S. high schools. With the wind at our backs we would recruit fourteen new freshmen for 2009.

Meanwhile, one of our supporters in Chapel Hill, Berkeley Grimball, asked if I could recommend a venue for a trip he wanted to take with his two sons, someplace different. I took the bait, glad to have their company. We flew to Guatemala in March. Our driver would be Luis Pop (*lwEESS POHP*), a friend of Jorge's and mine who speaks both Spanish and Q'eqchí'.

We drove first to El Rancho in the *departamento* of El Progreso (see map on page 84). Desert-like conditions prevail there. Hence the residents are builders and *ladino*, not farmers like the Maya.

Teresa (teh-RAY-suh)

Because there is no public high school in El Rancho, ninth grade would have been Teresa's last. Her mother supplements her husband's meager income by selling tamales door to door. One day she and Teresa stopped at the local school during recess to sell tamales to the students. Jorge, thinking she had come for the group interview, ushered the bewildered Teresa inside.

In Teresa's crowded little *bajareque* house (page 107) you see the stove below an open window; well, actually, a hole in the wall.

The street in front of Teresa's house (right) illustrates the neighborhood.

Brandon

Brandon, lived on the same street as Teresa. He alone, among our applicants, knew the multiplication tables but other considerations prevented his participation in GSSG's program. His mother's stove (right) is made of cement.

Walter

Walter lived with his grandmother and his mother, who cleans houses (but few families are wealthy enough to hire a cleaning lady). Their house had three and a half walls. Walter told us that he had no father.

Ladinos are typically thought of as middle class but in fact many are as poor as the Maya. Walter's situation was extreme but by no means exceptional.

Rafael

Rafael hails from Chiquimula, almost as dry as El Progreso; hence most of the residents are *ladino*. Rafael's father had abandoned the family many years earlier and his mother attempted to feed her children by cleaning houses. Rafael slept all of his life on the bed you see at right but, taciturn by nature, made no comment when I took the picture.

Rafael was in ninth grade in a public school but would not have been able to advance further because there are no public high schools in Chiquimula.

Yesenia

Yesenia, the fifth of ten children and Rafael's cousin, also hails from Chiquimula, Not surprisingly, the older part of Yesenia's home is made of adobe; a newer part, cement block.

When we met Yesenia, she was at first a bit nervous but, when I commented, she acknowledged with a little laugh that, yes, she was shy. That little laugh was all she needed to relax, even bantering with me a little about my Spanish. That beautiful smile endears her to everyone.

Wilmer

Wilmer, also *ladino*, the middle child of seven, lived in an exceedingly remote area. A road (at right) took us within a long-and-difficult walking distance of his house.

Abandoning the car and with Wilmer as our guide, we proceeded up a creek bed for a couple of miles until his residence came

into view.

Wilmer's father's face was deeply scarred because he had once been attacked by thieves who slashed both sides of his head and his right hand with a machete.

Elmer

Elmer, who is Mayan, was eleven when his father died of alcoholism; his mother died soon thereafter. The lad lived with an uncle and a grandfather, in the grandfather's house (below). There were no working appliances and almost no furniture in the

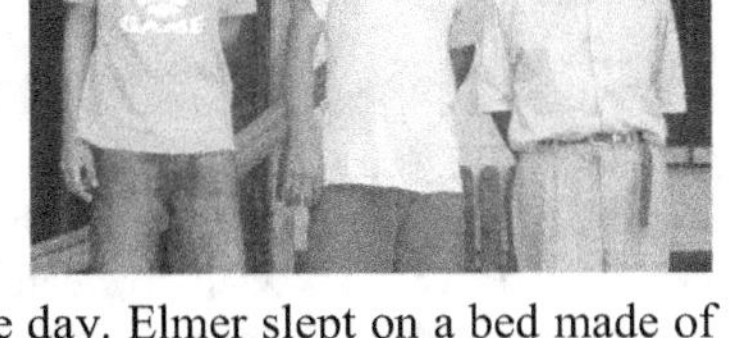

house. On coming home from school, Elmer would go to a neighbor for

his only meal of the day. Elmer slept on a bed made of boards with a piece of cardboard for a mattress.

For a Mayan teen in his circumstances, Elmer was unusually conscious of environmental issues. Though he appeared to be malnourished, he scored highest of all the applicants on our math test.

Having completed our recruiting in the desert-like conditions noted above, the Grimballs, Luis, and I journeyed to El Estor (see map on page 84), where Jorge and I had recruited José, Luis Coc, Ana, Abner, Mario, Sandra Coc, Griselda, and Fritman, along with Marley and Judith from their villages, the year before, only to have them turned away at the embassy (page 84). We were now returning to recruit more students.

Mirian

Mirian's family (nine children, six living at home) inhabits a small house made of rough boards with a tin roof and no electricity (below). Her parents are functionally illiterate. One of her five brothers has been severely crippled since birth, unable to speak or walk. He had never seen a physician and the family had no idea what was the matter with him or what, if anything, could be done about it, until an American physician traveling with us in 2009, Kim Swain de Pop, examined him. Her diagnosis—  cerebral palsy. Nothing could be done. Despite incredible poverty, smiles reign.

Mirian once had a tooth that hurt so badly she tried to pull it herself but only managed to break it off. I learned later that the tooth had abscessed. We would have it extracted in the U.S. Subsequently an American physician told me that without treatment she would eventually have died, in great pain.

Mirian's father works when he  can find work. Her mother cooks on an open fire, outside (right). Mirian had one pair of shoes, for school, which her mother wore on weekends when she went to clean houses. The rest of the family wore plastic sandals or went barefoot.

When we first met her, Mirian was in ninth grade. Her gaunt frame betrayed serious malnutrition. She would gain wait in the United States.

Niceh (*NEE-say*)

Niceh, born in Puerto Barrios (see map on page 84), has no memory of her Q'eqchí-speaking mother, who abandoned her family when Niceh was four. Niceh's father, very likely a descendant of African slaves brought to the Caribbean in the eighteenth century, would often disappear for weeks at a time, leave his four children on their own.

When she was six, Niceh and two of her brothers wended their way to their maternal grandparents' home in El Estor, where they would sleep on boards and cook in a kitchen outside (left). Although she consistently earned the best grades in class, the other students, including the Maya, treated Niceh with contempt, because she was black.

Niceh badly needed orthodontics.

Tita

Tita's father had abandonned his family but continued to live in El Estor and would sometimes see his children. Tita's mother worked as a nurse's aid, when she could find work.

Tita, her mother and two sisters, *ladinas*, lived in the Habitat house pictured above, their monthly payments seriously in arrears. They had a gas hot plate but could not afford gas and so cooked on an open fire behind the house.

They did have running water, but it was polluted. A concrete sink behind the house served as washing machine and dishwasher. They had electricity but no appliances.

Carlos

Carlos, the fifth of nine children, lived with his parents, two unmarried siblings, his grandmother, a married sister, her husband and their children, bringing the total to eleven. All except the grandmother were bilingual; both parents, illiterate.

Carlos' home consisted of two structures, made of *tañil*. The structure you see above is the main house, which includes the kitchen (left). Grandmother's house was smaller. When Carlos was home, he slept in grandmother's house and looked after her. Ironically Carlos home had no electricity though it is located within yards of a power station.

Rolan

Rolan, the second of four boys, had recently moved with his family to the house you see below, that had no appliances, though his father, who worked as a day laborer, had a cell phone. Both of Ro-

lan's' parents, but not the boys, are illiterate.

Rolan was born in a village called *El Bongo*, not far from Judith's home. His family move to El Estor, apparently in search of work, must have been recent, for his father was still building the house when we arrived for the Family Interview.

Johnny

Johnny has an engaging personality and scored well on our tests but he had problems not initially revealed in our interviews, as we will see in a moment.

Sandra Bolom (SAHN-drah)

Sandra hails from Socelá, Marley's village (page 184). As was the case with Marley and Judith, Sandra would get up at 4:00 A.M. to help her mother make enough tortillas for the day and later, when necessary, go with her

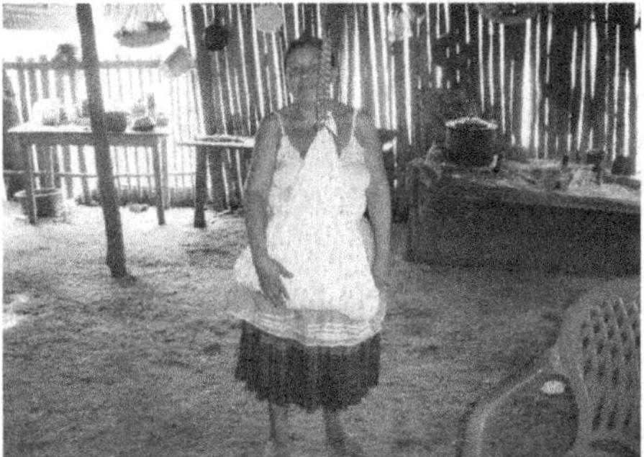

mother to do their laundry in the river.

Sandra's father, like all the men in the village, worked on the banana plantation and, like them, was fired (page 196). He found work as a security guard far away and seldom gets to see his family.

Sandra's house would fall down three years after the picture above was taken.

Trekking our way from Marley's to Sandra's house

Sandra's neighborhood in Socelá

Having completed our mission, the Grimballs, Luis, and I drove to Peten (map on page 84) to tour the Mayan ruins at Tikal, one of the most famous archaeological sites in the Americas (page 11), while many similar sites in Guatemala remain to be excavated.

Flores, the capital of the *departamento*, is located on an island in the largest lake in Peten. The island was discovered by the Spanish in 1524 but its fierce inhabitants successfully resisted the invaders until 1697 when the Kingdom of Guatemala sent an expedition to subdue the island, the last military engagement of the Spanish Conquest. But the conquest, here as elsewhere in Guatemala, proved to be incomplete, for the natives, living in isolated pockets, retained their indigenous culture and speak Itzá.

At Tikal we spent the better part of the day viewing the ruins, put up at a hotel in Flores, where there is an airport, and then went our separate ways, the Grimballs to fly home, Luis and I to Guatemala City.

Luis Pop (lwEESS POHP)

In the morning, Luis and I drove to San Lucas to find out why the lawyer I had engaged to do Blanca's legal work had not produced the documents we needed. Luis, who had worked in a lawyer's office, suspected foul play as soon as my lawyer started talking. We left and hired a different lawyer. After visiting Blanca, we returned to Guatemala City.

Luis' specialty in *diversificado* (page 85) had been accounting, though he candidly admitted he knew nothing about the subject. He had taken the required courses but had nearly failed the first and gotten a 60 in the other, a grade given to failing students just to get rid of them, he said. I surmised that the problem had been systemic rather than personal.

I wanted Luis to keep GSSG's books in Guatemala, for Jorge was frequently overwhelmed. With this objective in mind I had invited Luis to spend some time in my home, a.k.a., GSSG's office, to learn our bookkeeping routine. He had trouble getting a visa but eventually prevailed. I bought him a plane ticket.

After he arrived, I set Luis to completing the AYA applications (page 169) for the students who would come in 2009, for it was a large group and required a lot of paperwork.

Visas and Departure, 2009

In May Jorge notified me that the visa appointments were scheduled for June 1 and 2. He took the students to the embassy and they got their AYA (Exchange) Visas (page 169) without difficulty.

On June 6, the students who were already in the United States, twenty in all, flew to Guatemala, as did I. Jorge had arranged for a bus to pick us up at the airport and take us to a hotel, where the new recruits were already waiting for us. For the next three days we had a highly productive workshop in Guatemala City.

After the workshop, those who had already been to the United State went home for the summer. The new students would fly to different airports in the U.S. the next day. In the photo below, the 2009 cohort marvel at seeing an airplane up close for the first time.

Back row: Walter, Brandon, Tita, Yesenia, Mirian, Niceh, Jorge
Front row: Wilmer, Carlos, Rolan, Johnny, Elmer, Rafael

On June 9 we all flew together as far as Houston. From there Juanita, a friend of Jorge's, flew with Tita and Walter to Philadelphia. Jorge took Brandon, Tita, Yesenia, Wilmer, Carlos, Rolan, Johnny, and Elmer to MSP. I flew with Niceh and Rafael to RDU. Mirian had to fly alone but we arranged for a Continental agent at JFK to meet her as she disembarked and make sure she found her host mom. She subsequently told me all went well.

Finding the right combination of host families and schools sometimes proved to be difficult. In this case, we had not yet been able to make arrangements for Teresa and Sandra Bolom and after the workshop, instead of flying, they went home to await developments, that did in fact materialize a few weeks later. Jorge, who was back in Guatemala by then, took the girls to the airport, where he met a bilingual nun who said she would help the girls find the right gate in Houston. When they arrived at MSP in the evening, Sandra's host mom was there to pick her up. Carolyn Barnes (page 192) and Kim Swain de Pop (who speaks Spanish) were also there, got Teresa on the right bus and told her where to get off. Her host mom would be waiting for her. Everything worked out as planned.

If you have trouble keeping all of the students straight, turn to Appendix H, Snapshots of the Students' Fortunes, page 261.

Wilmer in Phase 1 (for Wilmer at home, see page 202)

When Wilmer arrived in Minneapolis, he was taken in by Jake and Cyril and their two adopted Guatemalan children.

During the summer, Jake and Cyril went all out to make Wilmer feel at home but after school started he became reclusive and morose. Cyril moved him to a private school, to no effect. They sought medical help—the diagnosis, depression. Initially Wilmer responded well to medication but over time and despite Jake and Cyril's best efforts his behavior became intolerable and in March I had no choice but to send him home.

Brandon in Phase 1 (for Brandon at home, see page 200)

Michael and Jennifer and their offspring happily received Brandon into their suburban home in the Twin Cities. A few days later I got a call from Michael saying that Brandon had kissed their eight-year-old daughter. Unsure of AYA regulations in cases like this, I called Melanie (page 170). She confirmed that he had to go. Jennifer agreed to let him stay one more day. I changed the return date on his ticket. Jennifer took him to the airport. Jorge contacted his mother. She picked him up at the airport in Guatemala City.

Elmer in Phase 1 (for Elmer at home, see page 202)

When I visited them, Jeff and Londa Somers rejoiced at the prospect of hosting Elmer but from the beginning he made it clear that he was unhappy, becoming despondent and unsociable. Coming home from school, he would lock himself in his room without even responding to Londa's greeting and refusing to come out even to eat. I called Elmer and gave him instructions on how he was to behave, what words he was to say in the morning, after dinner, when going to bed, etc., that he was to apologize for his bad behavior and offer to help with the dishes, taking care of the little ones, etc. I ended the call by telling him that I would call Londa in two days to see if he was behaving. I did. He was.

Jorge and I made our rounds in October. We first went to Elmer's school and found him searching environmental issues on the Internet (left); he was genuinely happy. ("Elmer is unusually conscious about environmental issues and also scored highest ever on our math test" [page 202]). Later we had dinner with the family. School had changed everything. Elmer was happy as a canary now and his family equally pleased to have him.

In March Jeff called to say that Elmer was accessing inappropriate sites on the Internet. A day or two later, Jeff reported that Elmer had apologized and they wanted him to stay.

Johnny in Phase 1 (for Johnny at home, see page 206)

Johnny was to live with Jean and Mark Deming and their children but soon got into trouble. First, he wanted his ears pierced. A little later he stole the money from their children's piggy banks. Johnny was given several more 'chances' but on December 3 Jean called to say that, with brazen disregard for the rules, he had used her laptop and broken it. When it was repaired, she found that he had used it to access a porn site and broke it in a fruitless attempt to conceal his offense.

Jorge called Johnny's dad, who worked in Guatemala City. The next day he picked up his son at the airport.

Niceh in Phases 1, 2, and 3 (for Niceh at home, see page 204)

When Niceh arrived, Randy and Amy Poteat and their children were overjoyed to meet her. In the fall Niceh started school at St. Thomas More Academy (page 172). At the end of the year, Randy told me that Any was expecting and asked me to find a new home for Niceh. I asked Bill Tschida, principal at Holy Trinity in Winsted, MN, to take her in.

In her senior year Niceh lived again with Randy and Amy and graduated from North Raleigh Christian Academy in 2013.

Niceh needed braces. In April of 2013, Dr. Charles Lohr, my dentist, recommended a course of treatment. He himself pulled four of her teeth and Dr. Uday Reebye, a dental surgeon, removed her four wisdom teeth. A month later Dr. J. Dempsey Smith applied braces. All three of these professionals provided their services pro-bono. Removal of the braces in July of 2015 revealed the beautiful smile (right) that typifies her spirit.

Niceh after orthodontics

In the fall of 2013, Niceh started Phase 3 at Durham Tech but the following year transferred to Wake Tech in Raleigh, while living with Tom and Marilyn Goehl (my successors at the helm of GSSG). In December, 2015, Niceh received her A.S. degree in civil engineering. Opting to forego the graduation ceremony, she returned to Guatemala and is now a full-time student in civil engineering at Mesoamericana University in Quetzaltenango, thanks to the generosity of Amy's parents.

Yesenia in Phases 1, 2, and 3 (for Yesenia at home, see page 201)

Denis and Kellie Anderson, who had an adopted Guatemalan son, joyfully picked Ye-senia up at the airport. For her birthday in August, they threw a party, in-viting all our students in the area and their families, as well as Jorge and me, to join them.

But Yesenia was inordinately shy and, try as Kellie and Denis might, they could not get her to talk. Eventually she came to live with the Pelzels (page 218), who were also hosting Blanca, and graduated in 2013. Yesenia is now studying psychology at the Chiquimula campus of San Carlos University, with support from GSSG.

Rafael in Phases 1, 2, and 3 (for Rafael at home, see page 201)

Rafael, Yesenia's cousin, was first hosted by Mick and David in Raleigh and in the fall registered at St. Thomas More Academy, where he would remain for four years. Six months after Rafael's arrival, Mick and David moved to Oregon. Sam and Princess took him in for the balance of the year.

At Byron's graduation (page 172) I met Tom and Debbie Lindsey, who readily agreed to host Rafael and did so until he graduated in 2013.

Rafael, like nearly all of our students, became in effect a member of his host family.

Today Rafael, though still laconic as a Greek bronze, has matured into a confident young man, self-directed and self-reliant. He is now studying computer engineering at the Chiquimula campus of San Carlos University. Like most of our students, he receives support from his host family and from GSSG.

The Lindseys' son Josh is a member of GSSG's Board of Trustees and maintains GSSG's Web site.

Mirian in Phases 1 and 2 (for Mirian at home, see page 203)

Mirian lived with different families over the years and attended various schools. In 2013 she graduated at Holy Trinity High School in MN.

Mirian is now studying judicial and social science at Rafael Landívar University, with help from GSSG.

Tita in Phases 1 and 2 (for Tita at home, see page 204)

In her freshman year, Tita lived with Dan and Lisa and their daughter in Trenton, NJ, took an ESL course over the summer and in the fall enrolled at a local high school. Tita's English improved rapidly and she seemed happy there.

As a sophomore, junior, and senior, Tita lived with Joe and Lily and their young, adopted Guatemalan son in the Twin Cities, while attending a private high school there. Tita struggled academically but refused to ask her teachers for help, although Lily and Joe repeatedly counseled her and went with her to the parent-teacher conferences. I too attempted to enkindle some enthusiasm for academe, without success.

Nevertheless, Tita graduated in 2013 and returned to Guatemala. She and Abner (page 189) are now married and have a child. She is not currently studying.

Walter in Phases 1, 2, and 3 (for Walter at home, see page 201)

Neil and Rosemary Jacob, having learned about GSSG, contacted me and expressed a desire to participate. The couple, married later in life, had no children and when Walter arrived in 2009, he filled a void in their family structure. Rosemary is a school teacher and Neil, in retirement, has two businesses, as a locksmith and knife sharpener.

Not long after Walter arrived, Neil and Rosemary discovered that he had something embedded in one eye. He recalled that he had once been hit in the face with a soccer ball and thought the problem might have resulted from that incident. Neil and Rosemary took him to a specialist who removed the object surgically.

In the fall Walter matriculated at Bishop McDevitt High School and remained there until he graduated in 2013. The pastor at the church introduced Walter to the parish early on and made known the circumstances in which he, his mother, and grandmother lived in Guatemala, in that house with three-and-a-half walls (page 201). One of the parishioners came forward and asked if Walter's home in Guatemala might be replaced for $5000. I passed the question on to Jorge who contacted the father that Walter had told us did not exist. The man, it turned out, was a bricklayer and offered to build a small, two-bedroom, cement block house for $5000. When he finished, he had enough left over to buy some furniture. Jorge and I visited the new house one day. It is small but attractively built and has both electricity and running water.

Walter graduated from high school and is now attending Montgomery County Community College with GSSG support.

Teresa in Phase 1 (for Teresa at home, see page 200)

Linda Coles had heard about GSSG and wanted to host. She and her husband Ron lived in rural Wisconsin and the local school had never sought approval to enroll exchange students. Linda got right on it.

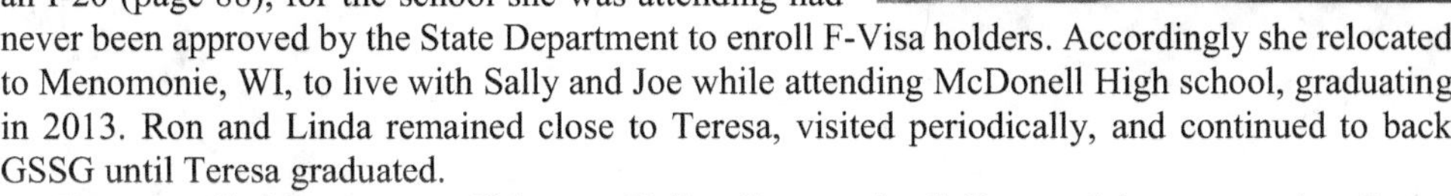

In September Teresa started at Cornell High. Early in October, Jorge and I made our rounds. When we visited Teresa, she was happy, well adjusted, and had no complaints.

Teresa would have to move to another school to get an I-20 (page 88), for the school she was attending had never been approved by the State Department to enroll F-Visa holders. Accordingly she relocated to Menomonie, WI, to live with Sally and Joe while attending McDonell High school, graduating in 2013. Ron and Linda remained close to Teresa, visited periodically, and continued to back GSSG until Teresa graduated.

Teresa studied for a year at Chippewa Valley Community College and then returned to Guatemala. She is now studying to be a professional translator at Galileo University in Guatemala City.

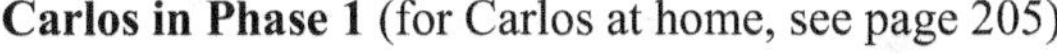

Carlos in Phase 1 (for Carlos at home, see page 205)

Juan and Evelyn had heard about GSSG and wanted to host. I visited, explained AYA, etc. and in June delivered Carlos.

At some point Carlos became ill. Juan and Evelyn took him to a local physician who referred the case to the Mayo Clinic. Carlos had a heart condition which, if not treated, could have cost him his life.

Carlos got into trouble trying to lie his way out of something and early in 2010 I had to relocate him to live with John and Julene. Though I never learned the details, Carlos got into trouble again. (For Carlos in Phases 2 and 3, see page 217.)

Reception in Minnesota

Sandra Bolom in Phases 1, 2, and 3 (for Sandra at home, see page 206)

When Sarah heard from Denis and Kellie that they were hosting Yesenia (page 201), she wanted to host as well. We met, followed the usual procedures, and got Sandra into a high school in the Twin Cities.

On Christmas Day, Sarah gave Sandra her cell phone and told her to go to her room and call her folks. She did. In January Sarah got a phone bill for $1,500. She admitted she should have checked on Sandra but insisted that I send her home at once and pay the phone bill. I had no place to put Sandra, so I sent her home but refused to pay the phone bill.

Sandra returned in 2010 to live with Susan and her teen-aged daughter, Elena (left). She graduated from Friendship Christian School in 2013 and is now studying business administration at Mariano Galvez University in Guatemala, with support from GSSG.

Rolan in Phases 1, 2, and 3 (for Rolan at home, see page 205)

In his freshman year, Rolan lived with Jim and Rose and their children in the Twin Cities but had trouble with one of their sons, how much of it attributable to Rolan I do not know.

When he came back for his sophomore, junior, and senior years, we placed him with Brian and Marisa Harrell and their daughters in Raleigh. Brian attended St. Thomas More Academy but did not do well there and in his senior year transferred to Friendship Christian School, where he graduated with honors in 2013. Rolan is now studying agricultural engineering at the Cobán campus of the San Carlos University, with support from GSSG.

On the invitation of Brian and Marisa, Rolan returned for a visit over Christmas in 2016 and I had an opportunity to talk with him. He is pursuing a licentiate in agronomy and doing well.

Raquel in Phases 2 and 3 (for Raquel at home, see page 117)

Because Raquel was only in fifth grade when she came for the six months of Phase 1 in 2005 (page 125), she was not eligible to return until 2009. By that time she had forgotten much of her English. No problem! Phase 1 was now a year long, the year with AYA (page 169).

On her return, Raquel first attended Liberty Classical Academy in St. Paul, MN, where she was at the head of her class—no kidding, the head of her class! Subsequently she transferred to St. Paul Preparatory School, a location more convenient for Kim Swain de Pop, her host mom. Kim knew about Raquel because of her close friendship with Carolyn, who was hosting Raquel's brother, Luis (page 192).

Raquel is a straight-A student and is as thoughtful and considerate as the day I met her (see page 117). Because of circumstances at home in Guatemala, she stayed here for the summer. Raquel is now a sophomore at Inver Hills Community College in St. Paul, MN. She recently married an American, the only one to do so. Kim is the physician who diagnosed Mirian's brother (page 203). She is also a member of GSSG's Board of

Raquel with Kim, Luis, and family

Trustees. Her husband, Luis Pop, the bewhiskered gent behind Raquel in the photo below, drove the Grimballs and me around Guatemala in 2009 (page 200).

Chapter XIV, GSSG 2010

Teresa had lived for two years with Ron and Linda (page 214). Linda recommended that Teresa transfer for her junior and senior years to Bishop McDonell High School in Menomonie, WI, where her niece, Cathy, worked in the office, and suggested that Cathy might host Teresa. The next time I made my rounds, I stopped at the school and met the principal, Br. Roger Betzold, a Christian

Brother (page 176, note), who not only admitted Teresa but Luis Coc (page 190), José (190) , and Carlos (214) as well, together with a break in tuition. I stopped in to see Cathy, who agreed that she would be glad to host Teresa and told me to visit Tom and Andrea Anderson (left) who might also be interested in hosting. Indeed they were; they would take all three boys.

In 2013 Teresa, Carlos, Luis, and José graduated from Bishop McDonell.

Teresa attended Chippewa Valley Community College for a year and then returned to Guatemala. She is now studying at Galileo University to become a professional translator, with GSSG support.

Carlos opted to become a high school teacher.

Luis enrolled at a university but after a year dropped out and got a job to help his mother financially.

José is studying engineering, off and on.

Carlos   Luis   Teresa   José

Blanca in Phases 1, 2, and 3 (for Blanca at home, see page 94)

I met Blanca, a *ladina*, in 2003 when I first went to San Lucas (page 94). In 2004, Jorge and I got her a birth certificate (page 111) certifying that she was eleven. About the same time, four American families came forward wanting to adopt her. To that end, she needed a legal guardian. To have her uncle play that role, we first needed evidence that her mother was deceased. Jorge tried to get her mother's death certificate, first at the records office in Guatemala City, without success, then in Santa Lucia (page 129) where the birth certificates of children born in El Jabalí are kept, but again came away empty handed. Guatemalan law provides for such a contingency—a social worker has to visit the siblings of the deceased to verify his or her demise. We tried that option, equally without success (page 169).

When Blanca turned sixteen, adoption was no longer possible (U.S. Law) and we offered her the opportunity to apply for GSSG's program. By now we had partnered with AYA (page 169) so that our students could come to the United States for Phase 1 as exchange students with a J (Exchange) Visa. U.S. Law stipulates that J-Visa applicants must be in at least ninth grade and no older than eighteen and a half. Guatemala Law stipulates that orphans without a legal guardian cannot get a passport until they turn eighteen. Theoretically we had six months between her eighteenth birthday and the eighteen-and-a-half J-Visa deadline, but her birthday is on May 28 and school would start at the end of August. In reality we had three months (June, July, and August).

On her eighteenth birthday, May 28, Jorge took Blanca to the passport office. From experience he estimated that the passport would probably be issued in two weeks. Instead she got it on the sixteenth of July. Now we had a little over a month to get her here. Jorge did the paperwork and took her to the embassy, where she got her visa. He bought plane tickets for Blanca and himself and they arrived at RDU two weeks before school started. The only English Blanca knew was "Thank You," which Jorge had taught her on the plane.

St. Thomas More Academy had agreed to admit Blanca. Dan and Thelma LeMarble and their daughter, Rachel, also a student at St. Thomas More Academy, made Blanca part of their family but Blanca could in no way handle the heavy reading load at St. Thomas More while still trying to learn basic English. Of course she failed her freshman year. I asked Bill Tschida at Holy Trinity in Winsted, MN, to admit her as a sophomore anyway. He did. Tracey and Roxanne Felder (left) and their two daughters took her in.

During her junior and senior years, Blanca lived with Ken & Lori Pelzel and their two daughters (right).

In 2014 Blanca graduated, ecstatic.

On her return to Guatemala, Blanca enrolled at Mesoamericana University in Quetzaltenango, majoring in educational psychology, and got a job with a call center that requires English. She also receives GSSG support.

GSSG's object had always been the poorest of the poor. Irrepressible Blanca was certainly one of them. When I first met her, she had little else but the clothes on her back, not even one parent. But she learned to love reading (page 129). After she got into GSSG, I began thinking about her future, fantasizing that, because of her affinity for books, she might someday get a Ph.D. in Spanish literature. But in Guatemala, education serves only as preparation for a job and literature is not taught. When I told Jorge about the idea, he pricked my balloon, replying, "Who would hire her?" Indeed, the vast majority of the Guatemalan population have never even read Gabriel García Márquez' *A Hundred Years of Solitude*, the *Popul Vuh*, Miguel Angel Asturias' *Men of Maize*, or *I, Rigoberta Menchú*, to say nothing of *Don Quixote*. Guatemala could surely use some Ph.D.s in Spanish lit.

Implications

In 2009 the economic meltdown of 2008, now well underway, seriously eroded our funding, all of it from the private sector. We had long sought corporate grants in vain. As long as the students were in high school, we managed but in 2012 that large 2008 cohort (page 185) graduated from high school, ready to start college, at around $40,000 a year, each, well beyond GSSG'S resources. So most of them returned to Guatemala and enrolled at one or another university there, where the cost of tuition is minimal but job training is all that's available.

Unfortunately, job training will do nothing to create from among Guatemala's poor a "network of knowledgeable leaders, of thinkers and writers, of professionals and entrepreneurs, in sufficient numbers to effect significant socioeconomic development in Guatemala."[295] Leaders are people with ideas and the attributes to attract a following. Ideas rule the world. Some ideas ameliorate the human condition; others shame humanity. Democracy is an idea; so is slavery. An I-Phone is an idea as was the printing press in 1453. Ideas are the products of a fertile imagination and nothing stimulates the imagination quite so well as reading; witness the children in my vignette on the public library in Chapel Hill (page 84). Madison, Jefferson, Adams, and Hamilton all read extensively not only in English but in Latin, ancient Greek, and often French as well. Without the stimulus provided by reading, the Founding Fathers would never have dreamed that numinous dream we now call the United States of America.

Today the ideas that rule Guatemala are little changed from those that inspired the Spanish Conquest in 1524—greed, oppression, abuse, contempt, genocide. As George Santayana famously observed, "Those who do not know history are doomed to repeat it." Without new leadership, Guatemala faces more of the same—greed, oppression, abuse, scorn, genocide—because without literature to generate innovation, the potential for leadership withers on the vine.

Public Servants

When Alba was rebuffed after jumping through the required hoops (page 161), Kelli Conlow (page 128) contacted Congresswoman Bachmann's office to ask for help. Subsequently Kelli called to tell me that she had received a reply from Jessica (in Congresswoman Bachmann's office) saying that Howard Betts, had replied to a query from Ms. Bachmann. Howard had told her that GSSG should send Alba back to the embassy and that he would interview her personally. I made the appointment and then called Jessica. She was very pleasant and, yes, she might be able to help with the larger issue; she would ask Howard if he would be willing to interview some of our other applicants as well. As it turned out, he was the head of the Visa Section at the Consulate in Guatemala and over the next couple of years would issue visas both to our individual candidates and to our groups, until he left that position. Of all the politicians we and others had contacted about our irregular treatment at the embassy, Michele Bachmann, alone made a sincere effort to help us, and she succeeded. To her and to Howard we and our students owe a debt of gratitude.

Government non-elected officials are sometimes maligned as incompetent and insensitive. Our experience with Sally, Abby, June, Jim, Stanley, Howard, and others suggests that U.S. Government staff, with rare exceptions like the difficult officer in the consulate (pages 159 and 166) are courteous, conscientious, and helpful.

---

[295] From GSSG's Mission Statement (page 91).

Chapter XV, Guatemala Today

Post Peace

The signing of the Peace Accords did, indeed, bring peace, albeit short-lived. A woman who had fought with the EGP (page 57), the most successful of the various guerilla organizations, remembered that, after the signing of the final peace accord in 1996, there was "peace, tranquility, a different life" but. . . . "Now we're even worse off than [during the conflict]."[296] In 2004, eight years after the Peace Accords, Beatriz Manz lamented that a deeply rooted violence still pervaded Guatemala and would "require a greater effort than a cessation of fighting."[297] Diane Nelson, writing in 2015, notes that, "war hovers close, violence a constant threat."[298] There is plenty of evidence to support their despondency.

Crime

Between 2001 and 2004 the homicide rate soared astronomically and in 2005 Guatemala had the steepest murder rate in Latin America. Between 2006 and 2008, five hundred and twelve city bus drivers and sixty of their assistants were killed, when armed gunmen stopped their vehicles to rob the passengers. By 2009, a hundred and forty-six bus drivers and their assistants were killed. No one has ever been tried.[301] During these years, Guatemala's homicide rate grew to exceed the "average number of Guatemalans killed each year" during the civil war.[302]

Military Control

One cannot talk about the Guatemalan military without raising the shade of Héctor Gramajo (page 61). Gramajo's goal, he meretriciously explained, was to reverse Clausewitz's strategy, "We want politics to be the continuation of war, and not that war be the continuation of politics."[305]

In 1996 the army numbered about 30,000 men. The Peace Accords specified that the army reduce its forces by one-third before 1997. In fact, the army has sought to increase its numbers to 50,000.[306] During the very first year after the signing of the Peace Accord, the army made it clear it had no intention of honoring the agreement.[307]

One would expect that the election of President Cerezo, a civilian, in 1986 (page 75) would have resulted in substantive change. But Gramajo was Cerezo's Chief of Staff and Gramajo's plan, known internally as the 'Project' (page 61), applied not only to military matters but to civilian affairs as well. Jennifer Schirmer quotes one of her sources: "The appearance is different, but inside it is the same old thing."[309]

---

[296] Kirsten Weld, *Paper Cadavers: The Archives of Dictatorship in Guatemala*, 2014, p.147.

[297] Beatriz Manz, *Paradise in Ashes: A Guatemalan Journey of Courage, Terror, and Hope*, 2004, p.30.

[298] Diane M. Nelson, *Who Counts? The Mathematics of Death and Life after Genocide*, 2015, p.

[301] Deborah T. Levenson, Adiós Niño: The Gangs of Guatemala City and the Politics of Death, 2013, pp.86–87.

[302] Kedron Thomas, Kevin Lewis O'Neill, and Thomas Offit, "An Introduction" in Kevin Lewis O'Neill and Kedron Thomas (edd.), *Securing the City: Neoliberalism, Space, and Insecurity in Postwar Guatemala*, 2011, p.11.

[305] Jennifer Schirmer, The Guatemalan Military Project: A Violence Called Democracy, 1998, p.236

[306] Ibid., p.7.

[307] Jennifer Schirmer, "Prospects for Compliance: The Guatemalan Military and the Peace Accords," in *Guatemala after the Peace Accords*, Rachel Sieder (ed.), 1998, pp.21–32.

[309] Ibid., p.31, citing an anonymous, "intellectual," source.

The National Police

CCities and towns in Guatemala do not have local police departments; counties, and hence county sheriffs, do not exist. The National Police provide protection for the entire population.

During the civil war at least 55,000 refugees, both Mayan and *ladino*, flooded into Guatemala City. With no jobs to absorb them, shanty towns became their refuge. Rampant corruption among the police beetled over the sultry metropolis.

The G-2 (page 61), the agency charged with implementing the reign of terror, controls the National Police. One former G-2 officer admitted, "What the G-2 says is what the National Police does, they carry out military orders."[311] And what is the result? Kirsten Weld reports that in 2014, the homicide rate in Guatemala City stood at more than 100 per 100,000, "exceeding the violent death rates of the war years."[312] She adds a well-known fact, that only a miniscule percent of reported crimes result in prosecution.

In 1997 the CEH asked President Arzú Irigoyen (page 77) for access to police records. He refused. In a surprise move, President Portillo Cabrera, just before leaving office in 2003, allowed access to some records. The whole bloody business took an unexpected turn when, in July of 2005, investigators from the Human-Rights Ombudsman's Office (page 75), while conducting other business, happened upon an enormous dump of old, musty papers in a labyrinthine warehouse, "a maze of rooms piled high with bundles of moldy records dating back more than a century,"[314] a trove of secret state documents. Kristin Weld's gripping account of the on-going reclamation and archiving of the documents, in large measure, police documents, and their emerging utility, may well keep the reader up at night.

Weld also retells a popular bit of sardonic humor, that Lucas García had a twin brother, who, however, was born dead, showing signs of torture.

Security Guards

Those 55,000 refugees (see above) did not necessarily evolve into criminals. Some became street vendors, some got menial jobs of various sorts, and quite a few found employment as security guards, who, by the way, far outnumber the police.[315] A guard's compensation barely provides room and board, leaving very little to send home to their families. Avery Dickens reports, for example, that Pedro, a Q'eqchí'-speaker from Alta Verapaz, in his third year of employment with a security firm, earned the equivalent of $227 a month, posted as a guard outside a Domino's Pizza in Guatemala City. Of that amount, he sends $67 to his family.[316] What family can live on $67 a month?

Gangs

Pedro was fortunate. He still had a home in his village. Most of those displaced by the plantations, the mines, and the massacres did not. The story of what happened to many of Guatemala's youth is narrated in spellbinding detail by Deborah Levenson in *Adiós Niño: The Gangs of Guatemala City and the Politics of Death*, published in 2013.

---

[311] Weld, op. cit., p.121.

[312] Ibid., p.122.

[314] Ibid., p.2.

[315] Avery Dickins de Girón, "The Security Guard Industry in Guatemala: Rural Communities and Urban Violence," in O'Neill and Thomas (edd.), *Securing the City*, p.104.

[316] Ibid., p.111.

In her Introduction, Levenson explains the title, *Adiós Niño*, relating how a soldier threw a new-born child into a river, calling out, 'Adiós Niño' ("Bye, bye, kid."). She goes on to relate how, during the war, the army had forced men and boys into the PACs (page 62) and made them torture and kill other Mayan men and boys, often in their own villages. The traumatized children who witnessed these horrors experienced life as death, killing and being killed. Thousands of them, orphaned, ended up in Guatemala City.[317] Some were brought to various shelters by the same soldiers that had massacred their parents and said that so and so was the only survivor of such and such a village. These children, she says, did not talk. At first the social workers thought they were deaf mutes, but little by little came to realize that the trauma of witnessing the assassination of their parents and the destruction of their community was in fact the cause.[318]

Levenson goes on to recount how, in one of the poorer neighborhoods of Guatemala City, a group of boys and girls in their teens who enjoyed *break* dancing had come to call themselves *Brek Las Cobras*. Soon other groups adopted the same *brek* moniker. By 1987 more than sixty such groups had evolved and many of them began calling themselves '*maras*,' a label apparently taken from a Brazilian movie. They were not evil, just kids who got together to have a good time, listening to the music of Led Zeppelin, Jethro Tull, and other groups from the States and elsewhere.

One time, for reasons unknown, a grenade exploded in Zone 1, the area around the National Palace (page 48). A National Police official clacked that the incident occurred in front of a discotheque where kids from *Mara* 33 hung out, that the group had been watching television programs from the U.S., and that the evil affecting the city's youth was the fault of irresponsible parents, troweling his narrative with loaded vocabulary like "drugs" and "foreign." Without any evidence, the newspapers embellished the story and blamed the *mara* for crime, prostitution, and the sale of drugs. The head of the Juvenile Delinquency Bureau further embellished the narrative, telling Levenson, "Rock music incites youth to fight."[320] A Pentecostal pamphlet weighed in, warning that the *maras* played rock music to promote "Satanic themes, pornography, materialism, and chaos" and that Michael Jackson cast spells of terror in his music and the video 'Thriller'," despite the fact that the Christian Democratic Party, to which many Pentecostals belonged, had published a study demonstrating that the *maras* were composed of ordinary urban youth who, at most, broke minor laws.

In the 1980s and '90s, tens of thousands of Guatemalan and Salvadoran youth escaped the carnage in their countries by migrating to the poorest Spanish-speaking neighborhoods in Los Angeles, where crack and guns had proliferated. There many of them joined existing gangs, two of which, M-18 and MS-13 (the latter called Mara Salvatrucha because of the large number of Salvadorans in its ranks) dominated the environment. These gangs, heavily into drugs and crime, fought and killed each other and committed other felonies. In time, the Los Angeles' jails, overflowing with foreign gang members, began deporting them; "what started as a trickle . . . in the early 1990s turned into a flood . . . by 1996."[322]

The newly returned gang members from Los Angeles and elsewhere took over the local *maras* in Guatemala City that then formed the base of the MS-13 and M-18 pyramids, the two largest and most lethal, criminal gangs. What had been an innocent rivalry about break dancing now became a violent contest over 'territory' that meant "neighborhood streets, stores, and women's bodies."[324]

---

[317] Others found their way to Spanish-speaking neighborhoods in Los Angeles where gangs from El Salvador and Honduras already existed.

[318] Levenson, op. cit., p.39.

[320] Ibid., p.58.

[322] Ibid., p.42.

[324] Ibid., p.47.

In 1987 Nora Marina Figueroa, a social worker, and Marta Yolanda Maldonado Castillo, a psychologist, joined Levenson in conducting a study of the *maras*. After they had spent several months talking with ten different *maras* (tree hundred and thirty youngsters in all), they concluded that most of the kids were "calm, well spoken, and thoughtful" and their greatest concerns were "love and acceptance." The youth came from poor families and most of them lived with their mothers, sometimes a grandmother, and father if he was alive. Often the alcoholic fathers or stepfathers beat the boys and raped the girls but most of the youth had good relations with their mothers or grandmothers, though sometimes girls did not get along with their mothers. Only one said that family life was excellent. Sometimes a working relative in the United States helped financially. One girl reported that at one point her *mara* had been all-girl.

The kids uniformly had little interest in mending relations with their biological families. Rather they felt that their *mara* was family because there they had someone "who loves you and tells you so." Even though they might sleep in the birth-family home, eighty percent consistently referred to their *mara* as "family." They spent time eating together, dancing, and smoking pot. All of them were openly sexually active, even those who were gay; "No big deal." All were literate and many helped put their siblings through school, though none were currently in school themselves. One said, "I want a different education, something that is really helpful and not a lot of crap," adding that it would be great if going to school was "not just dictation after dictation"[326] (see page 85). Working in many cases meant stealing, but not from the poor. They described President Cerezo (page 75) as "a greedy asshole" and had negative comments about President Reagan, but positive comments about the archbishop of Guatemala. All were conscious that peer pressure played a role in prolonging their adherence to their *mara*, where life offered friendship, love, music, dance, sex, money, leisure, and excitement but, above all, a sense of identity and community. By their late teens or twenties, most of the gang members interviewed earlier had subsequently left their gangs and entered the everyday life of the urban poor.

Levenson observed a "sharp contrast" between the gang members she had met in the 1980s and those in the late 1990s and early 2000s. The former enjoyed "open-ended conversation," while the latter liked to kill. Tattooing had replaced the designer clothes of the 1980s.

In the absence of governmental care, members of the well-funded Pentecostal Church assumed responsibility for the care of many impoverished youth in Guatemala City. The Church's program advocated mental discipline and physical punishment. One facility that Levenson visited, *Casa Mi Hogar* ("My Home"), housed more than 150 youngsters, including some 20 girls. Every time she visited, all of them were standing in the patio, looking distressed. The director explained that they stood for hours "to achieve discipline and formation."

More serious is the commuting of gang members to adult penitentiaries, where they are subject not only to abuse inherent in the system but also to exploitation by older mobsters who, from their cells, run criminal rackets on the outside. The most powerful of these older mobsters was reputed to be Byron Lima Olive, imprisoned for the assassination of Bishop Gerardi Condera.

Anthony W. Fontes, in a short paper, focuses on the adult gangsters' control of prisons.[327] "Ultimately," he says, "Maras are not the problem." He attributes "contemporary out-of-control urban violence" to two interrelated issues: first "the problem of porous prisons" and second "extortion–the most feared and despised illicit business in Central America." With respect to porous

---

[326] Ibid., p.68.
[327] Anthony W. Fontes, "Beyond the Maras: Violence and Survival in Urban Central America," https://www.wilsoncenter.org/sites/default/files/Fontes_2014_FINAL.pdf

prisons, he writes that prison staff, who earn about $250 a month, "receive a steady flow of bribes," that can double or triple their income.

On June 7, 2016, Judge Claudette Domínguez of Guatemala's High-Risk Crimes Court ordered eight former top military officers to stand trial for crimes against humanity committed between 1981 and 1987. The case against them is built on eyewitness accounts, documentary evidence, and the testimony of forensic anthropologists, who examined the physical remains of more than 560 bodies found in eighty-four graves during exhumations conducted at a military base near Cobán, many showing signs of torture and of being buried blindfolded. DNA evidence positively identified the remains of more than 120 as belonging to communities in the area.[329]

On July 13, 1988, Roberto Xol, a civilian with a wife and children, 'disappeared.' In July, 2014, his family was notified that a DNA match had been made with one of the bodies exhumed at Cobán. Fredy Peccerelli, a forensic anthropologist, together with an assistant, made arrangements to bring Roberto's bones to Campur, where the family lived. Peccerelli and his assistant first arranged, in a coffin, the clothes that the family was providing for the funeral. Next, taking the bones, they carefully reconstructed the skeleton inside the clothes, Roberto's skull resting on a small pillow. Finally Peccerelli took the clothes that Roberto had been wearing the day he died and gave them to Roberto's daughter, who, as a child twenty years earlier, had picked out those very clothes for her father to wear that fateful day; she buried her face in the bundle, weeping "Papa! Papa! You're back. You're back." Peccerelli closed the lid on the coffin.[330] The Maya believe that a bond remains between them and their ancestors but to maintain that bond, burial must observe ancestral customs, that Peccerelli had been careful to preserve.

Years later, when I showed the *New York Times* article detailing the process to Heydi (page 32), she remembered that her mother had attended the funeral of Gabriel Chitay Quej, whose remains had also been found at the same site and whose funeral was conducted in the same way. Gabriel was the son of Heydi's great aunt.

At the head of those eight former top military officers standing trial for crimes against humanity (see above) is Benedicto Lucas García, brother of and Chief of Staff for his brother, the dictator Romeo Lucas García (page 60). Earlier, in 2008 or 2009, Jorge had pointed out Benedicto for me in church.

The Murder of Bishop Gerardi

On April 26, 1998, Bishop Juan Gerardi Conedera was bludgeoned to death in his garage, attached to the rectory at San Sebastián Parish in central Guatemalan City, not far from the National Palace (page 48). Gerardi had been head of the Archdiocese' Office of Human Rights (ODHA) since its founding in 1989 and had published ODHA's report, *Guatemala: Nunca Más!* (*"Guatemala: Never Again!"*) two days earlier (page 2). A piece of concrete had been used to smash his skull, apparently after a struggle.

The government arrested a number of people, including Carlos Vielman (a homeless man), Father Mario Orantes (the bishop's assistant), and Margarita López (the parish cook). The trial dragged on. In January, 2000, Colonel Bryan Lima Estrada, his son, Captain Byron Lima Oliva, and Sergeant Obdulio Villanueva were arrested. In November, a gang member, Carlos García Pontaza was arrested as well but died the next day in prison (in other words, he knew too much). In June, 2001, Colonel Byron Lima Estrada, Captain Byron Lima Oliva, and Sergeant Major Villanueva were sentenced to thirty years in prison; Father Mario, to twenty years; and Margarita

---

[329] INTERNATIONAL JUSTICE MONITOR, "A project of the Open Society Justice Initiative."
[330] https://www.nytimes.com/2016/07/03/magazine/the-secrets-in-guatemalas-bones.html?_r=0

López, the cook, was freed. The verdicts were overturned the next year, only to be reinstated by the Guatemalan Supreme Court two years after that. In 2005, an appellate court upheld the verdicts against Colonel Lima and his son and, the next year, the Supreme Court reinstated the convictions. Colonel Lima died in prison; my friend, Jorge Paque, commented, "He probably knew who the killer was."

Back in 2001, Claudia Méndez Arriaza, a reporter, recorded that, during an interview with the elder Lima, he reminded her that, during the war, some ecclesiastics had allied themselves with the guerrillas. She asked if he meant Bishop Gerardi. He answered, "He had his line." She asked what was the bishop's line. He replied, "Ask the priests. . . . They'll tell you: liberation theology" (page 59). He went on to tell her that everything having to do with the Gerardi case, even the murder itself, perhaps, was a "continuation of the war by other means [see page 220]. The war wasn't over,"[335] a remark evocative of Héctor Gramajo's "we want war to be a continuation of politics, and not that politics be a continuation of war" (page 61); Gramajo's Project (page 61) was the army's Bible.

To succeed Bishop Gerardi as head of the Catholic Church's Office of Human Rights, the archdiocese chose Bishop Mario Ríos Montt, a man with views quite the opposite of his brother. Efraín Ríos Montt (page 64).

Public Institutions

On Thursday, March 9, 2017, the *New York Times* reported that the previous day a fire at a public orphanage for girls in Guatemala City had taken the lives of at least twenty and left at least forty injured. The article went on to expose the fate of the 750 girls housed there, that they were subject to sexual abuse by the very staff who were supposed to be protecting them, that the facility had been built for a capacity of 500, that one girl reported seeing worms in the food, that some of the girls, trying to escape had struggled with the guards and that the previous year a number of the residents had succeeded, that two of the girls had hanged another, and that the government had failed to act on a petition to close the facility. The next day, the *Times* reported that the death toll had risen to thirty.

Historically, Guatemala has been the third-largest supplier of children adopted in the United States, after China and Russia, but the cost is very high; in effect, Guatemalan children are for sale.

---

[335] Francisco Goldman, *The Art of Political Murder: Who Killed the Bishop*, p.241.

Epilogue

Homo sapiens, having subjugated its natural predators and extended its lifespan by several decades, is unwittingly painting itself into a corner. Inevitably mankind will someday have insufficient land to feed itself. Under these circumstances, overpopulated countries with a disenfranchised indigenous population and an elite upper class necessarily resort to genocide.

Observations

1. In Guatemala, genocide has already begun (page 65). Absent some radical change in U.S. policy, the resultant human tsunami will overwhelm any physical deterrent on the U.S. southern border.

2. By having the Mexican government turn back refugees at its border with Guatemala, the United States government is only adding to the power of that tsunami.

3. The only way to resolve behaviors offending human nature is to develop the human capital inherent in all of us.

4. The volume of foreign students in our colleges and universities demonstrates that developing nations around the world send their youth here as the surest path to development at home.

5. The population of Guatemala in 1979 was 6,843,875; today it is 16,856,938.[336] Given the shortage of farmland, young Mayan men and women, in desperation, flood into the major cities looking for work, where unemployment and underemployment must be near 50%. And what do they find there? Crime! Gangs! Drugs! Homelessness! Starvation! Rape! Racism! Torture! Police corruption! Criminal Immunity! Death! Human beings deprived of basic human rights will do anything to escape. In the mountains of Guatemala, the destitute and desperate landless Maya constitute a human tsunami, doubling with each generation, to overwhelm any physical deterrent designed to contain them. Indeed, living in the jaws of hell, they are already defying death itself! Only ameliorating the quality of life at home will keep them there.

Leadership

The Maya have always identified themselves not by their common, genetic ethnicity but by the various languages they speak. As a result, no Alaric after the death of Tecún Umán (page 14) ever arose to unite them against a common enemy. Today linguistic identity is breaking down, simply because the Maya are coming to see the value of formal education and the language of formal education in Guatemala is Spanish. The other major component of cultural identity, religion, has also given way, in this case, to Christianity. Where then can the commonality requisite to leadership be found, if not in ethnicity or religion?

Analogously, the United States is a country of immigrants, all of whose ancestors spoke one or another language in a linguistic potpourri from around the world and worshipped in a variety of faiths. Their descendants now universally identify themselves as "Americans," speak English, and are led not by a modern Alaric but by a constantly evolving "network of knowledgeable elected officials, of thinkers and writers, of professionals and entrepreneurs" (see "Mission" on page 98).

---

[336] Source, http://www.countrymeters.info/en/Guatemala

Root Cause–Two Perspectives

The root cause of the Guatemalan Civil War was the shortage of land or, from another perspective, overpopulation—two sides of the same coin. Long before the war, the Maya had been dispossessed of so much land that not enough remained for them to feed themselves, even as their numbers doubled with each generation. The one thing neither the United Nations nor the United States government could do, the one thing not even a successful revolution could have done, was create more land. The government of Guatemala sought to resolve the problem through genocide, and failed.

The United States and other so-called 'First-World' countries have in recent times developed a quality of life undreamed of anywhere else in history through what we call 'higher education.' The solution to Guatemala's problem, then, lies in providing Guatemalan youth with an opportunity to acquire an equivalent level of academic development. The Servicemen's Readjustment Act of 1944, a.k.a. the 'G.I. Bill of Rights,' provides a model for creating a "network of knowledgeable elected officials, of thinkers and writers, of professionals and entrepreneurs" (page 98) in Guatemala.

The G.I. Bill of Rights

Before the Second World War, most people in the United States were poor and poorly educated, not just people in remote areas but townsfolk as well, like my parents and grandparents, and possibly yours. Higher education saw its first wave of expansion into the ranks of the poor as a result of the G.I. Bill of Rights, the 'The Servicemen's Readjustment Act of 1944.' The program provided an opportunity for those who had served in the military during the Second World War, mostly young men, to get a college education, previously a prerogative of the wealthy. In consequence, more than two million veterans, largely from impoverished backgrounds, attended college. The resulting surge in America's stock of human capital created such long-term social, political, and economic growth as to propel the United States into world-wide hegemony. Recipients of the program include, prominently: elected national officials like George H.W. Bush, Gerald Ford, Daniel Inouye, Bob Dole, George Mitchell, Daniel Patrick Moynihan, John Warner, Sedgwick William Green; Cabinet Secretaries, Henry Kissinger and James Schlesinger; Ambassadors Herbert J. Spiro and William Harrop; Supreme Court justices William Rehnquist, John Paul Stevens, and Byron White; journalists Jonathan Spivak and William Graves; astronaut John Glenn; author Lawrence Osgood; artist Edward Gorey; entertainers Clint Eastwood, Paul Newman, and Walter Matthau; inventor Douglas Engelbart, who developed hypertext, invented the computer mouse, and has a law named after him;[337] and others, including my brother, Robert, who readily acknowledges that without the G.I. Bill he could never have gone to college. After working for someone else for a couple of years, Robert, like many others, started his own business and, again like many others, become a highly successful businessman and community leader.[338]

In the peak year of 1947, veterans accounted for forty-nine percent of college admissions. By the time the original G.I. Bill ended in 1956, 2.2 million G.I.s had taken advantage of the opportunity the program afforded.

Tom Brokaw, the award-winning NBC "Nightly News" commentator, in his *New York Times* best-seller, characterizes the men and women of that era as *The Greatest Generation*, writing in

---

[337] Engelbart's Law, the observation that the intrinsic rate of human performance is exponential.

[338] He is also a reader, having read more than a thousand books, not in his field of expertise but for pleasure and interest.

part: "A grateful nation made it possible for more of them to attend college than any society had ever educated, anywhere. They gave the world new science, literature, art, industry, and economic strength unparalleled in the long curve of history."[339] Focus for a moment on the breadth of the fields he calls "new": science, literature, art, industry, and economic strength unparalleled in all of history.' Creating something new requires innovation.

Innovation

What is it that makes it possible for human beings to innovate? Creating something new begins in the mind, of course, specifically in the faculty we call 'imagination' (page 86). The imagination, like all our faculties, needs to be used in order to be useful.

Every innovation begins as an idea, something created by the imagination. The major portion of a college student's time is spent reading, reading widely over a wide variety of subjects—English and American literature, American, European, and world history, mathematics, two and often three of the hard sciences (prominently physics, chemistry, biology, astronomy, and geology), again two or three of the so-called 'soft sciences' (prominently anthropology, geography, psychology, sociology, and political science), and the humanities (prominently philosophy, foreign languages and literatures, art history, music appreciation), and a variety of electives—computer science, theater, debate, religious studies, oratory, and others. In addition, friends and classmates take some subjects other than one's own and in dorm rooms, dining facilities, and social engagements transmit a fair amount of information about the classes they are taking, information that gets absorbed and becomes part of the cerebral content of everyone in the group, ultimately the entire college or university population, to be chewed on, dissected, modified, rejected, accepted, published in the campus newspaper, taken up by the student senate, condemned, and reworked, all the while influencing the thinking of the students, the faculty, the families, and subsequent history. That's what college is all about. That's what makes college so exciting.

The stimulus to the imagination by going through college made those G.I.s into the "Greatest Generation," a generation of innovators, and they passed their creativity on to their children and grandchildren, taking them into their laps and reading to them, putting them through grade school and high school, and then sending them off to college. Is it any wonder that in 2015 alone the United States Patent Office granted 140,969 patents? Guatemalan patents in 2015 totaled 3; a scant 76 in the nation's entire history.[340]

What can be done about Guatemala? Money thrown at it will only be absorbed in graft and other forms of corruption. We could bring some kids here as exchange students but the J Visa (page 88) is only for high-school students and is valid for one year only. What about bringing some Guatemalan youth here for college? Would a college education here in the United States have the same effect in Guatemala as it did here; would it create a country that everyone wants to get to and nobody wants to leave? Why not? Human nature is the same everywhere.

Thanks largely to the Harvard model, general-education subjects are the norm for the first two years of college. They provide the breadth of perspective requisite to the development of *innovation*. In fact, fewer than half of all college graduates ever end up employed in the field of their major. No matter, by the time they graduate they have the basic cerebral skills to innovate, to create something new, and they do. The implications for Guatemala are staggering.

---

[339] Tom Brokaw, *The Greatest Generation*, 1998, dust jacket.
[340] http://www.uspto.gov/web/offices/ac/ido/oeip/taf/h_at.htm#PartA1_1a

Women in College

The second wave of new college entrants followed as night the day and, by the '60s, women had come to represent fifty percent of college graduates. One of the consequences of women delaying marriage until after college is a steep decline in the birthrate. Today, in the course of their child-bearing years, on average, American women give birth to 1.9 children,[341] not even enough to maintain the current level of the population.

Demographics of Guatemala generally include the whole population. One study, however, focused on an indigenous community and found that "the average Atiteco family has approximately 8 live births during its reproductive period."[342] Most observers familiar with circumstances among the Maya would probably find that number about right. Judith's mother (page 183) had 12 children; Marlyn's mother (page 184), 7; Byron's mother (page 135), 10; Sandra Bolom's mother (page 206), 7—an average of 9. There is no reason to doubt that a college education for Mayan women would produce results similar to those of American women.

Replacing CARSI

The U.S. Government currently funds two major sets of programs in Guatemala, those of the USAID and the NIL, through CARSI (page 6). Conditions in Guatemala have not improved because none of those programs can create more land or reduce the birthrate, and they certainly have nothing to do with cerebral development. At best, they provide low-paying jobs for a miniscule portion of the population.

As will be evident, an education program for Guatemala modeled on the G.I. Bill and GSSG's experience can accomplish what all the CARSI programs combined have not remotely approached.

The Combined G.I. Bill of Rights and GSSG Program

Background

In light of U.S. complicity in the carnage of Guatemala's Civil War, the United States Government is obligated to some form of compensation, as acknowledged by President Clinton's apology (page 1). This study proposes the adoption of a program designed specifically to promote innovation among the progeny of that carnage as a vehicle for compensation commensurate with that obligation and at the same time invalidate the reason for the carnage (insufficient innovation to raise the majority population out of poverty), and thus eliminate the need for illegal emigration.

When the Servicemen's Readjustment Act of 1944 (the G.I. Bill of Rights) became law, the population of the United States stood at about 138 million. More than two million veterans, about 1.5% of the population, took advantage of the opportunity thus provided. The population of Guatemala today is about 16 million; 1.5% of 16 million is 246,462. One may reasonably assume that the same proportion as produced the 'Greatest Generation' in the United States would have the same effect in Guatemala, human nature being the same everywhere.

College in the United States generally consists of two years of general education and two years of training in a specific field. The universities in Guatemala do not provide the general education

---

[341] http://www.census.gov/hhes/fertility/data/cps/2014.html

[342] John D. Early, "Demographic Profile of a Maya Community: The Atitecos of Santiago Atitlán," *The Milbank Memorial Fund Quarterly*, Vol. 48, No. 2, Part 1 (Apr., 1970), p.168.

component of a college experience but they do provide the experience of training in a specific field (page 84). A Guatemalan Student in the Combined Program would, therefore, study for two years in the United States to acquire a liberal education here and then return to Guatemala for training in a "major" there because the context in Guatemala differs significantly from the context here; for example, studying to be a teacher here would not prepare one to be a teacher in Guatemala (primary teachers in Guatemala have to teach Spanish, not English; secondary school teachers need be teaching Guatemalan history, not American history; accountants have to know Guatemalan law, not U.S. law; and so on).

Costs

Responsibility for the carnage of Guatemala's Civil War does not fall exclusively on the United States Government. The fact is that neither the U.S. nor the Guatemalan government could have conducted the war by itself and both are responsible for compensation.

In the program proposed here, the direct cost to the U.S. Government is to consist of providing, once a year, round-trip airfare for selected students and paying high-school tuition (if any) for four years and college tuitions for the two years of general education, the direct cost to the Guatemalan Government consisting of covering all expenses related to studying for the *licenciatura* (professional job training), a modest investment since tuition at San Carlos University and its many branches is free.

Selection

Since Guatemalan youth graduating from high school in Guatemala are not qualified to enter college in the United States (see page 85), of necessity those selected to participate in the Combined Program will first attend a high school in the United States for four years, while living with American, natively English-speaking families, as did GSSG's students. Further, since high schools in the United States often will not admit freshmen who will turn twenty-one before graduating, entrants into the program may be no older than fifteen when school starts in the fall. To exemplify the importance of law, anyone who has ever entered the United States illegally shall be ineligible. As a counter to gangs, individuals with tattoos shall be ineligible.

The United States Government is not equipped to identify qualified Guatemalan youth, arrange for them to live with American families, and monitor their progress. Such being the case, the Combined Program must necessarily rely on sponsoring organizations.

Sponsoring Organizations

"On the ground" aspects of the Combined Program shall be conducted by Section 501(c)(3) Sponsoring Organizations that, like GSSG, shall report to the U.S. State Department as do other programs involving foreign students. Churches, very likely, would embrace an opportunity to play such a role; they have structure, built-in leadership, and they do not worship the almighty dollar. Parents of adopted Guatemalan children[343] were particularly active in GSSG and may well form Sponsoring Organizations in various areas of the country. (Several families did in fact assume total responsibility for their Guatemalan guests; see, for example, Kelli and Rick Conlow (pages 161 and 171) and Mary and Scott VanderVeen (pages 162 and 175). Fraternal organizations might also serve in that role. In any case, GSSG as it functioned between 2003 and 2013, provides a model.

The mechanism for tracking the students already exists in the SEVIS program (page 89).

---

[343] Guatemala has historically been the third largest supplier of adopted foreign children, after China and Russia.

Details

Note. The Combined Program will require a variation of the F visa (page 88). For the sake of discussion, 'F-G' will do here.

1) In light of the socioeconomic effects of the Guatemalan Civil War (page 1), eligibility for participation in the Combined Program shall be apportioned 83% Mayan and 17% *ladino* (page 1).

2) Selection of and responsibility for participants in the Combined Program shall be vested in Section 501(c)(3) Sponsoring Organizations (see above).

3) The Combined Program shall consist of three phases in which the participants will, in:

> Phase 1, arrive approximately three months before school starts in the fall to learn English by immersion while living with American, natively English-speaking families, and then attend public or private high schools during the ensuing four years, returning home every summer to maintain their national and cultural identity;

> Phase 2, attend college for two years of general/liberal education in the United States while living with an American, natively English-speaking families and then return to Guatemala permanently;

> Phase 3, attend a university in Guatemala to the completion of the *licenciatura* (page 85).

4) Students in Phase 1 may not have salaried employment; they may do odd jobs like mowing grass and baby-sitting. Students in Phase 2 may work on campus only.

5) To ensure the desired results, the participating Phase 1 youth must maintain at least a C average and earn scores on the ACTs or SATs acceptable to the colleges meeting the standards specified in #18 below. Students not meeting these requirements shall be returned to Guatemala by the Sponsoring Organization(s) forthwith.

6) Students in Phase 2 must register for no fewer than 12 credit hours per semester and maintain at least a 2.0 GPA, living again with host families. Students not meeting these requirements are to be returned to Guatemala by the Sponsoring Organization(s) forthwith.

7) Ancillary conditions:

> a) Sponsoring Organizations are responsible for all expenses except airfare (see 8 below) incurred by students in Phases 1 and 2 but students in Phase 2 may find full-time, summer employment in the United States; in that case they shall return to Guatemala for the Christmas season.

> b) If a student matriculates at a state college or university, it shall be the responsibility of the Sponsoring Organization to pursue the issue of residency;

c) Pregnancy, marriage to an American, and/or the birth of a child disqualifies the parent(s) from further participation in the program and the Sponsoring Organization shall return the student(s) to Guatemala immediately upon learning of the pregnancy or birth.

8) In phases 1 and 2, the United States government shall provide round-trip airfare once a year.

9) Sponsoring Organizations shall provide room and board, health insurance, clothing, books and school supplies, allowances, and transportation within the United States.

10) Sponsoring Organizations shall be responsible for ensuring the return of their students to Guatemala within thirty days after the termination of the student's formal education in the U.S.

11) If the Combined Program brings 1000 students in year 1 and increases that number by 32% each year for 17 years and then allows those in the pipeline finish, 246,462 students will have graduated from high school in the United States, after allowing for those who wash out (see Appendix F, page 257).

12) In GSSG's experience, out of the 31 students selected in 2008 and 2009,[345] 22 (71%) graduated from high school in four years. From these data, it is fair to conclude that about 71% of the students brought to the United States for high school in the Combined Program will graduate from high school in four years.

13) To ensure that students in the Combined Program do not remain in the United States, the law shall specify that: a) individuals issued an F-G Visa will never be eligible for: i) a Green Card, not even if married to an American, ii) citizenship, or iii) a Social Security number (with the exceptions in 14 below).[346]

14) Graduates of the program may be issued a visa and a Social Security number if engaged by a Section 501(c)(3) Sponsoring Organization in furtherance of the Combined Program, so long as they are thus actively employed.

15) Neither Sponsoring Organizations nor host families may engage in proselytizing and the students are expected to return to Guatemala with the same religious persuasion as their biological parents. Sponsoring Organizations failing to enforce this provision shall lose their authorization.

16) All Sponsoring Organizations must adopt the mission statement articulated on page 98. If they have multiple programs, this provision would apply only to the Combined Program. In addition, the local Chief Executive Officers or Executive Directors of the Sponsoring Organizations participating in the Combined Program must have spent a significant amount of time in Guatemala, know something of its history and socioeconomic structure, be able to communicate in both Spanish and English, and be either U.S. citizens or have a green card.

---

[345] The only years in which GSSG functioned as an appropriate model for the program envisioned here.
[346] GSSG's students were not inclined to remain in the United States and none remained illegally. Two girls married an American and stayed.

17) Each Sponsoring Organization shall hire at its own expense a facilitator, i.e., a Guatemalan employee responsible for the functions performed by Jorge Paque for GSSG (see the Index, *s.v.* Jorge).

18) All high schools, colleges, and universities enrolling students in the Combined Program, whether public or private, must be in good standing with the relevant accrediting agencies recognized by the U.S. Department of Education. Trade schools, chiropractic schools, podiatry schools, Bible schools, seminaries, and other specialized institutions shall not qualify, either because they are not accredited or because their curricula lack the requisite breadth of a normal college education. Community colleges shall <u>not</u> qualify because they lack important social experiences and resources: residence halls, dining halls, theater, famous speakers, Greek life, artistic performances, intercollegiate athletics, alumni associations, elective student offices, student newspapers, the active practice of civil discourse, and, finally, the stimulus of college life on campus.[348]

19) GSSG's workshops proved to be invaluable. Sponsoring organizations are responsible for creating such workshops (see Appendix C, page 249) and report result to the State Department.

20) GSSG, as it functioned in 2008 and 2009 provides a model for Sponsoring Organizations.

21) GSSG brought 17 new students in 2008; 3 did not return for their sophomore year; one did not return for his junior year; 1 senior washed out in mid-year. GSSG brought 14 new students in 2009; 4 did not return for their sophomore year. All the others graduated.

22) Expenses associated with the two years of college taken in the United States (tuition, books and school supplies, and a modest allowance) shall be paid for by the United States Government as its compensation for its role in the Guatemalan Civil War. The Guatemalan Government, for its role in the carnage, shall pay for all the expenses associated with the students' education in Guatemala to the completion of the *licenciatura* (tuition, if any, books and school supplies, room and board, transportation, and a modest allowance).

23) Sponsoring organizations failing to perform as required shall be decertified by the U.S. State Department.

24) In 2016 the Board of Trustees of the Guatemalan Student Support Group adopted a new mission, "to partner with impoverished Guatemalan communities to provide greater educational opportunities for their children and young adults," certainly a worthy cause (see pp.84ff.), but it does not address the central, overwhelming issue, Guatemala's catastrophic shortage of land/overpopulation. As a result, GSSG would not be eligible to participate in the Combined Program.

25) The Combined Program assumes that all high-school graduates will continue to Phases 2 and 3.

26) The Combined Program assumes that the United States Government will negotiate an agreement with the Guatemalan Government to formalize item 3), Phase 3 above.

---

[348] "The college 'experience' was not just a sum of the lectures heard, seminars attended, or research conducted; 'student life' was said to be a vital component of what was learned in the undergraduate years. The model for this was the residential college, promoting the four years of work toward a bachelor's degree as a way of life that encouraged habits of learning. . . . Student newspapers, glee clubs, literary societies . . . all would be brought under the increasingly important administrative function of 'student life'." Michael S. Roth, *Beyond the University: Why Liberal Education Matters*, 2014, pp. 122 and 124.

Conclusion

The Combined Program, if adopted by the governments of both countries, will ultimately transform Guatemala into a 'first-world' country, thereby not only eliminating the need for Guatemalan citizens to emigrate to the United States but also converting Guatemala into a haven for refugees from other countries in Latin America as well, prominently, El Salvador, Honduras, and Mexico. It will also eliminate the need for a wall.

Appendix A, The Recruiting Manual

[Documents in Spanish are here translated into English]

DEFINITIONS:

team = a group of Guatemalans and Americans authorized by the Board of Trustees to determine which applicants will become candidates in any given year;

contact = a Guatemalan principal or teacher who selects applicants for a group interview;

applicant (*aspirante*) = a student who has been selected by the contact for a group interview;

candidate (*candidato/a*) = an applicant who has been selected by the team to participate in GSSG's program;

participant (*participante*) = a candidate who has come to the United States in GSSG's program;

team leader = the Guatemalan team member chiefly responsible for conducting GSSG's affairs in Guatemala;

American = the team member authorized to represent the board of directors in Guatemala;

poverty [350] = inadequacy of income, nutrition, housing, clothing, education, cerebral stimulation, self-esteem, and communication skills;

honesty = no lying, no cheating, no stealing;

integrity = conduct consistent with highly moral values;

personality = the quality that others find attractive, the image an individual presents to others as his or her real self—confident, caring, thoughtful on the one hand, or proud, haughty, self-centered on the other;

character = one's behavior when he or she thinks no one is looking or cares; its components include justice, fortitude, prudence, temperance, self-discipline, courage, and compassion;

intelligence = the ability to engage in abstract reasoning;

imagination = the ability to generate new ideas;

will = the ability to make decisions, especially a preference for reason rather than emotion in the process;

leadership potential = the combination of honesty, integrity, personality, character, intelligence, imagination, and will [see page 99].[351]

GROUP INTERVIEW

When the applicants have assembled, the contact introduces the members of the team to the applicants. The team leader has the applicant arrange their chairs in a semi-circle. The team members then help the applicants write their names, birth dates, and grade level in large letters on a sheet of paper and pin them to their shirts. The team members seat themselves at the open end of the semi-circle. The team leader then tells the applicants that the purpose of the visit is to select individuals for a scholarship [no details] and emphasizes that GSSG has three primary rules—no lying, no cheating, no stealing.

The team next administers a series of five tests.

---

[350] See 'Seven Criteria,' page 86.

[351] Communication skills, the ability to speak and write effectively, are certainly a component of leadership but impossible to assess at this early stage of development. The acquisition of those skills is one of the program' objectives (see page 82).

1) IMPROMPTU SPEAKING TEST (to assess Personality and Leadership Potential)

While the team members take notes, the team leader asks each student to rise and tell the team something about himself or herself, his or her family, and anything else that he or she wishes to say. If the applicant does not mention the following, the team leader will ask: whether the home is *bajareque* [page 107], *madera* [wood], block, or something else, whether the floor is concrete or dirt, and what appliances are in the home. During the entire Group Interview, all of the applicants' demeanor should be noted—what they are doing while someone else is speaking, to whom do the others listen, which speakers are nervous and which speak easily, which speak randomly and which organize their thoughts, choose their words, have a sense of humor, look to others for help, etc. Team members should interrupt the speaker any time they have questions or comments or want to pursue a particular point. Team members keep their notes in the following table.

TABLE I
[here modified as if only two applicants were involved]

School: Date:	Notes
Name:	
Name:	

When the last student has spoken, the team administers the Aptitude Test.

2) APTITUDE TEST (to assess Intelligence and Imagination)

The test is conducted orally. The team members record a "1" for each correct answer on Table II [below] and a "-1" for each incorrect answer.

1.	Do they have a September 15 in the United States? [352]
2.	How many birthdays does a person who lived 50 years have"?
3.	Some months have 31 days. How many have 28?
4.	If a hole is one foot square by one foot deep, how much land is in the hole?
5.	Is it o.k. for a man to marry the sister of his widow?
6.	A doctor prescribes three pills and tells you to take one every half hour. How many minutes will have passed when you take the last one?
7.	A farmer has seventeen sheep. They all die except nine. How many are left?

---

352 September 15 is Independence Day in Guatemala.

8.	How many animals of each sex did Moses put in the ark?
9.	How many two-cent stamps are there in a dozen?
10.	Two men play five games of checkers. Each wins the same number of games. There are no ties. Explain.
11.	½ is the same as $^4/_?$. What is the value of "?"?
12.	Is it legal for a man who is living in Guatemala to be buried in Antigua?
13.	When was the year 1?
14.	What is the least number of soccer players on a soccer field at one time?
15.	A woman gives a dollar to a beggar. The woman is the sister of the beggar but the beggar is not the brother of the woman. Explain!
16.	[While the applicants deal with that question, the American writes the following list of numbers on the black board: 121034115612.] When the previous question has been answered, the team leader asks, "If you wanted to continue the list, what would the next four numbers be?"
17.	[While the applicants deal with that question, the third member of the team draws the following figures on the board. When the previous question has been answered, the team leader asks, "Which of the figures on the board does not belong to the group?"

TABLE II

[here modified as if only two students were taking the test]

School: ________________________   Date: ________________

Name	1	2	3	4	5	6	7	8	9	10	11	12	13	14	15	16	17

The Aptitude Test is collected and the IQ test is administered.

3) IQ TEST (to assess Intelligence)

The IQ Test consists entirely of sets of four objects, each differing from the others in shape and color. The test taker is directed to match a fifth object with one of the four. The test booklet provides two examples to illustrate what is called for and walks the test taker through the process of arriving at the right answer. As the test progresses, the differences become increasingly subtle.

When the students have finished, IQ Test is collected and the Math Test is administered.

4) MATH TEST (to assess the need for remediation) [The Math Test is an American seventh-grade test translated into Spanish. The applicants are in ninth grade.]

When the students have finished, the Math Test is collected and the team leader asks the American to conduct the Character Test.

5) CHARACTER TEST 1 (to assess self-discipline and courage, both functions of character)

The American tells the applicants that he is going to ask several questions and that, when they know the answer to any particular question, *they must raise their hand and be called on before answering* (self-discipline). They may <u>not</u> use pencil and paper to work out their answers. Team members enter in their copies of Table III (below) a "2" for each student who is called on and answers correctly, a "1" for each student who is called on and answers incorrectly, a "-1" for each student who answers correctly without having been called on, a "-2" for each student who raises his hand but cannot answer when called on, and a "-3" for each student who answers incorrectly without having been called on.

    A calculator will supply the answer to the first question, that is, .0179104476, but no one will know that. The purpose of the question is not to find out if anyone can do the math but rather to find out who has the courage to try. The American must recognize at least once each student who raises his or her hand. Notice should be taken of those who never raise their hand. [The answers are here supplied in brackets.]

1) How much is: *1*) three sixty-sevenths divided by three twelfths; *2*) 8 x 8 [64]; *3*) 7 x 8 [56]; *4*) 9 x 9 [81]; *5*) 11 x 11 [121]; *6*) 11 x 12 [132]; *7*) 12 x 12 [144]; *8*) 13 x 13 [169]; *9*) 13 -7.5 [5.5]; *10*) 7.5 -13 [-7.5]; *11*) half of 67 [33.5], 1*2*) half of -29 [-14.5], *13*) half of 137 [68.5], *14*) half of 1/8 [1/16], *15*) half of 2/8 [1/8], *16*) half of 3/32 [3/64], *17*) How many months are there in one-fourth of the year?

TABLE III
[here modified as if only two students were taking the test]

School: _______________________________________ Date: _________________

Name	*1*	*2*	*3*	*4*	*5*	*6*	*7*	*8*	*9*	*10*	*11*	*12*	*13*	*14*	*15*	*16*	*17*

The team leader then calls on the third member of the team to conduct the Creativity Test by asking the following questions to test the students' ability to think outside the box, that is, outside their own experience of reality.

6) CREATIVITY TEST [team members ask for details] (to assess the students' imagination)

1)   How many of you take charge when something needs to be done and no one else is doing it.
2)   Who has made plans for Christmas?
3)   Do any of you ever think that there is a better way of doing something that someone else is doing?

238

4) Is there a shortcut to making tortillas?.
5) Do any of you get angry when you don't get your way?
6) Do any of you sometimes tell your mom or your dad how to do something?.
7) Do any of you agree with the old adage, "To get along, go along"?
8) Who among you are satisfied that things are as they ought to be?
9) Do any of you ever dream of doing something really big? What?
10) Do any of you ever fail to finish a project?
11) What three words best describe you?
12) Is there any way to improve your lot in life?
13) Would you say that you are practical and predictable?
14) Do any of you ever waste time dreaming of something that will never happen?
15) What would you do with Q10,000,000?

TABLE IV [here modified as if only two students were taking the test]
[In each box, the team member writes the name of the student, the question number, and the applicant's answer.]

When the tests are finished, the team leader tells the applicants to return at such-and-such a time. The team members score the tests and decide whose homes should be visited for the Family Interview. When the students return, the team leader thanks those whose homes are not to be visited tells them that, regrettably, they have not been selected to participate in the program and may leave.

The students who remain are then given a copy of the *Forma de Datos Familiares* ("Family Information Form") and asked to fill it out as best they can. When they have finished they are told to take it home and complete it with the help of their parents. The students are also given a copy of the *Documentos Requeridos*, a list of required documents: a Birth Certificate, the most recent Grade Report, the Family Information Form, and the Parental Authorization Form. The team leader advises the students that these documents are required and makes arrangements to visit the homes.

FAMILY INTERVIEW

The purposes of the family interview are: a) to rate the poverty level of the family, b) to win the confidence of the parents, c) to learn the applicant's health history, d) to assess the quality of the applicant's upbringing, e) to assess the prevailing estimate of the applicant among other family members, f) to assess the prospect of other children becoming applicants, g) to take note of the applicant's function in the family, and h) to make sure the family has realistic expectations.

Following initial introductions with the parents and the older children, if available, the team leader introduces the team members and explains that GSSG is a non-denominational, non-political organization that brings impoverished Guatemalan youth to the United States for schooling.

The American then explains the purpose of the program and its three phases. In his explanation the American should make the following points:

1) there will be no cost to the biological family,
2) neither will there be any immediate, economic benefit to the family,
3) the purpose is to give selected youth an opportunity to attend high school and college in the United States and thus acquire, in concert with the other students in the program, the leadership skills necessary to bring about socioeconomic development in Guatemala,
4) selection is based on seven criteria: poverty, honesty, integrity, personality, character, intelligence, and leadership potential,
5) success is not guaranteed and the parents must agree not to hold GSSG responsible if the student's participation is terminated at any time, for any reason,
6) the student will lose credit for *tercero basico* [ninth grade] and may have to start *tercero basico* over again if he or she returns to school in Guatemala,
7) GSSG may use photos, stories, and other data regarding the family at its sole discretion, whether the student is selected or not,
8) parents may not accompany their son or daughter to the airport, and that
9) they, the parents, will not hold GSSG, the host family, or any other entity responsible for anything that may happen to the student during his or her stay in the United States, even death.

The team leader should make the point that, if the child is not selected, the reason may not be that the student has failed in any way, as a number of students selected is determined by GSSG's Board of Trustees.

Next the team leader reads the *Family Authorization Form* to the family and secures the necessary signatures.

The team leader then reads the *Parental Authorization Form* to the family, asks if there are questions, and secures the necessary signatures.

PARENTAL AUTHORIZATION FORM

____

                     Applicant's name

We, the parents or guardians of the individual named above, understand that the purpose of the Guatemalan Student Support Group, whose acronym is GSSG, is a charitable organization and that its program is designed to help poor Guatemalan youth as a way of promoting socioeconomic development in Guatemala. We affirm that our family is very poor. We understand that in the United States our son or daughter will be exposed to ideas and values different from our own.

We understand as well that the principal objective of Phase 1 of GSSG's program is fluency in English and that if, in the judgment of GSSG, our son or daughter does not speak satisfactory English at the end of Phase 1, he or she will not be permitted to continue to Phase

2, that advancement to the next phase is not automatic and that GSSG has no obligation of any kind to keep our son or daughter in its program.

In addition we understand that GSSG's objective is not the personal enrichment of our child or our family. Therefore we declare that we will use such authority as we have with our son or daughter to insure that he or she never seeks to live in the United States permanently, legally or illegally, and that failure to observe this condition will obligate GSSG to report the case to civil authority in the United States and further that, if this condition is violated, GSSG may seek compensation from us and/or our child.

With these considerations in mind, we authorize the Guatemalan Student Support Group and its representatives as well as any organization, group, school, church, or other entity authorized by GSSG, and our child's host parents:

a) to require our son or daughter to obey all the laws of the United States and its component polities;

b) to collect personal and confidential, and educational documents and information about our family and home, to take pictures and/or videos of us, our home, work, and way of life, and to use these materials to promote the organization and its program, whether our child is selected to participate in the program or not (reserved to GSSG);

c) to act as appropriate in seeking medical treatment and in any other circumstances that warrant attention and resolution;

d) to require our child to participate in such activities as GSSG officials and other persons authorized by GSSG may deem appropriate, not only medical or dental care but also cultural and recreational trips, religious, academic, and sporting events, and the like.

e) to use such legal, medical, dental, optical documentation, other personal documents as we have with respect to our child;

f) to impose on our child high standards of morality, hygiene, and self and to require our child to concur with the objectives of GSSG's program;

g) to require our child to return to Guatemala if he or she fails to conform to GSSG's standards and that we will reimburse GSSG the transportation costs involved (reserved to GSSG.);

For our part, we agree not to telephone our child more than once a month and, whenever we do speak with him or her by phone, we will be happy and never cry or complain.

Further we hold GSSG, its officials and representatives, the host families, and any organization, group, school, church or entity in whose activities our son or daughter was engaged, harmless in case of accident, injury, sickness or any other unfortunate development, including death, whether in the course of his or her time in the United States or during the trip to and from the United States. Further, we will do our best to defend GSSG and such organizations, entities, and persons already mentioned from judicial adversity. We understand that GSSG may, at its own discretion and for its exclusive benefit, provide such forms of security as it sees fit.

Finally, we have been given the opportunity to request an explanation of all aspects of this document that we did not initially understand and we affirm our satisfaction with the explanations provided and we have no further questions.

The team leader then reads the *Participant Commitment* form, advises the parents that students who do not behave in accordance with their commitment are sent home, noting that in the past most of the boys who were sent home had accessed pornography on the Internet. Having answered any questions, the team leader secures the student's signature and the father's signature as witness. The team leader also signs the form as a witness.

The team leader then reads the *Participant Commitment* form to the family.

PARTICIPANT COMMITMENT FORM

I, ____, fully understand that participation in the program of the Guatemalan Student Support Group (GSSG) is intended primarily to give me and other impoverished Guatemalan youth an opportunity to acquire an education meeting higher standards than those which generally prevail in the schools available to the poor in Guatemala. GSSG 's purpose, I understand, is the creation of a corps of knowledgeable leaders, of thinkers and writers, of professionals and entrepreneurs, in sufficient numbers to effect significant socioeconomic development in my country. By signing this document I hereby affirm my commitment to this objective and I solemnly swear, before God, that I will never seek to remain in the United States, legally or illegally. I further understand that if I engage in inappropriate behavior or if I do not succeed in each phase of the program, I will not be permitted to continue.

Finally, I understand that good character is a necessary component of success in any field, as in life itself, and that any evidence to the contrary will disqualify me from further participation in the program. Specifically, I affirm that I will never seek to access a pornographic site on the Internet, read or look at pornographic literature, send or receive "sexy" pictures, talk about sex with others, kiss on the lips, or touch anyone inappropriately or permit others to touch me inappropriately. Rather, I shall always dress modestly and in all respects conduct myself like a lady or gentleman. [Signatures and date required.]

After answering any questions, the team leader obtains the required signatures collects the documents.

Next the team leader explains that the final selection will be made later and, if their son or daughter is among the finalists, the remaining documents named in the "Required Documents" list must be available by such-and-such a date.

The team leader then tells the family that he himself or another team member will conduct a personal interview with the applicant and asks where they may speak privately.

PERSONAL INTERVIEW

The purpose of the personal interview is to assess the honesty, integrity, personality, character, intelligence, imagination (creativity), will (ability to make decisions), and leadership potential of the candidate. While other members of the team engage other members of the family in other activities, such as picture taking, asking about health and work, cooking and cuisine, crops and finances (not just as a distraction but to learn more about the family and the student), one member of the team, the woman if the applicant is a girl, conducts the personal interview.

The personal interview should be just that, personal. A effective interview begins by gaining the student's trust and respect, by being a sympathetic adult interested in listening and helping. You, the interviewer, might lead off by telling the student something about yourself and then inviting the interviewee to tell you about himself or herself. When trust has been established, turn to asking personal questions of the student. You might lead off with something the student has not volunteered, like "What grade are you in?" or "What's your favorite subject?" and then getting a little more personal, "Tell me about your best friend." You are not really interested in his or her best friend but the answer will tell you something about the speaker, because likes attract. The answer will likely say much about the candidate's *personality*. *Integrity* is a little more difficult. "I notice you are not wearing a watch. How come?" If the answer is, "I don't have the money," you might follow up with, "You can buy nice watches cheap on market day [see page 28]. How about if I give you the money; will you go and buy one?" This question addresses the issue of *integrity* because everyone knows that those cheap watches spread out on a blanket on Market Street are all the result of robbery. Their former owners were tourists, busloads of whom make relatively easy targets. Everyone knows that. Knowingly buying stolen property hardly suggests "highly moral values." Again, you might say, "Tell me about something you would like to have, something you have never seen and cannot buy," a topic related to *imagination*. "Have you ever lied?" If the answer is 'yes,' the student is probably *honest*. "Do you love Guatemala?" Almost anyone would instinctively feel obligated to say 'yes,' but deep inside everyone knows that Guatemala is a terrible place to live. The issue is not only about *honesty* but also whether the student is *intelligent* enough to distinguish love of family from love of country.

These questions might well lead to more revealing answers.

Is life sometimes difficult?
What's the most honest thing you've ever done?
Are you happy?
If your mom were going to die without a certain medicine and there is no way that you could buy it for her, would you steal it to save her life? [Make sure you know what your own answer would be, and why and how you will react to either answer.]
What is your observation about boys in general?
What is your observation about girls in general?
What is the most wonderful thing that has ever happened to you?
What is the most terrible thing that has ever happened to you?
What wonderful thing would you like to happen tomorrow?

Vis-à-vis *imagination*, you might ask if there is a better way of doing something that has attracted your attention in the home or the village. Again, you might ask, "What is 13 x 13?" to see if the individual is disciplined enough to have worked out the answer when the same question was asked in the Group Interview, a *character* issue. Other indirect questions might include: "What would you like to become as an adult?" to judge whether the student is mature enough to have dealt with the issue, a matter of *will*, making decisions. Again, the you might ask, "Why is Guatemala so poor?" to see if the student thinks that responsibility for poverty lies exclusively with others (corruption, injustice, racism, etc.) or may also lie within ('We are ignorant,' 'We are afraid to take chances,' etc.), again a matter of *character*. If you see a vista opening up in the respondent's consciousness, pursue it, "Where do ideas come from" and/or "Tell me some of your ideas." Above all, be sensitive to the student's interests and pursue them by asking, for example, what he or she would do to achieve such-and-such a goal, what the implications of pursuing such-and-such course of action might be, like the possibility of being killed for trying to found a Mayan political party. My favorite is, 'What does it mean to be human?' Such a line of questioning will do more than any number of math questions to identify the thinkers, that is, those with an active *imagination*. If the boy or girl enjoys being challenged, he or she is probably not only bright (*intellect*) but also *confident*, a *personality* issue. Another measure will be the extent to which the applicant asks questions of you. Their quality will differ from student to student and tell the team much not only about the student's *intelligence* but also his or her *personality*, and *imagination*.

The interviewer must make written notes during the interview and review them frequently as the process develops.

The personal interview is the most important of all and the interviewer's assessment of the applicant will likely carry the most weight in the evaluation of honesty, integrity, personality, character, imagination, and will, while leadership potential is best measured in the Group Interview and poverty, in the Family Interview, inside the home.

FINAL SELECTION

When all of the steps have been completed, the team meets to determine which of the applicants shall become candidates, that is, eligible to apply for visas. The team leader passes around the results of the Aptitude Test, the Math Test, and the IQ Test. The team members then express what observations they have made on the various Tables, while they review the photos relevant to each applicant in succession.

Next each team member compiles a list of his or her own rank-ordering of the applicants according to the seven criteria, without consulting the other team members. The lists are compared. If there is agreement on the suitability of x-number of applicants, regardless of the team members' individual ordering, and that number is equal to the number authorized by the Board of Trustees, the work of the team is finished.

If there is no agreement, the members of the team share their reasons for voting as they did with a view to persuading the others to change their ranking of the applicants. When they have finished, they vote again. If there is agreement, regardless of differences in ranking, the work of the team is finished. If not, those applicants enjoying the support of all three team members are moved to candidate status. If the final list does not suffice to satisfy the number authorized by the Board, the team visits one or more additional schools. Meanwhile, the team leader notifies the new candidates of the next step and the unsuccessful applicants of the results. The American provides the Board of Trustees with the names of those who have been selected, with profiles (page 208) to follow.

Appendix B, Host-Family Orientation

Introduction

- Welcome. Do all of you know each other?

- To contact us in Guatemala, send an email to _________________________________.

- We will e-mail you the date, time, and flight number as soon as we have bought the tickets.

Things to Do the Day of Arrival

- Please meet us at the airport.
- Guatemalans like to hug. They students will understand the word "Welcome." If you want to say *bienvenido* (*bee-en-ven-EE-doh*), they will be pleasantly surprised.
- Each of the students will have a English/Spanish dictionary. So you may want to look up a word, point to it, and say the word. In any case, a GSSG officer can translate for you.
- When it is time for bed, take your guest to the bedroom, open a dresser drawer or two and act out putting clothes in the drawer while you say, *ropa limpia* (*ROH-pah LEEM-pea-ah*), which means "clean clothes"; then show him or her the hamper and say *ropa sucia* (*ROH-pah SOO-see-ah*) "dirty clothes."
- Show your student the bathroom and where to put the toothbrush, where the towels are, and say, *Para usted* (*PAH-rah ooss-TED*), "For you." Demonstrate how to adjust the water temperature, especially in the shower and illustrate what to do with the shower curtain.
- Before leaving the student, say, *La llamaré para desayunar* (*la yah-mah-RAY PAH-rah day-sah-you-NAR*), if a girl or *Lo llamaré para desayunar*, if a boy, both of which mean, "I will call you for breakfast," and "Good night!" in English.

Everything Else

- For the first few days, do not leave your guest alone, except in his or her bedroom. Home sickness will set in soon enough. Take your student with you wherever you go.

- Your Guatemalan youngster will need some clothes. GSSG will reimburse you for your purchases up to $200. Please get what you can at Goodwill or thrift shops. Send your receipts to us.

- Insurance procedure: 1) get medical care and prescriptions as you would for your own child, using the student's insurance card; 2) pay the bill when asked to do so; 3) file the insurance claim form, making the youngster the beneficiary but giving your address as the youngster's address on the form; 4) send us a copy of the claim form and a copy of the bill; 5) GSSG will cover the deductible and co-pay.

- Please take the child to the county health department soon after arrival for a physical and shots. We will give you an immunization record from Guatemala, which may or may not have anything on it. In any case, the students will all need boosters.

- Give your youngster a card with your name, address, and telephone number.

- Shortly after your youth's arrival, get his or her passport and keep it in a safe place. Please make sure your spouse also knows where it is.

- Your Guatemalan child should live as a practical member of your family; treat him or her as your own. Include him or her in your family travels within U.S. If you have house rules, make sure they are understood and enforced. Many host moms recommend, "No eating or drinking except in the kitchen or dining room." Since most of the kids live in one- or two-room homes, often with a dirt floor, they have no concept of such a rule; much less the reason behind it.

- Expect some homesickness, but don't immediately reach for the telephone. Some hugging will probably do more good.

- GSSG does not allow physical punishment.

- It will probably be a good idea to set out the next day's clothes the night before. Most of our clients probably wear the same outfit for a week, while their other outfit is being washed. They will be glad to conform to your schedule.

- Before going to church or out to dinner, etc., make sure your guest is wearing appropriate attire.

- Do not expect the youngsters to be noticeably different. They do not live in the Stone Age. There are cultural differences but they will not be apparent at first. Over time you will notice something and think, "That's strange." If it's an isolated incident, just let it pass; if it's repetitive and socially unacceptable, explain what the usual practice is here, without suggesting that their behavior is bad or inferior; it's just different.

- You will have to do some parenting. Like all youngsters, yours will need and has a right to expect guidance and love. There will be a honeymoon period when you and the students are both trying to please. Make it short! From the first day, if your guest forgets to put the shower curtain inside the tub, explain gently. If he/she forgets again the next day, remind again. By the third day, remind again but forcefully or call us.

- Put strict limits on phone calls. The best way is to give your student an international phone card for some special occasion. Do not give him or her unlimited time. Your youngster should write thank-you letters to people who give them gifts. These kids have never before written or received a letter; they must learn.

- Under no circumstances should the students have a television set in their bedroom. Do not allow them to spend an inordinate amount of time alone in the bedroom.

- These kids are normal teens. Keep your expectations realistic. When you teach your youngster something new, like using a vacuum cleaner, walk him or her though the process. Explain that the cord, for example, must not get sucked into the machine. Remember that they have never even seen such a machine before, much less used it.

- When you take your youngster shopping, do not be afraid to say "No!" The students come here with the unrealistic expectation that everybody in the United States is rich, and so we are in comparison with their parents. You must show them that even we cannot have everything we want and neither can they.

- We will give you a copy, in English and Spanish, of what we tell them during the orientation in Guatemala. Your student also has a copy. Please refer to it as necessary.

- Forms of address. We tell the students to address adults outside the family as Mr. __________ and Mrs. __________. In Guatemala it is customary for youngsters to address older people by title and first name, for example, "Mr. John." Please insist that in English they use our system of title and last name: Mrs. Smith, Dr. Jones, etc.

- Avoid the word *Indian*; it is a racial slur in Guatemala.

- English: Print uses spaces to separate words; speech does not. At first be careful to speak very slowly, pausing after each word to give your youngster a chance to process each word in turn. If he or she does not understand, DO NOT EXPLAIN! That only adds more unfamiliar words to the problem. Rather, repeat exactly the same words, slowly, and give him or her a chance to look up words in the dictionary. When he or she doesn't understand, do not increase the volume; just say it again, very slowly.

- Please avoid: gonna, wanna, hafta, shoulda, dunno, $_m{}^m{}_m$, b'cuz, ahr, yer, layder, lemme, doin', etc. "Jeat jet?" will be unintelligible to your youngster; just say it and you will understand.

- The sound *uh*, as in *cup*, *but*, *up*, etc. does not exist in Spanish or in any Mayan language (so far as we know). The same is true of the sound *er*, as in *her*, *blur*, *early*, etc. These are the most common sounds in English. Please insist on the correct pronunciation. Be persistent!

- We are not just interested in language; we want to give our clients the tools they need to bring Guatemala out of poverty. The most important tool is reading, far more important than any physical skill. If you have children's books, get your Guatemalan started reading very soon. If necessary, read to them, as you did with your own children. Little by little they should make the transition to more adult reading. Newspapers are helpful because they tend to use the same words day after day.

- Get them into the habit of writing: a diary, letters, "thank-you"s, etc. They will never have written anything before. It's time to start.

- Show them where the linen is kept and when it comes time to change it, demonstrate. Indicate how often to change the bed clothes and get a clean towel. They will never have used a washcloth. Demonstrate its use if you like, but don't insist.

- Do not ask much about poverty; generally the poor are ashamed of being poor. After you have gained their confidence, then they may want to share their feelings about being poor.

- Contrary to what you may have heard, TV is not an effective instructional aid. If you watch a movie on DVD, turn on the Spanish subtitles for a few weeks, after that, English subtitles.

- A day or two before departure, make sure you still know where your child's passport is.

- Departure date will be __________. The flight will probably leave about 6:30 AM. That will put the youngsters in Guatemala City about noon, time enough to get home before dark. Girls should not be wearing expensive jewelry when they arrive in Guatemala.

- One final note, about religion, a sensitive subject. GSSG does not allow proselytizing. We expect the children to return home with the same religion as their biological parents.

<h1 style="text-align:center">Appendix C, Workshops (samples)</h1>

Guatemalan Student Support Group
June 2010 Workshop—Leadership

Abbreviations: JB = Bodoh; JP = Paque; KS = Swain de Pop; LP = Pop; LC = Choo; JE = Eide

<h3 style="text-align:center">Tuesday, June 8</h3>

N.B. I am not scheduling a chat with the eleven who live in NC, as I get to chat with them often.

Time	Event
c.05:30 AM	All students in the U.S. depart, most meeting up in Houston for the flight to Guatemala.
10:48 AM	All except the MI group arrive in Guatemala & take the bus or van to the hotel. JP
12:00-01:00	Introductions, lunch, distribution of 3-ring binders & summer-reading books. JP & JB
12:30-02:00 01:00-02:00 01:00-02:00	LP & JB go to the bank and then to the airport to meet the MI group. Sophomores: "English Grammar & Diagramming," Session 1. JP Juniors & seniors: start reading *Economics for Dummies*. LP & JB go to the airport.
02:00	LP & JB meet the MI group and take the bus or van to the hotel, arriving c.02:30.
02:00-03:00	Sophomores: "English Grammar & Diagramming," Session 2. JP Juniors & seniors: continue reading *Economics for Dummies*.
03:00-03:15	Break, distribution of 3-ring binders & summer-reading books to MI group, JP & JB
03:15-04:00	Chat with JB: Alba, Luis F., Raquel. 15" each; please be waiting. Sophomores: "English Grammar & Diagramming," Session 3. JP Juniors & seniors: continue reading *Economics for Dummies*.
05:00-06:00	Chat with JB: Sandra Bolom, Teresa, Yesenia, Rolan. 15" each; please be waiting. Sophomores: "English Grammar & Diagramming," Session 4. JP Juniors & seniors: continue reading *Economics for Dummies*.
05:45-06:00	Break.
06:00-06:45	Dinner.
06:45-07:45	Opening Session & First General Session: "What Is the Problem with Guatemala?" JB
07:45-09:45	Movie: *Amadeus*, Part I. JB
08:53	KS, her boys, & JP or LP pick up LC at the airport.
9:45-10:45	Chat with JB: Abner, Mario, Wilmer, Walter. 15" each; please be waiting. All others: read or go to bed.
10:30	Lights out (except Wilmer and Walter who still have to talk with JB).

<h3 style="text-align:center">Wednesday, June 9</h3>

Time	Event
07:45-08:30	Breakfast.
08:30-08:45	Discussion of the contents of the manila envelopes. JB,
08:45-09:45	Second General Session: "What Can Be Done about It?" JB
09:45-10:00	Break.
10:00-12:00	Sophomores: SLEP test. JP 1st session for Juniors & Seniors: "Leadership." JB
12:00-01:00	Lunch.
01:00-02:00	2nd session for Juniors & Seniors: "Economics & Happiness." JB Sophomores: "English Grammar & Diagramming," Session 5. JP
02:00-02:45	Third general session: "Practice Speaking English without an accent, 1." JB, LC, JE, JP

249

02:45-03:00	Break.
03:00-04:00	Fourth general session: "Writing a Letter" JB & JP
04:00-05:00	Sophomores: Test on "English Grammar & Diagramming," Session 6. JP Chat with JB: Lily, Ana, Marly, Rossy. 15" each; please be waiting. Juniors & seniors: read the book of your choice.
05:00-06:00	Fifth general session:: "Practice Speaking English without an accent, 2." JB, LC, JE, JP
06:00-06:45	Dinner: JP
06:45-08:00	Speeches: Alba, Nataly, Byron, Luis Fernández, Abner.
08:00-08:15	Break.
08:15-10:00	Sixth general session: "Don't leave your brains at the door, 1" *Amadeus*, Part II. JB
10:00-11:00	Chat with JB: Tita, Mirian, Carlos, Elmer. 15" each; please be waiting. All others: read or go to bed.
11:00	Lights out.

Thursday, June 10

Time	Event
08:00-08:45	Breakfast.
08:45-09:45	Seventh General Session: "Reading—Connecting the Dots." JB
09:45-10:00	Break.
10:00-11:00	Speeches: Pablo, Nancy, Lily, Pedro.
11:00-12:00	Speeches: Rossy, Heidi, Ana, Griselda.
12:00-01:00	Lunch.
01:00-02:00	Speeches: Judith, Sandra Coc, Marly, Mario.
03:00-06:00	Movie: *My Fair Lady*. JB
06:00-07:00	Dinner.
07:00-07:30	Measurements: girls, LC; boys, JP Miscellaneous activities. JB
07:30-08:00	Eighth General Session: "Don't leave your brains at the door, 2" *My Fair Lady*, JB
08:00-10:00	Party, dance. JP
10:30	Lights out.

Friday, June 11

Time	Event
08:00-08:45	Breakfast.
08:45-09:45	Ninth General Session: "Writing a Book Report." JB
09:45-10:00	Break.
10:00-10:45	Tenth General Session: "Post GSSG." JB
10:45-11:00	Pack up to leave.
11:00-12:00	Lunch. JP
12:00-12:15	Break.
12:15-12:30	Load the vehicles. Security vehicle arrives.
c.12:30	Everybody leaves.

Please note: Everyone is responsible for making his/her bed before breakfast every day, sitting with someone not sat with before at every meal, and taking his/her dishes to the kitchen after each meal. When you are assigned to wash dishes, go to the kitchen as soon as you have finished eating.

Tuesday, December 25

Time	Event
07:10 PM	Pablo arrives at RDU, Delta 1607.
08:41 PM	Walter arrives at RDU, Delta 743.

Wednesday, December 26

Time	Event
01:56 PM	All MN/WI students arrive at RDU.
02:30–03:00	Lunch for MN/WI students at Wendy's near the airport.
03:00	NC students, Pablo, Pedro, and Walter arrive at Wendy's. All leave for Manteo, NC.
07:00	As soon as we arrive, everybody gather around Dr. Goehl to draw your bed assignments, Judith and Tita go first and then go to the kitchen to help Mrs. Goehl prepare for dinner.
07:30–08:15	Dinner. (Sit with someone you haven't seen for a long time.) Judith & Tita wash dishes.
08:15–08:30	Free time. Alba & Blanca sweep.
08:30–09:30	Opening Session: distribution of materials.
09:30–11:00	Arrange your documents in your new 13–compartment folder & Free time.
11:00	Lights out. Total silence.

Thursday, December 27

Time	Event	
07:00–07:45	Breakfast. José and Walter wash dishes.	
07:45–08:00	Free time.	Nancy, talk w/ Dr. Goehl.
08:00–09:45	*Experiencing the Humanities*, Chapter I.	
09:15–10:00	Free time.	
10:00–11:30	*Experiencing the Humanities*, Chapter I, cont'd.	
11:30–12:00	Free time. Carlos & Blanca help prepare for lunch.	
12:00–12:45	Lunch. Carlos & Blanca wash dishes.	
12:45–01:00	Free time.	José, talk w/ Dr. Goehl.
01:00–03:00	Time to study for the test to follow.	
03:00–03:30	Test on *Experiencing the Humanities*, Chapter I.	
03:30–04:45	John Gardner, *On Leadership* 1, discussion.	
04:45–05:45	Speeches: Alba, Pablo, Byron, Sandra Coc, & Pedro. (10" each).	
05:00–06:00	Nancy & Raquel help prepare for dinner.	
05:45–06:00	Free time.	
06:00–06:45	Dinner. Nancy & Raquel wash dishes.	
06:45–07:00	Free time. Pablo & Teresa sweep.	Byron, talk w/ Dr. Goehl.
07:00–09:00	Documentary 1: "Inside 9/11" (2006), 1 hr., 45", discussion.	
09:00–09:15	Free time.	
09:15–10:15	Video: "Victor Borge" (60").	
10:15–11:00	Free time.	
11:00	Lights out. Total silence.	

Friday, December 28

Time	Event	
07:00–07:45	Breakfast. Sandra Bolom & Raquel wash dishes.	
07:45–08:00	Free time.	Tita, talk w/ Dr. Goehl.
08:00–09:00	Post–GSSG 2: Name & Bylaws; "Core"; "*Problema*"; thinking outside the box.	

09:00–10:00	John Gardner, *On Leadership* 2, discussion.	
10:00–10:15	Free time.	
10:15–11:45	Writing 1: Applying for college and scholarships (Dr.Goehl).	
11:30–12:00	Alba & Pablo help prepare for lunch.	
11:45–12:00	Free time.	
12:00–12:45	Lunch. Alba & Pablo wash dishes.	
12:45–01:00	Free time.	Sandra Coc, talk w/ Dr. Goehl.
01:00–01:30	Technical terms in "Islam: Empire of Faith," Part 1.	
01:30–02:30	Documentary 2: "Islam: Empire of Faith," Part 1 (1982), 55".	
02:30–03:00	Time Line 1, discussion.	
03:00–03:15	Free time.	
03:15–05:15	Documentary 3: "Inside Islam" (2002), 1 hr. 40", discussion.	
05:00–06:00	Niceh & Mirian help prepare for dinner.	
05:15–05:45	Speeches: Judith, Nancy, & Niceh (10" each).	Carlos, talk w/ Dr. Goehl.
05:45–06:00	Free time.	
06:00–06:45	Dinner. Niceh & Mirian wash dishes.	
06:45–07:00	Free time. Pedro & Carlos sweep.	Luis, talk w/ Dr. Goehl.
07:00–08:00	Writing 2: "Some English Idioms" & "Vocabulary" from *Experiencing the Humanities*.	
08:00–08:25	Speeches: Rafael, & Walter (10" each).	
08:25–08:40	Free time.	
08:40–10:40	Movie: "Roman Holiday," 2 hrs.	
11:00	Lights out. Total silence.	

Saturday, December 29

Time	Event	
07:00–07:45	Breakfast. Sandra Coc & Niceh wash dishes.	
07:45–08:00	Free time.	Rafael, talk w/ Dr. Goehl.
08:00–09:00	Speeches: Tita, Raquel, Mirian, Yesenia, & Teresa (10" each).	Alba, talk w Dr. Goehl.
09:00–10:15	Writing 3: Writing and Thinking (pp. 4–22).	
10:15–10:30	Free time.	
10:30–11:00	Writing 4: Evaluating (p. 22).	
11:00–11:45	Writing 5: Outlining (p. 24).	
11:30–12:00		
12:00–12:45	Lunch. Sandra Coc & Pedro wash dishes.	
12:45–01:00	Free time.	Mirian, talk w/ Dr. Goehl.
01:00–02:00	Documentary 4: "Islam vs. Islamists" (2007), 53", discussion.	
02:00–03:00	John Gardner, *On Leadership* 3, discussion.	
03:00–03:15	Free time.	Judith, talk w/ Dr. Goehl.
03:15–04:45	Writing 6: Revising & Rewriting (pp. 25–26).	
04:45–05:45	Speeches: Carlos, Luis, José, Sandra Bolom, & Blanca (10" each).	Pablo, w/ Dr. Goehl.
05:00–06:00	Rafael & Yesenia help prepare for dinner.	Raquel, talk w/ Dr. Goehl.
05:45–06:00	Free time.	
06:00–06:45	Dinner. Rafael & Yesenia wash dishes.	
06:45–07:00	Free time. Byron & Yesenia sweep.	Niceh, talk w/ Dr. Goehl.
07:00–10:30	Movie: "My Fair Lady," 3hrs. including intermission.	
11:00	Lights out. Total silence.	

Sunday, December 30

Time	Event
07:00–07:30	Breakfast. Nancy & Luis wash dishes.
07:30–08:00	Christian Terminology.
08:00–08:15	Free time.
08:15–08:30	Travel to: Ocean View Baptist, 902 S. Virginia Dare Trl., Kill Devil Hills; drop off Evan.
08:30–08:45	Catholics go on to Holy Redeemer, 301 W. Kitty Hawk Rd., Kitty Hawk.

10:00–10:30	Catholics return to Kill Devil Hills; pick up Evangelicals; return to Kitty Hawk.	
10:30–11:30	Visit Monument: 5230 N. Croatan Highway, The Bypass, MP 1, Kitty Hawk; return home	
11:30–12:00	Sandra Bolom & José help prepare for lunch.	
11:30–12:00	Free time.	
12:00–12:45	Lunch. Sandra Bolom & José wash dishes.	
12:45–01:00	Free time.	Teresa, talk w/ Dr. Goehl.
01:00–02:00	Documentary 6: "Obsession" (60").	
02:00–02:45	Time Line 2, discussion.	
02:45–03:00	Free Time.	
03:00–05:00	Documentary 7: "Islam: What the West Needs to Know." (2006), 1 hr. 40", discussion.	
05:00–06:00	Free time.	
05:00–06:00	Walter & Teresa help prepare for dinner.	
06:00–06:45	Dinner. Walter & Teresa wash dishes.	
06:45–07:00	Free time. Rafael & Mirian sweep.	Pedro, talk w/ Dr. Goehl.
07:00–09:00	Movie: *Not without My Daughter*, 2 hrs.	
09:00–09:15	Free time.	
09:15–10:15	Discussion.	
10:15–11:00	Free time.	
11:00	Lights out. Total silence.	

Monday, December 31

Time	Event	
07:00–08:00	Breakfast. Make up beds, vacuum, dust, etc.	
08:00–08:15	Free time. Tita & Judith wash dishes.	Blanca, talk w/ Dr. Goehl.
08:15–09:00	Writing 7: Composing a group letter to Mrs. Davis.	
09:00–10:00	Writing 8: Composing a letter to your sponsor(s).	
REMINDER: Be prepared to deliver a speech at the June Workshop. [Think outside the box.] Before you start, read the section on Unity and Coherence, pages 46 to 53. In choosing your vocabulary and your idioms, remember that your audience is bilingual. Be able to tell us what tone you are using and why.		
10:00–11:00	Women's laundry time. Boys do some housework.	
11:00–12:00	Men's laundry time. Girls do some housework.	
11:30–12:00	Byron & Luis help prepare for lunch.	
12:00–12:45	Lunch. Byron & Luis wash dishes.	
12:45–01:30	Rearrange the furniture and towels to their original set-up; vacuum, dust, etc.	
01:00–01:30	Pablo and Dr. Bodoh, return folding chairs to the Center.	Yesenia, talk w/ Dr. Goehl.
01:30–02:00	Load luggage in the vehicles.	
02:00–06:00	All travel to Raleigh, Durham, & Chapel Hill.	
06:00–07:00	Dinner with host families.	
07:00–	Evening with host families.	

Tuesday, January 1

Time	Event
07:00 AM	MN/WI group assembles at RDU
07:15 AM	Walter departs RDU, Delta 1165,
08:20 AM	MN/WI group departs for MSP, Delta 3318.
09:28 AM	Pablo departs, Delta 6187.

Appendix D, Higher Education

Formal education has its origin in ancient Greece, around 500 B.C. The Greek word for education is *paideia* (*pie-DAY-uh*). A school was called a *gymnasion* and physical education played a significant role in the curriculum. No one word corresponded to our *teacher*; anyone might make a profession of teaching. Success was measured not by certificates, like our bachelor's degree, but by the success of one's pupils. The Romans followed the Greek model.

After the fall of the Roman Empire, around A.D. 500, formal education ceased to exist in Western Europe. Its return can be credited to Charlemagne who, though himself illiterate, hired an Irish monk[353] to teach his children and grandchildren in the royal palace and himself sat in school with them (around A.D. 800). The Thirteenth Century witnessed the rise of most of the great Medieval universities: Cambridge (1209), Salamanca (1218), Montpellier (1220), Padua (1222), Toulouse (1229), Paris (1231), Orleans (1235), Sienna (1240), and Coimbra (1288). Latin had long since become the language of instruction everywhere in Western Europe and teachers at these institutions were called 'doctor,' the Latin word for *teacher*. In the Fifteenth Century these institutions and others began issuing documents certifying academic achievement: prominently the Bachelor of Arts degree. Subsequently the Master of Arts degree and the Doctor of Philosophy degrees would come into being.

All three of these titles represented the level of knowledge acquired; they were not licenses to do anything. Accordingly, the church began issuing such licenses, called the *licentia docendi* in Latin (which in Spanish became *licenciatura*; in English, *licentiate* or simply *license*), on the recommendation of the local university; eventually the state would assume that function itself. The distinction remains to this day: a *degree* represents an academic achievement; a *license* is authorization to market one's knowledge.

The last half of the nineteenth century witnessed a significant change, with the introduction of new inventions beguiling everyone's attention—the battery, the telephone, the cash register, celluloid, photography, electric lighting, the gyroscope, the fountain pen, the zipper, the radio, safety matches, and many more. The faculty in the School of Philosophy at the University of Berlin reasoned that these inventions represented new knowledge for, philosophically, know-ledge necessarily precedes the construction of any new thing—you have to have an idea first, a model in your head, so to speak, before you can make any new physical object. And how do you create new knowledge? By research. The particulars of research differ from one field to another—research in medicine, for example, requires expertise in physiology and chemistry, while research in engineering requires expertise in physics and mathematics. Accordingly the School of Philosophy at Berlin began requiring research resulting in new knowledge in the field of philosophy, demonstrated in a dissertation (a written document in which the researcher explains how he created the new knowledge), as a condition for awarding the doctorate in Philosophy, the Ph.D. (*Philosophiae Doctor* in Latin).

The idea caught on. Other schools at Berlin and other German universities followed suit and began requiring a dissertation. Because the Department of Philosophy had been the first, the others fell in line and also called their new degree *Philosophiae Doctor*, "Doctor of Philosophy." Fairly quickly the German universities began attracting foreign students, notably students from the United States who had already earned a bachelor's degrees at an American institution. In 1861 Yale University started granting the Ph.D. to students who, after earning a bachelor's degree, had

---

[353] Ireland, never having been part of the Roman Empire, was largely unaffected by its fall.

completed a prescribed program of graduate courses and successfully defended a dissertation resulting in new knowledge in science or the humanities. Soon the title, Doctor of Philosophy, became common for all research-based doctorates in all fields, in Europe and North America.

The M.D. has a different history going back to the late Middle Ages as a certificate of superior knowledge in the field of medicine but involving no research. Many universities today offer a program known as the M.D./Ph.D., in which the individual first gets a Ph.D. in biology or engineering (rarely other fields) based on his or her having created new knowledge in that field as demonstrated in a dissertation. After additional years of study, an M.D.is awarded certifying that same individual is qualified to practice medicine.

Research has now become the dominant influence in the transformation of Western culture. From the universities it quickly spread to industry. For example, the three great research universities in North Carolina—UNC in Chapel Hill, NC State in Raleigh, and Duke in Durham—form a triangle geographically, in the middle of which is situated the Research Triangle Park, where dozens of commercial enterprises employ thousands of Ph.D.s doing research—high-tech firms like IBM, pharmaceutical companies like Glaxo, Smith, Kline, and many others. Such research centers dot the landscape all over the United States, Silicon Valley being only the most prominent.

The old European model terminating in the licentiate still prevails in much of Latin America and there is little chance of significant change any time soon. Research is expensive. The libraries at the University of North Carolina at Chapel Hill house a total of more than eight million books, including a separate collection of first editions and rare books; science facilities include four hospitals, each with state-of-the-art equipment; a planetarium; two theaters; an off-campus botanical garden; and an on-campus arboretum. The government of Guatemala simply lacks the resources to compete at such a level and San Carlos University does not grant Ph.D.s,[354] that is, its purpose is not to produce new knowledge, only practitioners of what is already known—job training.

---

[354] An official in the Guatemalan system of education tells me that the Ph.D. is something "new" but I have not been able to identify any recipients.

Appendix E, Internships

As GSSG's students progressed through high school, we learned a good deal from experience. One particularly knotty problem became apparent when we realized that in four years of high school our students were not developing sufficient fluency in English. Many years earlier I had done a study of optimum ages for learning a foreign language. Best of all, of course, is learning a language early childhood. The trouble is that a language learned before about seven or eight is forgotten just as quickly as it had been acquired, unless it is maintained. As a result of my investigation I concluded that a window of opportunity for learning a foreign language and retaining it extends from about twelve or thirteen to about fifteen or sixteen.

A colleague of mine, who taught linguistics at Texas Tech, had emigrated from Algeria and spoke Arabic and French natively. His wife, from Belgium, spoke French natively. They both were also fluent in English; he, in fact also spoke German, Spanish, and Russian. They had two young children. Visiting their home one day, I learned that they were raising their children to be natively trilingual—Arabic, French, and English. I knew from my previous study that mixing up multiple languages can create psychological problems later in life. I enquired how they were managing that issue. They said they knew about the potential for trouble but had a plan—he spoke only Arabic with the children, she only spoke French, and the kids learned English by playing with other children in the neighborhood.

With these experiences in mind, I conceived a plan for an internship in which our students would be obliged to live five days a week during the summer vacation teaching in *primaría* (page 85) in English (school is in session in Guatemala from January to October), not one GSSG student per village but many in as many villages as our limited number of students could accommodate, teaching the usual subjects but in English, with American textbooks, and we would do this every summer into the indefinite future, in the same villages. We would start with *primaría* but add *basico* as the years went by so that, by the time the original first-graders had received our instruction for nine years and were eligible now to apply for GSSG, they would already be fluent in English.

In this program, the GSSG students would be free to go home on the week-ends. The Guatemalan teachers would still be officially the teacher of record, receive their regular pay, and assign grades to the students.

I first discussed this plan with Rick Conlow (who was at the time GSSG's president), his wife, and Alba (page 161), when the four of us were having dinner one night in the course of making my rounds. We tweaked it a little but overall it seemed like a good idea to everyone. Back home, I ran it past Sandra Coc (page 194), because I knew that she had a brother who was teaching in a village, and asked her to discuss the plan with him. He replied that he thought it was a great idea and would like to sit in as a student. The next time I went to Guatemala, I talked about it with Jorge, who was also enthusiastic. Louise LeGrand, who was affiliated with GSSG and had come to Guatemala with me, also liked the idea. So I had Jorge get the superintendent of schools for the *department* of Izabal on the phone. I explained the proposal to him and then turned the phone over to Jorge, who answered his questions. When he hung up Jorge told us the superintendent had replied, *el programa se aprobó* ("the program is approved"). We were at our motel. I said to Jorge and Louise, "We've got to get this in writing." So we sat down in the open-air lobby. I dictated, Louise typed on Jorge's laptop, and Jorge corrected my Spanish. We composed a cover letter to the superintendent and asked him to sign the proposal and return it to us. He never replied. We concluded that the program would require consideration at a higher level.

Appendix F, Calculating the Number of High-School Graduates

On page 229 we observed that "When the Servicemen's Readjustment Act of 1944 (the G.I. Bill of Rights) became law, the population of the United States stood at about 138 million. More than two million veterans, about 1.5% of the population, took advantage of the opportunity thus provided. The population of Guatemala today is about 16 million; 1.5% of 16 million is 246,462. One may reasonably assume that the same proportion as produced the 'Greatest Generation' in the United States would have a similar effect in Guatemala, human nature being the same everywhere." The table below illustrates that the goal of 246,462 would be realized in twenty-one years.

Assuming an initial cohort of 1000 students, an analysis of the success rate of GSSG's students who first came to the United States in 2008 and 2009 yields the following percentages:

Freshmen: 31 in all, 7 washed out, $7 \div 31 = .23$
Sophomores: 24 in all, 1 washed out, $1 \div 24 = .04$
Juniors: no juniors washed out.
Seniors: 23 in all, 1 washed out, $1 \div 22 = .04$
Graduates: the result of these calculations.

In the table below, the columns contain the following information:

Column A = New freshmen, increasing by 32% each year.
Column B = Freshmen attrition, 23% of A.
Column C = Sophomores, A minus B.
Column D = Sophomore attrition, C times .04.
Column E = Juniors, no attrition.
Column F = Seniors, same as E.
Column G = Senior attrition, F times .04.
Column H = Graduates = F minus G.
Column I = Cumulative number of graduates.

Translating the formulae above into the table below yields the following results:

Year	A	B	C	D	E	F	G	H	I
	New fresh-men = previous year +32%	Fresh-man attri-tion (A x.23)	Soph-o-mores (A-B)	Soph-o-more attri-tion (C x.04)	Juniors (C - D)	Sen-iors (same as E)	Sen-ior at-tri-tion (F x.04)	Grad-uates (F - G)	Total gradu-ates H + I of preced-ing year
	A	B	C	D	E	F	G	H	I
1	1,000	230							
2	1,320	304	770	31					
3	1,742	401	1,016	41	739				
4	2,300	529	1,342	54	976	739	30		
5	3,036	698	1,771	71	1,288	976	39	710	710
6	4,007	922	2,338	94	1,700	1,288	52	937	1,646

7	5,290	1,217	3,086	123	2,244	1,700	68	1,236	2,883
8	6,983	1,606	4,073	183	2,962	2,244	90	1,632	4,515
9	9,217	2,120	5,377	215	3,910	2,962	118	2,154	6,669
10	12,166	2,798	7,097	284	5,162	3,910	156	2,844	9,513
11	16,060	3,694	9,368	37	6,813	5,162	206	3,754	13,267
12	21,199	4,876	12,366	495	8,993	6,813	273	4,955	18,222
13	27,983	6,436	16,323	653	11,871	8,993	360	6,451	24,763
14	36,936	8,495	21,547	862	15,670	11,871	475	8,364	33,397
15	48,757	11,214	28,441	1,138	20,685	15,670	627	11,397	44,793
16	64,359	14,803	37,543	1,502	27,304	20,685	827	15,043	59,836
17	84,954	19,539	49,556	1,982	36,041	27,304	1,092	19,857	79,694
18			65,414	2,717	47,574	36,041	1,442	26,212	105,905
19					62,798	47,574	1,903	34,599	140,505
20						62,798	2,512	45,671	186,176
21								60,286	246,462

Appendix G, An Outline of Guatemalan History

(The final month [January] of American president's terms is discounted.)

DATE[355]	DICTATORS PRESIDENTS	U.S. PRESIDENTS	NOTEWORTHY EVENTS and DEVELOPMENTS
1524–28	Hermán Cortés, conqueror of Mexico, sends Pedro de Alvarado to conquer an area to the south called 'Guatemala.'		
1537	Francisco Marroquin ordained first bishop of Guatemala.		
1542	Spain organizes the area from Chiapas in Mexico to the border of Panama into an *audiencia* called the 'Kingdom of Guatemala,' with its capital at Santiago, later moved to a new city called 'Guatemala.'		
1773–75	Earthquakes wreck the city of Guatemala. Population relocates to present-day Guatemala City. The abandoned site comes to be called 'Antigua Guatemala' (Old Guatemala), now 'Antigua.'		
1524–1991	Governors appointed by the Spanish Crown.	1789 George Washington; 1797 John Adams; 1801 Thomas Jefferson; 1809 James Madison; 1817 James Monroe	
1821	Kingdom of Guatemala joins Mexico in declaring independence from Spain. Chiapas subsequently becomes part of Guatemala and later reverts again to Mexico.		
1824–26 1827–29	Juan Barrundia Mariano de Aycinena	1825 John Quincy Adams	
1829–30 1831-37	Pedro Molina Mariano Galvez	1829 Andrew Jackson 1837 Martin van Buren	
1838 1838–44 1838–65 (two governments from 1838 to 1844– civil war)	Pedro Valenzuela Mariano Rivera Paz Rafael Carrera	1841 John Harrison 1841 John Tyler 1845 James K. Polk 1848 Zachary Taylor 1850 Millard Fillmore 1852 Franklin Pierce 1856 James Buchanan 1861 Abraham Lincoln	Although the years 1838 to 1844 were fraught with turmoil, Carrera, an illiterate *ladino*, led an uprising that ultimately prevailed. Though crude and brutal, the Province of Guatemala enjoyed, under his autocratic rule, a long period of stability and respect for private property. In 1840 he declared Guatemala independent of the United Provinces. The other provinces soon did the same and the United Provinces of Guatemala ceased to exist.
1865–71	Vicente Cerna	1864 Andrew Johnson	Cerna y Cerna continues Carrera's policies.
1871–73	Miguel Garcia	1869 Ulysses S. Grant	Garcia Granados initiates liberal movement.
1873– 1885–92	Justo Rufino Barrios	1988 Rutherford Hayes	Period of *reforma*. Barrios confiscated Church property, laicized schools, expropriated Mayan communal land and sold it at favorable rates to investors, mainly German, to start coffee plantations, then a booming industry, forcing Mayan labor into debt bondage, built roads, railroads, ports, and telegraph lines (page 42).
1892–97	José María Reina Barrios	1885 Grover Cleveland	Barrios was killed in El Salvador trying to reunify the United Provinces of Guatemala.
1898– 1920	Manuel Estrada Cabrera	1897 William McKinley 1901 Theodore Roosevelt 1909 William H. Taft 1913 Woodrow Wilson	
1920 1921–25	Carlos Herrera José María Orellana	1921 Warren G. Harding	

---

[355] The names and dates of Guatemalan presidents who served less than three months are not represented. The dates of service of all Guatemalan presidents are rounded to exclude service of less than three months.

1926–30	Lázaro Chacón		1923 Calvin Coolidge 1929 Herbert Hoover	1929–1932 The Great Depression in both the United States and Guatemala
1931–44	Jorge Ubico y Castañeda	1933 Franklin Roosevelt		Ubico attracts the United Fruit Co. to purchase huge tracts of land. As a result, United Fruit controls forty two percent of the land in Guatemala.
1944 1945–50 1951–54	Federico Ponce Juan José Arévalo Jacobo Árbenz		1946 Harry S. Truman 1953 Dwight D. Eisenhower	1945–54 Guatemalan Spring (page 48) 1945 Arévalo initiates reforms. 1952 Árbenz purchases land from United Fruit and others for distribution to the poor.
1954–57 1958–62	Castillo Armas	1954 U.S. CIA outs Árbenz, installs Castillo Armas. Árbenz' reforms reversed. 1957 Castillo Armas assassinated. 1959 Fidel Castro becomes dictator in Cuba.		
1963–66 1966–70 1970–74	Enrique Peralto Asurdia J. Méndez Montenegro Carlos Arana Osorio	1961 John F. Kennedy (†11/22/1963) 1963 Lyndon B. Johnson 1969 Richard Nixon (resigned 8/9/1974)		1960–96 Guatemalan Civil War 1961, April, Bay of Pigs Invasion 1964 Pan-American Highway in Guatemala completed. 1967 Asturias wins Nobel lit. prize. 1968 Medellin Conference (page 59)
1974–78 1978–82	Kjell Laugerud Garcia Romeo Lucas García 1977 Jimmy Carter	1974 Gerald Ford 1976 earthquake kills 23,000		1977 Carter cuts aid to Guatemala. 1978, May 28, Panzós massacre 1980 Spanish Embassy in Guatemala burned. Archbishop Romero murdered in El Salvador.
1982–83	Efraín Ríos Montt	1981 Ronald Reagan		1982 Reagan restores aid to Guatemala.
1983-85	Oscar Mejia Victores			1983 Pope John Paul II visits Guatemala. 1985 New Guatemalan Constitution
1986–90	Vinicio Cerezo Arévalo	1989 George H. W. Bush		1989 Nov. 9, Fall of the Berlin Wall 1989, Nov. 16, Six Jesuits murdered in El Salvador. 1990 Sandinistas lose election in Nicaragua, accept results without violence.
1991–93	Jorge Serrano Elias			1992 Rigoberta Menchú awarded Nobel Peace Prize.
1993–95	Ramiro de León Carpio	Bill Clinton		1994 U.N. establishes MINUGUA. 1995 Clinton suspends training of Guatemalan officers in U.S.
1996–99	Alvaro Arzú Irigoyen	9/11/96 Myna Mack murdered. 12/31/1996 Guatemalan Peace Accord signed. 1997 Pope John Paul II visits Guatemala 2nd time. 4/26/1998 Bishop Juan Gerardi murdered. 11/1/1998 Hurricane Mitch 3/10/1999 Clinton apologizes for U.S. complicity in Guatemala's Civil War.		
2000–03	Alfonso Portillo Cabrera	2001 George W. Bush		9/11/2001 World Trade Center in New York and the Pentagon in D.C. attacked by Al Qaeda. 3/20/2003 Iraq war begins.
2004–-8	Oscar Berger Perdomo			Berger signs agreement with U.N. creating CICIG.
2008–11	Alvaro Colom	2009 Barak Obama		2008 Wall Street crash cripples GSSG.
2012–15	Otto Perez Molina			3/24/2013 Portillo and his vice-president convicted of money laundering
2016	Jimmy Morales	2017 Donald Trump		2017 U.S. tax reform, first in more than 30 years.

Appendix H, Snapshots of the Students' Fortunes

N.B. This table includes only the students who completed their freshman year of high school here and came back to continue their education. All, except Raquel and possibly Pedro, returned to Guatemala permanently. For more detail on any given student, please consult the Index.

Abner lived with his father and sister in El Estor (page 179), came here in 2008 as part of the large group that went to high school in Michigan and graduated four years later. He is now married to Tita Caal and has a child (page 189).

When **Alba** was born, her father took his other five daughters and moved into the slums of Guatemala City, leaving Alba with his sister (page 138). The saga of finding her father, who was living on the wrong side of the law, and persuading him to accompany Alba to the Guatemalan passport office and to the U.S. Embassy for a visa challenged our resourcefulness (pages 150ff.). Ultimately Alba became the first Guatemalan youth to graduate, after four years of study, from an American high school, while maintaining continuous residency in Guatemala (page 171).

Ana Macz proved to be a very poor hostess at big party arranged by her host parents. She became the only GSSG student to be sent home in her senior year without graduating (page 190).

Ana Pop, happy but not enthusiastic about leadership, chose not to return to the United States after her freshman year and got back into a school in Guatemala (pages 119 and 123), where her English teacher, who does not know English, gave her a failing grade!

I first saw **Blanca**, through the viewfinder of my camcorder, among a group of kids who were learning how to read in one of the parish projects in San Lucas Tolimán (page 94). She had no personal documentation of any kind). Four American families wanted to adopt her but we could find no death certificate for her mother. After she turned sixteen and was no longer adoptable, we squeezed her in before she turned sixteen and a half (maximum for exchange students). She arrived two weeks before school started, knowing no English, failed her freshman year, changed schools, graduated three years later (page 218), and now has a full-time job at a call center in Guatemala and is a part-time student at Mesoamerican University.

Byron and his cousin Ericka came in 2007, the only two we could get visas for that year after the catastrophe of 2006 (page 166). He graduated in 2011, started at Wake Tech but took a year and a half off to care for his terminally ill mother. During this time, Byron started a coffee business for the indigenous in his area, cutting out the middleman, and founded an English Academy as well (page 172). After his mother passed away, Byron returned to Wake Tech and graduated with an AS degree in business 2017 and returned to Guatemala.

Carlos, during his freshman year, developed a heart condition that could have taken his life (page 214). He graduated in 2013, along with Luis Coc, Teresa, and José (page 217) and is now a teacher in Guatemala.

Ericka and her cousin Byron came in 2007. She graduated in 2011, returned to Guatemala, and now has a child. She is not in school.

Giovanni, along with Nataly, Edgar, and Karina, came in 2004 (page 112), made no attempt to integrate into his host family, returned for a second year and offended his host mom, who had given him a camera for Christmas, by buying a better one (page 129). He did not return to the United States again but did serve as our credibility factor at Chitomax (page 143).

According to **Griselda**, her stepfather has a bullet in his head. Griselda, the party girl, and Sandra lived with the Heusers for four years and graduated from the Emerson Waldorf School in 2012. Griselda loved parties (page 193). She is now married and has a child.

Heidi made tamales on a wood fire for a Christmas bash every year, while living with the Hathaways in Raleigh, NC, for four years (page 196). Subsequently she got a degree in nursing in Guatemala, is now married, and has a child.

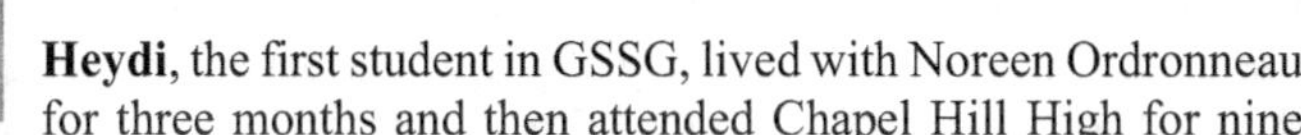

Heydi, the first student in GSSG, lived with Noreen Ordronneau for three months and then attended Chapel Hill High for nine months. Because she had only been here three months, her advisor at Chapel Hill High placed her in subjects not requiring much English (page 100) but, well into the semester, the superintendent moved her into the regular freshman classes. As a result, she failed the year. Getting a job in her home town, Tactic, she began taking classes on Saturday. With GSSG support she is now well on her way to completing a *licenciatura* (page 85) in Social Work at San Carlos University while simultaneously writing her autobiography, in English.

José's father was murdered by security guards at a mining company (pages 82 and 178). After graduating from high school here, he returned to Guatemala but has not elected to continue his education there.

Judith and Marley (see below) were the first village students in GSSG. Judith's father put up his parcel as collateral and borrowed money from a bank to put his children through high school but then lost his job (page 195). Judith found employment and helps support her family while continuing her studies in Business Administration.

I first met **Lily** when she, her mother, and a sibling were packaging calendars at Christmas time (page 139). The family often had nothing to eat except tortillas and salt. Lily is on track to graduate from Cornerstone University in 2017 and will return to Guatemala to attend medical school, thanks to the generosity of Mary VanderVeen and others in MI.

Luis Coc's father died in 2001; his mother has no skills and sells tortillas on the street to feed her five children (page 178). After graduation Luis studied for a year in Guatemala but gave it up to work full time to help is mother. Luis recently married a girl with an engaging personality and a character as fine as his own.

Luis Fernández, Raquel's brother, driving home late one night crashed his host parents' car. Some compromising images on Facebook led me to discharge him from GSSG. My successor reinstated him. He is now studying medicine in Guatemala.

Mario was raised by his great grandmother (page 177). Removed from GSSG for misconduct as a junior, he got a job with the mining company in El Estor and was once sent to the Ukraine. Likeable as ever, he and his host family maintain friends. Mario appears to be a responsible father.

Marley's father was also fired (see Judith above) but got another job. Thanks to the generosity of Mary VanderVeen and others in MI (page 187), Marley is on track to earn a degree in International Business in 2017.

Quiet and unpretentious, **Nancy** graduated at St. Thomas More Academy (page 197), studied for two years at Wake Tech, and is now pursuing a degree in forensic criminology in Guatemala with some support from GSSG. Nancy leads by example.

Nataly, a reader, came initially in 2004, was refused a visa several times but eventually graduated from Cardinal Gibbons High School (page 173), returned to Guatemala, and is now (2017) in her fifth year of medical school.

Niceh, GSSG's only black student and unusually bright, had eight teeth pulled in preparation for braces (page 211). After graduation from high school here, she enrolled at Wake Tech community college. After graduation she returned to Guatemala and enrolled in engineering at Mesoamericana University in Quetzaltenango, full funding provided by private sources in the United States. After a year of studies, she left her studies, returned to the United States, and married a young man she had met at Wake Tech.

When **Pablo** was asked to give a speech soon after arriving in the United States, he said he wanted to be the president of Guatemala. He attended Sienna College in Loudonville, NY, working on campus to pay his bills (page 198) but the pressure became impossible. GSSG did not have the resources to provide the funds he needed. After his first year, Pablo returned to Guatemala and is now studying engineering at the Cobán campus of San Carlos University, with some support from GSSG.

I removed **Pedro** from GSSG for what I judged to be arrogant opportunism and racism. My successor reinstalled him. In 2016 he became the only GSSG student to graduate from an American college/university (page 198), funding provided by private sources. I do not know what he has been doing since then nor do I know, perhaps he does not know, whether he will stay in the United States permanently or return to Guatemala.

Raquel initially came to the U.S. in Phase 1 in 2005 when she was eleven (page 117). In Phase 3 (page 216) she attended a community college and married an American. She is the only student we know for sure will stay permanently in the United States.

Rolan graduated Friendship Christian School with honors (page 215). He is now studying agricultural engineering at the Cobán campus of San Carlos University with some GSSG support and, during his vacation, teaches English with a non-profit, environmental organization.

Access to **Rossy**'s home is provided by a narrow passage through buildings on the street. An 'A' student, Rossy earned a degree in Social Work at Cornerstone University in 2016 (page 189) and is going on the graduate study with the assistance of private funding.

Sandra Bolom got up at 4:00 in the morning to help her mother make tortillas for her father and brother who left at six, trekking for two hours to get to work on a banana plantation. Later she would go with her mother to wash clothes in a river nearby. Sandra's house fell down while she was here. Sandra graduated at Friendship Christian (page 206) and is now studying business administration at Mariano Galvez University in El Estor.

Sandra Coc, artistically talented (194), graduated from Emerson Waldorf in 2012 and is now studying Social and Legal Sciences at Mariano Galvez in El Estor.

Teresa came to GSSG almost by happenstance, when she and her mother came to sell tamales at the school in which we were recruiting (page 200). Teresa is now studying to be a licensed translator at San Carlos in Cobán. As part of her studies, she has to read some English and some Spanish literature. She is the only Guatemalan I know who has read any English or Spanish literature while studying in Guatemala, at any level.

Tita's parents are separated but her father lives in the same town and occasionally sees her. Tita, her mother, and her sisters lived in a Habitat house with no utilities except polluted water (page 204).

Walter, his mother, and grandmother lived in a house with three-and-a-half walls (page 201). An American donated $5000 to build a new house.

Yesenia, with her pretty smile, lived in a desert area of Guatemala, cement being its principal product (page 201). She is now studying psychology at Mariano Galvez University in Chiquimula, with some GSSG support. Yesenia recently married.

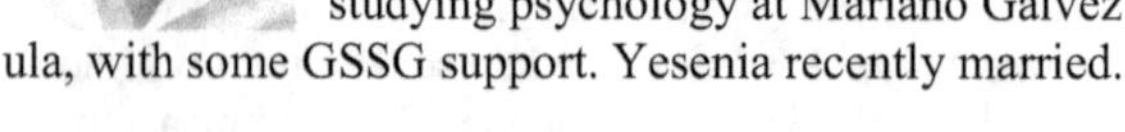

Check the Index for additional information and photos for each student.

Bibliography

Adams, Richard E. W., *Prehistoric Mesoamerica*, Third Edition, University of Oklahoma Press, 2005.

Annis, Shelton, "Story from a Peaceful Town: San Antonio Aguas Calientes," in Robert W. Carmack, *Harvest of Violence: The Mayan Indians and the Guatemalan Crisis*, University of Oklahoma Press, 1988.

Black, James, https://nacla.org/article/scorched-earth-time-peace

Brokaw, Tom, *The Greatest Generation*, Random House, 1998.

Cambranes, J.C., *Coffee and Peasants: The Origins of the Modern Plantation Economy in Guatemala, 1853-1897*, Stockholm, Sweden : Institute of Latin American Studies, 1985.

CEH, *Guatemala: Memoria del Silencio*, 1999 [both Spanish and English].

Chavez, Debbie, "Libraries in Quetzaltenango: A librarian's experience in Guatemala," https://www.library.pima.gov/blogs/post/libraries-in-quetzaltenango/

Chishti, Muzaffar, and Faye Hipsman, "Increased Central American Migration to the United States May Prove an Enduring Phenomenon," *Migration Policy Institute*, February 18, 2016.

Costello, Patrick, *Guatemala: Displacement, Return and the Peace Process*, WRITENET, 1995.

Cullather, Nicholas, *Operation PBSUCCESS: The United States and Guatemala*, Tipografía Nacional, 1999.

Dabb, Curtis W., James H. McDonald, and Walter Randolph Adams, "A Land Divided without Clear Titles: The Class of Communal and Individual Land Claims in Nahualá and Santa Catarina Ixtahuacá" in Hawkins, John P., James H. McDonald and Walter Randolph Adams (edd.), *Crisis of Governance in Maya Guatemala: Indigenous Responses to a Failing State*, University of Oklahoma Press, 2013.

Davis, Shelton H., "Introduction: Sowing the Seeds of Violence," in Robert M. Carmack, *Harvest of Violence: The Mayan Indians and the Guatemalan Crisis*, University of Oklahoma Press, 1988.

Demarest, Arthur, *Ancient Maya: The Rise and Fall of a Rainforest Civilization*, Cambridge University Press, 2004.

Dickins de Girón, Avery, "The Security Guard Industry in Guatemala: Rural Communities and Urban Violence," in O'Neill and Thomas (edd.), *Securing the City: Neoliberalism, Space, and Insecurity in Postwar Guatemala*, Duke University Press, 2011

DuBois, W.E.B., *Darkwater: Voices from Within the Veil*, AMS Press, 1969.

Early, John D, "Demographic Profile of a Maya Community: The Atitecos of Santiago Atitlán," *The Milbank Memorial Fund Quarterly*, Vol. 48, No.2, Part 1 (Apr., 1970).

Falla, Ricardo, *Massacres in the Jungle: Ixcán, Guatemala*, Westview Press, 1994.

Fitzpatrick-Behrens, Susan, https://nacla.org/news/angels-guatemala-confronting-legacy-official-terror

Fontes, Anthony W., "Beyond the Maras: Violence and Survival in Urban Central America," https://www.wilsoncenter.org/sites/default/files/Fontes_2014_FINAL.pdf

Forster, Cindy, *The Time of Freedom: Campesino Workers in Guatemala's October Revolution*, University of Pittsburgh Press, 2001.

Foster, Lynn V., *A Brief History of Central America*, Facts on File, 2007.

______, Foster, *Handbook to Life in the Ancient Maya World*, Facts on File, 2002.

French, Brigittine M., *Mayan Ethnolinguistic Identity: Violence, Cultural Rights, and Modernity in Highland Guatemala*, University of Arizona Press, 2010.

Gleijeses, Piero, *Politics and Culture in Guatemala*, University of Michigan Press, 1988.

______, *Shattered Hope: The Guatemalan Revolution and the United States, 1944–1954*, Princeton University Press, 1991.

Goldman, Francisco, *The Art of Political Murder: Who Killed the Bishop?*, Grove Press, 2007.

Grandin, Greg, "Five Hundred Years," in Carlota McAllister and Diane M. Nelson (edd.), *War by Other Means: Aftermath in Post-Genocide Guatemala*, Duke University Press, 2013.

______, *The Blood of Guatemala: A History of Race and Nations*, Duke University Press, 2000.

______, *The Last Colonial Massacre: Latin America in the Cold War – Updated Edition*, University of Chicago Press, 2004.

Handy, Jim, *Revolution in the Countryside: rural Conflict & Agrarian Reform in Guatemala, 1944–1954*, University of North Carolina Press, 1944.

Immerman, Richard, *The CIA in Guatemala: The Foreign Policy of Intervention,* University of Texas Press, 1982.

International Justice Monitor, "A project of the Open Society Justice Initiative."

Johnson, Paul, *Churchill*, Viking, 2009.

Jonas, Susanne, *The Battle for Guatemala: Rebels, Death Squads, and U.S. Power*, Westview Press, 1991.

Jones, Maggie, "The Secrets of the Bones," https://www.nytimes.com/2016/07/03/magazine/the-secrets-in-guatemalas-bones.html?_r=0

Kristof, Nicholas, "We're Helping Deport Kids to Die," *New York Times*, July 16, 2016.

LaFeber, Walter, *Inevitable Revolutions: The United States in Central America*, 2nd edition, W.W. Norton, 1993.

Landa, Friar Diego de, *Yucatan Before and After the Conquest*, trans. William Gates, Maya Society, 1937.

Levenson, *Adios Niños: The Gangs of Guatemala City and the Politics of Death*, Duke University Presss, 2013.

Mackie, Sedley (ed.), *An Account of the Conquest of Guatemala in 1524 by Pedro de Alvarado*, Cortes Society, 1924. [Includes an introduction, a piece on the 'Aborigines,' and biographical notes by Mackie, followed by translations of the relevant primary sources: the two letters written by Alvarado to Cortez, the "Annals of the Caqchiquels," two accounts by Bernal Diaz, and one by Las Casas.]

Malkin, Elizabeth, *Toppling a President*, New *York Times*, September 16, 2015.

Mann, Charles, *New Revelations of the Americas Before Columbus*, Knopf, 2005.

Manz, Beatriz, *Paradise in Ashes: A Guatemalan Journey of Courage, Terror, and Hope*, University of California Press, 2004.

______, *Refugees of a Hidden War: The Aftermath of Counterinsurgency in Guatemala*, State University of New York Press, 1998.

______, *Repatriation and Reintegration: An Arduous Process in Guatemala*, Georgetown University, 1988.

McCreery, David, *Rural Guatemala*, Stanford University Press, 1994.

Melville, Thomas R., *Through a Glass Darkly: The U.S. Holocaust in Central America*, Xlibris, 2005.

Menchú, Rigoberta, *I, Riboberta Menchú: An Indian Woman in Guatemala*, Verso, 1984.

Monetejo, Victor, *Voices from Exile*, University of Oklahoma Press, 1999.

Nelson, Diane M., *Reckoning: The Ends of War in Guatemala*, Duke University Press, 2009.

______, *Who Counts? The Mathematics of Death and Life after Genocide*, Duke University Press, 2015.

______, *A Finger in the Wound: Body Politics in Quincentennial Guatemala*, University of California Press, 1999.

Perera, Victor, *Unfinished Conquest: The Guatemalan Tragedy*, University of California Press, 1993.

REHMI, *Guatemala: Nunca Más*, 1998 [both Spanish and English].

Roth, Michael S., *Beyond the University: Why Liberal Education Matters*, Yale University Press, 2014.

Rothenberg, Daniel, *Memory of Silence: The Guatemalan Truth Commission Report*, Palgrave Macmillan, 2012.

Saxon, Dan, *To Save Her Life: Disappearance, deliverance, and the United States in Guatemala*, University of California Press, 2007.

Schirmer, Jennifer, *The Guatemalan Military Project: A Violence Called Democracy*, University of Pennsylvania Press, 1998.

______, "The Guatemalan military project: an interview with Gen. Hector Gramajo," *Harvard International Review*, Vol. 13, Issue 3 (Spring 1991).

______, "Prospects for Compliance: The Guatemalan Military and the Peace Accords," in Sieder, Rachel (ed.), *Guatemala after the Peace Accords*, Institute of Latin American Studies, 1998.

Schlesinger, Stephen and Stephen Kinzer, *Bitter Fruit: The Story of the American Coup in Guatemala*, Expanded Edition, Harvard University Press, 1999.

Seelke, Clare Ribando, "U.S.-Mexican Security Cooperation: "The Mérida Initiative and Beyond," *Congressional Research Service*, February 22, 2016, 1 and 2.

Shae, Maureen, *Culture and Customs of Guatemala*, Greenwood Publishing Group, 2001.

Sieder, Rachel, "War, Peace, and Memory Politics," in Alexandra Barahonda de Brito,k Carmen Gonzáles-Enríquea, and Paloma Aguilar (edd.), *The Politics of Memory: Transitional Justice in Democratizing Societies*, Oxford University Press, 2001.

Simon, Jean-Marie, *Guatemala: Eternal Spring – Eternal Tyranny*, Norton, 1987.

Thomas, Kedron, Kevin Lewis O'Neill, and Thomas Offit, "An Introduction" in Kevin Lewis O'Neill and Kedron Thomas (edd.), *Securing the City: Neoliberalism, Space, and Insecurity in Postwar Guatemala*, Duke University Press, 2011.

U.S. Department of State, *Background Note: Guatemala*, May 2002.

Wallace Fuentes, Myrna Ivonne, "The Spanish Embassy Occupation and Assault: History and the Partisan Politics of Memory Since 1980 in Guatemala," *A Contra Corriene: A Journal of Social History and Literature in Latin America*, Fall 2012.

Weld, Kirsten, *Paper Cadavers: The Archives of Dictatorship in Guatemala*, Duke University Press, 2015.

Wilkinson, Daniel, *Silence on the Mountain: Stories of Terror, Betrayal, and Forgetting in Guatemala*, Houghton Mifflin, 2002.

Index

N.B. The names of the Guatemalan students are alphabetized by their first name or nick name only, unless two have the same first name or nickname; other Guatemalans, either by first name or last name, depending on which is more commonly used; Americans, by their last name.

A

Abby, 165
Abner, 179, 189
Accord for a Firm and Lasting Peace, 1, 77
Accord on Human Rights, 77
Accord on Strengthening of Civilian Power and the Role of the Army in a Democratic Society, 1
Accord on the Establishment of the Commission to Clarify Human Rights Violations, 77
Accord on the Identity and Rights of Indigenous Peoples, 1
Accord to Search for Peace by Political Means, 1
Adelman, Dr. Richard, ii
Adiós Niño, 221
Adolfo Ich, 82
AFS, 37, 98
Agrarian Reform, 51
agriculture, 39
Alba, 138, 150, 156, 161, 171
Alfhem Affair, 53
Alfonso, 132
All of them!, 36
Allen, Shari and Kevin, i
Alliance for Progress, 57
Alliance for Prosperity Plan, 6
Alta Verapaz, 7
An, Eunice, 93, 101
Ana Macz, 180, 190
Ana Pop, 119, 123
Anderson, Andrea and Tom, i, 217
Anderson, Denis and Kellie, 212
animism, 16
Antigua, 13, 23
Apellido, Hannah, ii
Apellido, Jack, ii
Apology, 1
Arana Osorio, Carlos, 58
Árbenz Guzmán, Jacobo, 49, 50, 74
Archaic Period, 39
architecture, 96
Arévalo, Juan José, 5, 49, 74
Arnoldo, 36, 95, 100
Arzú Irigoyen, Alvaro, 77, 221
Assassination of Fr. Stan Rother, 69
astronomy, 11
Atkinson, Dawn and Rob, i, 197
AYA, 169

B

babies, Mayan, 14
Bach, Margie and Jens, i, ii
bachillerato, 85
Bachmann, Michele, 219
Background to the Combined Program, 229
Background to President Clinton's apology, 1
bajareque, 107
Ballet Gran Folclórico de Mexico, 96
Bananas and Railroads, 46
Barnes, Carolyn and Joe, i, 192
Barrios, José María Reina, 45
Barrios, Justo Rufino, 42, 45, 59
baseball, 19
base-line requirements, 114
basico, 85
Battigelli, Giovanna and Mario, i
bananas, 46
Belden, Diane and Art, i
Belize, 3, 9, 12, 39
Benedicto Lucas García, 224
Benoit Salemi, Carrie, ii
Berger Cabrera, Oscar, 82
Bering Strait, 9
Bernardina, 105
Bernays, Edward, 52
Bernhard, Matt, 163
Berninger, Jeff and Joe, 22
Betts, Howard, ii, 173, 219
Betzold, Br. Roger, ii, 217
Biden, Vice-President, 6
Bingo, 30
Biotopo, 30
Bitter Fruit, 27
Black, Eli M., 47, 74
Blanca, 94, 111, 128, 129, 158, 169, 217
Bodford, Brenda and Alvin, i
Bodoh, Robert and Mary, ii, 227
Bolshevik Revolution, 51
Bondhus, Mary Kay, ii
Bonds, Judy and Thomas, ii
Bonds, Michelle and Tom, i, ii, 124, 157, 161, 198
border, iv
break dancing, 222
British Commonwealth, 3
Brokaw, Tom, 227
Brooks, Connie and Jim, i, 188

Burning of the Spanish Embassy, 60
burning people alive, 2
Burns, Jodi and Joe, ii
Burr, Senator Richard, 161
Bus-Fare Protest, 60
Bush, George W., 6
Bush, George W., 5
Byron Center High School, 189
Byron, 135, 166, 167, 172

C

Cabot Lodge, Henry, 53
Cabot, John, 53
Cajal y López, Ambassador Maximo, 61
Calderón, Felipe, 5
Caledonia High School, 189, 190, 191, 194
calendar, 11
Calhoun, Greg H., 52
CALs, 51
cane and cornstalk homes, 109
Caq'chikel, 9
Carchá, 118
Cardinal Gibbons High School, 173, 195
cardinal points, 10, 16
Carlos, 205, 214, 217
Carrera, Rafael, 40
CARSI, 6, 229
Carter, President Jimmy, 60
Castillo Armas, Carlos, 23, 53, 55
Catastrophe, 159
Catastrophe 2, 166
Catholic Action, 59
Catholicism, 17
communal land, 39
community colleges, 233
cornstalk homes, 109
crime, 220
CEH, 2, 62, 68, 83
Central America, 3
Central American Regional Security Initiative, 6
Central Intelligence Agency, 1, 23, 53
Cerezo Arévalo, Vinicio, 75
Cerna y Cerna, Vicente, 40
Chamíl, 130
Chapel Hill High School, 100
Charles I of Spain, 40
Charles V, 27
Chiapas, 71
children's books, 84
Chiquimula, 8, 54
Chiquito, Lea and Paulo, i, ii, 197
Chitomáx, 143
Chixoy Dam, 117
CIA, 1, 53, 55
CICIG, 83

cities, 39
Civil Patrols, 62
Civil War, 1, 57
civilian presidents of Guatemala
    Arévalo, Juan José, 49
    Arzú Irigoyen, Alvaro, 77
    Berger, Oscar, 82
    Cerezo Arévalo, Vinicio, 75
    Colom, Alvaro, 83
    de Leon Carpio, Ramiro, 77
    Jimmy Morales, 83
    Serrano Elias, Jorge, 76
Classic Period, 10
Classic Period of Mayan History, 10
Claudia, 110
Clausewitz, 220
Clements, John, 53
Clinton, President Bill, 1
clothing, Mayan men's, 14
clothing, Mayan women's, 14
Cobán, 34, 41
Cobán and Carchá, 43
Cobán, German dominance, 43
Cochrane, Bob and Pam, i, 198
Cody, Patricia and Ed, 113
Cody, Patricia and Ed., i
CoEd, 20, 22, 33
coffee, 40, 41
coffee production in German hands, 43
coffee, San Lucas, 91
cofradias, 16
Coleman, Linda and Jon, i, 99, 195
college education, 229, 233
colleges in Guatemala, 85
Colom, Alvaro, 83
Colombia, 3, 59
Columbus, 27
Colvin, Stanley, ii, 169
Combined Program, 229
Comisión para el Esclarecimiento Histórico, 2
Commission for Historical Clarification, 2
communal land, 42
communism, 51
communist infiltration in Latin America, 1
compensation, 3
Conclusion, 234
Condon, Kathy and Jim, i
Conlow, Rick and Kelli, i, ii, 128, 137, 156, 157, 161, 169, 171, 219, 256
Conquest of Central America, 12, 40
corn, 39
Cornerstone University, 188, 189
cornstalk homes, 14
Cortés, 12
Costa Rica, 1, 12, 46, 76
costumbre, 12, 16
courtship and marriage, 18

Coyle, Marguerite and Francis, ii, 37, 95, 96
Crider, Kelly, ii
crime, 65, 72, 77, 82, 222, 224
Crocco, Dori and Francis, i
crosses, 16
Cuarto Pueblo, 63
Cultural Genocide, 73
Cultural Vitality, 18
culture, 37
    American, 18
    Japanese, 18
    mind-set, mind, or mentality, 19
    the way we think, 19
currency, 39
Currens, Joy and Dave, i, 112
Curtis, Diane and Russell, i, 189
Czejkowski, Rosemary and Joe, i, ii, 195

D

Danos, Barbara and Joe, ii
Davenport University, 187
Davis Library, 96
Davis, Jo Ann, ii, 115
Davis, Pete, ii, 37
de Alvarado, Pedro, 12, 14
De La Salle, 176
de León Carpio, Ramiro, 76
Death Squads, 58
death toll, 2
debt peonage, 44
Decree 170, 78
Decree 243, 45
Decree 900, 47, 51, 52
DeGiralamo, Susan, i
degrading Mayan culture
    disparaging Mayan customs, 45
    disparaging traditional dress, 45
    prohibiting burial, 67, 68
    punishing for speaking a Mayan language, 73
Del Monte, 74
Deming, Jean and Mark, i, 211
departamentos, 7
Department of State, ii, 1, 15
Departure 2008, 185
Departure 2009, 209
Dermody, Bob, ii
DeTitta, Pat, ii
dialects, 9
Díaz, Colonel Carlos Enrique, 54
Diego de Landa, 39
disappeared, 58
disease, 45
diseases brought by conquerors, 26
diversificado, 85
dogs, 39
Dole, Senator Elizabeth, 160, 161

Doran, Judy and Bill, 188
Doran, Judy and Bill, i
DOS, ii, 1
Dowe, Mary, ii
Dr. Tun, 91
DuBois, W.E.B., 86
Dulles, Allen, 53
Dulles, John Foster, 52, 53, 55
Dwyer, Rex, ii

E

earthquakes
    1773–76, 13
    1976, 59
    1997, 14
Eastman, Tim and Jill, i, ii
Edgar, 103, 112
education for a Mayan woman, 23
Education in Guatemala, 84
Edy, Edy, and Sergio, 105
Efraín Ríos Montt, 64, 65
Efrat, Lisa and Dan, i, ii
EGP, 57, 60, 66, 76, 220
EIN, 98
Eisenhower, President, 53
Eismann, Suzanne, ii
El Chapo, 5
El Estor, 38, 175
El Salvador, iv, 4, 9, 12, 25, 39
elders, 39
elders, village, 39
Elio's brother, 104
Elmer, 202, 210
Emerson Waldorf School, 193, 194
Engagement in Central America, 6
English, 9
Ericka, 136, 168, 173
erosion, 91
Escuela Claridad, 52
Esquipulas II, 1, 76
Estrada Cabrera, Manuel, 46
European descent, 12
Evangelical radio station, 54
Excerpts from CEH and RHEMI, 68
Exchange Visa, 88

F

Family Interview, 114
FAR, 57
farmland
    background, impossible, 80
    foreground, good, 80
Felder, Roxanne and Tracy, i
Ferrall, Dr. Isabel, ii
fetus extraction, 2

farmland
    poor, 81
fund-raising, 199
fingernails, 2
Flor, 191
Flores, Francisco, 207
Form I-539, 157, 161, 172, 173
Fort Leavenworth, 53
forty-two percent of Guatemalan land, 1
Francisco, Alejandro, ii
Francisco, Francisco, ii
Franz, Lynn and Joe Krueger, i, ii
Franz, Marion, ii
Franz, Peter, ii
Freedman, Sarah, ii
Freedman, Virginia, ii
French, Melanie, ii
Freud, Sigmund, 52
Fritman, 180, 191
funding, 219

G

G.I. Bill of Rights, 227
G-2, 75
Galu, Tish, ii
Gangs, 221
Garcia Granados y Zavala, Miguel, 41
Garcia, Karen, ii
Gellings, Christine, ii
Gendler, Joyce and Dr. Steven, i
genocide, 227
Geography of Guatemala, 7
Gerardi Conedera, Bishop
    Chairman of REHMI, 2
    murder of, 224
German investors, 43
genocide, 71
Giovanni, 101, 112, 129, 143
Glazier, Jim, ii
Gleijeses, Piero, 81
glyphs, 11
Gockerman, Dorothy, i, ii
Goehl, Tom and Marilyn, i, ii, 211
Goldcorp, 82
Golden, Jennifer and Michael, i
Good Friday, 16
Goodling, Nancy, ii
Gossman, Bishop, 124
Gramajo, Héctor, 61, 75, 220
Grand Rapids Christian High School, 188, 189
Grand Rapids Community College, 187
Grandin, Greg, 52
Gray, A. C., i
Gray, Bret, i
Gray, Shannon, ii

Grazen, Amy and Greg, i
Greatest Generation, 227
Green Hope High School, 100
Greenseth, Cathy and Rik, i
Grimball, Berkeley, i, 200
Griselda, 181, 193
GSSG, ii, 20, 34, 37
GSSG news, 98, 147
GSSG's Mission Statement, 98
Guatemala, 4, 5, 9, 12
Guatemala City, 21, 22, 46, 56, 110, 152, 211
Guatemala City slum, 21
Guatemala Today
    population, 12
    railroads, 12
    roads, 12
Guatemala: Memoria del Silencio, 1
Guatemala: Nunca Más, 2
Guatemala's annual vacation, 36
Guatemala's upper class, 43
Guatemalan currency, 14
Guatemalan military, 1
Guatemalan population, iv
Guatemalan Spring, 49
Guatemalan Student Support Group, 37
Guatemalans, iv
Guatemala's System of Education, 84
Guerrillas, 57
Guokas, Terri, ii
Gutenberg, 37
Guzmán, Jacobo Árbenz, 5

H

haciendas, 40
Hadden, Veronica and Robert, ii
Haiti, 23
Hamilton, 139, 162
Hammer, Richard and Alma, i, 198
Hamrick, Ann, i
Haney, Colonel Albert, 53
Hanna Mining Co, 81
Harrell, Marisa and Brian, i, 215
Hathaway family, 100
Heidi, 142, 196
Heil, Kevin, ii
Heiser, Brent, ii
Helm, Wendy and Randy, i
Hernández, President of Honduras, 6
Heuser, Carolyn and Jim, i, ii, 193, 199
Heydi, 224
Heydi and Arnoldo in Phase 1, 95
Heydi, 32, 100
Hillsgrove, Dr. Donna, ii
historic liberal, 41
Homo sapiens, 1

Honduras, iv, 4, 9, 12, 39, 53
horses, 26
Host Family Orientation, 100
Houlihan Smith, Mary Jane, i
Howes, Nora, i, 199
HudBay Minerals, 81
Hudgins, Dr. Donathan, ii
huipil, 14, 15
Human Rights Ombudsman, 75, 77
human tsunami, iv
human-rights violations, 2
hunter-gatherer, 39

I

Ice Age, 9
illegal immigrants, iv
illegal immigration, 4, 39
illiteracy, 23
imagination, 228
immigrants by country, 4
immigration
   illegal, 39
  tables, 4
Implications, 219
income, distribution of, 15
Independence from Spain, 40
independent countries, 40
Indian, iii
INL, 6
innovation, 228
Instituto Mixto, 33
insufficient land, 1
INTA, 57
Internet, 37
intolerable conditions, iv
Invasion, 54
IQ test, 114
iron fist, 82
Isabel, Dick, ii
Islam, 115
Issues, 193
Izabal, 8

J

Jabalí, 111, 129
Jacob, Rosemary and Neil, i, 213
Jacobo Árbenz Guzmán, 49
Jairo, 121, 124
Japanese, 19
Jennings, Pilar and Steve, i
Jimmy Morales, 83
Johnson, Dr. Margaret and Gene, ii
Jorge Paque, ii, 34, 35, 88, 89, 90, 110, 111, 114,
   123, 128, 129, 133, 134, 137, 141, 142, 143, 150,

   157, 158, 162, 166, 168, 169, 175, 177, 182, 185,
   192, 208, 210, 212, 213, 214, 217, 256
Jorge Serrano, 75
Jorge Ubico y Castañeda, 47
José, 217
José Manuel Fortuny, 52
José María Reina Barrios, 45
Josefina, 25
José, 178, 190
Juan José Arévalo, 5
Judith, 183, 195
Justo Rufino Barrios, 5, 42, 45, 59

K

Kaisei School in Tokyo, 19
Kapping, Wes, ii
Kapuscinski, James, ii
Karina, 104, 113
keeping the mortally tortured in agony, 2
Kennedy, John F., 57
Kingdom of Guatemala, 12
kingships, 39
Klein, Klara, ii
Kohls, Linda and Ron, i
Konsler, Gwen and Tom, ii
Krueger, Joe, ii
Kunsman, June, ii, 169

L

La Aurora, 22
La Reforma, 42
Labor, 44
Labor Relations, 41
ladinos, 12
LaFeber, Walter, 60
Lake Atitlán, 8, 69, 97
Lam, Loree and Paul, i
Lambeth, Cathy and Conn Harrington, i, 112
land, 1, 6, 39, 80, 227
   statistics, 78
Land of Eternal Spring, 20
land ownership, by
   natural right, 40
   right of conquest, 40
land registry, 79
Landa, Diego de, 39
Las Casas, Bartolomé, 27
Laugerud García, Kjell Eugenio, 59
Layton, J. McLane, ii, 169
leadership, 226
Learning by Doing, 114
Learning How to Study, 168
LeGrand, Louise, 191
LeMarble, Thelma and Warren, i

Lensing, Dr. George, ii
Leo XIII, Pope, 59
Leonard, Jennifer and John, ii
Leonardo, 133
Levenson, Deborah, 221
Lewis, Kelly and Kirby, i, ii, 167
Lewis, Marie and Jack, i, ii, 125
Liberal Governance, 41
Liberation Theology, 59, 60
Libraries, 37
libreta, 45, 50
licenciatura, 85
Lily, 139, 188
Lind, Bob, ii
Lindsey, Debbie and Tom, i
Lissner, Will, 52
LoBuglio, Joe and Shannon Jordon, i
Lohr, Dr. Charles, ii, 211
Loss, 43
Low, Dr. William and Family, i
Lucas García, Fernando Romeo, 60
Luddy, Robert, i, 172, 195
Luis Coc, 179, 190, 217
Luis Fernandez, 117, 123, 192
Luis Pop, 208, 216

M

MacDonald, Amy, ii
Macgillivray, Sr. Lois, ii, 98
Machost, Ann and Milton, i, 113
Madriz, Ana, ii
magisterio, 85
Magnuson, Richard, ii
mankind, 1
Manley, John, i
mano duro ("iron fist")., 82
Manuel Estrada Cabrera, 46
Manz, Beatriz, 220
Mao Tse-tung, 51
Map of Central America, 3, 12
Map of Departments and Towns, 84
Map of Guatemala, 7
Marcos Tun, 92
Margaret and Gene Johnson, 98
María, 31
Mario, 177, 189
market day, 28
Marley, 184, 187
marriage, 18
Marvin, 192
Marx, Karl, 52
Marxism, 53
massacres, 62
   Cuarto Pueblo, 63
   San Andrés Ixtapa, 75, 76

San Francisco, 66
Santa María Tzejá, 63
Sebep, 66
Xamán, 75
math test, 114
mathematics, 11
Matt, 163
Mattson, Kristin and Kent, i, 190
Maximón, 16
Maya, iv, 5, 9, 25, 26, 27, 36, 58, 59, 60, 76, 78, 101, 141, 143, 182, 201
   allowed to vote, 49
Maya of the Classic Period, 11
Maya Today, 14
Mayan astronomy, 11
Mayan calendar, 11
Mayan culture
   babies carriage, 14
   calendar, 16
   cardinal points, 16
   care for aging parents, 19
   corn, 19
   courtship and marriage, 18
   dress, 14
   farming, 16
   formal education, 19
   inheritance, 39
   portage on head, 15
   relationship with ancestors, 73
   religion, 16
   women's attire, 15
Mayan glyphs, 11
Mayan handicrafts, 13
Mayan housing, 36, 102, 119, 135, 138, 145, 177, 178, 179, 180, 183, 184, 205, 206
Mayan Languages, 9, 10
Mayan mathematics, 11
Mayan population doubling with each generation, 6
Mayan royalty, 26
Mayan religion, 16
Mayan villages
   Chamil, 130
   Chiallí, 135
   Chijulhá, 105
   Chitomáx, 143
   Jabalí, 169
   Nueva Ezperanza, 183
   Pasmalón, 36
   Santiago Atitlán, 69
   Socelá, 184
McElcar, Donna, ii
McElcar, Donna and Robert, i, 196
McKee, John, ii, 37, 95
McManus, Joe, i
Medical care in a village, 93
Mejía Victores, Óscar Humberto, 72
Memory of Silence, 2
Menchú, Rigoberta, 79
Méndez Montenegro, Julio Cesar, 58

Mérida Initiative, 5
Mexican refugees, 5
Mexicans, iv
Mexico, iv, 4, 5, 9, 39, 71
Middle Ages, 37
Milenski, Tara, i
Military Control, 220
Minerva, 46
Mining, 81
Minor, Keith, 46
MINUGUA, 78
Mirian, 203, 213
missionaries, 12
MLN, 55
Motivation, 34
Mommy! Mommy! Mommy!, 72
Morales, Jimmy, 6
Moran, Barbara, ii
Morrissey. Cathy and Jim], i
most-favored-nation status, 43
mountains of Guatemala, 9
Mulanix, Tracey and Steve, i, 190
Mulhall, Amy and Brian, i
Mulhall, David and Kevin, i
Muller, Darci and Bruce, 192
Mulry, Kelli and Patrick, 194
Mutual of America, ii
Myrna Mack, 83

N

Nancy, 140, 197
Nataly's Interview, 160
Nataly, 109, 112, 173
National Academy of Sciences, 89
National Bank of Guatemala, 42
National Institute for Agrarian Transformation, 57
National Palace, 48
National Police, 221
Nelson, Diane, 75, 220
Neuman, Melissa and Joe, i
New Students in 2004, 101
New York Times, 12, 52
Newhof, Susan, ii
Newhouse, Margaret, ii
Nicaragua, 12
Niceh, 204, 211
nine criteria, 114
Nixon, President, 58
Northern Transversal, 82
Nordhagen, Denise and Beaver, i, 162
North Carolina Museum of Art, 96
North Raleigh Rotary Club, 113
Novak, Joannie, ii
Nueva Esperanza, 182
Nutcracker, 96

O

Obama, President, 5, 6
Observations, 226
Ocampo, Tracey, ii
October Revolution, 49
oil, 82
Old Ways, 12
Ollis, Marcie and Dave, ii
Ombudsman, 75
Operation PBSUCCESS, 53
Ordronneau, Noreen, i, ii, 37, 95, 105
Organization of American States, 54, 77
orientation, 115
Óscar Humberto Mejía Victores, 72
Oslo Accord, 1
Otto, Priscilla, 199
overpopulation, 227
Oxton, Julene and John, i

P

Pablo, 118, 124, 198
PACs, 62
Panama, 3, 12
Pan-American Highway, 12
Pannone, Mercedes, ii
Panzós, 59
parcel, remote, 80
parcels, 39, 78, 79
Partido Guatemalteco de Trabajo, 52
Passports and Visas, 88
patents, Guatemalan, 228
patents, United States, 228
PBSUCCESS, 53
peace, 1, 65, 77
Peace Accords, 1, 81, 83
    Accord for a Firm and Lasting Peace, 1, 77
    Accord on Human Rights, 77
    Accord on Resettlement of Displaced Persons, 77
    Accord on the Establishment of the Commission to
        Clarify Human Rights Violations, 2
Pedro de Alvarado, 14, 24, 25, 26
Pedro, 141, 198
Pella Christian High School, 190
Pelzel, Lori and Ken, i
Peña Nieto, 5
peonage, 42
Peralta Azurdia, Enrique, 58
Pérez Molina, President of Guatemala, 6, 83
perraje, 14
Peru, 26
Petén, 7
Peterson, Margo and Roger, i, 112
phases
    three, 99
Phases, 231

Phases 1, 2, and 3, 98
Phillips, Julie and Greg, i
Pieri. Lori and Chris, 189
pila, 102
Pittsburgh Zoo, 126
Planetarium at UNC, 96
Pocomchí', 9
police, 6
Ponce, Frederico, 49
Pool Party, 99
Pop, Kim and Luis, i
Pop, Luis, 200
Popul Vu, 25
Porter, Beth and Don, i, 189
Portillo Cabrera, Alfonso, 82, 221
Post Peace, 220
Post-Classic Period, 10
Postma, Loreen and John, i, ii, 188
Poteat, Randy and Amy, i, 211
poverty, 15, 99, 109, 131, 132, 149, 171, 180, 195, 235, 239, 240, 244, 248
Powers, Ann, i
Project, 220
Pre-Classic Period, 10
Preferential Option for the Poor, 59
prescription, San Lucas, 93
Presidential Apology, 1
Price, David, 161
primaria, 85
Pritchett, Jim, ii, 169
Program Details, 231
Project, Gramajo's, 61
Proto-Mayan, 9
psychological violence, 61
Public Institutions, 225
public lending libraries, 85
Public Servants, 219

Recruiting Manual, 114
red tiles, 54
Reeber, Val and Dr. Robert, i
Reebye, Dr. Uday, ii, 211
Reed, Rev. Douglas, i
refugees, 71
regret, 33
REHMI, 2
Reina Barrios, José María, 45
religion, Mayan, 16
religious brotherhoods, 16
Renaissance, 37
reparations, 2
Rerum Novarum, 59
Reynolds, Anna Louise, i
Rich, Dr. Gabrial, ii
Rigoberta Menchú, 16, 17, 18, 26, 45, 67, 72, 79, 106, 109
Ríos Montt, Efraín, 64
roads in Guatemala, 12
Rodgers, Jeannie, ii
Rodriguez, Yadira, i
Rojas, Evelyn and Juan Ramirez, i
Rolan, 205, 215
Root Cause, 6
Root Cause–Two Perspectives, 227
Rosaria Godoy, 72
Rossy, 140, 189
Rotary Club of North Raleigh, ii
Roth, Mick and David, i
Rother, Fr. Stan, 69
railroads, 46
Rubén, 120, 125
ruins, 23
Ruiz, Ursula and Rod, i, ii
Rupp, Abby, ii, 165
Ruston, Mark, i

Q

Q'eqchí', 9
Quakers, 89
Quetzal, 14
Quiché, 7
Quiché', 9
Quint, Steve, i

R

Rafael Carrera, 40
Rafael, 201, 212
railroads, 12, 46
Raquel, 117, 125, 216
reading, 228
Recollections, 69
Recovery of Historical Memory, 2

S

Saldanha, Peter, i
Sam the Banana Man, 47
Sambrick, Diane, i
Sambrick, Kelly, ii
San Antonio Aguas Calientes, 25, 58
San Cristóbal Verapaz, 137
San Francisco, 66
San Lucas Tolimán, 91
San Pedro Carchá, 118
Sánchez Cerén, President of El Salvador, 6
Sandra Bolom, 206, 215
Sandra Coc, 181, 194
Santa María Tzejá, 80
sawdust and sand paintings, 16
Schirmer, Jennifer, 75, 220
Schlesinger and Kinzer, 50

school in San Lucas, 91
School of the Americas, 64, 96
schools, in rural areas, 22
schools, upper-class, 87
Schweickert, Dr. Lori, **i**
seasonal workers, 44
Sebep, 66
Second Vatican Council, 59
Security Guards, 221
Selection, 230
Sequel, 74
Serrano Elias, Jorge, 76
Servicemen's Readjustment Act, 227
Seven Criteria, 99
SEVIS, 89
Shaffer, Fr. Greg, 69, 91
Siberia, 9
Sierra Madre mountains, 8
Siwiecki, Matthew, i
Skye Resources, 81
slavery, 26
smallpox, 26
smashing children's heads, 2
Smith, Bedell, 53
Smith, Debbie and Lee, i, 168
Smith, Dr. J. Dempsey, ii, 211
Socelá, 184
Sololá, 8
solution, iv
Somers, Londa and Jeff, i, 210
Soviet Union, 52, 76
Spanish Embassy, 60
Spencer, Nancy and Bill, i, 172
Sponsoring Organizations, 230
Spontak, Josie and Richard, i
seasonal workers, 44
St. Anthony Messenger, 20
St. Thomas More Academy, 195, 196, 197, 198, 211,
    212
Stankard, Francis, i
Starr, Cliff & Nancy, 92
starvation, 79
Stasheff, Jim, i
Stella María Valverdi, 134
Strategy for Engagement in Central America, 6
strategy of terror, 1
strip mining, 81
Student Visa, 88
suicide, 69
Sulzberger, Arthur Hays, 52
Summit of the Americas, 6
Swain de Pop, Kim, 203, 216
syncretism, 12, 16

T

Tactic, *28*, 41
Takei, Dr. Frank, i
Tavana, Saeed, ii
Tavana, Saeed and Tiersa, i
Tax, Maria and Petrus, ii
Taylor, Clark, ii
Taylor, Jeff, i, 113
teachers, qualifications, 23
tectonic plates, 8
Tecún Umán, 14, 24
Tecún Umán (school), 24
temporary workers, 44
Teresa, 200, 214, 217
Terror as a Strategy, 61
terrorizing Mayan children
    beheading them, 68
    eviscerating them, 68
    raping them, 68
    shooting them, 69
    shooting them, 67
    slicing them with machetes, 68
    smashing their heads, 67
terrorizing Mayan men
    forcing PACs to torture and kill in their own
        villages, 73
    forcing them to kill, knowing they would be next,
        66
    hanging them in stocks, 44
    killing their wives and children, 44
    shooting them, 67
    slicing them with machetes, 66
terrorizing Mayan women
    rape, 64, 67, 68, 73
    skewering them on a spit, 68
    slicing them open to extract the fetus, 73
    torturing to death, 73
terrorizing the Maya
    burning them alive, 68
    burning them to death, 67
    'disappearing' them, 69
    dismembering them, 67
    through genocide, 72
textbooks, 20
The Many and the Few, 128
Thomas, Joan and Chuck, i, ii
Thrivent, ii
Through a Glass Darkly, 27
Tidball, Richard, ii
Tikal, 207
Tita Arrué, 34
Tita, 204, 213
titles, 39
Toriello, Guillermo, 49
tortillas, 19
torture, 61
Traje, 15
trees, 50,000, 91

Trejos, Dr. Sandra, ii
Tropical Trading and Transport Company, 46
True Peace, 27
Tschida, Bill, ii, 211, 218
tsunami, iv
temporary workers, 45
tumpline, 26
Turcios Lima, Luis, 57
Turner, Fitzhugh, 52

U

U.N., 53, 77, 78
U.S. Agency for International Development, 6
U.S. Bureau of International Narcotics and Law
    Enforcement Affairs, 6
U.S. military supplies, 2
U.S. State Department, 51, 53
Ubico y Castañeda, Jorge, 47, 48
Ukraine, 189
unaccompanied immigrant children, 4
Unidos and *Casados*, 30
United Fruit Company, 1, 5, 46, 47, 51, 57, 74
United Fruit's Response, 52
United Nations, 1, 71, 227
United Nations Security Council, 54
United Nations Verification Mission in Guatemala,
    78
United Provinces of Guatemala, 40
United States, 1, 2, 3, 19, 27, 34, 53, 54, 64, 75, 84,
    86, 87, 98, 219, 225, 226, 227, 228, 229, 232, 233
UNRG, 76
upper class, 43
USAID, 6
usufruct, 39

V

vagrancy law, 47
Van den Heuvel, Joanne, i
Van Lenten, Paige and David, i, 195
VanderVeen, Mary and Scott, i, ii, 162, 187
Vatican, 47
Vicente Menchú, 67
Vietnam, 58
Vietnam War, 2
Villages, 182
visa appointments, 123, 153, 158, 173
visa denials, 89
visa types, 88
Visitor's Visa, 88
volcanoes, 8, 20
volunteers, San Lucas, 92
visa appointments, 160

visa appointments, 185

W

Wagner, Rosie and James, i
Wake Tech, 100, 164, 172, 211
wall, iv
wall, cost of, 6
Wall, Rev. John, i
Walters, General Vernon, 60
Walter, 201, 213
Watsabaugh, Dave, i
Weber, Karrie and Richard, i
Weld, Kirsten, 221
Wells Fargo, ii
Werner, 121
White, Dwayne and Nicole, i, 126
White, Dwayne and Nicole, 124
Whitesell, Marisa, ii
Whitman, Anne, 53
Wilkinson, Daniel, 46
Wilson Library, 96
Wilson, Elizabeth and Ross Jackson, 100
Wilson, Horace, 19
Wisner, Frank, 53
Wiwel, Sharon and Tim, i, 196
Wolfe, James, i
Women in College, 229
workers
    colones, 44
    seasonal, 44
    temporary, 44
Workshops, 115
Worthington, Michele and Brad, i, 190

X

Xmucané', 16

Y

Ydigoras Fuentes, Miguel, 55
Yesenia, 201, 212
Yesulaitis, John and Pat, ii
Yesulaitis, Pat and John, 37
Yohan, 132
Yujá Xoná, Gregorio, 61

Z

Zacapa, 54
Zamora, Manuel, 28
Zemurray, Sam, 47
Ziemer, Ellen and Jerry Waddell, i
Zoila, 25, 58